RELIGION AND SPIRITUALITY

SPIRITUALITY

GLOBAL PRACTICES, SOCIETAL ATTITUDES AND EFFECTS ON HEALTH

RELIGION AND SPIRITUALITY

Additional books in this series can be found on Nova's website under the Series tab.

Additional e-books in this series can be found on Nova's website under the e-book tab.

RELIGION AND SPIRITUALITY

SPIRITUALITY

GLOBAL PRACTICES, SOCIETAL ATTITUDES AND EFFECTS ON HEALTH

EDITH C. ROBERTS
EDITOR

nova publishers
New York

Library of Congress Cataloging-in-Publication Data

Spirituality : global practices, societal attitudes, and effects on health / editors, Edith C. Roberts.
pages cm. -- (Religion and spirituality)
Includes index.
ISBN 978-1-63482-370-8 (hardcover)
1. Spirituality. 2. Mental health--Religious aspects. I. Roberts, Edith C., editor.
BL624.S6933 2015
204--dc23 2015006785

Published by Nova Science Publishers, Inc. † New York

CONTENTS

PREFACE

Spirituality has only recently been conceptualized as a distinct construct from religion or religiosity. For centuries, the term religiosity referred to both personal and public attempts to relate to the divine essence of the universe. More recently, and first among the layperson, the term spirituality has been recognized as a private phenomenon and the term religion as a public phenomenon. This book discusses global practices of spirituality. It also examines societal attitudes toward spirituality and the effects it has on human health.

Chapter 1 – Over the past seven decades, a growing body of evidence suggests a modest yet consistent and statistically significant association between spirituality and mental health. This relationship is important given that a great majority of Americans report high levels of spirituality. In this chapter, The authors will review the current evidence of the association between these constructs (including but not limited to our own work). However, the bulk of this research has often confused spirituality with religiosity, or focused on the traditional construct of religion rather than the emergent construct of spirituality. In addition, the majority of these studies have been exclusively correlational in nature, without exploring the mediating or moderating effects of spirituality on mental health. These lapses are both theoretically and clinically problematic for a variety of reasons. In this chapter the authors will summarize a more recent body of research that has started to explore spirituality in more complex designs (e.g., moderated mediation). The authors will make recommendations for future research that will help the field mature and develop a fuller understanding of the role of spirituality in mental health, and discuss the challenges and opportunities for using spirituality as a resource in mental health care. Finally, there is growing evidence that younger generations have different attitudes towards religiosity; these changes have implications for spirituality. The authors will explore this trend and what it means for the mental health of future generations.

Chapter 2 – Alzheimer's disease (AD) is a growing issue in the United States and globally, raising serious concerns about the future of the world's aging population. Most frequently seen in adults over the age of 65, AD is a degenerative neurological disorder that causes behavioral changes and the loss of memory, thinking, and language (Alzheimer's Association, 2014). AD is the most common type of dementia. Currently there is no known cure for AD, yet scientists have learned that AD progresses due to an attack on the brain's neurons that produce the neurotransmitter acetylcholine. This attack causes nerve cells to break connections and die (Alzheimer's Association, 2014). Further, abnormal lesions and neurofibrillary tangles develop outside the neurons and inside nerve cells; first damaging the brain's hippocampus where short-term memory is lost, and then developing in the cerebral cortex resulting in the loss of language and judgment (Alzheimer's Association, 2014). This attack on the brain's neurons can be rapid or progress very slowly. For example, deaths caused by AD can range anywhere between three to twenty years. The Centers for Disease Control and Prevention (CDC, 2014) estimated that the average life expectancy after receiving an AD diagnosis is approximately eight to ten years. Experiences for AD patients can vary according to the speed in which the disease progresses, but the disease remains terminal.

National data in the United States emerged in the late 1970's when Robert Katzman became one of the first to publish national estimates on AD in the 1976 editorial, *Archives of Neurology* (George, 2006). Katzman estimated that approximately 1.2 million cases of AD existed in 1976, causing about 60,000-90,000 deaths per year (George, 2006). Current estimates of AD have shown an immense increase in the prevalence of the disease since the 1970's. Currently, the Alzheimer's Association (2014) estimates that 5.2 million Americans are diagnosed with AD and 500,000 people die a year from this disease. Further, an astounding 16 million Americans are predicted to have the disease by 2050 (Alzheimer's Association, 2014). Current global rates and predictions are consistent with the prevalence rates of AD in the United States. Alzheimer's Disease International (2014) estimates that 44.4 million people have AD worldwide, and 135.5 million people will by 2050. Therefore, both globally and in the United States, the prevalence of AD is predicted to nearly triple in the next 40 years. The rising growth of expectant AD patients will undoubtedly have a major impact, both socially and economically, on those caring for these older adults.

Chapter 3 – To be confronted with tragic, critical incidents on a daily basis. To face human destructiveness and suffering, to defend society, standing between chaos and order in defense of peace; All require a unique type of individual. It is what we, as a society, demand from our law enforcement officers.

Currently in the United States, we are seeing our police officers questioned for using excessive levels of force. There are increasing numbers of violence erupting within our communities from its members who feel our law enforcement officers are "out of control." In a study of 350 United Kingdom police constables, the cost of PTSD, burnout, and stress was in excess of £99 million or $152 million. Forty percent were deemed to be of medium or high risk of PTSD and 13% of respondents had been signed off work with PTSD one or more times usually for 4+ months costing £11,538 per officer per instance.

In this chapter, the authors explore the budding importance of spirituality as a coping mechanism in police work, a path through the suffering and disorder. If our police officers are feeling isolated, under valued, and sick then how can they protect and serve our communities? Crime and disorder become pronounced in environments where law enforcement becomes dysfunctional. In the authors research on spirituality and policing in the United States and the United Kingdom common themes illustrate the importance of this coping mechanism, whereby officers feel "connected" to their profession, their work, and their communities. Can we extend this research toward the communities served to connect our police officers with its members to lessen crime and disorder?

Chapter 4 – Compassion is a widely recognized virtue across cultural, political and religious divides. Compassionate teaching is not new, however the topic is receiving renewed interest as educators around the world endeavour to respond empathetically and practically to students' complex holistic needs. This paper reports on a qualitative inquiry into the meanings, challenges and practice of compassion as experienced by ten participants, within a range of New Zealand Christian school contexts (primary and secondary), and one pre-service teacher training programme in Thailand with mainly Karen refugees from Myanmar. The rich data was obtained through a triangulated research design which involved four teachers in a collaborative action research project over a semester, three teachers and two principals in an online survey, and one principal in a semi-structured interview.

A reflective, inductive and iterative analysis of the textual data was used to gain in-depth understanding of what compassion meant to participants and how they enacted compassion in their respective educational contexts. The findings show that the teachers and principals were motivated towards compassion, having eyes to see people's needs and hearts willing to move from apathy or judgment, towards supportive action. However, the findings provide evidence that compassion in teaching could be a challenging decision-making and relational process, requiring wisdom, resourcefulness and resilience. Through critical reflection and trialling interventions, participants in the collaborative action research process became more intentional about viewing interpersonal issues and learning needs through a compassionate lens which positively impacted their professional practice. The findings from these participants showed that judicious and relational expressions of compassion can have a transformational effect in students' *behaviour and learning*, supporting the sacred injunction, 'and of some have compassion, *making a difference*' (Jude 1:22).

Chapter 5 – This chapter provides an analytical review of nearly 300 ways in which people have attempted quantitative assessments of spirituality or spiritual health/well-being (SH/WB) over the last 40 years.

They range from single-item to multi-item measures. Each item in these measures has been classified using the theoretical framework provided by the author's four domains model of spiritual health & well-being.

Some considered thoughts are presented relating to the purpose and ways of assessing spirituality and spiritual well-being. Types and forms of spirituality and spiritual well-being measures are discussed. Single-item measures are compared with multiple-item measures.

A summary table is then presented containing 260 studies with distinct multi-item measures which pertain to spirituality, spiritual well-being and related measures in general populations, university student groups, school students and teachers, and in healthcare settings.

These measures are all critiqued for content against the four domains model of spiritual health and well-being.

This chapter is an essential resource for anyone contemplating quantitative research in spirituality/well-being, as it provides access to available measures, some of which are hidden in obscure places.

Chapter 6 – There is evidence that spiritual attachment may confer psychological benefits associated with secure interpersonal attachments. Spirituality, perceived relationships with God, meets all the defining criteria of attachment relationships. Religion itself may be seen as a dynamic attachment process. God or other supernatural beings may act so a to substitute the role of an attachment figure. In this healing relationship, God is the "*Secure base*" and the "*Safe Haven*, which may relieve the wounds of bereavement and other kinds of loss. Attachment to God may confer emotional benefits associated with secure interpersonal attachments.

This chapter offers both qualitative and quantitative insight to the issue of spiritual attachment. The results of an anthropological field work with charismatic religious visionares are presented in context of their confessed close and intimate spiritual attachment mirrored by their narratives, life stories, texts and sacred dialogues. The prominent role of attachment in sacral communication is demonstrated.

The health aspects of the spiritual attachment are explored by the results of two consecutive behavioral epidemiological studies called Hungarostudy. The health psychological significance of spirituality is summarized by comparing the authors results with the data of studies and metanalyses of this field. Regarding religious attitudes and adult attachment features the 2013 Hungarostudy data helped us uncover relationships between sociality, spirituality and the mental health gains. The authors found significant differences regarding avoidant, dismissive attachment between the religiously indifferent and those practicing their religion. Their findings proved that religiosity can be classified as a life - enhancing factor. The positive relationship between religiosity and health psychological indicators have gained broader multidimensional significance as the authors could demonstrate it.

Chapter 7 – This chapter outlines potential interactions of God with humanity from the dawn of time through to attaining spiritual well-being. It briefly mentions alternative theories of origin, which connect to questions of ultimate reality, origin of human beings and our spiritual well-being.

The nature of spirit and its relationship with soul and mind is then canvassed, followed by an account of historical developments in 'spirituality'. The author's Four Domains Model posits that Spiritual Health/Well-Being is reflected in the quality of relationships that each person has in up to four areas, namely with themselves, with others, with nature and/or with a Transcendent Other (commonly referred to as God). A critique of available measures of spirituality and spiritual well-being reveals a decline in the number of instruments assessing human relationships with God from earlier to more recent times.

In contrast to this current trend of researchers selecting more humanistic emphases in spirituality/well-being in their research instruments, evidence is provided from recent findings that show that relating with God is the most important of the four sets of relationships for spiritual well-being. Further evidence is provided that God is the most influential Transcendent to enhance people's relationships with themselves and others. Although researchers are free to choose the nature of questions raised in their projects, findings presented here clearly show that any research that cuts God out of the equation is excising the foundation of spirituality/well-being.

Chapter 8 – Against a background of the relative numbers of advocates and chaplains in England, the nature of advocacy practice is considered. Changes in the law through the Mental Capacity Act (2005) (MCA) and the amendments to the Mental Health Act (1983) in 2007- which came into effect respectively in 2007 and 2009- made it a statutory duty in England and Wales for the National Health Service (NHS) and local authorities to refer to advocacy services, both Independent Mental Capacity Advocates (IMCAs) and Independent Mental Health Advocates (IMHAs). The MCA specifically facilitated the involvement of IMCAs in safeguarding adults' procedures and alongside other vulnerable groups, and in relation to Deprivation of Liberty Safeguards matters (DoLS). Both independent advocates and chaplains use advocacy skills, and for IMCAs, social, cultural and spiritual factors are influential. In combining interviews with over 40 advocates, chaplains and service users, and by comparing numbers in the field, I argue that emotion and spirituality should be considered more by advocates as part of their analytical process-audit role. This is also the case for those who are non-standard practitioners of advocacy, and may therefore have an impact in the community. The growth in advocacy coincided with an increase in literature on mental health and spirituality, of which a refreshed faith-based social conscience will want to be aware; the 'rediscovery of the spiritual dimension in health and social care' thus highlighted some shortcomings in the professionalisation of advocacy in relation to these areas, and possible advantages in a conversation between faith activists and advocacy practitioners. The question is left open as to whether such a fresh synthesis of knowledge and skills could be useful in improved safeguards for the most vulnerable in society.

Chapter 9 – The article seeks to present how the universe of the Paiter Suruí is conceived and organized by this ethnic group. The construction follows the arrests and experiences of the action space of this ethnicity who inhabiting the States of Mato Grosso and Rondônia, which during the ritual Mapimaí – "the creation of the world" - in phenomena and symbolic representations meeting their identities, so that in the event becomes more noticeable the spirituality, of which the territoriality is integral, and therefore materialized. The design of this study is empirical basis (experience in Mapimaí) and theoretical frameworks that discuss the indigenous question. It is noteworthy that the ritual as representation and cultural event, due to factors external to ethnicity has been "dormant" for several years and was taken over since the understanding of Paiter Suruí strengthens its identity as a people and it provides spiritual and affective ties strengthening, which allows ensuring the territoriality, considering the constant threats to Indigenous Land Paiterey Garah (Setember Seven).

Chapter 10 – Throughout history, the terms spirituality and religiosity were often used interchangeably until the constructs were separated due in part to the rise of secularism and a shift in Western culture during the last few decades (Hill et al., 2000; Zinnbauer et al., 1997). Many researchers, theologians, and philosophers now consider these two terms as connected but separable constructs, and studies now endeavour to clarify this distinction (e.g., Emmons & Paloutzian, 2003; Hill et al., 2000; Holder, Coleman, & Wallace., 2010). However, researchers have yet to reach a consensus on the distinct meanings of the two terms (Emmons & Paloutzian, 2003; Hill et al., 2000; Zinnbauer et al., 1997). This lack of consensus contributes to inconsistencies in the literature and difficulty comparing findings across studies. To address these concerns, the present chapter compares a range of definitions for both spirituality and religiosity before proposing the following new definition of spirituality: "Spirituality is a feeling of Connectedness to something greater experienced by cultivating a relationship with oneself, one's community, one's environment, and one's perception of the transcendent." Using this definition as a reference, we examined current assessments of spirituality and religiosity, focusing on each one's ability to capture the construct on a global level. Additionally, the benefits of religiosity and spirituality, especially concerning subjective well-being and health, are discussed. Together, these considerations lead to ideas and possibilities for future directions of spirituality research.

Chapter 11 – In Western societies, many people call themselves spiritual but not religious; this emerging religious stance inevitably gives rise to various societal attitudes and spiritual practices. Nowadays, many argue that spirituality is perceived as being highly personal and subjective. Some authors suggest that it can also be part of collective practices and shared beliefs which are not explicitly associated with conventional or institutionalized religions but rather, to a so called "implicit religion" (Gollnick, 2005). In light of this new paradigm, this chapter on being "spiritual but not religious" has three main objectives. First, it aims to provide reference points in order to contextualize the emergence of the term "spiritual but not religious" (SBNR) by presenting aspects of contemporary social contexts such as secularism and other new forms of spirituality. The second objective is to present factors which appear to be associated with this religious stance, SBNR, and its related emerging spiritual practices. Notably, three factors, trends or approaches will be discussed: a) the importance of holistic health; b) the socio-ecological approaches to spirituality and c) the influence of Eastern philosophy, such as the growing interest in mindfulness practices, in Western societies The third objective is to discuss the positive impact of these factors, trends and approaches on health, as well as some possible limitations to the understanding of a "healthy" spirituality in secular Western societies, particularly with respect to SBNR.

Chapter 12 – *Background:* Spirituality and asceticism are relevant characteristics of patients suffering from anorexia nervosa.

Objective: To describe the evidence on spirituality and asceticism in anorexia nervosa related to clinical features and therapeutic approaches.

Method: Medline/Pubmed, Scielo databases and specialized textbooks were used to look for evidence on asceticism and spirituality in anorexia nervosa and its clinical and therapeutic implications.

Results: From a historical perspective, spirituality and ascetic behaviours showed by medieval saints, and those observed in modern anorectics, share common features; however, the former wanted to reach sainthood and the latest seek thinness so valuable in Western sociocultural context. Contemporary Protestantism and anorexia nervosa display distinctive characteristics of protestant ethics, mainly self-discipline, self-control, self-sacrifice, rationality, efficiency and goals achievement. Although asceticism in these patients has been significantly correlated to worse outcome, more treatment dropouts, perfectionism, immaturity and purging, it is also associated to creative and adjustment skills and its connection to spiritual and religious proneness might improve the outcome of psychopathological and/or behavioural symptoms in anorexia nervosa.

Conclusions: The timeless occurrence within the historical Western framework of the anorectic syndrome pathogenic essence suggests that factors like age, personality and/or psychosocial environment pathoplastically model it. Spirituality would stimulate the motivation, contention and increase therapeutic adherence in patients suffering from anorexia nervosa. It should be considered as a helpful and eventually routine therapeutic tool in the treatment of anorectic patients.

Chapter 13 – This study compares the religiosity of representative samples of the Chilean psychiatrists, psychologists and psychoanalysts with the general population. A questionnaire inquiring into religious and spiritual beliefs was anonymously applied through a web based survey: there were more non-believers among psychoanalysts (62, 8%) than among psychiatrists (42,8%) and psychologists (33,6). The three professional groups were less religious than the Chilean population (87%). Results are compared with the study by Shafranske et al in the U.S: 73% of psychiatrists and psychologists believed in God, compared with 96% of the population, and by Hofman & Walach in Germany, where 57% of the psychotherapists belonged to a religious denomination.

This research was done receiving a grant in aid of the Research Advisory Board of the International Psychoanbalytic Association.

In: Spirituality
Editor: Edith C. Roberts

ISBN: 978-1-63482-370-8

Chapter 1

SPIRITUALITY AND MENTAL HEALTH: CURRENT UNDERSTANDING AND FUTURE TRENDS

Kirby K. Reutter, PhD, and Silvia M. Bigatti, PhD *

Gateway Woods Family Services
Indiana University Richard M. Fairbanks School of Public Health

ABSTRACT

Over the past seven decades, a growing body of evidence suggests a modest yet consistent and statistically significant association between spirituality and mental health. This relationship is important given that a great majority of Americans report high levels of spirituality. In this chapter, we will review the current evidence of the association between these constructs (including but not limited to our own work). However, the bulk of this research has often confused spirituality with religiosity, or focused on the traditional construct of religion rather than the emergent construct of spirituality. In addition, the majority of these studies have been exclusively correlational in nature, without exploring the mediating or moderating effects of spirituality on mental health. These lapses are both theoretically and clinically problematic for a variety of reasons. In this chapter we will summarize a more recent body of research that has started to explore spirituality in more complex designs (e.g., moderated mediation). We will make recommendations for future research that will help the field mature and develop a fuller understanding of the role of spirituality in mental health, and discuss the challenges and opportunities for using spirituality as a resource in mental health care. Finally, there is growing evidence that younger generations have different attitudes towards religiosity; these changes have implications for spirituality. We will explore this trend and what it means for the mental health of future generations.

* Corresponding author; sbigatti@iupui.edu; kirby.reutter@gatewaywoods.org.

INTRODUCTION

Prevalence of Spirituality and Religiosity in the United States

A plethora of polls conducted over many years suggest that the majority of Americans remain one "nation under God." A brief review of a few representative surveys in recent years adequately demonstrates this point. For example, a 2013 Gallup poll states that 56% and 22% of Americans regard religion as very or moderately important in their lives, respectively [22]. In the same year, a Harris poll found that a "strong majority of Americans (74%) professed belief in a deity" [26]. LifeWay Research reports universal personal participation in prayer, irrespective of religious identification or affiliation [49].

Furthermore, findings over the past several decades indicate a notable increase in America's interest in spirituality. For example, 58% of the American population expressed interest in spiritual maturation in 1994, while 82% of the population acknowledged this interest in 1998 [63]. In a survey conducted in 2009, three out of four Americans self-identified as "more spiritual than religious" [49]. Similarly, the Pew Forum on Religion found that 70% of individuals who were religiously unaffiliated expressed a belief in God or a Universal Spirit [51].

Spirituality As a Distinct Construct

Spirituality has only recently been conceptualized as a distinct construct from religion or religiosity. For centuries, the term religiosity referred to both personal and public attempts to relate to the divine essence of the universe [27]. More recently, and first among the layperson, the term spirituality has been recognized as a private phenomenon and the term religion as a public phenomenon. In their study of moral maturity, Walker and Pitts found that lay participants characterized spirituality in terms of "personal affirmation of the transcendent" while describing religion in terms of "institutional church organizations" [87; pp.409]. Thus, most researchers now define spirituality in terms of the inner, personal, subjective, and private, while defining religion in terms of the collective, institutional, visible, and public [95, 14, 48, 82].

A number of researchers have examined the distinctive roles of religiosity and spirituality on a variety of physical and mental domains, including symptom reduction of trauma victims [55]; the emotional resilience of young adults raised by depressive parents [71]; the mental health of young adults [93] and British families [41]; the psychosocial adjustment of adolescents (i.e., intrapersonal well-being, quality of parent-child relationship, substance use, and academic orientation) [24]; and self-actualization, meaning in life, and personal growth initiative [32]. More recently, our research team examined the distinctive roles of religiosity and spirituality in stress, anxiety, and depression [67]. In each of these studies, the distinctive nature of these constructs was confirmed by the data.

Zinnbauer and Pargament believe that the emergence of spirituality as a distinct construct in the United States has resulted from increments in the criticism of traditional religious organizations, religious pluralism of Western culture, personalized expressions of faith, overall individualism, and the overall rejection of traditional authority and cultural norms—all of which have served to diminish the influence of traditional religious organizations [94].

Changes in the definition of religiosity that explain the emergence of spirituality have occurred in a number of dimensions. First, religion was originally defined in terms of both substantive and functional dimensions [94]. The object of religious pursuits (e.g., worshipping the sacred) was the substantive dimension, while the purpose of religious pursuits (e.g., dealing with existential issues) was the functional dimension. More recently, religion has been increasingly defined only in substantive terms, while spirituality is now conceptualized almost exclusively in functional terms. Many of what used to be the functional aspects of religion (e.g., the pursuit of meaning, truth, wholeness, self-actualization, and interconnectivity) now fit the current definition of spirituality.

Similarly, religion was originally conceptualized in terms of both static and dynamic dimensions [94]. Static descriptions of religion only convey "what religion is," while dynamic aspects portray "what it does or how it works" [94; pp. 25]. More recently, however, "what it does or how it works" fit within conceptions of spirituality more than religion. Furthermore, original definitions for religion also included both cognitive and experiential dimensions. Over time, conceptualizations for religion have become reduced to cognitive aspects (e.g., creeds, dogmas, and theologies), while conceptualizations for spirituality have been associated with direct experience [94]. Finally, and perhaps most significantly, religion was originally defined in terms of both public and private dimensions [94]. Now, however, religion is most frequently described in terms of groups, organizations, and institutions—while spirituality is characterized in terms of personal, inner, and subjective phenomena.

In spite of these recent distinctions between the terms, most Americans describe themselves as both religious and spiritual [42]. Although there is overlap between the constructs (including problems of clarity of definition across studies), this chapter will focus on spirituality as an individual / experiential phenomenon.

Measuring Spirituality

The Daily Spiritual Experiences Scale (DSES)—developed by Underwood to provide a measure of ordinary, everyday spiritual experiences that transcend specific religious traditions, orientations, or denominations—may be the most frequently employed measure of spirituality [85, 87]. The DSES includes 16 items with both theistic and non-theistic themes. For example, Item 8 is theistic ("I feel guided by God in the midst of daily activities") while Item 11 is non-theistic ("I am spiritually touched by the beauty of creation").

Researchers have utilized this instrument within a wide scope of populations, ranging from social workers [83] to drug addicts [75], and from elderly Jews [38] to Indonesian Muslim youth [17]. The DSES has been translated into nine different languages and is currently utilized for research in countries as diverse as India, France, Korea, and Vietnam. A number of studies have also confirmed both the validity and the reliability of this instrument. For example, Underwood and Teresi reported the following forms of reliability: Pearson product-moment correlation for test-retest reliability = .85; intra-class correlation coefficient for internal reliability = .73; Cronbach's alpha estimate of internal reliability = .91-.95; and inter-rater reliability = .64-.78 [87]; these findings have been confirmed by others with comparable reliabilities [50]. In addition, the concurrent validity of the DSES was confirmed with a number of instruments, including the State-Trait Anxiety Inventory, Cohen Perceived Stress Scale, Scheirer's Optimism Scale, Berkman's Scale of Perceived Social Support, and the Watson and Clark Positive and Negative Affect Scale [87].

Growth of Research in Spirituality and Mental Health

A sampling of research in recent years suggests that empirical interest in the construct of spirituality and its relation to mental health continues to increase globally across a wide range of demographic groups. For example, within just the last few years, researchers have examined spirituality and mental health among adolescent sons of alcohol-dependent fathers [37]; juvenile victims of violence in Brazil [31]; homeless mothers [29]; college students [47]; and aging prisoners [1]. In addition, spirituality has been correlated with risk behaviors among Christian, Jewish, and Muslim secondary/post-secondary students, and also correlated with optimism, depression, and fatalism in Mexican-American stroke victims [5, 78]. Thus, recent research regarding spirituality and its relation to mental health variables seems to span the spectrum of nationality, race, religion, age, and gender.

Furthermore, spirituality has been examined with quality of life among those undergoing mindfulness-based stress reduction [25]; cancer patients and their spouses [40]; and substance abusers [81]. In each of these correlational studies, spirituality was associated with better mental health and quality of life. More specifically, research using the Daily Spiritual Experiences Scale (DSES) as a measure of spirituality has found the outcomes listed below:

- Married individuals provided greater assistance to spouses with traumatic injuries (in fact, the DSES was the strongest predictor of all variables examined) [53].
- Both males and females reported higher levels of marital satisfaction [3].
- Elderly individuals reported higher levels of social integration with less stress [77].
- Widowed individuals reported better recovery from the death of their spouses [15].
- Mid-life individuals demonstrated more altruistic behaviors, especially towards strangers [16].
- Chinese hospital workers reported less anxiety, depression, and burnout [57].
- Teachers in Nigeria reported less work-family conflict [2], while teachers in England reported more internal resources and greater significance in their vocation [91].
- Among 854 American employees, only the DSES (and not a host of other religious / spiritual factors) was related to favorable workplace conditions [80].
- American employees participated in fewer negative behaviors, including ethical infractions [68].
- Young adult cancer patients reported greater participation in health-related behaviors (e.g., better nutritional intake, medication adherence, and sleep hygiene) [61].
- Patients with heart failure reported greater self-efficacy [60].
- Lithuanian college students reported more physical activity, healthier diets, greater creativity, greater resiliency, greater self-care, and other "health-oriented lifestyles" [64].

- African Americans reported fewer HIV-related risk behaviors [92].
- Elderly patients reported shorter durations of hospitalization in addition to greater physiological / psychological wellbeing [44].
- Arthritis patients reported more energy, more positive mood states, and less emotional negativity [39].
- Individuals with previous alcoholic dependence reported less post-treatment recidivism [69].
- A variety of individuals (e.g., French adults, inner-city seniors, urban juveniles, incarcerated inmates) reported better psychological wellbeing / adjustment and more positive emotionality (e.g., excitement, self-esteem, optimism, happiness, life satisfaction) [86, 88].
- A variety of individuals (e.g., Korean immigrants, heart attack victims, survivors of domestic violence, chronic disease patients, physically isolated elderly) reported fewer symptoms of depression and/or anxiety [85].
- Older adults with high levels of stress reported less negative moods, greater "stress-buffering" and greater positive moods [33].
- Young adults raised by depressed parents reported greater resilience [71].
- Daily spiritual experiences have also been associated with greater post-traumatic growth and less distress after bereavement [13].

This sampling of recent research reflects the rich applicability of daily spiritual experiences across a variety of health variables. It is further noteworthy that in many of these studies, daily spiritual experiences were far better predictors of favorable outcomes than religious variables.

HOW SPIRITUALITY RELATES TO MENTAL HEALTH

Spirituality may relate to better mental health and quality of life because it helps individuals cope with stress and adversity. Gall and colleagues utilized Lazarus' Transactional Theory to conceptualize spirituality as a distinct resource for coping, and referenced decades of research to support this hypothesis [20].

For example, spiritual causal attributions have been associated with general coping, positive reframing, greater use of problem-focused coping, greater use of emotion-focused coping, and better adjustment to negative life events [18, 58]. In addition, a spiritually collaborative coping style was found to offer a sense of empowerment in light of stressful circumstances [59], while a spiritually-surrendering coping style was found to offer a sense of relief, comfort, and security [12]. Similarly, spiritually-oriented meditation was more effective in reducing levels of anger, anxiety, and tension than non-spiritual relaxation techniques [7]. Finally, both theistic and non-theistic spiritual meaning-making were associated with greater subjective satisfaction [52].

Spiritual attachments have been particularly recognized as an efficacious resource for coping. For example, perceived support from divinity was associated with decreased depression and increased self-esteem among individuals experiencing high levels of stress [54]. In addition, a secure relationship with divinity was associated with increased life satisfaction in conjunction with decreased loneliness, depression, and anxiety [43]. Similarly, relationships with divinity have been associated with elevations in comfort, social support, sense of belonging, empowerment, and control—as well as reductions in emotional distress and specific fears [19, 76]. Finally, relationships with divinity have also been associated with increased optimism, hope, inner strength, and focus on personal growth [21, 23, 27, 62].

SPIRITUALITY IN COMPLEX STATISTICAL MODELS

While bivariate correlational research has proliferated for decades [45], an increasing number of researchers have started to examine spiritual variables in more complex moderation/mediation models—i.e., sometimes as the moderating/mediating variable, and sometimes as moderated/mediated by other variables. For example, spiritual well-being moderated traumatic life events, mental health, and substance abuse among African American women [81]—while enhanced mindfulness partially mediated the association between increased daily spiritual experiences and improved mental health / quality of life [25]. In addition, intrinsic spirituality mediated the relationship between institutional activities and mental well-being, while moderating the relationship between violence exposure and mental health problems (all in the same dataset) [31]. Similarly, perceived control both moderated and partially mediated a variety of variables, including spiritual coping and subjective wellbeing [34].

The ability of spirituality to serve as both moderator and mediator seems to have significant implications. In our own work, we combined moderating and mediating variables by pursuing a moderated mediation design. Relevant to this chapter, we examined the following variables: perceived stress, religiosity, daily spiritual experiences, and symptoms of anxiety and depression (mood) [67]. We found that religiosity moderated and spirituality partially mediated the relationship between stress and mood. Interestingly, religiosity did not mediate stress and mood; in addition, levels of religiosity did not moderate the mediating effects of spirituality. Based on these findings [67], we concluded:

> …not only does spirituality contribute a pivotal link between stress and psychological adjustment, but also continues to facilitate this relationship once it has emerged. It does not seem that stressful life circumstances would result in improved psychological functioning without the presence of mediating factors such as spirituality. However, once present, it seems that spirituality continues to foster ongoing psychological improvement. Thus, perhaps it is reasonable to speculate that spirituality both initiates and enhances psychological well-being—even in light of adverse conditions.

These more complex designs further elucidate the relationship between spirituality and mental health, as distinct from religiosity. Studies of this nature seem to suggest that spirituality plays the primary role in psychological wellbeing, while religion plays a secondary role. Thus, spirituality may provide the "efficacious agent" by which religiosity also becomes ameliorative. More research using complex designs and focusing on process variables (i.e., the "how" and "why" of these relationships) will help the field move forward.

Clinical Recommendations

This extensive, longstanding, and rich body of research on spirituality as a resource should not remain within the walls of academia. Rather, it is our hope that practical applications can and will flow from the work that is being done in this field. Below we identify several practical recommendations for the mental health clinician in regards to incorporating spirituality—and when appropriate, religiosity—into the treatment of clients or patients.

First, religiosity seems to exert a favorable therapeutic effect on the majority of clients—but not for all. In fact, some studies continue to report that religiosity exerts no effect at all—or even effects that are clinically adverse. Reeves, Beazley, and Adams (2011) are perhaps the most comprehensive researchers in recent years to examine the differential effects of religiosity [66]. These investigators reviewed more than 700 studies that demonstrated the correlation between religion and mental health. In particular, nearly 500 studies indicated a positive correlation—while the remaining studies did not. This team concluded the following regarding these results: "Religion and spirituality unquestionably have a place in the treatment of many mental health patients" [66; pp. 6]. However, "religion may be seen to, at times, produce adverse effects in some mental health patients" [66; pp. 7]. Therefore, "religion may be incorporated into mental health treatment in circumstances that are appropriate—but should be avoided where it may worsen a patient's status" [66; [pp. 7].

Of course, this conclusion all but begs the question: When exactly are religious / spiritual interventions clinically indicated—and when are they not? Furthermore, how can we know the difference? Weber and Pargament seem to pick up where the previous researchers left off [90]. In their own review of the literature, Weber and Pargagment note the following: "Studies indicate that religion…can promote mental health through positive religious coping, community and support, and positive beliefs" [90; pp. 358]. However, "research also shows that religion…can be damaging to mental health by means of negative religious coping, misunderstanding / miscommunication, and negative beliefs" [90; pp. 358]. Therefore, these researchers recommend the incorporation of the "assessment of patients' spiritual needs" [90; pp. 358] within the therapeutic process.

Chidarikire further emphasizes the imperative to provide spiritual assessments within clinical practice: "In recent times strong evidence has been presented to suggest that incorporating spiritual care in treatment plans helps recovery, reduces relapses, and improves quality of life. Mental health patients have consistently identified spiritual needs as an important issue to them, and several studies have found that spiritual care positively contributes to symptom relief and general well-being. *Therefore, as part of providing holistic care, mental health patients should be offered a spiritual assessment followed by attempts to include their spiritual needs incorporated in care planning"* [9; p. 298] (emphasis added).

The benefits of incorporating spiritual assessments into clinical practice are multifaceted. First, spiritual assessments administered during the intake process may alert the clinician as to which clients may—or may not—benefit from religious / spiritual interventions in the first place. Secondly, the repeated administration of a spiritual assessment at recurring intervals may also provide salient longitudinal information regarding the ongoing valence of spiritual / religious interventions. Thirdly, the administration of a spiritual assessment on a "pre-test /

post-test" basis may additionally offer important indicators regarding the efficacy of these interventions for any given client.

Earlier we described the DSES as an excellent measure of spirituality; here we recommend clinicians incorporate this brief instrument into their intake assessments. Underwood has reviewed scores of studies that have employed this instrument [85]. According to this review, daily spiritual experiences are positively correlated with the following variables: favorable psychological states, greater well-being, life satisfaction, resiliency, better recovery from / prevention of addictive behaviors, healthier dietary intake, better adherence to treatment regimens, and better social / interpersonal functioning.

Generational Differences in Religiosity and Spirituality and Their Implications for Health

The Pew Research Foundation, along with PBS, conducted an in-depth study of trends in changes in religiosity in the US, noting a steady decline in the percentage of Americans that consider themselves religious [51]. The percentage of adults of all ages who report non-affiliation to a specific religion increased from 15% to 20% in just 5 years, and is mostly composed of whites, of various income levels, and across all areas of the country. These changes in religious beliefs are supported further by a Harris poll from 2013 which found that 82% of the population reported belief in God in 2005, 2007, and 2009—while the percentage dropped to 74% in 2013. Other religious beliefs also declined, such as belief in miracles (79% in 2005 vs. 72% in 2013) and heaven (75% in 2005 vs. 65% in 2013), among others [26].

This decline does not seem to result from individuals becoming less religious; in fact, religiosity seems to remain relatively constant over the lifespan. Whereas among older adults (65+) the percentage reporting a specific religious affiliation is 90%, it is 84% among 50 to 64 year-olds, and 77% among 30 to 49 year-olds [51]. These statistics suggest the decline is across generations—and not across time within the same cohorts.

Research indicates similar findings when focused exclusively on youth [51]. The percentage of 18 to 29 year-olds who report a specific religious affiliation is 68%, which is lower than any other group—and lower than other generations at that age. In the 1970's, 12% of adults ages 18 to 29 reported no specific religion; that percentage rose to 16% in the 1990's, and is now 32% among today's cohort. The National Survey of Youth and Religion (NSYR) has assessed a cohort of adolescents every three years since 2002-2003. Among the teens surveyed, one third was highly religious; one third was involved; and one third was completely uninvolved / unaffiliated [71]. Although the groups differed in religious involvement, they did not necessarily differ in their beliefs regarding God, life after death, heaven and hell, or miracles.

Given that organized religion provides many benefits to those affiliated (including support, sense of community, and a common set of values, among others), why would individuals who believe in a god or deity choose to do so outside of organized religion? The Pew Research Forum suggests several factors, including the growing involvement of religious organizations in politics at the national level (especially the Religious Right) [51, 30]—and therefore, the perception that money and power are a major focus of religious organizations. Another factor may be that the unaffiliated seem much more socially liberal than the affiliated; evidence of this is their high support for abortion (72% vs. 53%) and same-sex marriage (73% vs. 48%) compared to the affiliated. For many young Americans, religion seems "judgmental, homophobic, hypocritical, and too political" [64; pp.121].

Religion and Outcomes in Adolescents

These changes in religiosity among Americans, especially with younger generations, may be problematic. As with adults, religion seems to be related to positive overall health in youth. Using data from the 2002 Panel Study of Income Dynamics and the Child Development Supplement, Chiswick and Mirtcheva found that religious affiliation was related to overall health quality, especially among adolescents 12 to 15 years of age [10]. Smith and Lundquist identified a number of ways in which religious teenagers fared better than their counterparts, using data from the initial 2002-2003 survey years of the NSYR [79]. These researchers categorized adolescents into devoted (8% of sample), regulars (27%), sporadics (17%), and disengaged (12%). For various problem behaviors (e.g., smoking, drinking, drug use, and lapsed schoolwork) the percentages increased across the continuum. For example, 0% of devoted, 4% of regulars, 7% of sporadic and 11% of disengaged reported weekly (or more) consumption of alcoholic products. Similar trends were identified for viewing pornography, playing action video games, and engaging in sexual intercourse (or other types of sexual experiences). These trends were comparable for problem emotions (e.g., low satisfaction with own body, depression, loneliness, and feelings of meaningless) in addition to other salient life factors (e.g., quality of family relationships, moral reasoning, and compassion). Both sets of authors rightfully point out that other factors may explain these relationships; however, given the research presented in our first section on religion and health in the general population, it seems clear that religion serves as a protective factor for both adults and youth alike.

Spiritual But Not Religious

Spirituality may offset some of the potential problems associated with loss of religiosity among adolescents. According to King, Carr, and Boitor, spirituality may develop as a natural consequence of adolescent maturation [42]. These authors show how the normal developmental tasks of adolescence (e.g., existential concerns, search for purpose, meaning, belonging, and self-definition) may lead to spiritual engagement and growth, especially as youth interact with the world around them.

Although not as prevalent as religiosity, spirituality, as a distinct phenomenon, is growing. The Pew study [51] found that among the general public, 15% report being spiritual only; among the unaffiliated, the percentage is 37%. Among young adults, 72% agreed with the statement "I am more spiritual than religious" [49].

Some researchers believe this high percentage may be misleading. Among adolescents, examination of the NSYR data suggests that teenagers are "friendly with the spiritual seeker's view of the world"—but only a minority are actually spiritual seekers themselves [79]. These conclusions were based on adolescents' inability to define "spiritual but not religious." However, it is also possible that this outcome resulted more from an ongoing spiritual development, than from any misunderstanding of terminology. Roeser and colleagues believe spiritual development is a process whereby the individual moves from a focus on self to a better understanding of shared aspects of human experience [70]. This is similar to Benson et al.'s definition, in which spiritual development is conceptualized as "the developmental engine that propels the search for connectedness, meaning, purpose and contributions" [4; pp. 454]. Studying 12 to 25 year-olds, these authors determined that although youth scored higher on spiritual practices than religious practices, and had grown more in spirituality than religiosity, they were not more likely to define themselves as more spiritual than religious. It is significant to note that spiritual development occurred, in the majority of the youth, without explicit religious involvement.

In fact, clear understanding of spiritual and/or religious self-identification may not emerge until post-adolescence—if at all. If so, Smith and Lundquist's findings (above) regarding the confusion of "spiritual but not religious" among 12-17 year-olds may reflect a transition from parental beliefs and behaviors to one's own—albeit without full definition [79].

A report based on the 2013 Aris National College Student Survey may be informative regarding the future of religion and spirituality [46]. This is a national survey of 1,873 students, representing 38 colleges and universities, both public and private. This report found three distinct and equally represented worldviews: religious (31.8%); secular (28.2%); and spiritual (32.4%)—while 7.7% could not classify themselves. Among the secular group, 70% reported no religious affiliation; among the spiritual group, only one third did. When examining beliefs, the religious and secular camps represented opposite extremes, with 70% of religious confident in the existence of God, and 77% of seculars confident in the non-existence, or unsure of existence. The secular and religious camps also seem to differ significantly in terms of belief in reason / rationalism, creationism vs. evolution, life after death, and belief in miracles—with the spiritual camp in the middle. Both the secular and spiritual groups differed from the religious group regarding attitudes towards homosexuality, abortion / women's reproductive rights, and global warming. Because this categorization was based on self-identification, and since there were distinct differences in beliefs among the three groups, this report seems to suggest that as teens transition into their young adult years, they are defining their beliefs systems more clearly. Unfortunately, no such data exists for the young adult population that does not attend college.

SPIRITUALITY IN MILLENNIALS

These trends toward spirituality are being recorded as millennials, the newest generation, mature into adulthood. Millennials, typically identified as those born between 1980 to 2003, have a number of characteristics that distinguish them from previous generations. They are a powerful force for change as they demand—more than any previous generation—that environments adapt to fit their needs.

Perhaps because they grew up with the Internet, this generation has a more global perspective, which may explain why as a group they value diversity more than previous generations. This global perspective may also contribute to their tendency to be more collaborative, more socially aware and responsible [35], and more civic-minded than other generations [73]. These characteristics may indicate millennials' capacity for spiritual transcendence, which "provides meaning and serves to motivate contributions to the well-being of the world beyond themselves" [42; pp. 171].

Access to the world at their fingertips may also account for their preferences for multitasking and their tendency to quickly become bored in an environment that is not highly stimulating [37]. This generation also expects flexible schedules and tends to resist stringent rules and regulations [74]. At universities, we have been adapting our teaching practices to match these characteristics, and much of the research on millennials focuses on how they learn and how best to educate them. Newer research discusses the challenges this generation presents to the traditional workplace. It is these same characteristics that may be shaping their religious and spiritual beliefs and behaviors.

For example, and similar to millennials in general, youth high in spirituality have somewhat more prosocial tendencies than those high in religiosity, as well as more openness to change and experience [72]. The NSYR data suggests they tend to be open to viewing all religions as equally valid, a phenomenon which Smith and Lundquist call "open and inclusive religious pluralism" [79; pp. 75]. This is a marked change from previous generations.

This change may be a result of a mismatch between the values of religious adults and millennials. A meta-analysis of 21 studies of several religions from across the world, including the US, found that religious adults tend to be more conforming to rules and traditions and less likely to seek change, novelty, or self-enhancement. They were also less likely than the less religious to believe in equality across humans [72]. All these characteristics are in contrast to what we know of millennials. It is possible that spirituality may provide millennials with an alternative to traditional religions whereby they are able to connect to a higher power without the constraints of religious dogma, or the confounding of religion with politics and power that occurs in the US today.

Research on youth's perception of what religion is and is not may also indicate such a trend. In general, the majority of religious adolescents do not view religion as a set of codes to follow (e.g., praying regularly, keeping the Sabbath, or repenting from sin). Instead, religion "teaches that central to living a good and happy life is being a good, moral person [and feeling] good about you" [79; pp. 163]. This, as noted by the authors, is not specific to any religion or to religion at all. In fact, many youth reported openness towards and acceptance of other religions. For example, God exists but is not closely involved in adolescents' lives—and is not demanding of attention and behavior, but is there when needed.

These findings suggest that millennials who eschew traditional views of religion may be re-conceptualizing the meaning of religion to fit better with their own personal preferences. Thus, they may be reshaping religion, as they have reshaped education and are reshaping the work environment.

CONCLUSION AND RECOMMENDATIONS

If religion and spirituality have such strong associations with better health, broadly defined, then what are the implications of these changes for the health of millennials—and more specifically with regards to mental health, which is the focus of this chapter? What can or should be done to reduce the exodus from religion? How do we fill in the gap?

As a first step, more research is needed to understand these questions. For example, there are not enough (and no recent) studies that focus on this population of unaffiliated, "spiritual but not religious" and their health; therefore, we cannot know for sure, among millennials, whether lack of religion is associated with poorer health across the lifespan. Moreover, it is not clear that youth who claim no religious affiliation will remain this way. In past surveys, 54% of individuals who claimed no affiliation as children belonged to a religion as adults [51].

However, the finding that millennials are reconceptualizing their ideas of relgion suggests an avenue for intervention. Instead of leaving religious beliefs behind, these youth are redefining them to fit their needs. This suggests that religious institutions may find ways to adapt to this new generation, as educational institutions and the workplace have been doing. Millennials' appreciation of diversity and interest in service may suggest programs that religious organizations can offer that may interest youth and give them a chance to experience religion in action. This would also address millennials' need for more stimulating environments. A less stationary and more active and mobile religious group may appeal to millennials' interest in positively impacting the world.

Although there may be ways to decrease the movement away from religion that seems to be transpiring, it is important to note that we may not need to be concerned. As mentioned earlier, most of the research on religion and health has been correlational, and may well be explained by other factors related to both. Our own more complex research design suggested that spirituality related to mental health more than religiosity [67]. Religion may be associated with better health because it provides individuals with factors such as social support systems, values, sense of community, sense of being part of something larger, and other assets. If so, and if millennials are able to obtain these assets through other means, we may find that their mental health remains unaffected.

In addition, secular approaches to provide millennials' these needed assets are available. One such approach is based on the framework of Positive Youth Development (PYD). PYD focuses on youth strengths, potential, and self-determination. This model categorizes strengths into the Five C's of competence, confidence, connection, caring, and character. Travis and Leech added two more (community and citizenship), both of which would also fit well with what might otherwise be provided by religious activities [84]. There are currently numerous programs and projects focused on promoting PYD among American youth, and overall they have been successful [8]. The framework has been employed worldwide, and reviews indicate efficacy in promoting the development of the various C's of PYD.

We believe PYD is a sound secular approach because of its focus on optimal development and because of the extensive evidence that PYD is associated with better mental health [42]. Evidence of success has been consistent enough that in 2013, Campbell and colleagues suggested there is "a strong economic case …for increasing public investment in positive youth development programs" [6; pp. 38]. PYD is also employed by the Search Institute, which is dedicated to improving the lives of youth, with a focus on assets, relationships, communities, and helping kids thrive.

Of course, PYD is not the only viable approach. Communities across the country are testing ways to get youth involved, and to help them connect, relate, and find meaning. Continued research, intervention efforts, and evaluation of programs will clarify the many questions that remain regarding spirituality and mental health, and how to maximize the benefits of this relationship.

REFERENCES

[1] Allen, R. S., Harris, G. M., Crowther, M. R., Oliver, J. S., Cavanaugh, R., & Phillips, L. L. (2013). Does religiousness and spirituality moderate the relations between physical and mental health among aging prisoners? *International Journal of Geriatric Psychiatry, 28*(7), 710-717.

[2] Ayo, H. T., Henry, S., & Adebukola, K. T. (2009). Psychosocial variables as predictors of work-family conflict among secondary school teachers in Irele local government area, Ondo State, Nigeria. *Pakistan Journal of Social Sciences, 6*(1), 11-18.

[3] Bell, D. J. (2010). *The relationship between distal religious and proximal spiritual variables and self-reported marital happiness.* (Doctoral dissertation, Florida State University).

[4] Benson, P. L., Scales, P. C., Syvertsen, A. K., & Roehlkepartain, E. C. (2012). Is youth spiritual development a universal developmental process? An international exploration. *The Journal of Positive Psychology, 7*(6), 453-470.

[5] Berry, D. M., Bass, C. P., Forawi, W., Neuman, M., & Abdallah, N. (2011). Measuring religiosity/spirituality in diverse religious groups: A consideration of methods. *Journal of religion and health, 50*(4), 841-851.

[6] Campbell, D., Trzesniewski, K., Nathaniel, K., Enfield, R., & Erbstein, N. (2013). Positive youth development merits state investment. *California Agriculture, 67*(1), 38-46.

[7] Carlson, C. R.; Bacaseta, P. E.; & Simanton, D. A. (1988). A controlled evaluation of devotional meditation and progressive relaxation. *Journal of Psychology and Theology, 16*, 362-368.

[8] Catalano, R. F., Berglund, M. L., Ryan, J. A., Lonczak, H. S., & Hawkins, J. D. (2004). Positive youth development in the United States: Research findings on evaluations of positive youth development programs. *The annals of the American academy of political and social science, 591*(1), 98-124.

[9] Chidarikire, S. (2012). Spirituality: The neglected dimension of holistic mental health care. Advances in Mental Health, 10(3), 298-302.

[10] Chiswick, B. R., & Mirtcheva, D. M. (2013). Religion and child health: Religious affiliation, importance, and attendance and health status among American youth. *Journal of family and economic issues, 34*(1), 120-140.

[11] Cohen, S.; Kamarck, T.; & Mermelstein, R. (1983). A global measure of perceived stress. *Journal of Health and Social Behavior, 24*(4), 385-96.

[12] Cole, B.; & Pargament, K. I. (1999). Re-creating your life: A spiritual psychotherapeutic intervention for people diagnosed with cancer. *Psycho-Oncology,* 8, 395-407.

[13] Currier, J. M., Mallot, J., Martinez, T. E., Sandy, C., & Neimeyer, R. A. (2013). Bereavement, religion, and posttraumatic growth: A matched control group investigation. *Psychology of Religion and Spirituality*, *5*(2), 69.

[14] Del Rio, C. M., & White, L. J. (2012). Separating spirituality from religiosity: A hylomorphic attitudinal perspective. *Psychology of Religion And Spirituality, 4*(2), 123-142.

[15] Easterling, L. W., Gamino, L. A., Sewell, K. W., & Stirman, L. S. (1999). Spiritual experience, church attendance, and bereavement. *Journal of pastoral care, 54*(3), 263-275.

[16] Ellison, C.G., Henderson, A.K., and Moore, T. (2012, November*). Daily Spiritual Experiences, Prosocial Attitudes, and Helping Behaviors among U.S. Adults.* Paper presented at annual meetings of the Society for the Scientific Study of Religion, Phoenix, AZ.

[17] French, D. C.; Eisenberg, N.; Vaughan, J.; Purwono, U.; & Suryanti, T. A. (2008). Religious involvement and the social competence and adjustment of Indonesian Muslim adolescents. *Developmental Psychology, 44*(2), 597-611.

[18] Gall, T. L. (2003). Religious and spiritual attributions in older adults' adjustment to illness. *Journal of Psychology and Christianity, 22*(3), 210-222.

[19] Gall, T. L.; & Cornblat, M. W. (2002). Breast cancer survivors give voice: A qualitative analysis of spiritual factors in long-term adjustment. *Psycho-Oncology, 11*(6), 524-535.

[20] Gall, T. L.; Charbonneau, C.; Clarke, N.; Grant, K.; Joseph, A.; & Shouldice, L. (2005). Understanding the nature and role of spirituality in relation to coping and health: A conceptual framework. *Canadian Psychology / Psychologie Canadienne, 46*(2), 88-104.

[21] Gall, T. L.; Miguez de Renart, R. M.; & Boonstra, B. (2000). Religious resources in long-term adjustment to breast cancer. *Journal of Psychosocial Oncology, 18*(2), 21-38.

[22] Gallup. (2013). 2013 Gallup Poll Religion Aggregate. [Online poll]. Retrieved from http://www.gallup.com/file/poll/166616/2013_GALLUP_POLL_RELIGION_AGGRE GATE_131224.pdf.

[23] Gaskins, S.; & Forté, L. (1995). The meaning of hope: Implications for nursing practice and research. *Journal of Gerontological Nursing, 27*(3), 17-24.

[24] Good, M., & Willoughby, T. (2014). Institutional and personal spirituality/religiosity and psychosocial adjustment in adolescence: Concurrent and longitudinal associations. *Journal Of Youth And Adolescence, 43*(5), 757-774.

[25] Greeson, J. M., Webber, D. M., Smoski, M. J., Brantley, J. G., Ekblad, A. G., Suarez, E. C., & Wolever, R. Q. (2011). Changes in spirituality partly explain health-related quality of life outcomes after Mindfulness-Based Stress Reduction. Journal of behavioral medicine, 34(6), 508-518.

[26] Harris Interactive. (2013). Americans' Belief in God, Miracles and Heaven Declines. [Online poll report]. Retrieved from http://www.harrisinteractive.com/NewsRoom/ HarrisPolls/tabid/447/ctl/ReadCustom%20Default/mid/1508/ArticleId/1353/Default. aspx.

[27] Highfield, M. F. (1992). Spiritual health of oncology patients: Nurse and patient perspectives. *Cancer Nursing, 15*(1), 1-8.

[28] Hill, P. C., & Pargament, K. I. (2008). Advances in the conceptualization and measurement of religion and spirituality: Implications for physical and mental health research. *Psychology Of Religion And Spirituality, S*(1), 3-17.

[29] Hodge, D. R., Moser, S. E., & Shafer, M. S. (2012). Spirituality and Mental Health among Homeless Mothers. *Social Work Research*, 36(4), 245-255.

[30] Hout, M., & Fischer, C. S. (2002). Why more Americans have no religious preference: Politics and generations. *American Sociological Review, 67*(2), 165-190.

[31] Huculak, S., & McLennan, J. D. (2010). “The Lord is my Shepherd”: examining spirituality as a protection against mental health problems in youth exposed to violence in Brazil. Mental Health, *Religion & Culture, 13*(5), 467-484.

[32] Ivtzan, I., Chan, C. P., Gardner, H. E., & Prashar, K. (2013). Linking religion and spirituality with psychological well-being: examining self-actualisation, meaning in life, and personal growth initiative. *Journal of religion and health, 52*(3), 915-929.

[33] Jackson, B. R. (2010). *Daily Spiritual Experiences: A Buffer against the Effect of Daily Perceived Stress on Daily Mood* (Doctoral dissertation, University of Notre Dame).

[34] Jackson, B. R., & Bergeman, C. S. (2011). How does religiosity enhance well-being? The role of perceived control. Psychology of religion and spirituality, 3(2), 149-161.

[35] Jenkins, J. (2008). Strategies for managing talent in a multigenerational workplace. *Employment Relations Today, 34* (4), 19-26.

[36] John, L., & Sharma, D. (2014). Spirituality as a Predictor of Positive Mental Health among Adolescents with Alcoholic Addicted Fathers. *Indian Journal of Positive Psychology, 5*(2), 98-108.

[37] Johnson, J. A., & Lopes, J. (2008). The Intergenerational workforce revisited. *Organization Development Journal, 26* (1), 31-36.

[38] Kalkstein, S., & Tower, R. B. (2009). The Daily Spiritual Experiences Scale and well-being: Demographic comparisons and scale validation with older Jewish adults and a diverse internet sample. *Journal of religion and health, 48(*4), 402-417.

[39] Keefe, F. J., Affleck, G., Lefebvre, J., Underwood, L., Caldwell, D. S., Drew, J., Egert, J., Gibson, J. and Pargament, K. (2001). Living with rheumatoid arthritis: The role of daily spirituality and daily religious and spiritual coping. *The Journal of Pain, 2*(2), 101-110.

[40] Kim, Y., Carver, C. S., Spillers, R. L., Crammer, C., & Zhou, E. S. (2011). Individual and dyadic relations between spiritual well-being and quality of life among cancer survivors and their spousal caregivers. *Psycho-Oncology*, 20(7), 762-770.

[41] King, M., Marston, L., McManus, S., Brugha, T., Meltzer, H., & Bebbington, P. (2013). Religion, spirituality and mental health: results from a national study of English households. *The British Journal of Psychiatry*, *202*(1), 68-73.

[42] King, P.E., Carr, D., & Boitor, C. (2011). Religion, spirituality, positive youth development, and thriving. *Advances in Child Development and Behaviour, 41,* 161-195.

[43] Kirkpatrick, L. A.; & Shaver, P. R. (1990). Attachment theory and religion: Childhood attachments, religious beliefs, and conversion. *Journal for the Scientific Study of Religion, 29*(3), 315-334.

[44] Koenig, H. G., George, L. K., Titus, P., & Meador, K. G. (2004). Religion, spirituality, and acute care hospitalization and long-term care use by older patients. *Archives of Internal Medicine*, *164*(14), 1579-1585.

[45] Koenig, H. G.; McCullough, M. E; & Larson, D. B. (2001). *Handbook of religion and health.* Oxford: Oxford University Press.

[46] Kosmin, B. and Keysar, A. (2013). Religious, Spiritual and Secular: The emergence of three distinct worldviews among American college students. [Online report based on the 2013 ARIS survey.] Retrieved from http://www.trincoll.edu/Academics/centers/isssc/Documents/ARIS_2013_College%20Students_Sept_25_final_draft.pdf.

[47] Kuo, B. C., Arnold, R., & Rodriguez-Rubio, B. (2014). Mediating effects of coping in the link between spirituality and psychological distress in a culturally diverse undergraduate sample. Mental Health, Religion & Culture, 17(2), 173-184.

[48] Lepherd, L. (2014). Spirituality: Everyone has it, but what is it?. *International Journal of Nursing Practice, 2014,* 1-9.

[49] LifeWay Research. (2009). American Millennials are Spiritually Diverse. [Online report]. http://www.lifeway.com/lwc/files/lwcF_LifeWay_Research_finds_American_Millennials_are_spiritually_diverse_pdf.pdf.

[50] Loustalot, F. V.; Wyatt, S. B.; Boss, B.; & May, W.; McDyess, T. (2006). Psychometric examination of the Daily Spiritual Experiences Scale. *Journal of Cultural Diversity,13*(3), 162-167.

[51] Lugo, L. (2012). Nones' on the Rise: One-in-Five Adults Have No Religious Affiliation. *Pew Research Center's Forum on Religion & Public Life [online report] (October 9, 2012). http://www.pewforum.org/Unaffiliated.nones-on-the-rise.aspx.*

[52] Mahoney, A.; Carels, R. A.; Pargament, K. L.; Wachholtz, A.; Leeper, L. E.; Kaplar, M., et al. (2002). *The sanctification of the body and behavioral patterns of college students.* Paper presented at the Annual Meeting of the American Psychological Association, Washington, DC.

[53] Maisel, N., Rauer, A., Marshall, G., & Karney, B. R. (2010). *Social support after a partner's traumatic injury: Situational, relationship, and individual difference predictors* (pp. 264-288). K. Sullivan, & J. Davila (Eds.), *Support Processes in Intimate Relationships.* New York: Oxford University Press.

[54] Maton, K. I. (1989). The stress-buffering role of spiritual support: Cross-sectional and prospective investigations. *Journal for the Scientific Study of Religion, 28*, 310-323.

[55] McIntosh, D. N., Poulin, M. J., Silver, R. C., & Holman, E. A. (2011). The distinct roles of spirituality and religiosity in physical and mental health after collective trauma: a national longitudinal study of responses to the 9/11 attacks. *Journal of behavioral medicine*, 34(6), 497-507.

[56] Ng, K.; Ang, S.; & Chan, K. (2008). Personality and leader effectiveness: A moderated mediation model of leadership self-efficacy, job demands, and job autonomy. *Journal of Applied Psychology*, 93(4), 733-743.

[57] Ng, S. M., Fong, T. C., Tsui, E. Y., Au-Yeung, F. S., & Law, S. K. (2009). Validation of the Chinese Version of Underwood's Daily Spiritual Experience Scale—Transcending Cultural Boundaries?. *International Journal of Behavioral Medicine, 16*(2), 91-97.

[58] Pargament, K. I. (1997). The psychology of religion and coping: Theory, research, practice. New York: Guilford Press.

[59] Pargament, K. I.; & Park, C. L. (1995). Merely a defense? The variety of religious means and ends. Journal of Social Issues, 51(2), 13-32.

[60] Park, C. L., Brooks, M. A., & Sussman, J. (2009). Dimensions of religion and spirituality in psychological adjustment in older adults living with congestive heart failure. In Ai, A. L. (Ed.), *Role of Faith in the Well-Being of Older Adults: Linking Theories with Evidence in an Interdisciplinary Inquiry* (pp. 112-134). Hauppauge, NY: Nova Science Publishers.

[61] Park, C. L., Edmondson, D., Hale-Smith, A., & Blank, T. O. (2009). Religiousness/spirituality and health behaviors in younger adult cancer survivors: does faith promote a healthier lifestyle?. *Journal of Behavioral Medicine*, *32*(6), 582-591.

[62] Park, C. L.; & Cohen, L. (1993). Religious and non-religious coping with the death of a friend. Cognitive Therapy and Research, 17(6), 561-577.

[63] Powell, L. H.; Shahabi, L.; & Thoresen, C. E. (2003). Religion and Spirituality: Linkages to Physical Health. American Psychologist, 58(1), 36-52.

[64] Pranckeviciene, A., Zasytyte, E., and Gustainiene, L. (2008). Relationship between Spirituality and Wellness in a Sample of University Students. *International Journal of Psychology: A Biopsychosocial Approach* 2, 1-2.

[65] Putnam, R. D., & Campbell, D. E. (2010). *American grace: How religion divides and unites us.* New York: Simon & Schuster.

[66] Reeves, R. R., Beazley, A. R., & Adams, C. E. (2011). Religion and spirituality: Can it adversely affect mental health treatment?. *Journal of Psychosocial Nursing and Mental Health Services, 49*(6), 6-7.

[67] Reutter, K. K., & Bigatti, S. M. (2014). Religiosity and spirituality as resiliency resources: Moderation, mediation, or moderated mediation?. Journal for the Scientific Study Of Religion, 53(1), 56-72. doi:10.1111/jssr.12081

[68] Roberts, S. and Jarrett, T. (2011, October). *Are Spiritual People Really Less Evil? A Study Exploring the Influence of Spirituality on Deviance in the Workplace.* Presentation at the Midwest Academy of Management Fifty-Fourth Annual Conference, Omaha, Nebraska.

[69] Robinson, E. A., Cranford, J. A., Webb, J. R., & Brower, K. J. (2007). Six-month changes in spirituality, religiousness, and heavy drinking in a treatment-seeking sample. *Journal of Studies on Alcohol and Drugs, 68*(2), 282.

[70] Roeser, R. W., Issac, S. S., Abo-Zena, M., Brittian, A., & Peck, S. C. (2008). Self and identity processes in spirituality and positive youth development. *Positive youth development and spirituality: From theory to research*, 74-105.

[71] Rounding, K., Hart, K. E., Hibbard, S., & Carroll, M. (2011). Emotional Resilience in Young Adults Who Were Reared by Depressed Parents: The Moderating Effects of Offspring Religiosity/Spirituality. Journal of Spirituality In Mental Health, 13(4), 236-246.

[72] Saroglou, V., & Muñoz-García, A. (2008). Individual Differences in Religion and Spirituality: An Issue of Personality Traits and/or Values. *Journal for the Scientific Study of Religion, 47*(1), 83-101.

[73] Saunderson, R. (2009). Is It Really So Hard to Reward and Recognize a Multi-Generational Workforce?. *Employee Benefit Plan Review, 63*(8), 6-7.

[74] Shaw, S., & Fairhurst, D. (2008). Engaging a new generation of graduates. *Education + Training, 50* (5), 366-378.

[75] Shorkey, C., Uebel, M., & Windsor, L. C. (2008). Measuring dimensions of spirituality in chemical dependence treatment and recovery: research and practice. *International Journal of Mental Health and Addiction, 6*(3), 286-305.

[76] Siegel, K.; & Schrinshaw, E. W. (2002). The perceived benefits of religious and spiritual coping among older adults living with HIV/AIDS. *Journal for the Scientific Study of Religion, 41*(1), 91-102.

[77] Skarupski, K. A., Fitchett, G., Evans, D. A., & Mendes de Leon, C. F. (2010). Daily spiritual experiences in a biracial, community-based population of older adults. *Aging & Mental Health, 14*(7), 779-789.

[78] Skolarus, L. E., Lisabeth, L. D., Sánchez, B. N., Smith, M. A., Garcia, N. M., Risser, J. M., & Morgenstern, L. B. (2012). The prevalence of spirituality, optimism, depression, and fatalism in a bi-ethnic stroke population. *Journal of religion and health, 51*(4), 1293-1305.

[79] Smith, C., & Denton, M. L. (2005). *Soul searching: the religious and spiritual lives of American teenagers.* New York: Oxford University Press.

[80] Sprung, J. M., Sliter, M. T., & Jex, S. M. (2012). Spirituality as a moderator of the relationship between workplace aggression and employee outcomes. *Personality and Individual Differences, 53*(7), 930-934.

[81] Staton-Tindall, M., Duvall, J., Stevens-Watkins, D., & Oser, C. B. (2013). The Roles of Spirituality in the Relationship between Traumatic Life Events, Mental Health, and Drug Use Among African American Women from One Southern State. *Substance Use & Misuse, 48*(12), 1246-1257.

[82] Stephenson, P. S., & Berry, D. M. (2014). Describing Spirituality at the End of Life. *Western Journal of Nursing Research, 2014*, 1-19.

[83] Stewart, C.; Koeske, G. F.; & Koeske, R. D. (2006) Personal religiousness and spirituality associated with social work practitioners' use of religious-based intervention practices. Journal of Religion &Spirituality in Social Work: Social Thought, 25(1), 69-85.

[84] Travis, R., & Leech, T. G. (2014). Empowerment-Based Positive Youth Development: A New Understanding of Healthy Development for African American Youth. *Journal of Research on Adolescence, 24*(1), 93-116.

[85] Underwood, L. (2013). *Spiritual connection in daily life: Sixteen little questions that can make a big difference.* West Conshohocken, NY: Templeton Press.

[86] Underwood, L. G. (2011). The daily spiritual experience scale: overview and results. *Religions, 2*(1), 29-50.

[87] Underwood, L. G., & Teresi, J. A. (2002). The daily spiritual experience scale: Development, theoretical description, reliability, exploratory factor analysis, and preliminary construct validity using health-related data. *Annals of Behavioral Medicine, 24*(1), 22-33.

[88] Van Dyke, C. J., Glenwick, D. S., Cecero, J. J., & Kim, S. K. (2009). The relationship of religious coping and spirituality to adjustment and psychological distress in urban early adolescents. *Mental Health, Religion and Culture, 12*(4), 369-383.

[89] Walker, L. J.; & Pitts, R. C. (1998). Naturalistic concepts of moral maturity. *Developmental Psychology,* 34, 393-412.

[90] Weber, S., & Pargament, K. (2014). The role of religion and spirituality in mental health. *Current Opinion in Psychiatry, 27*(5), 358-363.

[91] Woods, G. (2007). The 'Bigger Feeling':The Importance of Spiritual Experience in Educational Leadership. *Educational Management Administration & Leadership, 35*(1), 135-155.

[92] Wutoh, A.K., English, G.N., Daniel M., Kendall K.A., Cobran, E.K., Tasker, V.C., Hodges, G., Brady, A.P., and Mbulaiteye, A. (2011). Pilot study to assess HIV

knowledge, spirituality, and risk behaviors among older African Americans. *Journal of the National Medical Association, 103*(3), 265-268.

[93] Yonker, J. E., Schnabelrauch, C. A., & DeHaan, L. G. (2012). The relationship between spirituality and religiosity on psychological outcomes in adolescents and emerging adults: A meta-analytic review. *Journal of adolescence, 35*(2), 299-314.

[94] Zinnbauer, B. J.; & Pargament, K. I. (2005). Religiousness and spirituality. In R. Paloutzian & C. Park (Eds.), Handbook of the psychology of religion and spirituality (21-42). New York: Guilford Press.

[95] Zinnbauer, B. J.; Pargament, K. I.; Cole, B.; Rye, M. S.; Butter, E. M.; Belavich, T. G.; Hipp, K. M.; Scott, A. B.; & Kadar, J. L. (1997). Religion and spirituality: Unfuzzying the fuzzy. *Journal for the Scientific Study of Religion,* 36, 549-564.

In: Spirituality
Editor: Edith C. Roberts

ISBN: 978-1-63482-370-8

Chapter 2

SPIRITUALITY, COPING, AND PSYCHOLOGICAL RESILIENCE AMONG ALZHEIMER'S CAREGIVERS

***Scott E. Wilks*[1*]*, Samantha M. Bates*[2] *and Amy L. Wright*[3]**

[1]PhD, LMSW, is a *John A. Hartford Foundation (New York) Faculty Scholar in Geriatric Social Work* and Associate Professor, Louisiana State University School of Social Work, Baton Rouge, Louisiana, US

[2]LMSW, is a PhD student, Louisiana State University School of Social Work, Baton Rouge, Louisiana, US

[3]LMSW, is a PhD student, Louisiana State University School of Social Work, Baton Rouge, Louisiana, US

Alzheimer's disease (AD) is a growing issue in the United States and globally, raising serious concerns about the future of the world's aging population. Most frequently seen in adults over the age of 65, AD is a degenerative neurological disorder that causes behavioral changes and the loss of memory, thinking, and language (Alzheimer's Association, 2014). AD is the most common type of dementia. Currently there is no known cure for AD, yet scientists have learned that AD progresses due to an attack on the brain's neurons that produce the neurotransmitter acetylcholine. This attack causes nerve cells to break connections and die (Alzheimer's Association, 2014). Further, abnormal lesions and neurofibrillary tangles develop outside the neurons and inside nerve cells; first damaging the brain's hippocampus where short-term memory is lost, and then developing in the cerebral cortex resulting in the loss of language and judgment (Alzheimer's Association, 2014). This attack on the brain's neurons can be rapid or progress very slowly. For example, deaths caused by AD can range anywhere between three to twenty years. The Centers for Disease Control and Prevention (CDC, 2014) estimated that the average life expectancy after receiving an AD diagnosis is approximately eight to ten years. Experiences for AD patients can vary according to the speed in which the disease progresses, but the disease remains terminal.

* Corresponding author: email: swilks@lsu.edu.

National data in the United States emerged in the late 1970's when Robert Katzman became one of the first to publish national estimates on AD in the 1976 editorial, *Archives of Neurology* (George, 2006). Katzman estimated that approximately 1.2 million cases of AD existed in 1976, causing about 60,000-90,000 deaths per year (George, 2006). Current estimates of AD have shown an immense increase in the prevalence of the disease since the 1970's. Currently, the Alzheimer's Association (2014) estimates that 5.2 million Americans are diagnosed with AD and 500,000 people die a year from this disease. Further, an astounding 16 million Americans are predicted to have the disease by 2050 (Alzheimer's Association, 2014). Current global rates and predictions are consistent with the prevalence rates of AD in the United States. Alzheimer's Disease International (2014) estimates that 44.4 million people have AD worldwide, and 135.5 million people will by 2050. Therefore, both globally and in the United States, the prevalence of AD is predicted to nearly triple in the next 40 years. The rising growth of expectant AD patients will undoubtedly have a major impact, both socially and economically, on those caring for these older adults.

Alzheimer's Disease Caregivers

Late life functioning and life expectancies have improved due to advancing medical technologies. As such, older adults have been living longer with terminal illnesses like AD, leaving families increasingly responsible for providing care to their loved ones. Because symptoms of AD can progress slowly over time, family and friends have been found to be the primary sources of care for people with Alzheimer's (Gitlin & Schultz, 2012). Family members and/or friends who care for those diagnosed with AD are called *informal caregivers*. Informal caregivers are defined as an individual that does not have professional training and is not paid to provide care. In this chapter, *AD caregivers* will reference those who provide informal care to their family members or friends diagnosed with Alzheimer's. Providing care, irrespective of payment or professional training, has been found to generate specific risks for AD caregivers' health and well-being.

Risks for Caregivers

Research has shown AD caregivers are at an increased risk for psychological, behavioral, and physiological health problems due to increased stress (Miller, Rosenheck, & Schneider, 2012). Similarly, increased risks of depression and anxiety have been found among those witnessing a loved one progress through the stages of AD; exacerbating risks to caregiver's psychological well-being (Shah, Snow, & Kunik, 2001). Poor mental or physical health can make managing caregiving responsibilities difficult, creating negative effects for the care recipient (Gonzales et al., 2011; Navaie-Waliser et al., 2002).

A recent study on the economic impact of AD showed that the cost of informal caregiving, estimated at 252 billion dollars, accounted for 42% of the total global cost of AD (Wimo et al., 2013). The total cost of AD worldwide was valued at 604 billion dollars (Wimo et al., 2013). Therefore, we cannot ignore the contribution of informal caregivers and its influence on global costs and the cost effectiveness of informal care. The negative impact of caregiving risks on the health and well-being of AD caregivers may cause a significant increase in the worldwide costs of AD. Broadly, if informal care dissipates, resources will become strained in countries where assistance programs fund formal health care. Protecting the health of AD caregivers has serious implications for reducing global costs. One way to protect against these risks for AD caregivers is to help them find ways to cope effectively with their stress, including coping techniques related to spirituality. First, it is important to understand the framework of stress and coping in order to understand what techniques promote healthy outcomes and reduce maladaptive behaviors for AD caregivers.

Stress-Coping Framework

Richard Lazarus and Susan Folkman (1984) established a stress-coping framework to explain how stress interacts with a person and their environment. This framework suggests that stress begins following a distressing event or situation and then proceeds into three cognitive processes: primary appraisal, secondary appraisal, and coping. Primary appraisal is an assessment by the individual to appraise whether or not they have anything at stake in the distressing encounter. Next, the individual engages in secondary appraisal by assessing what can be done to overcome, prevent harm, or maximize the benefits of the distressing event or situation (Folkman et al., 1986). Within the cognitive process of secondary appraisal, various coping techniques are evaluated to determine how to manage the situation. For the purpose of this chapter, *coping* is defined as the final cognitive and behavioral process of managing internal and external demands that are taxing or exceeding the person's resources (Folkman et al., 1986). Often, stress and diminished resources create increased burden for AD caregivers. *Burden* refers to the extent in which caregivers perceive their own emotional or physical health, social life, or financial status affected by caring for an ill friend or relative (Zarit, Todd, & Zarit, 1986; Vilchinsky et al., 2014). In order to buffer stress and burden, individuals – in this discussion, specifically AD caregivers – engage in different techniques of coping.

Coping Techniques

AD caregivers have been found to engage in numerous coping techniques to combat stress and burden. In the past, researchers first recognized that increased burden was affecting AD caregivers when support groups emerged in the mid-1970's. The first known AD support group, the Family Survival Project was establish in San Francisco in 1976, followed by the establishment of the Alzheimer's Association in 1979 (LoboPrabhu, Molinari, & Lomax, 2006). These programs were the first to offer much needed support and education to AD caregivers. Their popularity and support offered to AD caregivers became an area of research interest, specifically identifying the role of social support to cope with burden. The literature on social support and other forms of coping grew immensely in the early 1980's.

In this chapter, coping techniques are the specific activities or behaviors AD caregivers use to cope with burden. A majority of the early studies on caregiving, in general, had large sample sizes and used survey methods to collect data (Nightingale, 2003). Within these early studies, researchers examined numerous coping techniques and their influence on caregivers' health, caregivers' perceived stress, recipient care, and the caregiving relationship (Chang, Noonan & Tennstedt, 1998; Tix & Frazier, 1998; Salts, Denham, & Smith, 1991; Segall & Wykle, 1989). The following coping techniques were among the first to be specifically examined among AD caregivers as a result of these early studies on caregiving: drinking, prescription medication, prayer, meditation, information seeking, avoidance, resource allocation, nonprescription medication, counseling, medical care, church, and support groups (Conway, 1985; Morycz, 1985; Taylor, 1982). Following these early studies, the effects of meditation, prayer, church attendance, and religious practices emerged as an area of research interest as these techniques have shown positive outcomes for caregivers (Nightingale, 2003). The identification of the positive effects of these coping techniques led to social scientists to further examine the importance of spirituality among AD caregivers.

SPIRITUALITY AS COPING AMONG AD CAREGIVERS

Spirituality encompasses both religious and existential concepts. For example, *religion* has been defined as the search for significance related to the sacred and the adherence to beliefs and practices of organized social and religious institutions (Koenig, McCullough, & Larson, 2001; Harrison et al., 2001). Religious behaviors and beliefs (e.g., prayer, reflective thought, going to church) are similar to existential practices that are philosophical in nature. Existential practices include searching for personal meaning, loyalty to values, and finding inner peace (e.g., meditation, tai chi, yoga; Koenig, McCullough, & Larson, 2001; Narasimhan, Bhaskar, & Prakhya, 2010). *Spirituality*, therefore, is broadly defined in this chapter as any mechanism in which an individual engages in a personal search for purpose and meaning in life, as well as a connection to a transcendent reality (Hill et al., 2000; Puchalski, 2002). Spirituality is a behavioral expression directed toward entities greater than the self. There are several reasons why spirituality is a useful coping technique for caregivers.

Spiritual thoughts, behaviors, and practices like meditation and prayer are easily available and accessible resources. The availability and accessibility of these spiritual techniques are particularly useful when resources become limited (Harrison et al., 2001). Since perceived burden increases for caregivers as resources become strained, the constant availability of spiritual coping techniques can be protective in reducing burden. Similarly, spiritual rituals like funerals, church attendance, and prayer seek to comfort emotional strain, promote hope, and give meaning to life. Religious institutions provide resources and structure to promote sense of community among members, often perpetuating forms of social, emotional, and physical support for caregivers. Spiritual involvement can also prevent risky behaviors such as use of drugs or alcohol, social isolation, and hopelessness (Stuckey, 2001). In sum, spirituality can be protective in helping caregivers reduce stress and burden, provide support, and prevent maladaptive behaviors. Research gathered in the last 30 years has yielded greater knowledge about the prevalence and impact of spiritual techniques on caregivers.

Prayer

One of the most important spiritual coping techniques that emerged in the literature was, and still is, prayer. Kaye and Robinson (1994) reported that 94% of caregivers engaged in private prayer everyday. Further, 77% of caregivers talked about spiritual matters with friends/family once a week and 88% read spiritual-related materials once per week (Kayne & Robinson, 1994). More recently, a national poll supported spirituality as a major coping resource as 73% of all caregivers reported using prayer to cope with the demands of caregiving (Caregiving in the U.S., 2004). Intercessory prayer, or prayer for others, has also been found among caregivers (Hanson et al., 2008), yet little research has observed the influence of this type of prayer on specific outcomes for AD caregivers. It is important to state that current research has shown that prayer remains the most commonly reported coping method among AD caregivers. These salient results show the prevalence of prayer and other spiritual coping techniques among caregivers. Studies have also shown the influence of church attendance on AD caregivers.

Church Attendance

Heo and Koeske (2001) and Haley et al. (1987) found religious attendance was consistently associated with lower rates of depression and lower burden. Church attendance has also been associated with individuals reporting less of a perceived need for social support (George & Gwyther, 1986). This finding may reflect the already available infrastructure of the church as a facilitator of preexisting social support. Further, in a study of 84 AD caregivers, Burgener (1994) found that church attendance was associated with better social functioning. Social functioning is important to AD caregivers in order maintain healthy relationships that may impacted as the demands of caregiving increase. Overall, studies have shown that church attendance as a coping technique can positively influence social activities for caregivers. Existential practices such as meditation and yoga as spiritual coping techniques have similarly been shown to impact AD caregivers.

Meditation and Yoga

Meditation and yoga are spiritual techniques that help individuals focus on a mind-body connection to help them understand and mediate stress. Several researchers have sought to examine these practices among AD caregivers. In a six-session yoga and meditation intervention, Waelde, Thompson, and Gallagher-Thompson (2004) used pre- and post-test measures to examine depression, anxiety, and self-efficacy among AD caregivers. Following the intervention, their results showed a significant reduction in depression and anxiety for caregivers, and improvements in their perceived self-efficacy. AD caregivers also reported subjective improvements in physical and emotional functioning (Waelde et al., 2004). Lavretsky et al. (2013) supported these findings found that yoga and meditation lowered depressive symptoms and improved cognitive functioning for caregivers. Finally, Oken et al. (2010) found, after implementing a mindfulness meditation intervention with AD caregivers, that the experimental group had lower levels of self-reported stress than the control-group.

These research studies show that the existential search for inner peace and personal meaning can improve mental health outcomes, reduces stress, and improve physical, emotional, and cognitive functioning for AD caregivers. Additional studies have examined the impact of spiritual coping techniques on burden and health outcomes for AD caregivers.

SPIRITUALITY AND CAREGIVER BURDEN

A major theme in the literature on spiritual coping is its association with lowering caregiver burden. Lowering caregiver burden can be protective for AD caregivers and promote positive outcomes. Spurlock (2005) assessed spirituality and caregiver burden among 150 AD family caregivers. Spirituality was measured using a spiritual well-being scale, comprised of religious well-being and existential well-being subscales. Findings showed that higher mean scores on the spiritual well-being measure was associated lower mean scores on a caregiver burden scale. Results also reflected findings of previous studies as Spurlock's sample reported high utilization of prayer, attendance to religious activities, and discussion of spiritual matters with family and friends.

Other research studies have supported these findings of spiritual coping lowering caregiver burden. For example, Karlin (2004) found participation in organized and non-organized religious practices was associated with lower burden. Wright, Pratt, and Schmall (1985) examined spiritual support among 240 AD caregivers and found higher spiritual support was predictive of lower burden as well. The reduction of caregiver burden as a functioning of spiritual coping is important because of its strong association with positive physical and physiological health outcomes for caregivers.

Studies have shown that lower caregiver burden can improve physical and psychological health outcomes for AD caregivers. In a multisite randomized control trial funded by the National Institutes of Aging (NIA) and Nursing Research (NINR), Heo and Koeske (2011) found the pathways between religious attendance, prayer/meditation, and religious coping were significant for AD caregivers. Further, pathways of high religious coping significantly predicted lowered levels of burden appraisal, resulting in lower levels of depression. Self-reports of physical health were also marginally related to prayer and mediation practices and negatively related to burden appraisal and depression (Heo & Koeske, 2011). These findings mean that those who used prayer and meditation perceived their health to be much better than those who did not use these practices. Numerous other studies have supported these findings and shown that spiritual coping was associated with better self-reported health perceptions and mental health outcomes for AD caregivers (Burgener, 1994; Haley et al., 1987; Hebert, Dang, & Schultz, 2007; Karlin, 2004).

In sum, a majority of the studies on spiritual coping for AD caregivers have shown that lower caregiver burden reduces depressive symptoms and other mental health risks. In contrast, those with high burden were found to have increased symptoms of depression and self-reported having poor physical health. It is important to note that not all individuals have positive outcomes when using spirituality as a coping technique. While the positive aspects of spiritual coping techniques have been consistently reported in the literature, adverse outcomes have also been found.

SPIRITUALITY AND ADVERSE OUTCOMES

For AD caregivers, spirituality may not always contribute to positive cognitions, behaviors, and practices. For example, in a study of AD caregiver's religious coping activities, Shah, Snow, and Kunik (2001) measured the extent to which a person turned to religion in both positive and negative ways in response to stress. Results showed that when AD caregivers experienced discontent with their religious beliefs they experienced greater burden and depression (Shah, Snow, & Kunik, 2001). Therefore, caregivers may feel anger toward God, distance from members of their religious group, and question their faith in times of stress. This reaction was associated with higher levels of depression and burden.

Other researchers have questioned whether spirituality hinders caregivers from seeking medical support for both the care recipient and themselves. These questions have arisen after studies have shown religious beliefs influence how individuals perceive and obtain medical care. For example, Meller (2001) measured religious faith and the number of times caregivers went to the doctor. Results showed that religious faith was associated with fewer doctor's visits by caregivers despite high self-reports of poor physical health (Meller, 2001). These findings may suggest that if a caregiver has a strict adherence to a belief system that God or a higher power will protect her/him against negative outcomes, it may increase her/his risks for poor health outcomes. These poor health outcomes will sustain themselves if the caregiver fails to seek medical treatment.

The historical background and literature review presented in this chapter thus far has focused on the specific risks and current knowledge about AD caregivers. The importance of AD caregivers in supporting the current, and future, population of older adults diagnosed with AD is definite. This chapter will now focus on how known risks and protective spiritual coping techniques have been found to promote psychological resilience among AD caregivers.

RESILIENCE AND SPIRITUALITY

Resilience is considered to be positive adaptation, competence and functioning in the face of any type of stressful experience, and is classified in certain research with at-risk populations as the "positive" end of the spectrum of psychosocial outcomes (Egeland et al., 1993, p. 517). AD caregivers with healthier adaptation skills (e.g., coping) are likely to appraise caregiving responsibilities as being less stressful and therefore may exhibit reduced susceptibility to the negative psychosocial effects of caregiver burden (Gonzalez et al., 2010). Thus, taken together, these findings seem to suggest the occurrence of resilience regarding AD care. Studies have been conducted in order to examine the interrelationships between spirituality as it relates to burden/stress and psychological resilience among AD caregivers.

Prayer

Wilks and Vonk (2008) assessed the extent to which AD caregivers utilize private prayer as a means of coping as well as whether prayer mediates caregiving burden on perceived resilience in a sample of 304 caregiver participants in caregiver support groups throughout the southeastern United States. Ai, Peterson, Bolling, and Koenig's (2002) scale, *Using Private Prayer as a Means of Coping* (UPPMC), was self-administered to each participant and assessed each participant's belief in the importance of prayer, the benefit of prayer in coping with burden, and the use of prayer to cope with burden. Responses were on a 4-point Likert-type format ranging from *strongly agree* to *strongly disagree*. The frequency of prayer was also measured on a 4-point Likert format consisting of responses of *never*, *daily*, *weekly*, and *monthly*. Additionally, the Connor-Davidson Resilience Scale (CD-RISC, Connor & Davidson, 2003, p. 76), measured resilience and consisted of 25 items each rated on a 5-point scale ranging from *not true at all* to *nearly true all of the time*. Examples of the items included: "I tend to bounce back after illness, injury or other hardships"; and "I am not easily discouraged by failure." Findings indicated that a large majority (95%) of participants reported that they engage in private prayer on a daily basis (Wilks & Vonk, 2008). Results from the UPPMC (Ai et al., 2002) suggested that the utilization of private prayer is a greatly relied upon coping method for AD caregivers. Findings also revealed a decreased effect of caregiving burden on perceived resilience with the inclusion of private prayer, which is suggestive of prayer being a mediator of the two aforementioned variables (Wilks & Vonk, 2008).

Intrinsic Spirituality

Another aspect of spirituality includes intrinsic spirituality, defined as the expression of spirituality as well as the overall encompassing sense of spirituality, frequently plays a key role in providing consolation to AD caregivers during stressful times (Hodge, 2003). Thus, intrinsic spirituality is classified as the nature in which spirituality is an influential moment in an individual's life whereby they find their ultimate purpose for their life within their spirituality (Hodge, 2003). Additionally, research has shown a moderately high level of intrinsic spirituality and its relationship to resilience among AD caregivers. For instance, Wilks (2006) assessed whether or not intrinsic spirituality was a predictor in perceived level of resilience among AD caregivers by sampling 304 AD caregivers in support groups in a southeast region of the United States. Through the utilization of measurements such as of Hodge's (2003) *Intrinsic Spirituality Scale* (ISS), a six-item instrument evaluating the level to which an individual taps into their internalized, spiritual commitment (Burris, 1999), in addition to the CD-RISC (Connor & Davidson, 2003), Wilks (2006) found that caregivers demonstrated a fairly high degree of perceived resilience. Additionally, he found that the greater the degree of intrinsic spirituality, the more likely the caregiver perceived a greater sense of resilience

Spiritual Support

The number of studies addressing the influence of religion and spirituality as personal resources in regards to caregiver stress is limited, even though these variables have been found to provide a pertinent set of coping tools for caregivers (Hebert et al., 2006). Research has suggested that spiritual support can lead to positive direct effects on caregiver burden

(Haley et al., 2001). Specifically, church attendance, higher levels of intrinsic religiosity and spirituality, and use of prayer have all been found to provide emotional comfort for caregivers undergoing difficult and stressful situations (Karlin, 2004). Studies have shown religiosity and spiritual support to mediate the negative effects of caregivers' burden as it relates to depression (Leblanc et al., 2004), suggesting that spiritual support serves as a protective function for AD caregivers.

IMPLICATIONS FOR HEALTH CARE PRACTICE

These findings of the aforementioned issues of spirituality bear several implications among the health care professional community in regards to its work with AD caregivers specifically as it relates to their coping and resilience. Coping is considered to be a *durational* strength whereby one is able to alleviate or successfully manage burden. Comparatively, resilience is considered to be an *outcome* strength; that is, an observed characteristic of effect after an experienced burden, usually resulting from effective means of coping (Masten, 1999). Clarification between coping and resilience invites social workers to recognize the difference between the two concepts as well as appreciate the findings of related studies (Wilks, 2006).

Acknowledging the strength of prayer, intrinsic spirituality, and spiritual support as it relates to the perceived level of resilience among AD caregivers is pivotal in the worker-patient/client (in this case, worker-caregiver) relationship (Wilks, 2006). The health care professional can recognize spirituality as a key resource, especially if the patient/client acknowledges it as such. Practitioners should be able to support the use of spirituality as a resilience-promoting technique among AD caregivers (Wilks, 2006) in addition to a healthy means of stress management. Additionally, the successful use of a strengths-promoting process of practice by integrating the caregiver's spirituality into the assessment depends upon the worker's level of competence in this area (Hodge, Cardenas, & Montoya, 2001). Given that past surveys suggest that practitioners may not have the necessary education and training to address spirituality concerns in a sensitive manner (Derezotes, 1995), Wilks (2006) argued the importance of addressing the spiritual nature and expression among AD caregivers within academic curricula among allied health disciplines, along with education in methods of spiritual assessment. Due to the rapid growth of the AD caregiver population, with 5 million families currently providing care for a family member (NAC/AARP, 1997), it is especially vital to understand the importance of setting forth a commitment to spiritual understanding within the classroom and internship settings (Wilks, 2006).

CONCLUSION

This chapter discussed the Alzheimer's caregiver population, the issues of spirituality, the coping methods of private prayer, intrinsic spirituality and spiritual support and their ability to mediate caregiver burden and stress on perceived resilience among AD caregivers. Numerous spiritual coping techniques have been found to be effective among the AD caregiver population, despite some of the adverse outcomes related to spirituality. Specifically, private prayer, church attendance, meditation and yoga have all shown to decrease depressive symptoms and reduce other psychosocial effects of caregiver burden, helping to promote psychological resilience among AD caregivers. Thus, studies have been conducted and findings have shown a decreased effect of caregiver burden on perceived resilience with the inclusion of private prayer among AD caregivers. Additionally, the presence of intrinsic spirituality seems to be moderately high among AD caregivers, suggesting its significance relating to resilience, given that the perceived sense of resilience increases as the degree of intrinsic spirituality increases among dementia caregivers.

REFERENCES

Ai, A., Peterson, C., Bolling, S., & Koenig, H. (2002). Private prayer and optimism among middle-aged and older patients awaiting cardiac surgery. *The Gerontologist, 42*, 70-81.

Alzheimer's Association. (2014). *Alzheimer's & dementia.* Retrieved from http://www.alz.org/

Alzheimer's Disease International. (2014). *Global information.* Retrieved from http://www.alz.co.uk

Burgener, S.C. (1994). Caregiver religiosity and well-being in dealing with Alzheimer's dementia. *Journal of Religion and Health*, *33*, 175-189.

Center for Disease Control and Prevention. (2014). *Alzheimer's disease.* Retrieved from http://www.cdc.gov/aging/aginginfo/alzheimers.htm

Chang, B., Noonan, A., & Tennstedt, S. (1998). The role of religion/spirituality in coping with caregiving for disabled elders. *Gerontologist*, *38*(4), 463-470.

Cohen, S., Janicki-Deverts, D., & Miller, G. (2007). Psychological stress and disease. *JAMA: Journal of The American Medical Association*, *298*(14), 1685-1687.

Connor, K. M., & Davidson, J. R. T. (2003). Development of a new resilience scale: The Connor-Davidson Resilience Scale (CD-RISC). *Depression and Anxiety, 18*, 76-82.

Conway, K. (1985). Coping with the stress of medical problems among black and white elderly. *International Journal of Aging and Human Development*, *2*, 39-148.

Cooper, C. G., Katona, C., Orrell, M., & Livingston, G. (2008). Coping strategies, anxiety and depression in caregivers of people with Alzheimer's disease. *International Journal of Geriatric Psychiatry*, *23*(9), 929-936.

Derezotes, D. S. (1995). Spirituality and religiosity: Neglected factors in social work practice. *Arete, 20*(1), 1-15.

Egeland, B., Carlson, E., & Sroufe, L. A. (1993). Resilience as process. *Development and Psychopathology, 5*, 517-528.

Folkman, S., Lazarus, R. S., Dunkel-Schetter, C., DeLongis, A., & Gruen, R. J. (1986). Dynamics of a stressful encounter: Cognitive appraisal, coping, and encounter outcomes. *Journal of Personality and Social Psychology*, *50*(5), 992-1003. doi:10.1037/0022-3514.50.5.992

Geldmacher, D. S., Kirson, N. Y., Birnbaum, H. G., Eapen, S., Kantor, E., Cummings, A. K., & Joish, V. N. (2014). Implications of early treatment among Medicaid patients with Alzheimer's disease. *Alzheimer's & Dementia*, *10*(2), 214-224. doi:10.1016/j.jalz.2013.01.015

George, L. K., & Gwyther, L. P. (1986). Caregiver well-being: A multidimensional examination of family caregivers of demented adults. *Gerontologist, 26*, 253-259.

Gitlin, L. & Schultz, R. (2012). Family caregiving of older adults. In T.R. Prohaska, L. Anderson, & R.H. Binstock (Eds.), *Public Health for an Aging Society* (pp. 181-204). Baltimore, MD: The Johns Hopkins University Press.

Gonzalez, E. W., Polansky, M., Lippa, C. F., Walker, D., & Feng, D. (2011). Family caregivers at Risk: Who are they? *Issues In Mental Health Nursing*, *32*(8), 528-536. doi:10.3109/01612840.2011.573123

Gonzalez, M., Lopez, J., Romero-Moreno, R., & Losada, A. (2010). Anger, spiritual meaning and support from the religious community in dementia caregiving. *Journal of Religious Health, 51*, 179-186.

Haley, W. E., West, C. A., Wadley, V. G., Ford, G. R., White, F. A., Barrett, J. J. (2001). Psychological, social and health impact of caregiving: A comparison of black and white dementia family caregivers and noncaregivers. *Psychology and Aging, 10*, 540-552.

Haley, W.E., Levine, E.G., Brown, S.L., & Bartoloucci, A. A. (1987). Stress, appraisal, coping, and social support as predictors of adaptational outcome among dementia caregivers. *Psychology and Aging*, *2*, 323-330.

Hanson, L. C., Dobbs, D., Usher, B. M., Williams, S., Rawlings, J., & Daaleman, T. P. (2008). Providers and types of spiritual care during serious illness. *Journal of Palliative Medicine*, *11*(6), 907-914. doi:10.1089/jpm.2008.0008

Harrison, M. O., Koenig, H. G., Hays, J. C., Eme-Akwari, A. G., & Pargament, K. I. (2001). The epidemiology of religious coping: A review of recent literature. *International Review of Psychiatry*, *13*(2), 86-93. doi:10.1080/09540260120037317

Hebert, R. S., Qianyu, D., & Schulz, R. (2006). Preparedness for the death of a loved one and mental health in bereaved caregivers of patients with dementia: Findings from the REACH study. *Journal of Palliative Medicine*, *9*(3), 683-693. doi:10.1089/jpm.2006.9.683

Hebert, R. S., Weinstein, E., Martire, L. M., & Schulz, R. (2006). Religion, spirituality and the well-being of informal caregivers. *Aging & Mental Health, 10*, 497-520.

Heo, G. J. & Koeske, G. (2011). The role of religious coping and race in Alzheimer's disease caregiving. *Journal of Applied Gerontology*, *32*(5), 582-604.

Hill, P. C., Pargament, K. I., Hood, J. W., McCullough, M. E., Swyers, J. P., Larson, D. B., & Zinnbauer, B. J. (2000). Conceptualizing religion and spirituality: Points of commonality, points of departure. *Journal for the Theory of Social Behaviour*, *30*(1), 51.

Hodge, D. R. (2003). The intrinsic spirituality scale: A new six-item instrument for assessing the salience of spirituality as a motivational construct. *Journal of Social Service Research, 30*(1), 41-61.

Hodge, D. R., Cardenas, P., & Montoya, H. (2001). Spirituality and religious as protective factors participation among rural youths. *Social Work Research, 25*, 153-161.

Hurd, M. D., Martorell, P., Delavande, A., Mullen, K. J., & Langa, K. M. (2013). Monetary costs of dementia in the United States. *The New England Journal of Medicine*, *368*(14), 1326-1334. doi:10.1056/NEJMsa1204629

Iavarone, A., Ziello, A. R., Pastore, F., Fasanaro, A. M., & Poderico, C. (2014). Caregiver burden and coping strategies in caregivers of patients with Alzheimer's disease. *Neuropsychiatric Disease and Treatment, 10,* 1407-1413. doi:10.2147/NDT.S58063

Karlin, N.J. (2004). An analysis of religiosity and exercise as predictors of support group attendance and caregiver burden while caring for a family member with Alzheimer's disease. *Journal of Mental Health and Aging*, *10*, 99-106.

Kaye, J., & Robinson, K. M. (1994). Spirituality among caregivers. *Journal of Nursing Scholarship*, *26*(3), 218. doi:10.1111/j.1547-5069.1994.tb00317.x

Koenig, H. G., Larson, D. B., & Larson, S. S. (2001). Religion and coping with serious medical illness. *Annals of Pharmacotherapy*, *35*(3), 352-359.

Lavretsky, H., Epel, E., Siddarth, P., Nazarian, N., Cyr, N. S., Khalsa, D., Lin, J., Blackburn, E., & Irwin, M. (2013). A pilot study of yogic meditation for family dementia caregivers with depressive symptoms: Effects on mental health, cognition, and telomerase activity. *International Journal of Geriatric Psychiatry*, *28*(1), 57-65. doi:10.1002/gps.3790

Lazarus, R., & Folkman, S. (1984). *Stress, appraisal, and coping*. New York: Springer. .

Leblanc, A. J., Driscoll, A. J., & Pearlin, L. I. (2004). Religiosity and the expansion of caregiver stress. *Aging and Mental Health, 8*, 410-421.

LoboPrabhu, S. M., Molinari, V., & Lomax, J. W. (2006). *Supporting the caregiver in dementia: A guide for health care professionals.* Baltimore: Johns Hopkins University Press.

Marin, M. F., Lord, C., Andrews, J., Juster, R. P., Sindi, S., Arsenault-Lapierre, G., Fiocco, A.J., & Lupien, S.J. (2011). Chronic stress, cognitive functioning, and mental health. *Neurobiology of Learning and Memory*, *96*, 583-595.

Masten, A. S. (2001). Ordinary magic: Resilience processes in development. *American Psychologist, 56*, 227-238.

Meller, S. (2001). A comparison of the well-being of family caregivers of elderly patients hospitalized with physical impairments versus the caregivers of patients hospitalized with dementia. *Journal of the American Medial Directors Association*, *2*, 60-65.

Miller, E., Rosenheck, R., & Schneider, L. (2012). Caregiver burden, health utilities, and institutional service use in Alzheimer's disease. *International Journal of Geriatric Psychiatry*, *27*(4), 382-393. doi:10.1002/gps.2730

Morycz, R. K. (1985). Caregiving strain and the desire to institutionalize family members with Alzheimer's disease. *Research on Aging*, *7*, 329-361.

Mucha, L., Fowler, R., & Bonafede, M. (2011). The incremental effect of Alzheimer's disease on direct health care costs and utilization in a Medicaid population. *Alzheimer's & Dementia: The Journal of the Alzheimer's Association*, *7*(4), 357. doi:10.1016 /j.jalz.2011.05.1033

Narasimhan, N., Bhaskar, K., & Prakhya, S. (2010). Existential beliefs and values. *Journal of Business Ethics*, *96*(3), 369-382. doi:10.1007/s10551-010-0472-7

National Alliance for Caregiving, & AARP. (2004). *Caregiving in the U.S.* Retrieved from www.caregiving.org/data/04finalreport.pdf

Navaie-Waliser, M., Feldman, P. H., Gould, D. A., Levine, C., Kuerbis, A. N., & Donelan, K. (2002). When the caregiver needs care: The plight of vulnerable caregivers. *American Journal of Public Health*, *92*(3), 409-413.

Nightingale, M. C. (2003). Religion, spirituality, and ethnicity. *Dementia: The International Journal of Social Research and Practice*, *2*(3), 380-391. doi:10.1177 /14713012030023006

Oken, B. S., Fonareva, I., Haas, M., Wahbeh, H., Lane, J. B., Zajdel, D., & Amen, A. (2010). Pilot controlled trial of mindfulness meditation and education for dementia caregivers.

Journal of Alternative & Complementary Medicine, *16*(10), 1031-1038. doi:10.1089/acm.2009.0733

Perry, G. (2006). *Alzheimer's Disease: Advances for a New Century*. Amsterdam: IOS Press.

Puchalski, C. M. (2002). Spirituality and end-of-life care: A time for listening and caring. *Journal of Palliative Medicine*, *5*(2), 289-294. doi:10.1089/10966210275364l287

Salts, C. J., Denham, T. E., & Smith, T. J. (1991). Relationship patterns and role of religion in elderly couples with chronic illness. *Journal of Religious Gerontology*, *7*(3), 41-54.

Segall, M. & Wykle, M. (1989). The black families experience with dementia. *Journal of Applied Social Sciences*, *13*(1), 170-191.

Shah, A. A., Snow, A. L., & Kunik, M. E. (2001). Spiritual and religious coping in caregivers of patients with Alzheimer's disease. *Clinical Gerontologist: The Journal of Aging and Mental Health*, *24*(3-4), 127-136. doi:10.1300/J018v24n03_11

Spurlock, W.R. (2005). Spiritual well-being and caregiver burden in Alzheimer's caregivers. *Geriatric Nursing*, *26*(3), 154-161.

Stuckey, J. C. (2001). Blessed assurance: The role of religion and spirituality in Alzheimer's disease caregiving and other significant life events. *Journal of Aging Studies*, *15*(1), 69.

Suehs, B. T., Davis, C. D., Alvir, J., van Amerongen, D., PharmD, N. P., Joshi, A. V., Faison, W. E., & Shah, S. N. (2013). The clinical and economic burden of newly diagnosed Alzheimer's disease in a Medicare advantage population. *American Journal of Alzheimer's Disease & Other Dementias*, *28*(4), 384-392. doi:10.1177/1533317513488911

Taylor, S. P. (1982). Mental health and successful coping among aged black women. In R. C. Manuel (Ed.), *Minority Aging* (95-100). Westport, CT: Greenwood.

Tix, A. P., & Frazier, P. A. (1998). The use of religious coping during stressful life events: Main effects, moderation, and mediation. *Journal of Consulting and Clinical Psychology*, *66*(2), 411-422. doi:10.1037/0022-006X.66.2.411

Vilchinsky, N., Dekel, R., Revenson, T. A., Liberman, G., & Mosseri, M. (2014). Caregivers' burden and depressive symptoms: The moderational role of attachment orientations. *Health Psychology*. doi:10.1037/hea0000121

Vitaliano, P. P., Zhang, J., & Scanlan, J. M. (2003). Is caregiving hazardous to one's physical health? A meta-analysis. *Psychological Bulletin*, *129*(6), 946-972. doi:10.1037/0033-2909.129.6.946

Waelde, L. C., Thompson, L., & Gallagher-Thompson, D. (2004). A pilot study of a yoga and meditation intervention for dementia caregiver stress. *Journal of Clinical Psychology*, *60*(6), 677-687.

Wilks, S. E. (2006). Intrinsic spirituality among Alzheimer's caregivers: A pathway to resiliency. *Advances in Social Work, 7*, 76-100.

Wilks, S. E., Vonk, M. (2008). Private prayer among Alzheimer's caregivers: Mediating burden and resiliency. *Journal of Gerontological Social Work, 50*, 113-129.

Wimo, A., Jönsson, L., Bond, J., Prince, M., & Winblad, B. (2013). The worldwide economic impact of dementia 2010. *Alzheimer's & Dementia*, *9*(1), 1-11. doi:10.1016/j.jalz.2012.11.006

Wright, S., Pratt, C., & Schmall, V. (1985). Spiritual support for caregivers of dementia patients. *Journal of Religion and Health*, *24*, 31-38.

Zarit, S., Todd, P., & Zarit, J. (1986). Subjective burden of husbands and wives as caregivers: A longitudinal study. *Gerontologist*, *26*(3), 260-266.

In: Spirituality
Editor: Edith C. Roberts

ISBN: 978-1-63482-370-8

Chapter 3

POLICING AND SPIRITUALITY: BRIDGING THE GAP TO THE END OF CRIME

***Dr. Ginger Charles*[1,*] *and Dr. Jonathan Smith*[2,#]**
[1]Institute for Spirituality and Policing,
Modesto Junior College in Modesto, California, US
[2]Devon and Cornwall Police, UK

ABSTRACT

To be confronted with tragic, critical incidents on a daily basis. To face human destructiveness and suffering, to defend society, standing between chaos and order in defense of peace; All require a unique type of individual. It is what we, as a society, demand from our law enforcement officers.

Currently in the United States, we are seeing our police officers questioned for using excessive levels of force. There are increasing numbers of violence erupting within our communities from its members who feel our law enforcement officers are "out of control." In a study of 350 United Kingdom police constables, the cost of PTSD, burnout, and stress was in excess of £99 million or $152 million. Forty percent were deemed to be of medium or high risk of PTSD and 13% of respondents had been signed off work with PTSD one or more times usually for 4+ months costing £11,538 per officer per instance.

In this chapter, we explore the budding importance of spirituality as a coping mechanism in police work, a path through the suffering and disorder. If our police officers are feeling isolated, under valued, and sick then how can they protect and serve our communities? Crime and disorder become pronounced in environments where law enforcement becomes dysfunctional. In our research on spirituality and policing in the United States and the United Kingdom common themes illustrate the importance of this coping mechanism, whereby officers feel "connected" to their profession, their work, and their communities. Can we extend this research toward the communities served to connect our police officers with its members to lessen crime and disorder?

Keywords: Spirituality, Crime, Policing, Resilience, Leadership

* E-mail: gingercharles@me.com or charlesg@yosemite.edu.
# E-mail: Jonathan.Smith3@devonandcornwall.pnn.police.uk.

INTRODUCTION

Recently in the United States, the topic of police use of force and protesting groups calling for "justice" has been foremost in all news media in this country. With the events that have occurred in the "officer involved shooting" of Michael Brown in Ferguson, Missouri, the "choke" hold and death of Eric Garner in New York City by NYPD, and the most recent police shooting of 12 year old Tamir Rice in Cleveland, OH, are demanding that we examine our police communities for accountability and fairness in ethnically diverse populations. Certainly what has occurred with these tragic events is the creation of an "opportunity" to open a dialogue about how police officers serve our communities. However, these events also implore that we delve into issues of what it means to be a police officer, how police officers survive and thrive in their work, and what can we, as society, do to promote healthier communities by fostering healthier police officers.

This chapter will draw from the authors' own research and experiences of working within the police culture in both the United States and the United Kingdom. Both authors have been researching within the police community since 2000, have interviewed well over a hundred and fifty police officers relating to spirituality, leadership, and police work, and have observed how these officers cope with the constant contact of human destructiveness and challenging nature of their work. The lead author is a retired police officer with over 27 years of experience in patrol, community services, and investigations. The second author served as a researcher/trainer within the police forces in the UK.

We will discuss the tremendous effects of police work on the police officer. We will define *spirituality* and how this may be important in opening communication with our communities in order to heal from these latest events in the United States, and perhaps worldwide. We will outline what the research has shown and why this may be an important focus for coping and communication between the police communities and the communities they serve. Finally, we will explore key points concerning the importance of supporting spirituality in police work within our police organizations as a way of enhancing an officer's survival in police work, which directly affects our communities, building health and understanding between both worlds.

EFFECTS OF POLICE WORK

There are over 633,000 police officers in the United States and over 220,000 police constables in the United Kingdom. These figures do not include other types of law enforcement officers, such as Federal officers, which accounts for an additional 100,000 + more in service. With a community this large, there appears to be resilience and officers who perform, serve, and cope well. Unfortunately, research within the police community is limited, as it remains a very closed society. As warriors for justice, they are strong, stoic, and stubborn and do not allow "outsiders" to view vulnerabilities. Certainly, this isolation can be part of the issue when exploring what does or does not work in the police community.

Because the police community is challenged in life and death encounters daily, the examples of coping (either positive or negative) are far more pronounced and, therefore, useful as examples to other in which to learn. There are four "ultimate existential concerns that plague" all human beings (Yalom, 1980). Officers are often confronted with all four of these existential concerns during most of their shifts: death, freedom, isolation, and meaninglessness.

An officer may respond to a violent domestic then on to a traffic accident without much time to process the events. Perhaps that officer must then skip a meal to problem solve a homeless person trespassing on someone's property and then respond to a murder involving a child. Each separate incident may take its toll on the officer and highlights why it is so important to help officers to explore and talk about existential questions. These existential concerns are being raised, unconsciously and continuously in their work. We need to provide the armor to shield them from the pain these questions may cause until they are capable to handle them or recognize they cannot. Potential implementation of some solutions will be discussed later.

With the current use of force events in the police community, it is important to explore police culture and how these events are challenging our communities. For example, the isolation and meaninglessness of constant conflict within a diverse community may build walls of resistance between the police and community members. The friction between the two communities may foster a lack of understanding from all members and, therefore, anger within that lack of understanding.

According to the National Institute of Justice website, it is difficult to estimate the frequency of excessive use of force (Alpert and Dunham, 2004). Additionally, excessive use of force by our police is rare. What is unknown is whether communities do not feel safe reporting use of force, the officers who abuse their police powers are few in numbers, or whether there are other reasons as yet undefined. As stated previously, the police culture is a closed community. Certainly diverse community may feel the need to be cohesed in their struggles as well. Again, this begs an opportunity for open communication.

What Is Spirituality?

The definition of spirituality used for the author's research was broadly defined as: "Related to meaning, purpose, and connectedness to what one considers sacred and how one aligns with that sacredness" (Charles, 2005). Other definitions of spirituality include concepts of "calling" and "membership" (Fry, 2003), a relationship with a higher or sacred presence (Jones, 2003), and Webster's Dictionary (1976) that describes the subjective experience of what one considers sacred or greater than self.

The authors acknowledge the difficulty in attempting to define such a complex and contentious topic. The broadness of the definiton provides inclusion of all spiritual beliefs rather than attempting to fit a multi-dimensional concept into a narrow interpretation, such as a religious meaning or a Christian perspective. The broader meaning of *spirituality* employed here provides the participant the opportunity to find shared meaning through practice and discussion.

According to Naimon, Mullins and Osatuke (2013, p94), "Spirituality is more inclusive and abstract than religiousity." There is a strong association with charity, community, hope, and meaning. Other research on spirituality has identified a link between spiritualtiy and forgiveness. Fry (2003, p705) states, "Spirituality reflects the presence of a relationship with a higher power or being that affects the way in which one operates in the world. Certainly this definition may include or exclude religiousity. However, the broadness of the definition provides a richness and deepens our understanding of the human "spirit" (Fry, 2003).

How does this elusive concept affect a police officer's work?

SPIRITUALITY AND POLICE WORK

The authors' research involved interviewing police officers regarding how their spiritual orientation is incorporated in their police work. Officers and constables were interviewed in the United States and the United Kingdom to explore how their faith helped them in their work as law enforcement officers.

Within the police culture there is still a code of silence (Violanti, 1999). A general distrust of those outside the community has markedly affected the amount of research within the police ranks. Because of the enormous responsibility assumed by the police role, it is not acceptable to show any weakness (Charles, 2009; Violanti, 1999; Waters and Ussery, 2007). Therefore, we sought to explore what is going right for these officers. Herein lies the purpose for our research. We sought to further the understanding of the importance of spirituality in an individual who performs the work of a police officer or police constable.

Spirituality was identified as a significant coping mechanism assisting police officers with sustaining health and survival within the toxicity of police work (Waters, 2007; Charles, 2009; Feemster, 2009; Smith, 2010). Essentially, the authors found there were similarities that did include parts of various definitions, such as: calling, membership, sacred, high power or God, prayer or meditation, and aligning with sacredness. The three core themes identified in the research were: Other-centered, Higher Justice-Peace, and Humanism/Calling (Charles, 2005; Smith and Charles, 2010; Smith and Charles, 2013; Charles, et al, 2014).

This exclusive community of police is selected from the human race and, therefore, vulnerable to the daily stressors and trauma they encounter. When these traumas are reflected in the police community we witness high levels of divorce, sickness, alcoholism, addiction, and other self-destructive behaviors (Violanti, 1999).

There are enormous costs associated with police officers that succumb to the pressures of police work. Beyond the personal toll, there are significant costs to the organization, community, and society. In an on-going study into stress, burnout and Post Traumatic Stress Disorder (PTSD), Liddell (2013) conducted one of the largest survey of police forces in England. She received 350 responses from several police organizations. Although there are some methodological weaknesses in the research the findings do reveal that 60% of police participants feel they have no one to talk with; 13% of the respondents were deemed to be suffering from PTSD and unable to work, costing the agencies over £11k an officer; 79% of officers felt their agency did not provide them enough support. These results suggest it is critical to examine what helps police officers survive and endure these challenges.

So how does the police community maintain their resilience with this amount of responsibility and power? Police officers carry a massive responsibility and level of power. Not many jobs or professions can have such a huge, immediate impact on another human being's life. What effect does this have on a police officer and what effect does it have on communities served by that officer? How does the police community maintain their resilience with this amount of responsibility and power?

According to the American Psychological Association, resilience is defined as, "the process of adapting well in the face of adversity, trauma, tragedy, threats or even significant source of stress." Southwick and Charney (2012) believe resilient individuals "tame" and "master" stress in their world. It is necessary to regulate emotions, remain physically fit, and sustain an active and healthy social network (Smith and Charles, 2013).

Police officers must very quickly master high levels of stress and emotions in their workplace. Their training necessitates the ability to confront stress and handle the situation in front of them. What we have not done well for our police officers and constables is "check in" or continue their training in this area, believing that once they are trained then they can "master" any situation, until the end result is a broken individual or one that has lost their moral compass. Certainly, there has been a introduction of debriefing counseling and peer support groups. However, the police community is a very exclusive one, which does not openly demonstrate personal vulnerability.

Because of the daily confrontation with human destructiveness and suffering, officers/constables may find difficulty in maintaining a positive outlook. Other police officers may not provide healthy role models to emulate. Finally, typically their social network can close down to encompass only fellow police officers. How then do many of our law enforcement maintain resilience in such an environment? It is our hypothesis that spirituality provides significant ways to maintain resilience in the face of such high levels of stress, human destructiveness, and suffering.

Recent research tells us some resilience is built through the mere experience with the trauma. A study of paramedic service demonstrated that levels of resilience increased with such experience (Gayton and Lovell, 2012). In another study, police constables were followed for 12 months, from entry into the police work. These constables benefitted positively from prior trauma events (Burke and Shakespeare-Finch, 2011). There is significant training for police personnel but there are no active "resilience training" programs for police personnel. Is this a variable unaccounted for in the research?

Other studies reflect that when service or crisis workers assume personal responsibility for their response to trauma then they are more likely to succeed and find the work healing (Bartone, Roland, Picano, and Williams, 2008; Clohessy and Ehlers, 1999; Maytum, Heiman, and Garwick, 2004; McGee, 2006). Many of these workers and soldiers find the work meaningful.

What is it that helps us find that resilience? How do we find the work meaningful. Certainly the research within spirituality in the workplace has reflected its importance in growth and maturity, and becoming other-centered versus self-centered (Maslow, 1968; Smith and Charles, 2010; Travis, 2009; Carlier, 1999; Conklin, 2012). When an individual finds meaning and purpose within work, then the hardships become a learning opportunity rather than a setback.

These setbacks or hardships provide the individual the opportunity to learn and grow beyond the trauma or failure. This "bouncing back" from adversity was seen many times in our research. Our recent study (Charles, et al., 2014) involving eleven police officers, from several different agencies in Colorado, followed these officers over the last three to five years of their careers. Almost every officer struggled through some trauma, suffered from addiction, experienced divorce, or was involved in an internal investigation. All of the officers were able to recover from the adversity and regain their footing.

When these officers discussed their misfortune or challenge, they spoke of the importance of working with supervisors and communicating with each other. They shared that it became a team effort with the supervisor to change behavior, receive support and resources, and regain balance. All of the officers demonstrated a high level of humility and insight. Many police officers recognize the importance of their work using their spirituality as a coping mechanism. They recognize how human connection and compassion is a powerful theme within their work. One participant from our research revealed:

> I had a guy I arrested for public intoxication and he was one of our regulars. I remember driving, he's in the back of the car, and I was driving to the jail with him. I said, "So, how long have you been a drunk?" And he replied, "I don't know, how long you been a pig?" And so that was the lesson for me. He pegged me on that one. I was definitely humbled (Charles, 2005, p110).

Another participant reflected his desires to serve with compassion. "You want to put the bad guys away, you want to help people be accountable, you want to let that other person know that I'm not going to let these people pick on you" (Charles, 2005, p111). The police officers who used their spirituality in their police work recognized their connection to those they serve (Charles, 2005; Charles, 2009; Smith and Charles, 2013; Charles, Travis, and Smith, 2014). Another police officer shared, "So we're connected. It doesn't matter what culture it is, we're connected somehow" (Charles, 2005, p112).

These are the police officers who have not been identified in the media recently, that serve with compassion and spiritual connectedness. These rich examples above illustrate the themes of compassion and humanism, of being other-centered, and a sense of being "called" to police work. So how do we best support or encourage police officers to use and/or develop spirituality as a coping mechanism in their work?

PROVIDING *SPIRITUAL* SUPPORT AND TRAINING TO POLICE OFFICERS

> "Everyone thinks of changing the world, but no one thinks of changing himself."
>
> Leo Tolstoy

Fry (2003) discusses the importance of "calling" and "membership" in spirituality in the workplace, that workplace spirituality enhances an employee's joy, peace, job satisfaction, and commitment. In our research, we found a resounding 100% believed they were "called" to police work. They found meaning in their work in protecting society from itself (Charles, 2009; Smith and Charles, 2010; Charles, et al. 2014). It becomes vital that our police organizations begin to recognize the importance of its membership and calling to police work. First steps toward supporting spirituality in police work should comprise all of the police leaders, supervisors, and management staff. Qualities of spiritual leadership include: vision, altruistic love, and hope/faith (Fry, 2003). Unfortunately, officers do not always feel supported by the police organization. The "man at the top" is often the problem within police organizations. This becomes the elephant in the room. When reviewing Liddell's (2013) survey of police respondents for example, 79% of officers did not feel supported by their organizations.

Police organizations supporting spirituality in the workplace need to develop from within the lead individuals in order to reflect out to the organization. Within our research, police officers could clearly articulate what it means to them to incorporate their spirituality in their police work (Charles, 2009; Smith and Charles, 2010; Charles, et al., 2014). This was not taught or trained, but was inherent in the officer, and was regardless of whether spirituality was supported within their organization. In fact a followup study of UK officers (Charles and Smith, unpublished), most participants described not being supported by their organizations but they chose to incorporate their spirituality in their work as it connected them to their communities served. The lead author's personal experience also demonstrated this unsupported approach from police leadership in many of the police agencies where officers were interviewed.

So what is the best way to bring in the topic of spirituality in a police organization when the problem is the "top cop" or the leaders of the organization? The person who holds the purse strings would be a possibility, and would need to be self-aware, secure, and open to issues within the organization. This police leader would be willing to build a framework of organizational values, such as: trust, a standard of excellence, humility, tolerance, and compassion for all members of the organization (Giacalone, 2003). Additionally, the workplace culture would inspire employees to experience transcendence through their work and encourage members to feel connected, allowing for expression of compassion and service to the community. Spiritual leaders would walk in front, behind, or beside their employees (Fry, 2003). This requires that our police leaders have insight and humilty in order to evaluate their organizations and themselves and, if necessary, begin again.

CONCLUSION

It is apparent that the challenges facing today's police officers around the world are many and varied. For many police officers, their work is a way of service and protection for members of our society. For most officers, it is not a goal to become involved in a deadly force encounter, having to make the ultimate choice of killing someone. As stated previously, excessive force by police officers is rare. Yet, there are several cases of police use of deadly force leading in the new media. Many communities around the United States have seen demonstrations, both violent and peaceful, and protests of inequality/unjust treatment by the police. The subject is timely and does not appear to be diminishing. Perhaps this is an anomaly or maybe it is an opportunity to explore what is happening within our police organizations.

There is more research needed and more funding needed to support such research within the police community in order to further our understanding of how best to support our police officers around the world. However, we have discussed how spirituality appears to be an effective coping mechanism for these officers. They were able to "bounce back" from adversity, demonstrate high levels of compassion and humility, and serve with integrity and love in their communities. These officers also demonstrated an ability to explore all options in a situation rather than struggling with a fixed point of view.

If we consider employing spirituality in the police workplace, actually incorporating it in the very walls of the organization, and reflecting spirituality from our police leaders to all members of the organization, how can we not have an effect on our communities? With police officers feeling supported and encouraged, there may be a shift in engagement with our communities. Police officers could respond to all members of the community with less defensiveness. Police officers might take action with more cognitive flexibility, seeing choices and alternatives in police encounters rather than narrowing a view point to just one perspective of winning the fight.

This is not an easy fix or a simple path for us. It requires much introspection, dedication, and work. However, it is a beginning in an exploration toward ending crime, which could be its own reward.

REFERENCES

Alpert, G. P. (2004). Understanding police use of force: Officers, suspects, and reciprocity. New York, New York: Cambridge University Press.

Bartone, P., Roland, R., Picano, J., and Williams, T. (2008). Psychological happiness predicts success in U.S. Army Special Forces. *International Journal of Selection and Assessment,* 16 (1), 78-81.

Burke, K., and Shakespeare-Finch, J. (2011). Markers of resilience in new police officers: Appraisal of potentially traumatizing events. Traumatology.

Carlier, I. (1999). Finding meaning in police traumas. In J. and. Violanti, Police traumas: Psychological aftermath of civilian combat (pp. 227-233). Springfield, Il: Charles C. Thomas.

Charles, G. (2005, August). How spirituality is incorporated in police work: A qualitative study. San Francisco, CA: Unpublished dissertation.

Charles, G. L. (2009). How spirituality is incorporated in law enforcement. FBI Law Enforcement Bulletin, 78 (5).

Charles, G., Travis, F., and Smith, J. (2014). Policing and spirituality: Their impact on brain integration and consciousness. *Journal of Management, Spirituality and Religion,* 11 (3), 230-244.

Clohessy, S., and Ehlers, A. (1999). PTSD symptoms, response to intrusive memories and coping in ambulance workers. *British Journal of Clinical Psychology,* 38, 251-263.

Conklin,T.A. (2012, September). Work worth doing: A phenomenological study of the experience of discovering and following one's calling. *Journal of Management Inquiry*, 309-317.

Dik, B., and Duffy, R. (2009). Calling and vocation at work: Definitions and prospects for research and practice. *Counseling Psychologist*, 37, 424-450.

Feemster, S. (2009). Wellness and spirituality: Beyond survival practices for wounded warriors. *FBI Law Enforcement Bulletin*, 78 (5).

Figley, C. (1999). Police compassion fatigue (PCF): Theory, research, assessment, treatment, and prevention. In J. and. Violanti (Ed.), Police trauma: Psychological aftermath of civilian combat (pp. pp. 37-53). Springfield, IL, United States of America: Charles C Thomas.

Fontana, D. (2003). Psychology, religion, and spirituality. Malden, MA: Blackwell.

Fry, L. (2003). Toward a theory of spiritual leadership. *The leadership quarterly,* 14, 693-727.

Giacalone, R. A. and Jurkiewicz, C. L. (2003). Toward a science of workplace spirituality. In C. L. Jurkiewicz, Handbook of workplace spirituality and organizational performance (pp. 3-28). New York, NY: M. E. Sharp.

Henry, V. (2004). Death work: Police, trauma, and the psychology of survival. New York, New York, United States of America: Oxford University Press.

Jones, J. (2003). The mirror of God: Christian faith as spiritual practice-lessons from buddhism and psychotherapy. New York, New York: Palgrave Macmillan.

Josipovic, Z., Dinstein, I., Weber, J., and Heeger, D. (2012). Influence of meditation on anti-correlated networks in the brain. *Frontiers in human neuroscience,* 5 (183), 1-11.

Liddell, E. (2013). Prevalence on PTSD, Compassion Fatigue and Burnout in the Emergency Services. Presentation to the Police Federation Health and Safety Conference. Police Federation Headquarters.

Maslow, A. (1968). Towards a psychology of being. New York, NY: D. Van Nostrand Co.

Maytum, J., Heiman, M., and Garwick, A. (2004). Fatigue and burnout in nurses who work with children with chronic condictions and their families. *Journal of Pediatric Health Care*, 18, 171-179.

McGee, E. (2006). The healing circle: Resiliency in nurses. *Issues in Mental Health Nursing,* 27 (1), 43-51.

Naimon, E. M. (2013). The effects of personality and spirituality on workplace incivility perceptions. *Journal of Management, Spirituality and Religion,* 10 (1), 91-110.

National Police Suicide Foundation. (2009). The work of the National Police Suicide Foundation. Beyond Survival: Wellness Practices for Wounded Warriors. Lansdowne: FBI.

Schmidt-Wilk, J. (2000). Consciousness-based management development: Case studies of international top management teams. *Journal of Transnational Management Development,* 5 (3), 61-85.

Smith, J. and Charles, G.. (2013). Developing leadership resilience: Lessons from the policing frontline. Farnham, UK: Ashgate Publishing Ltd.

Smith, J. and Charles, G.. (2010). The revelance of spirituality in policing: A dual analysis. *International journal of police science and management*, 12 (3), 1-17.

Travis, F. (2009, May). Brain functioning as the ground for spiritual experiences and ethical behavior. FBI Law Enforcement Bulletin.

van Heugten, K. (2013, January 24). Resilience as an underexplored outcome of workplace bullying. Qualitative Health Research. Sage.

Violanti, J. M. (1999). Trauma in police work: A psychosocial model. In J. Violanti, and D. Paton, Police trauma: Psychological aftermath of civilian combat. Springfield, IL: Charles C. Thomas.

Waters, J. and Ussery, W.. (2007). Police stress: History, contributing factors, symptoms, and interventions. *Policing: An international journal of police strategies and management*, 30 (2), 169-188.

Yalom, I. (1980). Existential psychotherapy. New York, NY: Basic Books.

In: Spirituality
Editor: Edith C. Roberts

ISBN: 978-1-63482-370-8

Chapter 4

TRANSFORMATIVE SPIRITUALITY: MEANINGS, CHALLENGES AND PRACTICE OF COMPASSION IN EDUCATIONAL CONTEXTS

Alaster Gibson**, *Ph.D.
Bethlehem Tertiary Institute; Tauranga, New Zealand

ABSTRACT

Compassion is a widely recognized virtue across cultural, political and religious divides. Compassionate teaching is not new, however the topic is receiving renewed interest as educators around the world endeavour to respond empathetically and practically to students' complex holistic needs. This paper reports on a qualitative inquiry into the meanings, challenges and practice of compassion as experienced by ten participants, within a range of New Zealand Christian school contexts (primary and secondary), and one pre-service teacher training programme in Thailand with mainly Karen refugees from Myanmar. The rich data was obtained through a triangulated research design which involved four teachers in a collaborative action research project over a semester, three teachers and two principals in an online survey, and one principal in a semi-structured interview.

A reflective, inductive and iterative analysis of the textual data was used to gain in-depth understanding of what compassion meant to participants and how they enacted compassion in their respective educational contexts. The findings show that the teachers and principals were motivated towards compassion, having eyes to see people's needs and hearts willing to move from apathy or judgment, towards supportive action. However, the findings provide evidence that compassion in teaching could be a challenging decision-making and relational process, requiring wisdom, resourcefulness and resilience. Through critical reflection and trialling interventions, participants in the collaborative action research process became more intentional about viewing interpersonal issues and learning needs through a compassionate lens which positively impacted their professional practice. The findings from these participants showed that judicious and relational expressions of compassion can have a transformational effect in

* Email: a.gibson@bti.ac.nz.

students' *behaviour and learning*, supporting the sacred injunction, 'and of some have compassion, *making a difference*' (Jude 1:22).

INTRODUCTION

Compassion is generally understood as an emotional response of genuine *empathy* towards someone who is suffering and a willingness to *do something kind and helpful* to ameliorate that suffering. Nussbaum (1996, p. 57) says compassion, 'provides imperfect citizens with an essential bridge from self-interest to just conduct.' Compassion is widely acknowledged as a virtue across diverse cultures, political spectrums and religions. It is strongly linked to care in school contexts (1992), and while not new to education, it is receiving renewed interest as teachers increasingly experience students who really struggle with learning and life in general.

LITERATURE REVIEW

The review of educational literature identified a wide range of professional issues relevant to compassion in teaching. For example, compassion is recognised as a characteristic of effective teachers (Hanover Research Council Report 2009; Onwuegbuzie, Witcher, Collins et al., 2007), and for those engaging in mentoring (Starr-Glass, 2005). Compassion is relevant to the concepts of care, inclusion and social justice, which are emphasized in the Ministry of Education New Zealand Curriculum (2007), and the New Zealand Teachers Council Code of Ethics for Registered Teachers (2004). Fostering compassion in school contexts can positively influence the development of student character and classroom climate (Kessler, 2002; McClain, Ylimaki, & Ford, 2010). Compassion is also linked to restorative justice practices relating to student misbehaviour (Adams, Cronin-Lampe, Cronin-Lampe, et al., 2003). Karakas (2011), even includes compassion within a model for positive institutional management in which staff and students are encouraged to move from self-centredness to interconnectedness, service and stewardship. Compassion in teaching is relevant due to increasing numbers of students with complex and diverse needs, including neglect, abuse, oppression and discrimination (Wolpow, Johnson, Hertel & Kincaid, 2009).

Compassionate pedagogy (Poppo, 2006), was another theme identified in the literature referring to ways teachers differentiate their planning, apply a repertoire of strategies and a choice of assessment products to cater for learners, including special needs and gifted students (Hao, 2011; Hartsell, 2006). Within the context of children's spirituality, Fraser (2014) also discusses how a student and school initiative modelled compassion by fundraising for a Samoan community badly affected by a tsunami. Compassion is also included within specific curriculum programmes such as Character Education, which Van Brummelen (2009, p. 235), describes as follows.

> Character education is intended to help students become ethically responsible, self-disciplined, and community-oriented persons who understand, accept and act on values such as respect, empathy, compassion, integrity, self-control, responsibility, justice, stewardship, humility, patience and prudential courage.

Some of the literature emphasized the need to exercise discernment when considering suffering and compassion. Jonas (2010, p. 52) suggests, 'the goal is not to see the end of suffering but to see the increase of self-mastery, which necessarily includes hardship and difficulty.' He cites research that shows it is not uncommon for teachers to *prematurely* intervene to alleviate the struggle and confusion students may be experiencing, thereby hindering self-development of perseverance and resilience. Mintz, (2013, p. 224) argues a case for teachers of social justice, to facilitate 'just primary suffering' in students. This 'self-inflicted suffering' is necessary for students to be transformed from apathy and support for oppressive social and institutional behaviour. Mintz (2013) contends that transformational learning will not occur, if we eliminate dissonance and 'teaching sensitive material' (p. 216). Freire (1970) recognised the emancipatory power of educating the poor in-situ, within their communities of suffering. Ill-considered expressions of compassion are described by Lupton (2011), as *toxic*, a term referring to support that fails to consider the long term re-integration of recipients into normal self-managed life.

The literature also described compassion as *both* an intrapersonal and interpersonal processes reflecting the dispositions, life experiences and relational connectivity between the teacher and student. Palmer (2000, p. 11) says, 'Good teaching cannot be reduced to technique; good teaching comes from the identity and integrity of the teacher.' Chubbuck & Zembylas (2008, p. 303), cite a case of a teacher who said, 'If you don't know how to be compassionate with yourself, then how can you know how to be compassionate for other people?' Teachers won't always 'feel' like being compassionate towards students who are particularly difficult. Sustaining compassion can result in compassion fatigue, a problem identified in the literature affecting people in both the teaching and medical professions as they seek to constantly give of themselves and provide resources to very needy people (Dudding, 2013; Zakrzewski, 2012).

Compassion is widely acknowledged as a virtue within diverse religio-spiritual perspectives (Moran & Curtis, 2004). Drawing on Buddhist teachings, Whang and Nash (2005, p. 79), discuss the need to reclaim compassion which they believe lies at the heart and soul of *teacher* education. Discussing the personal characteristics of Christian teachers, Van Brummelen (2009, p. 50), says, 'Our commitment to Jesus Christ leads us to being Spirit filled… Love is the undergirding characteristic that all teachers must possess… true love is compassion.' Form a Biblical perspective, compassion and mercy are said to be characteristics of God. Psalm 145:8 says, 'The LORD is gracious, and full of compassion; slow to anger and of great mercy'.

The Biblical narrative also provides a range of examples of compassion such as the contrite prodigal son being welcomed home by his father (Luke 15:20), the Samaritan's care of a victim of a highway robbery, (Luke 10:30-37), and Pharaoh's daughter adopting the abandoned baby Moses in Exodus 2:6. Compassion was a characteristic of the life of the Jesus Christ; sent to 'heal the broken-hearted' (Isaiah 61:1) and to 'save his people from their sins' (Matthew 1:21). His expressions of compassion were diverse, measured and intermittent, sometimes self-initiated and discreet to an individual (John 5:2), at other times involving thousands (Matthew 14:21). Jesus' compassionate response to the suffering of Mary and Martha was protracted over several days (John 11: 11-43) and the Syrophenician woman's request for help was initially rejected (Mark 7:25-30).

In the parable of the king who 'was moved with compassion' and forgave the monetary debt of a particular servant (Matthew 18:27), there was an expectation that the servant would do likewise in his relationships with others (Matthew 18:32-34). Compassion should be motivated by love (1 Corinthians 13:3) and given as an expression of God's love in our lives; 'But whoso has this world's good and sees his brother have need, and shuts up his bowels of compassion from him, how dwells the love of God in him? (1 John 3:17). Jesus, in his story to a Jewish lawyer (Luke 10:33-37), said the compassionate actions of the Samaritan towards a victim of crime, illustrated neighbourly love, and to go and do likewise.

Each of these illustrations is applicable to educational contexts today as teachers endeavour to respond empathetically and practically to students in need, many of whom are rebellious, abused, oppressed; searching for hope and a future. These meanings of compassion suggest it will need to be wisely considered and lovingly enacted. In conclusion to this review of the literature, compassion can be seen not as an optional extra, but as an integral dimension of effective, humane, and transformative spirituality in teaching.

METHODOLOGY

Because I sought to *understand* the meanings, challenges and practices of compassion in Christian faith-based educational contexts, I decided on a qualitative, interpretive, constructivist research *paradigm* (Denzin & Lincoln, 2003). The inquiry was also inclusive of a theistic epistemology and view of reality (Savantakos, 2005). This stance allowed authentic descriptive analyses of the textural data as presented by participants within their faith-based educational contexts.

RESEARCH DESIGN

To strengthen the credibility and trustworthiness of the research findings (Bryman, 2004; Creswell, 2003), I triangulated the research design in several ways; recruiting participants from diverse educational contexts (primary, secondary and tertiary); recruiting participants involved in diverse roles (teachers, teacher-leaders and principals); and engaging participants in diverse methods (collaborative action research, online survey, semi-structured interviews and reflections).

The collaborative action research (CAR) method was conducted with four participants in three distinct faith-based educational contexts. CAR is understood as a flexible, recursive, iterative and spiralling *inquiry* process (Pine, 2009). It is designed to engage participants with their own needs, leading to valued insights and improved professional practice. CAR provides inquiry opportunities for teachers to 'reflect in action, on action and for action' (Ministry of Education, 2008, p. 77). Importantly, it allows teachers to learn from *both* the process and outcomes of their inquiry. The modified CAR approach used by the four participants engaged them in two cycles of planning, implementing, and evaluating compassionate teaching interventions across a two term period. An hour long, semi-formal interview was conducted at the beginning and where possible at the end of the process. I kept in email contact with the participants, receiving two emailed reflections and progress reports as well as exchanging reading material related to compassionate teaching.

In analysing the data, I looked for meanings, themes, relationships and differences, rather than frequency and statistical significance. It was an iterative, non-linear and recursive process spanning the duration of the research. The method I used was based on Creswell's (1998, p. 143) data analysis spiral, 'a cyclical, inductive and interpretive process.'

PARTICIPANTS AND INSTITUTIONAL DEMOGRAPHICS

The goal of finding 'plausible and credible explanations, is central to all research' (Morse, Barrett, Mayan et al., 2002). To achieve these outcomes within a qualitative framework, I decided to recruit a small but purposeful sample of teachers, teacher- leaders and principals (Bryman, 2001). The ten participants, whose demographics are outlined in the table below, provided multiple viewpoints and a variety of critical incidents. The data was collected over the equivalent of a semester during 2013.

Table 1. To show the demographics of the research participants

Collaborative action research participant demographics	
Type of faith-based institution	**Participant characteristics**
N.Z. suburban school (Y1-13)	Secondary school teacher, female, experienced
N.Z. suburban school (Y1-13)	Middle school (Y7) male, experienced
Thailand rural pre-service teacher training institute with mainly Burmese refugees	Tertiary level diploma programme, 1 male and 1 female beginning teachers
Online questionnaire participant demographics	
Type of institution (N.Z.)	**Participant characteristics**
Suburban Private Middle school (Y7-10)	Teacher and Syndicate leader
Suburban Private Intermediate school (Y7-8)	Principal
Suburban Integrated Primary school (Y1-6)	Principal
Suburban Integrated Primary school (Y1-6)	Class teacher
Suburban Integrated Primary school (Y1-6)	Class teacher
Principal interview demographics	
N.Z. suburban school (Y1-13)	Experienced female Head of the Primary School

BACKGROUND

My interest in *compassionate teaching* can be traced through experiences as a primary teacher in two public schools and a private faith-based school. More recently I have served as a pre-service teacher educator at a private faith-based tertiary institution in New Zealand. This position has also involved me teacher education in the Polynesian state of Tonga and north-west Thailand with mainly Karen refugees from Myanmar. My doctoral research into spirituality in principal leadership and its influence on teachers and teaching (Gibson, 2011), drew attention to the importance of care in school communities. I have also been married for nearly twenty years and my wife and I have three children ranging from 11-18 years of age.

FINDINGS

Introduction

En route to Auckland for my first interview with a participant in this study, I offered a ride to two young people hitch-hiking on the outskirts of a small Bay of Plenty township. During the ensuing conversations the young woman asked me why I was researching compassionate teaching. After sharing my explanation, I invited her to share any experiences she could recall of compassion from teachers at school. The young woman explained that she had had a very troubled home life growing up, went to lots of different schools, and arrived at college 'known' as a really difficult student. I asked, what helped her? Her reply was, teachers who focussed on what she was good at… what she could do. She also described being caught smoking by a science teacher at high school. The teacher knew she was already in lots of trouble but used discretion not to report the incident. Instead the teacher used the experience to encourage the young woman to engage in her science class later that day. The young woman said she hadn't taken her books out of her bag for probably six months- but that day she did, and thereafter, because of the compassionate response of this teacher.

Collaborative Action Research Participant 1: A Secondary School Teacher

> I just left it and I said to the Lord, 'Can you please show me – I mean this girl through your eyes, can you please give me an insight into her… can you please reveal this girl to me this day. (P1, interview 1, p. 7)

Meanings of Compassion in Teaching

Tension between Justice and Mercy

The experienced, female, secondary school teacher's initial thoughts on compassion were based around a biblical text in the Old Testament of the Bible, Micah 6:8, which she applied to her context in terms of school discipline. In her explanation, mercy is used interchangeably with compassion. Emphasis is placed on the *love* of mercy. However the quote below shows a paradox, on the one hand loving mercy, while at the same time upholding the required consequences of student misbehaviour within the school.

> The LORD says, … you have to exercise justice and practice mercy but love mercy, and that probably in a sense sums up what Christian compassion is within a teaching perspective because you can't disassociate the exercising of compassion from the requirements within a school to exercise consequences. (P1, interview 1, p. 1)

Self-Confrontation

The teacher described the volitional aspects of compassion and the diverse contexts in which it might be expressed – individually through to whole classes. The quote below shows there is a tension in the decision making self-talk as to whether a student receives mercy when they *deserve* justice. There is also the concomitant challenge to be impartial, basing one's judgment on the current misdemeanour, not the student's reputation or one's past experiences of the student. For this participant, the volitional process involves critical self-reflection about motives in the light of what the Bible teaches about compassion.

> So it's using or choosing to use mercy when they deserve justice – you know, that can be a whole class, that can be a student by student thing… it shouldn't have anything to do with that child's reputation or your history with that child. That is what is so amazing about biblical understanding of compassion, because it requires you to confront yourself and think, 'Am I dumping justice on this child because they're a rat bag, you know, am I giving grace and mercy to this child because they're a goodie-goodie?' (P1, interview 1, p.2)

Seeing the Child through God's Mercy on Me

The participant intuitively reflected on her own imperfections of behaviour when she was a high school student as she engaged with decisions about compassion in her teaching. This sense of conviction through a spiritual prompting attributed to *'my Lord'*, helped her to empathize with the student who was misbehaving for her. Seeing a child through this other lens- personal *failings* and God's *mercy on me,* helped this teacher check emerging negative thoughts, allowing greater likelihood of a compassionate response.

> Sometimes I'll be thinking of a child in a negative way, and my Lord is brilliant in bringing to mind specific sins or failings in my teenage years, and oh it's sooo good, because it is so humbling. All of a sudden I'm just in that child's head, and I'm thinking, 'I did that – I was you, I responded that way, I slacked off in that way, I lied to you that way… and yet God still had mercy on me…' (P1, interview 1, p. 3)

Challenges with Compassion

Stress and Failure

The teacher knew what she wanted to *be* and yet acknowledged an occasion when compounding antecedents; a difficult previous class, collegial communication problems and her current class being off-task, triggered an inappropriate verbal response. Humility was subsequently illustrated when the teacher asked the class for their forgiveness, essentially seeking a compassionate response. This excerpt below illustrates the reciprocity of compassion between teacher and students. The teacher's self-reflection shows an awareness of the pre-requisite virtues of being *longsuffering* and patient- qualities which are integral to compassionate teaching.

> This week I had to apologise to my Y11 class because I just came in, they were mucking around, they weren't getting on with it, I just let fly because I'd had an earlier problem with my Y9-10 class... I'd had a major communication cross wires with a teacher, and as I said to my Y11's I said, 'You got it all.' (P1, interview 1, p. 3)

Personal Suffering

The teacher participant had developed insights and empathy for student suffering through significant personal and family experiences of suffering. However, these issues also contributed to ongoing fatigue and a lowering of resilience towards stressful situations. In these ways, the teacher's personal well-being was both positively and negatively influential on the sustained practice of compassion. In the edited quote below, it shows how this teacher *veiled* her own suffering, while *negotiating* a compassionate behavioural response from the students, albeit under the guise of a light-hearted threat.

> Like anyone I have a huge amount going on in my life... and it's not been a good week for me either... last year when my ... I sort of made a joke of it but I'd say, 'My ____'s still in hospital. This means what?' And they'd say [the class], 'This means that you will ____ if we put a foot wrong' and I would go, 'That's right!' And off we go... If I'd actually told them how I was really feeling, it would have been far too much [for the age group]. (P1, interview 1, p. 4)

The Child I Don't Like

Inquiring further into the challenges the participant experienced in showing compassion in her Christian school context, the teacher revealed the following honest and candid admission.

> You suddenly wake up one day and you don't like a student... I mean, I don't like sneaky students, I don't like attitude students, those are probably my big ones. You know the gum chewing, eye rolling ones... just deceitful students (P1, interview 1, p. 6-7).

Probing into this challenge, the teacher explained her compassionate response to these real and 'natural' feelings. 'So at the moment, I'm waking up in the morning and I'm praying for the students I don't like... I would never say to them, 'I don't like you' (P1, interview 1, p. 7). The purpose of the teacher's prayer was to seek 'insight and discernment' (P1, interview 1, p. 7). In the following excerpt is a profound insight into the life-world of compassionate teaching- the tension between the natural and spiritual, and this teacher's desire to see a student, through God's eyes. The source of motivation to act compassionately was brought about by her sense of conviction of being unjust towards the student.

> I had an incredible example of this just the other day, I was writing up a Y10 student's report doing the comments, and I looked at them, she's a... I don't like her... and I looked at this general comment and I said to the Lord, I was at school and said to the Lord, 'No, I'm not treating this girl justly- my dislike for her is coming through in what I'm saying... and I just left it and I said to the Lord, 'Can you please show me – I mean this girl through your eyes, can you please give me an insight into her... can you please reveal this girl to me this day. (P1, interview 1, p. 7)

Following this self-reflection and prayer, the teacher left the staffroom and immediately had a positive encounter with the particular student. 'It was unbelievable, it was a miracle' (P1, interview 1, p. 7). What transpired was an opportunity to recognise and interact with the disliked student in a special way which in turn, led to recognition of the student before the class and a renewed relational connection between teacher and student. In the following excerpt the teacher reveals how she engaged with self-talk that challenged presuppositions and attitudes, leading to transformed behaviour.

> I was almost in tears of gratitude … it's incredible that is the Lord at work in this school, isn't it? Yeah it always starts with us, with self-confrontation and searching our own hearts and just that realization hey, if you don't like this student, you don't trust them and you're suspicious of their motivations, because that will define everything that you say to them… that will define how you interpret actions. It's really neither righteous or merciful to actively dislike any student – even if he did deserve it, sort of thing… That's a big thing for me, that's where the Lord is really working with me at the moment… and it's extraordinary and recently I've just started smiling and saying hello to the students I dislike the most. (P1, interview 1, p. 7)

Blind Spots

The teacher provided understanding as to *why* she valued praying to God for the students. 'He [God] sees the heart, and I'm not privy to what's going on in the background of these children's lives' (P1, interview 1, p.8). The excerpt below shows the teacher is aware of the wider societal challenges students are struggling with. Prayer is a tangible expression of support; God's help could make a difference in the children's well-being as they sojourned in her classroom.

> I mean they can come in [the students], you don't know they've just got out of the car and had a filthy fight, you don't know if the parents' marriage is on the rocks… they've got this avalanche of materials and consumerism and social networking and stuff just bowling them over,… and Christian kids are drowning in that…
>
> My prayer before the Lord is, really that I can't, I can't solve that, I can't do anything about the rest of their lives … But my prayer before the Lord is that when my kids come into my class, they feel that here they're safe, here they're valued, here they're listened to … here their opinion will mean something… here they have a place. (P1, interview 1, p. 8)

Practice of Compassionate Teaching

Humility, Wisdom and Self-Control

Spirituality was integrated into the teacher's espoused practice of compassionate teaching. For example, the teacher identified the importance of humility during the interpersonal aspects of working with a student who has misbehaved. This implies recognition of the need to hold her identity, position and power as the teacher carefully and not to hypocritically assume moral superiority. Linking back to the passage in Micah 6:8, the teacher referred to the importance of humility in the way a teacher interacts with and *values* a student.

> … to walk humbly before your God… I think that sums up the whole concept of compassion. Because when you're a teacher, I have pulled up genuine troublesome kids and I've said to them, 'OK you've been caught out, OK I'm going to leave it at that, because I want to be proud of you, I want you to take this on board, because I know you're better than this- you know… I've done that too, because they are used to being berated and told off for the same old thing. But again, it's a form of wisdom. (P1, interview 1, p. 3)

Furthermore, the teacher explained a sense of responsibility *before* God and communion *with* God in the pursuit of a *just* outcome. The teacher emphasizes the disposition to *desire* wisdom as a pre-requisite for compassion. The implication being that the exercise of compassion in her teaching would not to be based on impulse and feelings alone.

> With me it's that constant sense before the LORD, and not only am I being just, but LORD, in this situation what is just? So I can't actually practice mercy and compassion without wisdom. In fact it's impossible. (P1, interview 1, p. 2)

The participant described how responding to student misbehaviour required self-control, a considered response, and an *open* stance toward student voice. These strategies were believed to be helpful in deriving truth about a misdemeanour and exercising mercy and/or consequences justly. However, the final comment acknowledges students don't always tell the truth, compounding the challenges this teacher faces when deciding whether or not to show compassion.

> It takes self-control, when you may feel at your wits' end with a child… It takes stepping back from pre-conceived notions … it takes practicing what you're going to say before you're actually in the situation… for me I always say to the child, 'OK, this is what I saw, this is what I was told, I would like you to tell me what you did, what happened, … because I want to do the right thing here… And if you give them that opportunity to defend themselves, then you know, they will do so with spirit and with truth usually. (P1, interview 1, p. 2)

Collegial Care

The teacher shared several other critical incidences that illustrated compassion in the life-world of her teaching at a Christian school. The first incident was contextualized around an after-school invitation from a colleague to discuss something of personal and professional significance. The teacher-participant had other important work to do and didn't feel physically well. However, out of the motive to bring her colleague joy, she generously gave 20 minutes of her time to listen and to provide critical friend feed-back. This example shows that a compassionate response in teaching, costs. It also illustrates that the motive to bless someone else can over-ride one's own suffering, linking *loving self-sacrifice* with compassion in teaching.

Compassionate Pedagogy

The second critical incident is contextualized around a student with special needs. Forethought, time and energy were required to adjust an assessment schedule to include this student and accommodate his individual needs. However, the compassionate efforts of the teacher were not easily converted into success for the student, with the result that the teacher felt frustrated and wondering, it would be *easy to give up*. This example of compassionate *pedagogy* shows the ongoing nature the teacher's involvement with the student and the *fatigue* that can occur as a result. This incident shows that compassion in teaching may not produce a *satisfying* outcome, which is consistent with the expressions of compassion by the Lord Jesus. It also raises the question of adequate support for this special needs student and the teacher – a compassionate challenge for the school's leadership.

> I have a boy… in Year _. I've had him all the way through [past three years] he has been diagnosed with mild Asperger's Syndrome. It's only been after two years of saying good morning ____, good afternoon ____ Finally this year he's started to respond. Now I'm helping him through NCEA [National Certificate of Educational Achievement]. It would be so easy to get frustrated and give up on ____, because you ask him for an essay and he'll give you two brilliant paragraphs and then just stop … and he'll write you another paragraph talking about what he might have written, but he hasn't actually written the task… I changed the whole NCEA assessments this year just for him. Because last year we did speeches and he has a speech problem, and I knew that he couldn't pass the speech one… And [he] sat there day after day after day, just staring at his piece of paper, and I was thinking, 'I changed the assessment for you.' (P1, interview 1, p. 5-6)

Compassionate School Culture

The findings showed that for this teacher, compassion was very much a part of the leadership and life-world of the school community, which she described, 'at the moment, it's pretty darn good' (P1, interview 1, p. 8). There was also a once a week meeting, for parents to come into the school and pray. The following excerpt describes the supportive input received by the participant through a morning staff devotion meeting and how it might happen for others if a need arose. The implication being that the teacher experiencing compassion within the culture of the school might be influenced to show compassion in teaching within her classroom culture.

> The Spirit just seems to be sovereign and in the mind of whoever is on devotions that morning. Yesterday I sat down and I just thought, I'm not even sure if I can get through today, I am so tired and so low, and devotions started with all these wonderful verses from Isaiah… You know, about the LORD is your strength, the LORD is your shelter, and your refuge and your strong tower… the whole devotion was just a warm bath of promises of God with us… of God upholding us, do not fear, do not be discouraged, and at the end of it every single teacher said, that was for me… If a teacher came in here and said, 'I'm here this has just happened [a problem or need] then we'd be around them like a shot praying for them. (P1, interview 1, p. 9)

Several other examples provide a rich understanding of compassion within the culture of the school.

> At the beginning of last year we lost an ex-parent [the person died] and then following that, we lost someone to a ____. So what normally happens is that, there is always a call for meals, you know just Christ-like practical compassion… we do 'koha' at times, monetary gifts, anonymous to staff or families, who are just- you know, besides themselves. (P1, interview 1, p. 9)

Goals and Action Plan

Several weeks later the teacher participant communicated by email her goals and action plans. She identified her husband and a colleague at school as her critical friends. The first goal stated, 'One is impatience and anger/judgmental attitude towards unlikeable students. I have identified two students who are currently causing division in a small class through rather petty power plays. I desire to combine discipline with gentle correction without anger,' (P1, emailed goals, August, 2013). While on the face of it, this goal doesn't use the word compassion, contextually it is directly linked to compassionate teaching. Dealing with anger and dislike of students are significant prerequisites for compassion and its associated terms, mercy and loving practical support.

Consistent with the collaborative action research process, the teacher explained her plan of *action* to achieve the goal. The plan integrated scripture, critical self-talk, the cessation of unhelpful behaviours and the practice of new behaviours consistent with what she described as the empowering work of the Holy Spirit.

> My action plan is to use the word of God in practical self-confrontation. I am not in control of the choices or behaviour of others, but I am charged by God to exercise self-control in thought, word and deed and that through the Word and the empowerment of the Holy Spirit. Therefore I will actively practise 'putting off' impatience and anger towards these students and actively 'put on' patience and gentleness, reproving and exhorting as required.

A second goal was focused on minimizing personal and student stress over loss of time to teach, due to a school production that was underway. The demands of the production were perceived to be putting pressure on the unity of the staff. The goal below identifies an area of personal and corporate suffering. The action plan embraces *self-compassion* and corporate compassion. There are five aspects to the plan; putting aside anxiety, faith-filled prayer, being intentionally positive with colleagues, mindfulness of biblical passages, and a detailed 'worksheet' to scaffold the teacher through the implementation process; 'I desire to be a peacemaker' (P1, email correspondence, 21st August, 2013).

> I will actively put aside my anxiety about my lesson times and petition the Lord that He will honour the hard work I have put into this term's planning so that my Year ____ class do get all their work done! I will actively seek to encourage my colleagues through a cheerful attitude and encouraging word 'in season'. I have a worksheet for each of these issues which is very detailed in terms of the 'how' to practise the 'put offs' and 'put ons'.These are the bible verses I have chosen as being significant for personal and on-going meditation: Philippians 4: 7 Do not be anxious about anything, but in everything by

prayer and petition, with thanksgiving, present your requests to God, and the peace of God, which transcends all understanding will guard your hearts and your minds in Christ Jesus. Proverbs 16:24 Gracious words are like a honeycomb… James 3:17 But the wisdom from above is first pure, then peaceable, gentle , open to reason, full of mercy and good fruits, impartial and sincere. Galatians 5:22-23 But the fruit of the Spirit is love, joy, peace, patience, kindness, goodness, faithfulness, gentleness and self-control. (P1, personal correspondence, 21st August, 2013).

Outcomes of Action Research

Conviction Around Speech

Seven weeks later the teacher described her progress with the action research process. The quote below refers to goal one and describes how spiritual conviction, combined with perseverance to enact new behaviours, led to improved interpersonal communication with students. Spirituality was perceived to be integrated into this example of transformational learning.

> In regards to the students: God really convicted me in terms of my speech – how it is so easy to wound or to apply a healing balm. Although it seemed a little forced at first I actively practised words of encouragement and focused praise on ALL my students. This became more important as the demands of the musical increased as I could see how much my encouragement meant to the class. (P1, personal correspondence, 10th October, 2013)

Self-Control and Collegial Support

In regard to goal two, the teacher affirmed the on-going significant levels of fatigue and stress among staff, including herself, due to the school production. The teacher was able to make herself available to needy people on staff, just listen to them, reflect back to them what they were saying, offer encouragement and sometimes just '*keep her mouth shut'*. The findings also show that someone else on the staff, an unlikely and unlooked for colleague, acted in a compassionate way towards the teacher in this time of vulnerability and weakness. Noteworthy is the way in which this colleague compassionately combined words of encouragement with correction and gentle reproof. This incident shows how compassionate teaching can extend beyond teachers and their students, to collegial compassion – within the life-world of the learning community.

> Our musical demanded far more of all of us than we expected and so fatigue and stress dominated in the second half of the term. God also sent me an unlikely and unlooked for support person at this time. By that I mean a staff member who I had always struggled to 'work out'. She showed incredible discernment in terms of my own stress levels and always said just the right thing by way of gentle reproof, correction or encouragement. (P1, personal correspondence, 10th October, 2013)

Self-Confrontation and Spiritual Transformation

Having explored this action plan and reflected on the influence of compassionate teaching, I asked what the teacher had learned in regard to compassionate teaching and what she would like to do differently next term and why?

> The biggest lesson is to continually remember how mighty the tongue is (for good or evil). Therefore engage very cautiously and wisely at all times! I think that my plan is part of the on-going process of continual refinement and transformation in my life and that only through the power and grace of the Holy Spirit. I am not planning to make any radical changes to it this coming term but rather my plan is to continue the process of self-confrontation. What do I need to say or do in this situation? What wisdom or encouragement or love can I offer at this time? Is advice needed or desired or just a listening ear? (P1, personal correspondence, 10th October, 2013)

Asked if she were to share one or two highlights from this exploration into Christian compassionate teaching with colleagues at a team meeting or staff meeting, what would share and why?

> The change in one boy in particular, who is just starting now to shine out of a dark place! Every time I encourage him he seems to grow another inch! (P1, personal correspondence, 10th October, 2013)

Non-Judgmental Inclusive Stance

In the second and final interview, late in the fourth term of the year, the teacher participant reflected on a critical incident involving a difficult situation with a support person involved in the school production. The teacher reflects how relational disconnection was overcome by inclusive and prayerful action. The excerpt describes the efficacy of the teacher's compassion rather than judgmental stance; being willing to consider the situation from the other person's perspective and being invitational.

> If you're looking at that whole sort of judgmental – compassionate thing , … we inherited one of the event 'techies' and he was really difficult to get on with… and at the end of the dress rehearsals we had major technical issues, and we were all sitting in one part of the auditorium and this guy's on the other side and I said well, … why don't we pray about it. And then I just turned around to this guy and said, 'Would you like to come and pray with us about the needs?' And he was in like a dime… and came straight over, sat down, got totally engaged and then went well beyond the call of duty that night.
>
> It just really made me think about how so quickly we pigeon hole people … maybe the guy was just tired, shy, had a bad day – you know… and when offered that chance to be part of what was going on he was on board …and it lifted a big burden off me because I played a central role in the whole thing… I gained a real lesson out of that… and also I gained a colleague… it really convicted me how quickly we can make a judgment on someone… and cut them out. (P1, interview 2, p. 16)

The teacher also reflected on the efficacy of enacting a compassionate management strategy towards two younger primary aged children during this school production process.

The excerpt below shows how close the teacher was to enacting discipline in which the result could have been very different. Significant is the teacher's self-talk regarding the age, ability and needs of the six year old boys in a manner not inconsistent with what the literature describes as compassionate pedagogy. The need to be just; to modify and to encourage, are indicative of compassion integrated within professional practice.

> I was one decision away from just saying, 'You're out!' And then I just thought, I don't want them to be out, they're six years old and they're boys and my expectation that they're little adults, so I thought (A) it's not fair to keep them in- 'cause we are expecting too much of them… or (B) I can modify what they have to do… and encourage them to take a part they can handle… and make them feel important enough, that they have a role… but it worked.

Inconsistencies and Spiritual Insights

These incidents provided meaningful insights into this teacher's *real* life-world not just an ideal life-world of compassionate teaching. The quote below describes the participant's integrated spirituality and highlights her humanity; a candid admission that some days were easier than others to maintain the intentionality of seeking keys to understanding difficult students.

> The LORD gives you insight into what's driving them [the students], what's going on in their lives, what's on their hearts, he has the key doesn't he to all of us? So that's the first stop, what is the key to this boy? What is the key to this girl? My approach isn't working, I'm having to come down hard, is that in fact what has to happen? Or is there a key here that I could be turning that would get much better results plus co-operation? I'm not saying that I manage to do that all the time. Today, this week has been particularly difficult… there hasn't been a lot of 'key searching' there's been a lot of immediate justice because they have to actually sometimes see that. (P1. Interview 2, p. 18)

Being Mindful and Teachable

The second interview concluded by inviting the participant to reflect on the collaborative action research process. Several transformational outcomes are described below.

> One of the greatest things about me doing this is that it started to act as a semi-permanent brake, I'll just be all puffed up like a bull frog about to let loose and I'll think compassion… and I'll sort of deflate like a balloon… Let's just think about this…
>
> I'm not saying that that's all the time, but it has definitely been there all the time, just compassion, … what that does is straight away I just close my mouth and start to engage my brain. It has made me very aware of my triggers with behaviour that is simply potentially just the way that child 'is'… but for whatever reason I could wax lyrical about that from my background … but so what… but it has made me very aware that there is some actions and reactions in my students that create a negative reaction in me… But that doesn't mean that the student needs to be reproached, it could simply be that I've got a problem interpreting the behaviour… so it's really made me aware.
>
> I used to be a lot quicker – especially with these two boys to jump on them. Now I'm much more likely to stand back and say, 'Well hang on, who's got the problem here? Was there a deliberate intent on their part, or is it just my fleshly –default. So this whole

exercise has made me really aware that I have this default position with certain behaviour and that I need to much more discerning … is the behaviour a fault of my interpretation of the issue? So that's actually been very useful. (P1, interview 2, p. 1)

Collaborative Action Research Participant 2: An Intermediate School Teacher

Compassionate teaching 'unlocked' this approach and gave me an alternative and an excuse for change. (P2, personal correspondence, November 2013)

Meanings of Compassionate Teaching

Parental Care and Neighbourly Love

The experienced, male, intermediate school teacher's explanation of compassion, cited below, was imbued with personalised values and dispositions underpinned by what is commonly referred to as the golden rule spoken by Jesus in Matthew 7:12.

Slow to anger and abounding in love, and faithfulness, charging no interest… as a father I have compassion on my children [students] just like Father God has compassion on his children. Feeling, showing sympathy- concern for others, pity, being tender hearted, having an understanding or empathy for the suffering of others. And I take from the Bible the scripture, 'do to others what you would have them do to you.' (P2, interview 1, p2)

Made in God's Image

The positioning of compassionate teaching was informed by an understanding of students as image bearers of the Creator and the reciprocal benefits for future planning.

I respond this way because each one is God's creation as well as myself. They're made in God's image and he has gifted each one. In doing such I am learning something about them that maybe I'd not bothered to find out or know of them. It helps me in my understanding of their need and what is required to help them.
(P2, interview 1, p4)

Challenges with Compassion

Avoiding Being Overly Compassionate

The participant recognised the need for balance between compassion and discipline in teaching children. Mistakes were viewed as learning opportunities. Culpability and justice were seen as integral to and having a balancing effect upon compassionate teaching. Being *overly* compassionate was understood as counter-productive, developing in students a sense of dependence on others for support.

> I learn from my mistakes and I'm telling the kids in my class it's one form of learning, we learn by our mistakes, we try not to make that same mistake and move on... justice must be meted out when justice is required... which balances the compassion. We can be overly compassionate and if we're overly compassionate we have students who are probably too soft. They've got to learn to be assertive, they've got to be able to stand up for themselves. (P2: Interview 1, p5)

I'm Not Always a Compassionate Teacher

The teacher acknowledged that compassion reflects all of who we are, even our 'baggage' accumulated through life's journey. In the quote below he says he doesn't always 'feel' like being compassionate; compassion in its initial phase, being understood as an emotional response. Notwithstanding, he also emphasized a professional goal to develop a compassionate *class*. The implications being to enhance the potential for compassion to be experienced, to pre-empt uncaring behaviour and to develop compassion in the students' lives, consistent with a Christian discipleship model of education.

> We all have different natures and personalities and emotions and we all come with baggage and some of us more so than others and we might not feel like wanting to be compassionate one day to the next. And I'm not always a compassionate teacher. I want to create a culture in my class that will emulate a compassionate class, a class where we care for each other, where we speak kindly, we have gentle hands, we don't hit or throw or anything like that... and we help each other... and so that's the culture I'm trying to build. It's a lovely sort of 'nest' to have class of compassionate people- not just a compassionate teacher but the teacher is part of that compassionate culture and so that's what I try to build (P2, interview 1, p6).

The emotional element of compassionate teaching was significant for this participant being related to the complexities and stressful demands of full time, class-based teaching. In the quote below there is a perception that responding disapprovingly of inappropriate student behaviour conflicts with his understanding of compassion. However, analysis of the hypothetical discourse shows that the reproof is augmented towards cultivating right relationships in the student's life.

> You have to adjust very quickly your emotions and what you say because sometimes, I slip up and I don't come to school feeling very compassionate at all... and I'll be grizzly and I'll be probably a little bit – my voice might rise a little bit or I might really come down hard on somebody- especially the behavioural ones- you know, 'I've just had enough...' 'I've had enough!' You know, and I'll tell them and then I'll turn around and probably later on say, 'Look, I want you to know that I say what I say because I want you to do what's right, ... I want you to think before you act. You want to make friends- you talk nicely to them... you don't swear at your friends- push-shove them around. (P2, interview 1, p6).

Conflict with Other Teachers' Approaches

The findings implied an on-going tension exists between discipline and compassion, when to exercise one or the other was not easy, requiring teacher judgment. Compassionate teaching may be further complicated by the preferred authoritative practices of some colleagues who view compassion as a 'soft option'. Within the context of learning focused behaviour management, compassion was understood by the participant as a negotiated construct built around trust. Compassion in such contexts meant giving a bit of slack, with clear expectations and accountability.

> In a school like this with so many staff, not everybody thinks that way. Not everybody's going to buy into your soft approach or your compassionate teaching approach because they're going to be more authoritative. [Speaking personally] I will give a bit of flexibility – bit of slack, but if they or someone misuses that privilege, then of course that slack tightens up.'
>
> Now as a compassionate teacher, that's OK. That's helping to teach that person something but in a compassionate way... And they have to gain your trust in order to allow you to give them a little bit of slack here and there. (P2, interview 1, p.7)

Being Fair and Consistent

In addition to the previous insights, the teacher participant described the challenge of being equitable and fair in the practice of compassion. In seeking to apply the passage in Romans 9:15 'For he says to Moses, I will have mercy on whom I will have mercy, and I will have compassion on whom I will have compassion,' the teacher recognizes his subjective freewill in being or not being compassionate. However, he describes over-riding professional ethical obligations to be impartial and non-discriminatory.

> I'll have compassion on whom I'll have compassion, ... that is very much a choice. And that comes with the freewill; I have the will to be compassionate with that person or not with that person. However if you are going to be a fair person then I don't like to make those choices- I'm only going to be compassionate upon this one or that one... for this reason, or that reason... if you're going to do that then you set a precedent ... I think if you're going to be compassionate to one you're compassionate to all- regardless of circumstances, Christian/non-Christian, bully/non-bully... horrible person or whatever the case might be. (P2, interview 1, p. 7)

The Difficult Student

In response to a follow-up question the teacher affirmed that *being* compassionate to students with significant behavioural issues is difficult. The participant's reflective thinking cited below highlights another tension with compassionate teaching - the natural man versus the spiritual man. Is compassion merited or undeserved, and what motivates or hinders our responsiveness to being compassionate?

> It's not easy to show compassion to my behavioural challenges because they're always challenging, they're always prodding, they're always going to be pushing you to your limit... But the human side, the flesh side of me says 'Yeah- you don't deserve the compassion and so therefore I'm going to be honest and say, 'Yeah, I feel like I don't want to be compassionate to you, but I feel obligated that I must. I must because as a Christian, and as a role model, and if I want to show the characteristics of Christ, my Lord and saviour then I must... whether I like it or not... the Bible tells me not to

conform to this world, and to transformed by the renewing of our mind. (P2, interview 1, p. 8)

Further understanding of the practice of compassion in teaching was explained by the participant in terms of socio-cultural influences in the form of changes to school policies and legal requirements, and the emphasis being placed on restorative justice programmes, rather than punitive action alone.

> [There are] laws and policies that restrict us from being more I suppose able to dish out consequences, punishments when it is necessary. We have to look more towards the forgiveness and the compassionate side of ourselves in order to replace what has been taken away. I'm talking about corporal punishment, those sorts of things. ... I believe kids today they know more about the law, they know more about what a teacher can or can't do, they use it against teachers, they will stand up to a teacher, use language at a teacher, language is terrible at times... and it just doesn't make it any easier for a teacher so it's no wonder a teacher may feel more compassion for one person than another if that's the sort of treatment one gets...

Practice of Compassionate Teaching

Compassionate Pedagogy

The participant's *practice* of being compassionate in teaching was contextualised around diverse learning and behavioural needs of students, professional virtues as well as the provision of peer support.

> Helping students in my class who struggle or do not understand fully instructions, who don't fully understand the work required or the task that must be completed... I have a child in my class that has dyslexia... and quite severely... and that child is a special needs [pupil]. I have an international student whose English is limited. I have a couple of students who are behavioural challenges. I show a lot of tolerance and patience. I use a normal voice. I try to be firm but fair at the same time. I show an interest in each one ... plenty of praise and positive affirmations, I may utilize peer tutoring or mentoring for those that are struggling. (P2, interview 1, p3)

Relational Teaching

The professional practice of compassion was also located within an intentional, authentic, relational style of teaching and a class culture of inclusion and mutual respect.

> I believe that I'm very relational in my relationships that I form with the children. I believe strongly that my getting to know each student, ... talking to a student at a level where they're not just kids. I find with kids, if you get to know them, they get to know you a little bit, the relationship- there's a respect there and you're more likely to get a better output from the students in their work and in their behaviour- but you've got to work on it. It doesn't come easy with some of them... you've got to be genuine. (P2, interview 1, p3-4)

Providing Extra Tuition

The teacher participant described a critical incident of compassionate teaching from three or four years ago. The following quote describes who was involved, the curriculum need, the personal cost, and the intrinsic factors motivating the teacher to respond with tangible and timely assistance. It also describes the reciprocal benefits of compassion in teaching, interpersonally and spiritually.

> Three or four years ago, a student in my maths class, she was having some difficulty in keeping up with the rest of the class and needed extra help… as a compassionate teacher, I got alongside this person and decided that I would give that person extra help where I could. I didn't care about oh it was eating in to my lunchtime or oh no I should be somewhere else or I don't want to do this, it was an act of my will to want to do this, it was my compassionate side- I empathised, I want to help you, I'm concerned that I don't want you to get behind, I don't want you to struggle as you go up… I just felt the blessing of God from that, from what I had done. (P2, interview 1, p. 10).

Goals and Action Plan

The interview concluded with an invitation to identify a goal for collaborative action research.

Critical analysis of the text below suggests the teacher's strong sense of professional ownership with the chosen goal. The target group is identified, out of an implied sense of dissonance and dissatisfaction over the way things are at present. Significant feelings of hurt and apathy are identified as obstacles to be removed. The participant is aware of the cost in terms of time, and describes mentoring this small group of male students as a tangible expression of teacher compassion. Mentoring is not a quick fix, easy option. Yet the teacher is self-motivated to embark on a significant, holistic, transformational journey.

> I want to spend more time in mentoring my behavioural challenges. Putting aside any hard felt emotions and sense of apathy towards these ones and to embark on a journey of change. Socially, spiritually, emotionally and academically… This one would probably be one of the biggest challenges, I think but then I want to be able to handle a bigger challenge, rather than a little challenge, which would hardly test me. (P2, interview 1, p. 12)

Outcomes of Action Research

Mixed Results

The following reflection was emailed near the end of the following school term. The quote highlights the specific behavioural changes, extra time and restorative justice processes that the teacher employed in seeking to manage the difficult students in a compassionate way. However, although these compassionate practices were deemed 'very useful' they did not satisfactorily transform the students' lives.

> With both boys I have used a quieter voice when dealing with them and taken the time to explain clearly their wrong behaviour and what is acceptable, correct behaviour. This is followed up by close monitoring and when wrong behaviour is displayed, a reminder of what we agreed was right behaviour… I often use restorative justice when dealing with the two boys. This has been very useful in calming the situation and hearing each perspective in the presence of all concerned. While this has been useful it has not always resolved the problem. The boys go home and the parents get their version which often results in parents wading into the fray. (P2, personal correspondence September 2013, p. 1)

Compassion Alone Not Sufficient

Notwithstanding, the teacher maintained a positive opinion of the potential of compassionate teaching so long as consequences for misbehaviour were enforced. He also remains committed to caring for the difficult student despite minimal improvements. In looking forward to the future, the teacher recognises the vulnerability of this student and expresses concern that he will continue to experience compassionate support, lest gains be undone.

> Compassionate teaching CAN have an effect on students' behaviour, bearing in mind, that consequences for ones actions must be completed, as an alternative to a harsh negative approach. My bully boy has, over-time softened to the Word of God and wants to pray and know more about Jesus Christ. I have noticed slight changes in his behaviour for better… He still displays unacceptable traits. But, I believe this coupled with a teacher, he knows cares about him is effecting change. This MUST be carried through his schooling. He will need teachers who teach compassionately. Otherwise he will revert to old habits and the good work is lost (P2, personal correspondence September 2013, p. 2)

Compassion Fatigue

The teacher described one more outcome from this *first term* of focusing on compassionate teaching. The quote below implies that the emotional and physical costs of compassionate teaching were impacting the participant's wellbeing. Secondary trauma is described in the literature as the stress a person incurs as a result of helping someone who is suffering (Figley, 1995). The issue raised has implications for school policy and those serving in school leadership.

> The other point I would iterate is vicarious secondary trauma. That a side effect to compassionate teaching can be the teacher becoming weighed down by taking on board the concerns and worries of their students and that there should be good support systems in place to help counteract this. (P2, personal correspondence September 2013, p. 2)

Listening to My Compassionate Side

Later in the year, at the end of the fourth term, the teacher again critically reflected on his engagement in the action research process. Maintaining self-control and consistency with compassionate teaching were issues that he had become aware of. The quote below is contextualised around a particularly difficult critical incident that erupted at the school between two male students. The conflict continued over several days and restorative justice processes were ineffectual as neither party would concede fault or accept responsibility. Of interest is the participant's self-talk which plays a vital part in his compassionate response.

> I felt like bashing their heads together but that was not an option and certainly not a compassionate one either. After much soul searching and diplomacy coupled with a listening ear, calm voice, careful wording and mediation, the matter was mostly resolved. My compassionate side said do not react, be patient, listen, and DO NOT get angry. This approach seemed to work for this situation.

Motivation to Explore Compassion Further

Another outcome described by the teacher was his desire to further explore compassion in teaching the following school year part of a Master in Education programme. His intentions described below are well considered and reflect a desire to understand the transformational effects of a relational pedagogy that includes compassion as opposed to a pedagogy enforced by strict discipline within a culture of fear.

> I would like to explore the relationship between compassionate teaching and the respect/obedience gained or not gained through this means as a viable alternative to a hard-line approach. The relationships forged between student and teacher being one of friendship, respect, honesty and integrity. In contrast to a relationship built on fear. (P2, personal correspondence December 2013, p. 1)

Unaware Until I Trialled It

Only through participation in the action research process, did the teacher begin to change, becoming aware that the dispositions and behaviours associated with compassion were better suited to his style of teaching. The quote below also affirms that this renewed focus in his teaching was perceived to be consistent with his identity as a Christian educator.

> I cannot say that this was something entirely new to me. Rather I chose to use a different approach and was 'locked' into it. Compassionate teaching 'unlocked' this approach and gave me an alternative and an excuse for change… although I was unaware of it at the time until I trialled it, it was a better fit of my nature…
>
> Thank you for the opportunity to take part. It has helped me to discover something about what shapes me and my style of teaching. It is the Who I Am in Christ. (P2, personal correspondence December 2013, p. 1)

Collaborative Action Research Participants 3 and 4: Two Teachers in a Pre-Service Teacher Education Programme- Thai Border with Myanmar

> I think compassion is often looked at in terms of a victim or someone down on their luck but we can use it to try and change a behaviour we don't like.
>
> (P4, personal correspondence October 2013, p1-2)

Participants 3 and 4, hereafter referred to as P3 and P4, are a married wife and husband couple. They are recently qualified primary trained teachers, serving voluntarily in a pioneer pre-service faith-based teacher education programme on the Thai border with approximately 40, mainly Karen refugees from Myanmar. The teachers and students live and study in a small rural campus. The action research data was gathered during the third quarter of the first, two year cycle of a diploma programme.

Meanings of Compassionate Teaching

Rationale for Compassionate Teacher Education

Their faith-based understanding acknowledges emotional, cognitive, and practical dimensions to compassion including selflessness and Christ-likeness. The reference to a verse in the Bible is significant in that the context explains how Christ took on the identity and position of a servant. Yet there is also a tension in terms of how to maintain discipline and compassion without compromise.

> I believe that compassion is… not only loving somebody with your head or your heart, but it's putting it into action… and going by the principle of Philippians 2:3 [Let nothing be done through strife or vainglory; but in lowliness of mind let each esteem other better than themselves] it's completely putting others above yourself so if somebody is hungry that means whether you're hungry you need to go out of your way to feed them… if you're tired and somebody needs support you need to go out of your way to support them… always about the other person and not about ourselves… I believe that's true compassion… the action. (P3, interview 1, p. 1)
>
> It's modelling Christ, the things he tells us we're supposed to live, and I think it also has dimensions of discipline in their also… to show compassion you have to – I think most people don't think that, there's two sides to compassion, 1. The discipline side where you still have to stand firm with what the Word says even though it might not possibly be showing compassion in that situation, so it's like a mixture of discipline and compassion. (P4, interview 1, p. 1)

Justice and Fairness

The integrated nature of compassion with disciple was contextualized by both participants around the life-world of their learning community. Compromising on discipline would undermine fairness and equality in the educational programme. Compromising discipline around kitchen duties would breed unfairness and selfishness.

> There's the educational discipline where students need to know that in order to have justice and fairness in the community we have to follow the same rules that everybody is governed under… so if they decide to turn up to class late or they don't want to hand in an assignment or things like that, within the education boundaries then we have to discipline… fairness and equality is quite a huge factor because you've got so many different personalities and aspects that you need to balance out otherwise there's always going to be someone left behind or feeling like they haven't been treated well or treated with compassion. (P4, Interview 1, p. 2)
>
> If somebody is not turning up to their cooking duties then they're not showing compassion on the other people, because it becomes unfair. (P3, interview 1, p. 2)

Challenges with Compassion

So Many Hurt Broken People

The situational context influenced P4's compassionate teaching. In the excerpt below, he explains how in coming to understand the students' life stories, as displaced people from Myanmar due to civil war, his compassion *changed.* Understanding the individual student enabled the development of empathy, two pre-requisite elements for compassionate teaching.

> Once you know the students and know their stories, and know their backgrounds then even though you are just in the classroom, even though you are fair and you discipline everybody together, because we talked about mercy in class the other day… it changes – your compassion changes based on the situation because of your background knowledge on their lives, you know like if you've had some students who've been through something like, not had schooling and had to leave their village, and you're asking them to do something in class and you have to put those two and two together and say oh well, I need to show compassion here. And I don't know, it seems to be on a daily basis because there are so many hurt broken people around us. (P4, interview 1, p. 3)

Ingratitude and Dependence

Another challenge identified by the participants was the negative effects compassion *was* having on some students, contributing to dependence and a sense of ingratitude and entitlement. This challenge was significant as it concerned *actual*, not hypothetical, negative effects of compassion. The problems created an ethical dilemma for the participants, requiring wisdom and discernment.

> P3: The other thing I was thinking in this community right now, with the move, with the students they've had a lot of things handed out to them, they've had free accommodation, eating really well, they've got basically education handed to them on a plate to them,…
>
> P4: We'll buy any medical needs they need,…
>
> P3: They've got into this point where they're expecting hand-outs- some of them, … and so we are also concerned with the compassion that we give, well is it giving another hand-out? Or is it being compassionate?
>
> P4: it's a really fine line… when they start to expect from you or even demand from you,
>
> P3: …and the gratefulness that they show, they're so used to receiving things, that they're not quite as grateful as much… (P3 and 4, interview 1, p. 7)

Avoiding Distortions of Compassion

P4 was aware from experience, that expressing compassion in teaching is not straightforward. Implied in the quote below, is a need for discernment to avoid distortions of the virtue of compassion; avoiding being excessively compassionate and thereby counter-productive. Discipline is understood as an integral, not separate expression of compassion.

> I don't think that compassion is as clear cut as we think it is… I get the dictionary definition of compassion says that you're always doing something nice or understanding the other person exactly, and for us when we're here for us to be compassionate with our

> students also means that we have to discipline them in the right areas... to show compassion . I just don't think it is as clear cut. It [compassion] doesn't stand alone, ... you can be over-compassionate and that's not helping the person that you're trying to be compassionate with. I mean we would class ourselves as compassionate people in what we're doing, and yet every day involves quite a lot discipline with people that we are being compassionate to.
>
> Someone who is compassionate might not be overly worried about the discipline side of things,... I don't think people put the two together when they talk about compassion it's always like- they're a lovely, lovely person but they never tell me off. (P4, interview 1, p. 2)

Cultural Misunderstandings

Inter-cultural misunderstandings were identified as a significant source of frustration to being compassionate. In the quote below, P3 describes intrapersonal insights into how she wrestled with certain student problems. She describes the effort needed to overcome negative feelings and a natural thought response that did not want to engage with a person compassionately.

> The cultural difference the Karen people we work with here in Noh Bo, they're very afraid to ask questions and actually find out how to do things. If they don't understand something they won't actually come to Graeme and I and ask for clarification, and so it frustrates me a lot and so that for me is one of the biggest challenges to remember that we've actually stepped into their culture and I cannot expect them to change overnight and so I have to show them more compassion when they don't come and ask for clarification and I just have to work it in with them... it's a continuous effort for me to show compassion in that area.
>
> When they've left it too late... My initial thought is well it's your problem and not my problem, go and deal with it yourself; which is my automatic response. (P3, interview 1, p. 5)

A War of Attrition-Transcending Self

Another theme from the findings was the participants' ability to sustain compassionate teaching. The high needs context where they served was tiring, leading to inconsistencies in showing compassion. This finding highlights the reality and human limitations of compassionate teaching. In the excerpt below P4 describes his critical reflective thinking as he processes the challenges and purposes to transcend self; choosing to 'model Christ.'

> I think almost the human nature side of things. It can become a war of attrition where, 'cause you are showing compassion a lot, in like ____ [female student] sick in bed, many of the students get sick and showing compassion to 40 students that really need compassion on a daily basis, like every day you are doing that... you've got to keep reminding yourself that you can let yourself get tired, you can let yourself get run down, and sometimes you might even have a response that you think I really didn't show compassion there... or I should have done it this way... and so a war of attrition.. You have to stop and say, there's no limit, your cup shouldn't fill up with how much compassion you have and then that's it, you have to remind yourself even when you're tired, and even when maybe the students are doing the same thing over and over again,

that it's still your job to be compassionate, still your job to model Christ and for the students to see that. (P4, interview 1, p. 6)

Practice of Compassionate Teaching

Laying Down Our Lives Before Christ

The participants described how spiritual disciplines; the practice of prayer and of being spiritually minded, were perceived as vital to their ability to sustain compassionate teaching. The findings below are not religious rhetoric; rather they are authentic descriptions of the participants' sense of self-sacrifice' - thousands of kilometres from family and home comforts, serving on a voluntary basis, displaced and broken people in sweltering tropical heat, in constant danger of malaria, dengue fever and scorpion bites.

> P3: For us over here, prayer time and <u>laying down our lives before Christ</u> every single day and saying hey Lord this is not my burden but your burden.
>
> P4: It's not about 'me'.
>
> P3: And it's not about me over here, so will you [God] give me that supernatural strength to be able to show compassion and serve to best of my ability in your strength and we certainly feel that. The days where we're lacking a bit and actually not handing over to God – you know…
>
> P4: Take it on your own shoulders and you quickly run out… quickly run out of juice… and we then have to get back on track. (P3, interview 1, p. 6)

Small and Large Compassion

Compassion in this context of teacher-education in Thailand was broadly expressed; individually and corporately, affecting the whole community. In the quote below, P4 explains critical incidents where compassion is shown discreetly in response to a basic need and intuitively through improvisation during a class session. In this sense a nuanced understanding was revealed; compassionate teaching not only provided what a student needed but avoided something the student didn't need.

> Small compassion to me would be seeing that one of the students doesn't have any footwear or his jandals are half the size of his feet so you actually go out and buy some jandals for them showing compassion on them because they don't have any income or money, and that's a small act of compassion. And then the larger act of compassion would be after you've known this student's background and you know that they might be struggling in an area or they're hiding or hanging on to hurt, that you can actually steer them away from some things showing compassion and certainly in a teaching context you can say well, this person isn't really going to gel with this or enjoy this so I will show compassion on that person… Give them an alternative or for the sake of that one person you might not do it for the whole class… showing compassion for what they've been through… and that's a snap decision sometimes. (P4, interview 1, p. 4)

Dignity and Life-Skills Integrated into Compassion

Another example of compassion in teaching within this context was described around avoiding giving money to the poor students as a hand-out. Instead the teacher participants designed jobs for the poorest students to do so they could earn their money with dignity and develop life-skills that would stand them in good stead for the future. In the excerpt below they refer to the dilemma they were faced with, how to be compassionate and just; not undermining the initiative and diligence of those who had found their own income sources. Significant is the teachers' careful deliberation and problem-solving process, that took three weeks. The rationale for getting it right was deemed crucial for sustaining community and interpersonal trust.

> P4: Being compassionate to their needs of having no money; we gave some students some jobs here and some students got their own jobs and some people back home gave us some money to sponsor some students so we were in a dilemma with being compassionate to the one's that needed the money but also a justice thing in the community where some people have actually got their own jobs and we didn't want it to look like these ones get a hand out and these ones have gone in and been pro-active. So knitting those two together, justice and compassion, we made jobs so everyone had jobs...
>
> P3: So they're all working for their money... we were not just giving the money out.
>
> P4: So it's not a hand out, lots of things give it value. We spent three weeks deliberating over different ways to do that because we wanted to still be compassionate but we had to be fair and just... The fastest way to begin a programme like this to ostracise yourself from the community would have been to treat some people differently than others... we'd lose their trust. (P3 and 4, interview 1, p.6)

Reciprocity of Compassion between Teachers and Students

Both participants recognized they needed to allow room for compassion. This was explained by the way they said Christ modelled it, 'when compassion is *needed* ... it's almost a case-by-case basis' (P4, interview 1, p. 3). The situational context or life-world in which these two teachers worked was critical to their enacting of compassion. P3 illustrated this around a critical incident whereby compassion was *expected* to be reciprocated by their students toward them.

> Last term ... we didn't actually have a classroom, so from day to day we were moving from class to class. Generally we would expect the students to be quite punctual, they have to be there on time every morning but last term we I guess you could put the grace and compassion together, we gave the students a bit more grace with being late, and showing that compassion, but they had to show it back on us as well, so it was a give and take. (P3, interview 1, p. 3)

Action Plans and Outcomes of Action Research

Wrestling with Own Social History

The participants were willing to engage in an action research cycle. P3 described her area of interest around a couple of students she found difficult to connect with relationally. In the quote below, she critically reflects on the issue acknowledging the contribution of her own social history to the problem and her emerging sense of selflessness; dying to self.

> There a couple of people I struggle showing compassion with. It's because of the maybe the connection with those people. It's not because I don't like them or because I don't want to show compassion on them but the relationship with them. If they're not going to put any effort in to having a relationship with me or putting any effort in, then it makes it a lot harder for me to do the same with them. If they're not showing that appreciation of my compassionate side, then well I don't really feel like it's appreciated.
>
> And that for me comes from my background, the social situation and the friends I've had, I've put a lot of effort in with my friends, and have never received that back, so it was always me giving and I felt that I was never getting anything in return, and till I got to a point in my life, where I got tired of giving, giving, but again God has brought me to a place where it's not about what I receive but still what I can give. (P3, interview 1, p.8)

Shifting One's Position and Attitude

Approximately 2 months later, I received an emailed critical reflection on their action research process. P3 narrowed her action plan to focus to one student who she described as, 'a challenge from the beginning; very needy… without knowing it [she] will cause tension between certain people.' The first step in her action plan was, 'Prayer for wisdom to know how to deal with ____ and prayer for ____. (P3, personal correspondence October 2013, p. 1) This led to a sense of internal transformation and shift in position and attitude. Of significance are the teacher's self-directed changes which facilitated improved relational connectedness with the teacher and the difficult student.

> As I began to pray for [the student] my heart began to soften and realised it was not up to me to judge [the student] , try to change [the student] or teach [the student] a lesson in each conversation we had. So instead of walking to the other end of the room to avoid [the student's] questions and complaints, I have prayed that God would use me to encourage [the student] if needed. I changed my attitude and made every effort to greet [the student] with a smile each morning. I went out of my way to ask specifically how [the student] and the family were. I believe because of my availability and openness toward [the student] _____ was able to come to me and share things that [the student] had not shared to others. Through those times I was able to encourage [the student] in a loving kind way because I wanted the best for [the student]; not because I was trying to change [the student] with a hard heart. (P3, personal correspondence October, 2013), p. 2)

Letting Go and Trusting God

The efficacy of the research action plan influenced a broader attitudinal change in P3 towards all students. In the excerpt below she describes her Christian responsibility as a teacher, her faith in God's sovereignty, and a willingness to be less controlling; preconditions that she felt enabled her to be more compassionate. P3 also connects her faith and action to obedience to teaching from Paul's epistle to the Philippians in the Bible.

> This term before I react or pass any judgement on anyone I may possibly feel frustrated with, it is my responsibility to pray for them first and trust that God will have it in control. By letting go of that control I am then able to be more compassionate in my teaching by showing love, grace and concern for the other person. Philippians 4:6, "Be anxious for nothing but through prayer and supplication make your requests known to God". If we are praying for others we have no reason to worry or be anxious for them because God instructs us to give it to Him and it is His responsibility. (P3, personal correspondence October 2013, p. 2)

Extreme Needs-Extravagant Compassion

P4's action plan developed around one particular high needs student. The problem involved significant issues that were compromising not only the student's health but also others associated with the learning community. Exploring compassionate teaching initially involved P4 flexibly applying the penalty rule regarding the student's late assignment because the student had made a real effort in the face of difficult circumstances. However, more extreme issues arose. In the scenario described below, compassion is extravagantly expressed concurrent with discipline- exclusion from the campus. P4 explains that his compassion did not condone the inappropriate behaviour.

> I sat with [the student] after we had moved [the student] to another area of the village, made sure [the student] had a net to sleep under, someone to talk with and water, I knew that showing [the student] compassion while at the same time never condoning what [the student] had done was going to be the key to bring healing to the whole family. I needed to show [the student] love in order to help [the student] with the next step. [The student] only agreed to leave and get help we had organised because [the student] trusted and respected me and I believe that was through the area of previous compassion being shown both in this episode and past events. (P4, personal correspondence October 2013, p. 1)

Transformational Potential

In this extraordinary incident P4 was able to hold simultaneously a range of opposing emotions demonstrating self-control. He says, 'I should have snapped, but I knew that I had to look after [the student].' In his reflections emailed to me towards the end of the academic year, P4 acknowledges compassion can be difficult to rationalize. He concludes the action research process by expressing a belief that compassion can be a transformative tool for the teacher.

> It's a strange thing I know; showing compassion to the one who has inflicted so much hurt and pain to someone close to me makes no sense but I believe if I had not then it was only delaying the healing process for all involved... In other words, I think compassion is often looked at in terms of a victim or someone down on their luck but we can use it to try and change a behaviour we don't like. (P4, personal correspondence October 2013, p. 1-2)

Interview with a School-Principal

'It was very hard to try and steer compassion for the [student] and what we needed [the student] to do. It's a privilege to be a part of that, because that's compassion. (P5, interview 1, p. 3)

The following findings from participant 5, a school principal, were derived from an hour long, semi-structured interview conducted on site in August, 2013. The principal contextualized her explanations and illustrations of compassionate teaching around a leadership role involving the implementation of an *anti-bullying* and *restorative justice* programme.

Meanings of Compassionate Teaching

Love Your Neighbour As Yourself

The anti-bullying and restorative justice programme supported the school's mission statement which emphasised the provision of a safe and caring learning environment for children. The programme utilised secular resource booklets, integrated with Christ-centred, biblical teaching.

I believe that with Christ at the centre … we could use a secular resource which are these books [showing them to me] that teaches children identifying, coping and preventing bullying behaviour. And it covers physical, social, emotional, types of bullying… we were dealing with the physical incidents but we were ignoring the emotional, the social put downs. So this is a vehicle which I've given the staff and … they've been working their way through and now what they're doing is they're finding specific lessons when a need arises. And just using the promise of what God said, 'to love your neighbour as yourself,' kind words heal and help, cutting words wound and maim.' The fruit of the Spirit, what it should look like, and what is goodness and kindness, gentleness… and teachers are able to use the bible on one hand to teach about how God tells us to live and then these wonderful secular resources which are just outstanding in terms of showing children the physical, verbal, social bullying- nasty rumours, all of the that. (P5, interview 1, p. 1)

Naivety and Need

The principal explained the need for a compassionate restorative justice programme in her Christian school. Children at the school were not perfect and although Christian teaching and values are prominent, many children faced real personal challenges as they journeyed through their school years.

There's a naivety that we're a Christian school and the children should be perfect here and our first priority is to teach them the bible and that should change their behaviour - straight away! But it's a life-long journey. I believe we teach the children scriptures, we teach them the commandments, so that they're on their hearts and minds, and when they are entering puberty and adolescence, and they're faced with different choices I'm hoping that they'll remember what God has said, and that they'll identify the difference between right and wrong. (P5, interview 1, p. 3)

Challenges with Being a Compassionate Teacher

Unpopular with Some Parents

The principal described the challenges she faced because understandably, some parents wanted the misbehaving students removed from the school. However, through the restorative meetings parents of children disaffected by the inappropriate behaviour were able to see the issues through different eyes. Later on, the high needs student began to experience progressive transformation and re-integration into the school community. One of the findings revealed in the quote below is the active role the students within the class played, as agents of compassion in the restorative process.

> For them [the parents] to go out of the room with a different lens on what been going on in this [student's] life. They wouldn't know all of those aspects that I've told you other than [the student's] a troubled child, ... we had to have [the child] supervised at all times at interval and lunch, we no longer have that supervision in place any more.
>
> We got the class involved in how to support this [student] relationally- particularly this year, and we set targets of 7 days without hitting, 14 days, one month... and we got up to 100 days. And yet I've had parents who say that kid shouldn't be in our school, and that's the biggest challenge I find. (P5, interview 1, p. 2)

Pain and Privilege

Another theme revealed in the findings is that compassion within this Christian educational context is costly in terms of people's patience, resources including time. Compassion in this context also implies hurt and disruption to innocent parties.

> Now this is all in support of our school counsellor, him and I working together with parents, the teacher. We have 'strengthening families' meetings, we have a whole lot of different agencies, three or four times a year where we've sat around and talked particularly about this [student], the support that's needed for the parents, what we need to do as a school and it's a privilege to be a part of that because that's compassion. (P5, interview 1, p. 2-3)

Staff Feeling over-Whelmed

Another finding from this field work was that the principal identified compassion fatigue within some of the teachers as they became involved with students and their parents who were experiencing marital problems. 'I've got some staff who are feeling quite over-whelmed with sad stories they're hearing and that is becoming more and more draining on our staff.' (p5, interview 1, p. 4) The principal was also very aware of her responsibility to be there for the teachers.

> Yes it's natural that teachers will be stretched and taxed and burdened and worn out, and they need to know they can come to us for support, that we can step in and give them

some release time, that's what I try to do practically... It's no use me having all the theory... I've got to make sure that practically I'm here. (P5, interview 1, p. 7).

Practice of Compassionate Teaching

Working with the Rejected and Broken-Hearted

The principal described that compassion in teaching could be short, simple and effective. However, students with high needs often required on-going monitoring and support. In the quote below, the principal paints a picture of just such a student. As a researcher, I found I was moved emotionally upon hearing this description of someone despised and rejected, wounded and broken-hearted. And yet, I also felt for the class teacher and fellow members who would be tested and challenged doing life together with the high needs student. Compassion in teaching costs. Also of significance is the principal's leadership role in helping the class teacher to see the student through a different lens.

> Some are not quick fixes. We've got another child, who again came from CAMHS (Child Adolescent Mental Health Service) and no one would take ___________ . [The student] was violent, came from an extremely difficult background, through the family court law system. And just a recent article said that when children are caught up in family court law they lose five years of their life because of the emotional taxing on those children to be subject to mum and dad and such acrimonious behaviour.... And if children can be kept out of that and mum and dad manage around the children to keep gracious... children are much more settled and calm... and so we have a lot of that too Alaster that I'm involved with and again it's trying to help a teacher with the lens, look this child's been in home A they've been there for three days, and now come to home B, they have to re-adjust to new routines and sometimes a new step mum or a new step dad or step children, yes bad behaviour is bad behaviour... we don't want to see disrespect but we also need to have a bigger understanding of what's it like when they're coming to school. And it's a challenge for us. (P5, interview 1, p. 4)

Getting Results

Within this context, P5 explained her role as a compassionate leader and the transformative effects the comprehensive intervention was having, citing a reduction of serious student misbehaviour across a twelve month period.

> You then asked me in terms of my role as a compassionate leader- we have had a number of students who have come into our school that have been referred to us by CAMHS, [Child adolescent mental health] an outside agency, and this folder here from 2012 represents all the interactions I've had with these students. And this is this year's [a much thinner folder], because what we do is work actively with the parents, outside agencies, the teacher. (P5, interview 1, p. 2)

Working with Grief and Loss

Compassionate teaching within this programme was illustrated through the complex restorative justice process involving the student, a range of stakeholders and support personnel. Compassion was initially expressed by not labelling the child, focussing instead on the specific inappropriate behaviours. Secondly, compassion was described through the way those involved sought to understand the reasons for the inappropriate behaviour. Thirdly, compassion was described through the desire to see positive improvement in the student's life, not simply the administration of a punishment.

> We had one student from a very troubled background, dad had died when [the student] was young, grandparent is gravely ill… is a big student, had [other] issues… manifested in outbursts of inappropriate behaviour … and rather than labelling him a naughty boy, his behaviour wasn't acceptable, we had to manage complaints from parents constantly, in fact I've got a folder from the year before, again with this type of correspondence, it was very hard to try and steer compassion for the [student] and what we needed to do, was to work with the teachers, to work with the parents, … so what we did was when we had some physical incidents we would have a restorative meeting, and we would call the parents in and sit around together and also have the school counsellor involved, and the privilege Alaster, of some of these fathers sitting at the meeting, being able to say to this [student] look this is what we need you to be able to do- I know you don't have a dad, but this is what a dad would want from his [child]. (P5, interview 1, p. 2)

Compassion Modelled through Leadership

The following edited critical incident captures the principal's personal engagement with compassion in leadership. The excerpt reveals commitment and perseverance, as well as a sense of frustration and even fatigue as she wrestles her way through a particular problem during work hours and in the middle of the night. Compassion in teacher leadership affects the spirit- moving the participant to intercession and for supernatural assistance.

> I woke up in the middle of the night concerned about one of our [students] who's in a home, where there's the split week arrangement [with parents] and we've been trying to access counselling for this [student] and we need both parents to consent… and one of the parents won't… the [student] is displaying behaviour at school which is disrespectful but I know it's because [the student] is caught up in this ugliness of the parents arguing- new step-parents on both sides, siblings… So I woke up in the weekend praying for him and what else do I do now? (P5, interview 1, p. 5)

Ability to Empathize

The principal's empathy for others and understanding how to engage compassionately with their needs was influenced by life-experiences. She said, 'I'm able to look at parents in the eye and say I know exactly where you're at, I ask you to keep focused on the children … And I've had some really good response from that.' (P5, interview 1, p. 5) In the quote below the principal demonstrates her heart-felt connection with suffering students.

> I've had to call the police [at school] because we've had parents arguing over whose house the children will go to. I've sat with children around this table till seven o'clock at night. I've had to go to a classroom and be present whilst one parent handed the children over to the other because a court order had just come through. And that's heart

breaking… absolutely heart-breaking… and my heart breaks – I know what it does to children. (P5, interview 1, p. 6)

Transformed Lives

The interview concluded with the principal describing the impact compassionate teaching could have, contextualized around the restorative justice process that was being implemented in the school. The scenario below is based on real experiences of transformed lives. She acknowledges personal satisfaction and gives credit to other teachers involved. Although compassion in teaching can have high costs, over time these may be reduced and even eliminated.

> When you see a child as part of the school community engaged in play, engaged in the classroom, beaming with a smile; that is the biggest reward you can get. From where you see them coming in hiding under tables, having to call parents to come and pick them up, working with outside agencies and slowly over a period of time, saying, 'we just don't need you [the agencies] to be involved with the school anymore… that is the most rewarding and it's because we've got dedicated teachers here who really are compassionate. (P5, interview 1, p. 7)

Findings from the online survey: Five participants, two principals, one primary teacher/syndicate leader and two primary class teachers from a range of small (student rolls less than 200), faith-based school contexts (Private and State Integrated[1]) within New Zealand.

> It is building relationship with the heart of an autistic child so for the first time they feel wanted at a school, and so they are peaceful and quiet and a 'different child' from how they were at their last school. (Online survey, question 3)

1. Describe your understanding of the term "compassion" from a Christian biblical perspective. Please include at least one biblical reference to support your description.

- I think that compassion means to take into account the heart of the person with whom you are dealing. Out worked, this involves being moved by a genuine expression or remorse or repentance by another person; responding to a person out of a real desire to seek their best, not from anger or hurt pride; taking care not to crush another with words or actions that hurt. A person with compassion still meets out justice, and speaks the truth, but does it in love.
- For me, Jesus is the best example of compassion in the Bible. His love of the 'unlovable' and his care for others around him is evident through all the Gospels.
- Compassion means choosing to understand and get beside those who are suffering or need help.
- Colossians 3:12 Therefore, as God's chosen people, holy and dearly loved, clothe yourselves with compassion, kindness, humility, gentleness and patience.

[1] A state-integrated school is a former private school which has integrated into the state education system while retaining its special character.

The perspectives listed above draw attention to the motives that inform compassion, the manners associated with seeking compassion (repentance and remorse) and expressing compassion- to seek the best for the person, without pride or desirous of vengeance. Jesus is set forth as a timeless and relevant role model for compassion today. Justice is not compromised, practice is informed by scripture and a vital disposition of being willing to get beside those in need, is affirmed.

2. Describe what you believe a compassionate teacher, teacher-leader or principal within 'a' Christian school context would do.

- I believe a compassionate teacher would not be quick to judge but to show understanding. A teacher like this would also walk alongside their students and be there for them in areas of need and guidance.
- Love their students and do all they can to show that.
  To know and understand our staff, families and young people as individuals and respond accordingly.
- To look for ways that bring about restoration and reconciliation when things happen.
- To know the needs of our community and seek with God's help to help, support, grow them.

The ideas listed above suggest that a compassionate Christian school educator would seek God's input, showing love and relational understanding, being orientated towards student re-integration rather than being quick to judge.

3. Describe an example or critical incident that you observed or heard about at your school this year (or last year) that illustrates the concept of compassionate teaching or compassionate leadership.

- Child Youth and Family agency child- a girl, mum deserted her. A parent of the school offered to take the child and the school offered to accept the challenge including giving sponsorship. Over 6 months of this year we have ministered to the child and seen many moves towards wholeness - very small steps , many 1 to 1 , many round table conversations, much prayer by all staff .Praying she will respond to the Lord one day in the meantime we live for her success.
- It is building relationship with the heart of an autistic child so for the first time they feel wanted at a school, and so they are peaceful and quiet and a 'different child' from how they were at their last school.
- When a child's pet died, the teacher let the child tell all about it, even though they had other things to do.
- When some boys were way out of line and deserved punishment (they did have to face consequences) but compassion was shown given that the boys had both experienced the loss of a father.

The above real life examples of compassion describe a wide range of student needs involving rejection, grief, and genetic neurological disability. Compassion within these Christian school contexts varies from significant planned and costly corporate care through to a one-off spontaneous decision by a teacher to allow a student to talk to the class about the death of a beloved pet.

4. Describe what you believe are the main challenges school leaders, teacher-leaders and teachers face engaging with compassion towards students and / or staff.

- The balance of Justice, mercy and humility.
- Busyness - it's easy to get too busy to take the time to make the heart connections.
- Pride - it's easy to get offended at bad behaviour rather than to see past it to the heart of the child.
- I believe the main challenge for showing compassion toward students is keeping a clear standard of discipline (a consequence of an action) but also knowing when to show compassion and understanding. This comes back to knowing your students.
- Time - expediency to get things done. We can easily miss what is really going on.
- Our own development of character that enables us to be compassionate.
- A clear understanding of God's compassion that is shown to us on a daily, moment by moment basis! We should be models of what Christ is!

Although the sample of five Christian teachers and principals is small, the challenges they describe above are real and noteworthy. Busyness and time pressure due to high workload are listed by two participants, one principal and one teacher, as a hindrance to responding compassionately within their school communities. Two participants highlight the difficulty of implementing compassion while maintaining justice and discipline, which are traditional indicators of well-run schools. One participant identifies pride as a problem, which in this case is linked to holding on to an offence, being unwilling to suffer wrong and forgive. The final bulleted point emphasizes the problem of not fully appreciating God's compassion and the mismatch between what *'we should be'* and what we often *are*.

5. Describe two practical ways that you personally have endeavoured to express compassion in your teaching and / or leadership. Please describe the contexts to help me understand your examples

- I really try to make a heart connection with each child, to know about them, who they are, what they like, to love them. Sometimes that means asking God to give you a love for them, but it also takes time - like being prepared to visit the house of a student who is upset or going through family difficulties.
- In my teaching, I have tried (and will continue) to hear my student's voice when sorting out a conflict or behaviour. While I know my students, I might not understand what they are going through in their life at that time or what motivated them to carry out an action. Through showing understanding I am not quick to judge or condemn but I am showing that I value their opinion.
- During a maths lesson, a child frequently becomes upset even before they are given their worksheet. I have changed my approach many times until we have reached an understanding of what he is expected to do little step by little step. I see him at every step rather than when he has completed the page like the rest.

- Young girl from a foster home has to deliver a speech and also has learning challenges. I took time to work with her individually during time when others were not around (so she would not be embarrassed by the extra support). I also wrote her a personal note to encourage her in work.

The rich and varied examples above show that compassion is inseparable from love, emotional connectedness, and the expending of self and resources towards the person being helped. Compassionate pedagogy can involve little steps in the mist of the class or discreet assistance and words of encouragement in private.

6. Describe what you perceive were the effects or results of your compassionate teaching / leadership on you personally and on the recipient(s).

- Respect and openness to ask for assistance and help when required
- A Year 8 boy with both a physical disability and ongoing family problems, whose house I have visited on more than one occasion, has shown a real effort to get up and be at school on time this term, he has expressed that he wants to work in our school when he has finished his schooling, and he is making academic progress. I think this is because we have dealt with him with compassion.
- The effects were that my students see that they are valued. They see that they can come to their teacher without feeling afraid or shut down. While it can take longer to sort out, overall it helps the teacher to gain understanding and builds respect.
- The student who did her speech stood and confidently delivered it - having never done this before (year 9 now), and WAS so proud of herself. Her dignity was kept and she felt she could do it. No one else knew what time had gone into it but it developed a closer bond between her and I. She is more willing to have a go at other things.

The effects of compassion listed above highlight firstly, improvements in interpersonal relationships between teacher/students and principal/staff and secondly, improvements in student performance and achievement. These findings affirm that compassion can make a positive difference.

7. Describe any or all of your schools' policies and practices which you believe support and encourage compassion within the life of the school learning community.

- We have a policy and procedure to involve parents early in any discipline issues. We work hard to teach the students team work and care for one another.
- Two of our school's values are respect and relationships. These show our students understanding and love for people.
- Children are encouraged to support each other, apologise when the hurt someone, think before they speak and talk kindly.
- Our principal has great chats with your kids that I believe show a compassion and desire for change and not just outcomes.
- Behaviour management programme –it gives students opportunities to work on areas of concern.

- We are very relational as a staff so we tend to talk with our kids, we know them incredibly well so are aware of what is going on or not going on so we can serve them best.

The findings to the above question show that although compassion was not explicitly included in the school policies, it was implied within management practices and school values. Furthermore, several participants identify the practice of developing a culture of relational care within their respective schools. The final bulleted point emphasizes an important quality of compassionate teaching; knowing students *'incredibly well'* in order to *'serve them best.'*

8. Describe ONE possible scenario involving a student, students or a staff member that you would like to be more compassionate towards during the school term. What specific actions might you take? Could you please implement this plan of action during the term and reflect on the outcome?

- One of our new staff members has been 'stand offish". I am working on daily prayer and deliberate regular touching base
- I'm always working on compassion - with everyone, but particularly with staff (I seem to be better with students!). All my staff (and my Board chair) know I am working on not letting my own busyness affect my responses... sometimes it just means thinking more before I speak.
- Two boys in my class have dominant personalities and often cause disruption, thus making my teaching interrupted. In the past, their rowdiness has caused me to snap when I thought they were being silly when in fact they were asking a question and I had shut them down. Lately, I have been working on teaching appropriate classroom manners and have also made an effort to these boys to show that they are valued. I apologised for shutting one boy down when he spoke and have made an effort to teach them in a way that honours their learning style, which will keep them engaged and motivated. We are all learners and do make mistakes but love and compassion should always come first!
- One child pushes all the buttons, have implemented a support programme where [the child] meets small targets with a reward.
- I have a staff member that I work with who is often very confrontational. I often find myself backing away from ____ because ____ is so in my face. I think I need to be more compassionate given that ____ came from a difficult school last year and is still working through those things. I often feel like I am being labelled with those ____ previously worked with and am misunderstood in my efforts to help. [The teacher's] cultural background also contributes to ____ very in your face style and I need to show greater understanding for this and be willing to show greater compassion rather than feeling personally affronted.

The open and candid descriptions above highlight real needs within the five participants' Christian school contexts. In the first scenario the principal's action plan integrates spirituality (prayer) with intentional efforts to build a rapport with the staff member that is disconnected. In the second scenario, the principal humbly acknowledges compassion as an area being worked on, with busyness in the leadership role identified as a major problem compromising compassionate responses to people's needs. The final bulleted scenario from the syndicate leader describes a complex collegial problem involving inappropriate and hurtful behaviour. The colleague's problems have several antecedents, a difficult previous school and culturally embedded habits. The action plan is significant in that the participant is willing to suffer wrong, and to show compassion towards the other person, characteristics of *spiritual maturity and leadership*. The primary teacher with a child that *pushes all the buttons* proactively implemented a behaviour modification plan. It does not ignore the misbehaviour, but compassionately seeks to transform the child's behaviour in a positive way. The other remaining scenario from a primary teacher with two challenging boys describes an action plan that embraces a willingness to re-build broken relationships and to explore alternative teaching strategies, better suited to the boys learning styles. This plan of action models two important characteristics of a *compassionate pedagogy*.

Likert Scale Survey Questions

The final set of data from the online survey was derived from seven Likert scale questions. The five participants felt very satisfied with their understanding of a biblical Christian perspective of compassionate teaching and four of the five positively agreed that they were known as compassionate practitioners. The syndicate leader gave a rating of 3/5. All agreed strongly that compassionate teaching/leadership can make a positive difference in people's lives and makes an important contribution to achieving the educational goals of their respective Christian schools. There was a consistent neutral rating of 3/5 in response to their belief in the benefit of professional development in biblical Christian understanding of being compassionate. All *disagreed* strongly that compassion was only seldom experienced by colleagues and students at their respective schools. The one question that drew a wide variation of responses was 'upon reflection, I believe there is a scenario in my school or class where I would like to explore being compassionate.' This was in contrast to the written responses to question 8 where each participant was able to describe a scenario where they would like to be more compassionate.

DISCUSSION

The findings from the ten participants in this qualitative research project share many consistencies with the themes discussed in the secular and religio-spiritual sections of the literature review. However, the findings also reveal nuanced understandings pertaining to the practice and challenges associated with compassion in faith-based educational contexts.

Meanings

Participants' meaning-making of compassion was inseparably linked to their own social, cultural, religious and economic life experiences; their own encounters with suffering, grief and loss, as well as the opportunities being experienced within their institutional contexts in which they currently served. Meaning was a reflection of *who they are*, their identity and integrity (Palmer, 2000). Participants understood compassion arose from their sense of empathy for someone in need, followed by their personal practical assistance or mercy (Nussbaum, 1996). That is, they recognized both an *affective* and *effective* dimension to compassionate teaching (Wolpow, R., Johnson, M., Hertel, R., Kincaid, S., 2011).

All participants related biblical principles or narrative to their meanings of compassion in teaching. These included the second great commandment to love your neighbour as yourself (Matthew 22:39), and the teaching in Micah 6:8 to love mercy, to do justly and to walk humbly with God. Several participants made sense of compassion through the life of Jesus, who they looked to as a role model. One participant described how compassion was a selfless response to someone's repentance and deep remorse – no doubt having in mind the story of the father's mercy shown to his prodigal son (Luke 15:20). Others linked compassion with the 'fruit of the Spirit' (Galatians 5:22) and being willing to 'get beside' the person in need, like the Samaritan did to the victim of robbery on the road to Jericho (Luke 10:30-37). Many participants described the need for a balance between compassion and discipline, consistent with the discussion in the literature review around God's character as well as the writings of Freire (1970) and Jonas (2010). Furthermore, compassion in teaching did not mean participants minimized future behavioural expectations of their students, which was similar to the expectations of Jesus' compassion in the New Testament narrative found in John 5:1-14 and John 8:3-11.

Challenges

Participants described various personal, institutional and even cultural challenges to being compassionate in their educational contexts. For example, some participants described concern about being too compassionate, while others described the challenge of compassion fatigue, the cumulative emotional and physical stress of responding to the needs of others over an extended period of time. Both of these concerns were identified in the literature review (Dudding, 2013; Mintz, 2003; Zakrzewski, 2012).

Several participants identified busyness and pride as real every-day challenges, while two participants explained how some parents and staff would prefer more punitive approaches to student behaviour problems. Some participants said they didn't always feel like being compassionate towards students or staff they found particularly difficult to relate to and that there was often a tension between compassion and discipline- how to be just and fair. Overcoming the natural self and putting on the spiritual self in Christ was identified as a challenge by some participants. These nuanced insights to compassionate teaching were not discussed in the literature review and are issues for teachers and educational leaders who share common faith-based perspectives to reflect on.

Practice

In terms of practice, the findings agreed with the literature reviewed that compassion was often a complex, interpersonal, situational, and holistic endeavour (Wolpow, Johnson, Hertel & Kincaid,2009). Participants provided examples of compassionate *pedagogy*, and compassion in *behaviour management* of students, two themes highlighted in the first section of the literature review (Adams, Cronin-Lampe, Cronin-Lampe, et al.,2003; Hao, 2011; Poppo,2006). Acts of compassion within the participants' Christian educational contexts varied greatly from discreet responsive adjustments during teaching, through to ongoing, costly, inter-agency support programmes. Although the findings affirmed that compassion could be transformational in terms of improvements in student learning and behaviour, this study also showed that some participants experienced mixed results. The student problems or needs remained as ongoing works in progress (Willis, 1996).

Several insights into compassion within faith-based educational contexts were revealed through this study. For example, becoming a compassionate teacher required participants to *be relationally connected* to their students, being aware of their needs and background circumstances, and to possess genuine empathy for their students' holistic well-being (New Zealand Teachers Council, Code of Ethics for Registered Teachers, 2007). Being compassionate necessitated *discernment* of how to show mercy and how to uphold justice. Enacting compassion required participants to show forbearance, humility, patience and kindness when responding to student misbehaviour, and to be flexible and adaptive to meet students' learning needs. Furthermore, the action research participants described their *intrapersonal* processing associated with compassion in teaching. This included critical and reflective self-talk, prayer to God for his insight into people and problems, wrestling with the conviction of their conscience about negative attitudes, self-confrontation about motives and justice, heeding what they referred to as the prompting of the Holy Spirit, and meditation on and obedience to Biblical teaching.

The findings also revealed new insights into the effects compassionate *teaching* could have on the participants in the action research component of the project. Their engagement with the topic of compassion while initially *informational*, led to the *formation* of new dispositions and skills which in turn *transformed* their practice. For example, one participant said, 'as I began to pray for [the student] my heart began to soften' (P3). Upon reflection, P1 said, 'One of the greatest things about me doing this [action-research] is that it started to act as a semi-permanent brake, I'll just be all puffed up like a bull frog about to let loose and I'll think compassion, and I'll sort of deflate like a balloon, let's just think about this.' Another teacher wrote, 'Compassionate teaching unlocked this approach and gave me an alternative and an excuse for change, although I was unaware of it at the time until I trialled it, it was a better fit of my nature… it is who I am in Christ' (P2).

Implications and Recommendations

Although these qualitative findings are not generalizable to statistical populations, it is hoped they will be of interest to secular and faith-based educators who value compassion as a transformational dimension to their teaching and because of the authentic life-world experiences described in the findings. Three implications arise from the findings. Firstly, compassion was understood not only as an important dimension to participants' faith-based *beliefs* but also as an important characteristic of *being* a teacher. This was expressed clearly by P4, who in the context of teaching needy displaced student-teachers from Myanmar and feeling tired said, 'it's still your job to be compassionate, still your job to model Christ and for the students to see that.'

Secondly, the findings emphasize the value of the integration of faith and spiritual disciplines to assist with the challenges *sustaining* compassion in Christian educational contexts. Participants described a wide range of practical, interpersonal and self-focused reasons why they found compassionate teaching challenging. However, their spirituality which included disciplines such as intercessory prayer and petition to God, application of the scriptures to their situation, daily denying of self, being willing to suffer wrong, and to give of themselves and their resources in an unmerited way, was perceived to be helpful. P3 described the importance of this *living spirituality* when she said,

> For us over here, prayer time and laying down our lives before Christ, every single day, and saying hey Lord, ... will you give me that supernatural strength to be able to show compassion and to serve to best of my ability in your strength and we certainly feel that.

Thirdly, the study affirmed the value of teachers as researchers. As a form of professional development and teacher-led inquiry collaborative action research was able to be responsive to the highly contextualized nature of the four teacher's practice. It engaged them in reflection in action, about action and for action. By doing so the teachers were able to learn from both the *process* and *outcomes* of their inquiry.

One recommendation arising from this research would be for Christian teachers and principals to engage in critical reflection *for action* around their own meanings, challenges and practice of compassion within their respective learning communities. A second recommendation would be to invite Christian educators to facilitate collegial prayer and biblically informed discussion around ways to strengthen compassion as a *lived characteristic* of their institutional cultures.

CONCLUSION

This article has reported on a qualitative research project inquiring into a dimension of transformative spirituality: the meanings, challenges and practice of compassion. The qualitative findings were derived from the lived experiences of ten participants in a range of faith-based school contexts within New Zealand and one teacher-education context in Thailand with displaced people from Myanmar. The four participants who engaged in the collaborative action research provided enriched triangulated data across a semester which actively explored the complexities of compassion as they journeyed with specific needy students. The teacher's engagement with the concept of compassion while initially informational, led to the formation of new dispositions and behaviours which in turn transformed their practice. Analysis of the data showed on-going evidence of the perceived importance of spirituality in both the decision-making process and acts of compassion in teaching.

Being *mindful* of and *enacting* compassion benefitted the action research participants by encouraging alternative decisions and behaviours, helping to re-build relationships with others and providing authentic opportunities to model their spirituality within professional practice. The case study of the principal who provided leadership in the implementation of a *Christ-centred* approach to restorative justice, affirmed the positive effects the programme was having on children with behavioural needs. While costly in terms of resources and personnel, compassion not only helped to re-integrate the children into the school learning community but also helped parents and teachers view those children through another lens. The three teachers and two principals who participated in the online survey described a heart-moving range of examples of compassion, from discrete responsive pedagogy to comprehensive community support.

On the other side of the equation, some participants said they didn't always feel compassionate, it was never described as easy, and it didn't always produce the desired results. However, all participants were able to cite examples of how judicious and relational acts of compassion were perceived to be transformative in students' lives, supporting an injunction in sacred text, 'and of some have compassion, making a difference' (Bible, Jude 1:22).

REFERENCES

Adams, H., Cronin-Lampe, K., Cronin-Lampe, R., Drewery, W., Jenner, K., Macfarlane, A., McMenamin, D., Prestidge, B., and Winslade, J. (2003). *Restorative practices for schools- a resource.* Hamilton, New Zealand.: School of Education, University of Waikato.

Bryman, A. (2004). *Social research methods.* Oxford, England: Oxford University Press.

Chubbuck, S. & Zembylas, M. (2008). The emotional ambivalence of socially just teaching: A case study of a novice urban school teacher. *American Educational Research Journal, 45*(2), 274-318).

Collins, C. (2013). *Christ-centred resources for education, edification and evangelism: The compassionate teacher.* Retrieved from http://www.bjupress.com/resources/articles/t2t/the-compassionate-teacher.php

Creswell, J. W. (2003). *Research design. Qualitative, quantitative and mixed methods approaches,* (2nd ed.). London, England: Sage Publications.

Denzin, N., & Lincoln, Y. (Eds.). (2003). *The landscape of qualitative research* (2nd ed.). Thousand Oaks, CA: Sage.

Dudding, A. (2013). *When doctors have compassion fatigue.* Retrieved from http://www.stuff.co.nz/national/health/9271509/When-doctors-have-compassion-fatigue

Figley, C.R. (Ed.) (1995). *Compassion Fatigue: Secondary Traumatic Stress Disorders from Treating the Traumatized.* London, U.K.: Brunner Routledge.

Fraser, D. (2014). The eternal yearning. *International Journal of Children's Spirituality 19*(1), 17-24. http://dx.doi.org/10.1080/1364436X.2014.886559

Freire, P. (1970). *Pedagogy of the oppressed.* New York, NY: Continuum.

Gibson, A. (2011). *Spirituality in principal leadership and its influence on teachers and teaching.* A thesis submitted in fulfilment of the requirements for the degree of Doctor of Philosophy at The University of Waikato, New Zealand. Retrieved from http://researchcommons.waikato.ac.nz/handle/10289/5176

Gibson, A. (2013). Exploring spirituality in teaching within a Christian school context through collaborative action research. *The International Christian Community for*

Teacher Education Journal, 9(1). Retrieved from http://icctejournal.org/issues/v9i1/v9i1-gibson/

Hanover Research Council (2009). *Best practices in online teaching.* Retrieved from http://www.uwec.edu/AcadAff/resources/edtech/upload/Best-Practices-in-Online-Teaching-Strategies-Membership.pdf.

Hao, R. N. (2011). Critical compassionate pedagogy and the teacher's role in first generation student success. *New Directions for Teaching and Learning, 127*, (Autumn), 91-98.

Hartsell, B. (2006). Teaching toward compassion: Environmental values education for secondary students. *Journal of Advanced Academics 17*(4), 265-271.

Holy Bible (2013) *King James Version: MySword Bible 4.1.1 for android devices.* RiverSoft Information System. Retrieved from http://mysword-bible.soft112.com/

Jonas, M. (2010). When teachers must let education hurt: Rousseau and Nietzsche on compassion and the educational value of suffering. *Journal of Philosophy of Education, 44*(1), 45-60.

Karakas, F. (2011). Positive management education: Creating creative minds, passionate hearts and kindred spirits. *Journal of Management Education, 35*(2), 198-226.

Kessler, R. (2002). Fostering connection, compassion, and character at school. *Independent School, 61*(2), 50-53.

Lupton, R. D. (2011). *Toxic charity: How churches and charities hurt those they help (and how to reverse it).* New York, NY: HarperOne.

McClain, L., Ylimaki, R., & Ford, M. (2010). Sustaining the heart of education: Finding space for wisdom and compassion. *International Journal of Children's Spirituality, 15*(4), 307-316.

Ministry of Education (2008*). Ki te Aoturoa. Improving inservice teacher educator learning and practice.* Wellington, New Zealand: Learning Media.

Mintz, A. (2013). Helping by hurting: The paradox of suffering in social justice education. *Theory and Research in Education, 11*(3), 215-230.

Moran, C. D., & Curtis, G. D. (2004). Blending two worlds: Religio-spirituality in the professional lives of student affairs administrators. *National Association of School Personnel Administrators Journal, 41*, 631-646.

Morse, J., Barrett, M., Mayan, M., Olson, K., & Spiers, J. (2002). Verification strategies for establishing reliability and validity in qualitative research. *International Journal of Qualitative Methods, 1*(2), 1-19.

New Zealand Ministry of Education (2007). *Guidelines for principals and boards of trustees on stand-downs, suspensions, exclusion and expulsions. Part 1: legal options and duties.* Retrieved from http://tinyurl.com/phgjust

New Zealand Teachers Council. (2007). *Code of ethics for registered teachers.* Retrieved from http://www.teacherscouncil.govt.nz/ethics/code-of-ethics-poster-english-4a.pdf

Nussbaum, M. (1996). Compassion: The basic social emotion. *Social Philosophy and Policy 13*(1): 27–58.

Onwuegbuzie, A., Witcher, A., Collins, K., Filer, D., Wiedmaier, C., & Moore, C. (2007). Students' perceptions of characteristics of effective college teachers: A validity study of a teaching evaluation form using a mixed-methods analysis. *American Educational Research Journal 44*(1), 113. DOI: 10.3102/0002831206298169

Palmer, P., J. (2000) *Let Your Life Speak: Listening for the Voice of Vocation,* San Francisco, CA: Jossey-Bass.

Pine, G.J. (2009). *Teacher action research: Building knowledge democracies.* Thousand Oaks, CA: Sage.

Poppo, K. (2006). A pedagogy of compassion: Janusz Korczak and the care of the child. *Encounter: Education for Meaning and Justice, 19*(4),

Starr-Glass, D. (2005). Review: From Teaching to mentoring: Principles and practice, dialogue and life in adult education. *Journal of Transformative Education 3*(2), 185-189.

Van Brummelen, H. (2009). *Walking with God in the classroom: Christian approaches to teaching and learning* (3rd ed.). Colorado Springs, CO: Purposeful Design Publications.

Whang, P. & Nash, C. (2005). Reclaiming compassion: getting to the heart and soul of teacher education. *Journal of Peace Education, 2*(1), 79-92.

Willis, S. (1996). Finding alternatives to control and compliance. *Managing Today's Classroom, 38*(6), 1, retrieved from http://www.ascd.org/publications/newsletters /education-update/sept96/vol38/num06/Managing-Today's-Classroom.aspx

Wolpow, R., Johnson, M., Hertel, R., Kincaid, S. (2011). *Compassionate Schools: The heart of learning and teaching.* Washington State: Washington State Office of Public Instruction. Retrieved from http://www.k12.wa.us/CompassionateSchools/Heartof Learning.aspx

Zakrzewski, V. (2012). *How self-compassion can help prevent teacher burnout.* Retrieved from http://greatergood.berkeley.edu/article/item/self_compassion_for_teachers

In: Spirituality
Editor: Edith C. Roberts

ISBN: 978-1-63482-370-8

Chapter 5

A CRITIQUE OF QUANTITATIVE MEASURES FOR ASSESSING SPIRITUALITY AND SPIRITUAL WELL-BEING

Dr. John W. Fisher [*]

Adjunct Associate Professor, Education & Arts,
Federation University Australia
Hon. Senior Fellow, Faculty of Medicine, University of Melbourne
Hon. Senior Research Fellow,
CRSE, Hong Kong Institue of Education
Visiting Professor, IHMSS,
University of Glyndŵr, Wales

ABSTRACT

This chapter provides an analytical review of nearly 300 ways in which people have attempted quantitative assessments of spirituality or spiritual health/well-being (SH/WB) over the last 40 years.

They range from single-item to multi-item measures. Each item in these measures has been classified using the theoretical framework provided by the author's four domains model of spiritual health & well-being.

Some considered thoughts are presented relating to the purpose and ways of assessing spirituality and spiritual well-being. Types and forms of spirituality and spiritual well-being measures are discussed. Single-item measures are compared with multiple-item measures.

A summary table is then presented containing 260 studies with distinct multi-item measures which pertain to spirituality, spiritual well-being and related measures in general populations, university student groups, school students and teachers, and in healthcare settings.

These measures are all critiqued for content against the four domains model of spiritual health and well-being.

[*] Email: j.fisher@federation.edu.au.

This chapter is an essential resource for anyone contemplating quantitative research in spirituality/well-being, as it provides access to available measures, some of which are hidden in obscure places.

2.1. Purpose and Ways of Assessing SWB

Assessment serves many purposes, one of which is to help identify the strengths and weaknesses of populations and individual people.

Suitable quantitative assessment instruments provide fast, efficient and effective means by which the views and self-reported experiences of groups of people or individuals can be screened to create awareness of concerns that can be acted upon by responsible authorities in order to lead to desired action.

Research reported in this chapter shows that the use of many attempts at assessing spirituality and SH/WB are reported in the literature (*e.g.*, Egbert, Mickley & Coeling, 2004; Hill & Pargament, 2003; King & Crowther, 2004; Koenig et al., 2001, 2011; MacDonald & Friedman, 2002; Moberg, 2002).

A major difficulty in trying to make sense of this mass of research is that the conceptual bases upon which the research is founded vary markedly between studies (Berry, 2005). Much of the research confuses spirituality and religion. Although there are commonalities between these two constructs, they are not synonymous.

All measurement devices are built on a values base (generally the researcher's), and most instruments produce norms for populations studied. Norms vary so much between groups that what appears to be positive for SWB in one group might have negative implications in another (Moberg, 2002).

Moreover, each group is likely to believe that its own criteria for 'true' spirituality are better than everyone else's, and should possibly be the normative base for all humanity. Moberg (2002) does not agree that, because all people are spiritual, it is possible to use identical procedures to evaluate SWB of diverse populations, especially religious and minority groups.

He asserts that investigating spirituality is complicated because no measure can be perfect, and any measure simply reflects the phenomenon or its consequences, because it cannot be measured directly.

Most measures rely on self-reports, but they might not reflect reality because "*feeling well* is not necessarily *being well*" (ibid., p.55). It is essential to check the validity of any instrument used.

Does it "genuinely measure spirituality or its components?" (ibid., p.56). Gray (2006) asserts that the power of a questionnaire depends on its theoretical base and the rigour with which it is developed and tested.

Nearly all available religiosity/spirituality measures ask people for a single response about their 'lived experience' on a series of questions (Ross, 2006). In the best instruments, these questions are built on theoretical frameworks of relationships between spirituality and health that are considered important by the developers of the scales.

The 'scores' thus obtained are arbitrary indicators of spiritual health or well-being, especially if they only have a handful of items (Boero et al., 2005).

The notion of a group norm for spiritual health is also problematic. People's spiritual health depends on their world-view and beliefs as well as lived experience (Fisher, 1999a; Hill et al., 2000), so development of a single measure, which purports to be an objective standard by which to compare people, fails to recognise the multifaceted nature of spiritual health.

Properly developed and tested research instruments can save valuable time in the initial screening of small or larger groups of people. The time that is saved can be used for pastoral care.

2.2. Results of Literature Searches

Literature searches were performed during 1998-2014 using the key words 'spiritual*' on its own and using the BOOLEAN terms AND with 'health' OR 'well- being', together WITH 'assess' OR 'instrument' OR 'measure' OR 'questionnaire' OR 'scale' OR 'survey.' Information was sought from journals in education, health – medicine and nursing, psychology, religion, social sciences and spirituality. Dissertation abstracts and Australasian and US theses were also searched.

Using Google Scholar yielded several research papers and theses not otherwise accessible. The searches revealed that qualitative methods are mainly used and reported in education. Houskamp, Fisher and Stuber (2004, p.233) claim:

'Although researchers have spent considerable effort developing paper-and-pencil self-report measures to assess aspects of spirituality in adults, there have been few researchers who have devoted their resources to studying spirituality in children.

As a result, the research in spirituality in children and adolescents is still at an early stage and is highly dependent on interviewing and other qualitative research techniques to generate hypotheses, with no established body of research to develop reliable and valid quantitative measures.'

Original references were sought and traced, where necessary, to obtain copies of quantitative spirituality measures. Several authors were contacted directly by e-mail to achieve this. Increasing interest in spirituality over the last two decades has spawned numerous literature reviews.

Overall, nearly 300 quantitative measures of spirituality and/or spiritual health or well-being were found in available literature published between 1967 and 2014. Many more religiosity measures have been reported elsewhere (Hall, Tisdale & Brokaw, 1994; Hill & Hood, 1999; Koenig et al., 2001, 2011).

All available spirituality measures are mentioned here in the hope that this summary will save future researchers time in tracking down measures which are most suited to their needs.

2.3. Types of Quantitative Spirituality Measures

Three types of measures are discussed in this chapter:

- those that focus on spiritual health, well-being or wellness (SH/WB), and
- those with specific mention of spirituality, and

- related/partial spirituality measures (reflecting key aspects of the four domains model of SH/WB, not often with a spirituality label).

Each item in these nearly 300 measures has been classified using the theoretical framework provided by the four domains model of spiritual health & well-being (Fisher, 1998):

- If the item indicates relationship with self, it is classified as P (for Personal SWB)
- If the item indicates relationship with other people, it is classified as C (for Communal SWB)
- If the item indicates relationship with environment, it is classified as E (for Environmental SWB)
- If the item indicates relationship with Transcendent Other/God, it is classified as T (for Transcendental SWB)

R is used to classify references to religion/ religiosity that do not express relationship with God (T) or other people (C).

Items which do not address relationships within P, C, E, or T, and are not classified as R, are labelled as O for Other.

As some items cross-load on more than one domain, some 0.5 scores have been allocated to represent this.

2.4. Format of Spirituality Measures

Single versus Multiple-Item Measures

There is no 'gold standard' for assessing or measuring spiritual well-being. The literature contains a smorgasbord of spirituality measures with content ranging from one to 156 items. The selection of an appropriate SWB measure depends on the purpose of the research for which it is intended.

The choice between a single- or a multi-item measure is not a competition. Qualitative and quantitative measures can inform different aspects of a concern, and single- and multi-item measures can be used in a study to provide complementary and/or confirmatory data (Sloan et al., 2002).

Sloan et al. (p.482) maintain that the following points are important in selecting an instrument:

- It must have the ability to discriminate between groups at a given time, and
- be able to detect changes over time.
- The concepts measured by it must be consistent with the purpose for which it is being used, that is, the 'research' question.
- It should not show floor or ceiling effects.
- A good measure indicates how large a change is necessary to declare that an important shift has occurred, or condition exists.

Selected Single-Item Measures

This section offers a critique of nine single-item measures which purport to address spirituality.

In an investigation with 11-14 year-olds, Ark (1997) used 'prayer as a coping strategy' as a measure of 'spirituality'. This is a prime case of conflating religiosity with spirituality. In a study with 13-18 year-olds, Good and Willoughby (2006) assessed religiosity with a single question related to church attendance, whereas they defined spirituality as 'personal beliefs in God or a higher power'. These authors criticized their own single-item measures and their 'theistic conceptualization' of spirituality, concluding, 'The scientific community must seek to produce indicators that accurately reflect how youth today experience spirituality in their own lives, rather than trying to categorize them according to outdated indicators of "religiosity"'(ibid., p. 53). In a study of Australian adolescent health issues, Stanton et al. (2000) used one item on religion, but none on spirituality. The National Survey of Young Australians (Mission Australia, 2007) asked respondents how highly they valued ten items, one of which was 'spirituality'. They ranked the items on a scale from 1 to 10. This could hardly be considered a comprehensive assessment of spirituality.

A self-rated health status survey of 15-90 year-olds conducted by Ratner et al., (1998) included, as question 7, 'Would you describe your spirituality as…' 'poor' to 'excellent' on a 5-point scale. The Spiritual Well-Being Linear Analogue Self Assessment (SWB-LASA) asked, 'How would you describe your overall spiritual well-being?' based on a scale from 0 = 'as bad as it can be' to 10 = 'as good as it can be' (Johnson et al., 2007). These single item measures are offered as global 'measures' of a complex construct.

Contemporary research among 15-16 year-olds being undertaken by the Universal Education Foundation (UEF) (Awartani et al., 2008) showed promise of providing a means of assessing spiritual potential in young people.

This project states that it is using material from the WHO Quality Of Life SRPB Group (2006). UEF's Voice of Children Questionnaire 1 (VOC1) contains 135 closed-item questions grouped into 25 clusters. The single SWB question Q1_7, prompts, 'Rate your satisfaction with your sense of inner peace'.

In VOC 2, 16 provisional indicators drawn from study 1 have been collapsed into nine domains. The only one to identify spiritual components, is 'Domain 7: Inner Strength and Spirit', which is described as 'feeling playful, alive, inspired by life, at ease with oneself, and zestful' (Awartani et al., 2008, p.63). Both of these expressions of SWB would be classified as P. It will be interesting to see what eventuates from the UEF project and whether a more expansive assessment of SWB ensues.

Researchers who use single-item measures justify their actions by saying, 'simply cueing the respondent into this area of their life and the aspect that is most salient to them within this area will form the basis of their response' (Wills, 2009). This argument has some merit because all surveys are built on the assumption that respondents make sense of the concept/s being investigated via a questionnaire.

The level of abstract thinking may be greater when using single-item measures compared with using many items to break a complex concept into relatively concrete questions, which is of particular import with surveys of young children. When two multi-dimensional constructs, such as religiosity and spirituality, are conflated into one question, any conceptual confusion among respondents could be exacerbated. Buckey (2007) used one self-report item to indicate 'the degree of importance given to individual religious or spiritual beliefs'.

The first Australian Unity Wellbeing Index to use a Religion/ Spirituality (R/S) question asked, 'How satisfied are you with your spiritual fulfilment or religion?'(Survey 16, October, 2006 in Cummins, 2008). In Survey 17 this was changed to, 'How satisfied are you with your spirituality or religion?' (Cummins, 2008). Wills (2007) modified this notion slightly to religio*sity* instead of religion. The problem remains, however, that if a person scored highly on a composite R/S question, it could indicate satisfaction with BOTH religion/religiosity and spirituality, OR either spirituality (but not religion) OR religion (but not spirituality). The conflation of spirituality with religion is even continued within a multi-item measure (for 32 of the 34 questions in the Spiritual and Religious Competency Assessment (SARCA) tool developed by Fluellen (2007)).

How do each of 'religion' and 'spirituality' relate to SWB? Using the 20-item SHALOM survey, data extracted from studies with secondary school and university education students reported small to high correlations between the items, 'How important is religion in your life?' compared with, 'How important is spirituality in your life?' The results also show very small ($r=\sim0.10$) to moderately large ($r>0.50$) correlations between the importance of each of religion and spirituality with SWB (Fisher, 2009).

Squaring the value of the correlation coefficient (r) indicates the percentage of variance that exists between two factors. For example, for state university Education students, $0.553^2=0.306$, that is, 31% of variance is explained by the correlation between their perceived importance of spirituality with that of SWB. For Christian university education students this is $0.107^2=0.001$, or 1%. With such variations between groups, it would be very difficult to interpret responses to a composite R/S question, such as those displayed above.

Performing correlations of composite single-item measures with other demographic, psychological or health variables could lead to questionable conclusions. Sloan et al. (2002) report, 'It is not uncommon for scores on a single-item index and a multi-item index to be reasonably correlated. It is more common, however, that scores on the multi-item index are more reliable (stable) than single-item scores' (p.485). With this in mind, the following sections deal with multi-item measures, that according to Sloan et al. (2002), one would expect to be more reliable.

Selected Measures with 2-4 Items

Measures with small numbers of items are not much better than single-item measures at providing a comprehensive cover of multidimensional SWB. The following examples show this lack of balance across the four domains of SH/WB:

Maton (1989) assessed 'spiritual support' with a 3-item scale:

- 'I experience God's love and caring on a regular basis', classified as T,
- 'I experience a close personal relationship with God,' classified as T, and
- 'Religious faith has not been central to my coping' classified as R/P with no C & E items.

Poston and Turnbull (2004) used themes of 'having spiritual beliefs' (P) and 'participating in religious communities' (R/C) as key components of a spiritual domain of quality of life (*i.e.*, no E and T items).

The Yellowstone Boys and Girls Ranch' Spiritual Assessment of youth was based on two items: 'reported previous spiritual/religious participation' (R) and 'assent to a higher power' (T) (Mayer, 2005). There were no P, C or E items in this measure.

Greenberger (2006) had difficulty trying to fit three items together to form one construct of religious/spiritual functioning (RSpF). The 3 items used were: 'attendance at religious events' (R), 'frequency of watching religious events on TV' (R), and 'importance of religious or spiritual beliefs' (R/S). The RSpF construct had to be eliminated from the measurement model and was replaced by the single observed variable 'importance of religious or spiritual beliefs', which is a compounded R/S variable.

Aird (2007) used four items to assess spirituality in a study with young Australian adults: 'belief in God' (R/T), 'belief in a spiritual or higher power other than God' (R/T), 'frequency of church attendance' (R/C), and 'maternal belief in God' (O). No P or E items were present here.

Lindholm and Astin (2008) assessed 'spirituality' as: 'consider myself a spiritual person', 'seek opportunities to grow spiritually', and 'integrate spirituality into my life' in a study of faculty in American universities. These four items fit in the Personal domain of SWB, with none for C, E or T.

When Land, Lamb and Mustillo developed the Foundation for Child Development Child Well-Being Index (FCD-CWI) (2001), they included three of their 28 National Indicators of Child Well-Being in a domain entitled 'Emotional/Spiritual Well-Being'. This domain comprised three items: 'suicide rate' (ages 10-19) (P), 'rate of weekly religious attendance' (Grade 12) (R), 'percent who report religion as being very important' (Grade 12) (R). There were no C, E or T items here. Subsequent child well- being studies *An overview of child well-being in rich countries* (UNICEF, 2007) and *The UNICEF Index of Children's Well-Being* (Ben-Arieh, 2008) both used the FCD-CWI.

None of these seven measures with 2-4 items mention more than two of the four domains of spiritual health & well-being.

Multiple-Item Measures

It is not possible for single-, or even the available two- to four-, item measures to adequately cover the four domains of spiritual health & well-being. In accord with comments by Sloan et al. (2002), it seems reasonable to suggest that multifaceted constructs would be best measured with multidimensional, multi-item measures of SWB. A summary of available multi-item spirituality measures follows.

The Table lists the three types of spirituality measures in this chapter within four sections:

- General (measures that have been used with adults, some university students and in health-related studies),
- University only (with most studies being performed with psychology students),

- Schools (for studies with students and teachers), &
- Health-only studies related to spirituality and well-being.

Rather than identify abbreviations as footnotes to this table, the organisational detail is presented here in the hope that it will help readers negotiate the considerable detail contained therein. Please remember that the items in each of the study/instruments have been classified on the basis of the four domains model of SH/WB, in which:

P=Personal SWB C=Communal SWB E=Environmental SWB
T=Transcendental SWB (including God) R=Religious variables O=Other variable
Some items cross-load over two factors so 0.5s are used to represent this.

- The first, that is, left-hand, column shows the Year in which the study or instrument was reported.
- A minimum of 3 items per factor is considered necessary to produce a sturdy measure for a given factor.
- The second column lists the study/instruments in chronological order in each section.
- Columns 3 to 8 show the allocation of items to each of the domains of SWB (P, C, E, T), plus R and O:

As SWB is seen as being relational, it is important to distinguish between religious belief statements (R) and expressions of religious faith, in practice, in relationship with God (T). Religious faith might also be expressed through relationship with other people, in which case it would be classified as R/C.

- Column 9 labelled FA, indicates the status of the instrument with respect to Factor Analysis (e.g., Y2 indicates that, Yes, the data generated by the study/instrument have been subjected to factor analysis with 2 discrete resultant factors. N indicates that No factor analysis was reported for the study/instrument. The symbol '?' indicates doubt about the validity of claims made relating to the factor analysis. For example, items cross-loading on factors but factors being treated as discrete entities, or, item-to-total correlations being too low to be considered (e.g. value < 0.3).
- Columns 10 to 12 show the Number of people in each study, the type of respondent and place (country) in which the study was performed.
- Column 13 lists the name of the first author.
- Column 14 lists the Source of a copy of the actual instrument:

C=Contact with author, H=Hill & Hood 1999, P=Publication, T=Thesis,
W=Web, Underlined = secondary source
Abbreviations: Afr-Am= African-American, alc= alcoholics,
Qol=Quality of Life; F=Female; stu = students; 1^0=primary; 2^0=secondary.

Composition of Original SH/WB, Spirituality and Related/Partial Measures

Listed chronologically in each section

GENERAL (including some *uni*)													
SH/WB measures		**SWB**											
1	2	3	4	5	6	7	8	9	10	11	12	13	14
Yr	**Study/instrument**	**P**	**C**	**E**	**T**	**R**	**O**	**FA**	**N**	**type**	**place**	**author**	**S**
83	Spiritual Well-Being Scale(SWBS)	10			10			Y2+	206	stu/adults	USA	Ellison	P
84	Spiritual Well-Being Questionnaire (SWBQ)	10	6		4	18	4	Y7	981	adults?	USA/ Swed	Moberg	P
94	Revised Spiritual Well-being Scale	10.5	4	1	5.5			Y3?	393	Cath srs	USA	Kelly	T
95	Mental Physical Spiritual Well-being Scale	5.5	2	1	0.5	1	20	Y3?	358	uni/adult	Aus	VellaBrodric	P
95	Spiritual Wellness Inventory (SWI)	24	9.5	4.5	5	3	9	Y10	515	adults	USA	Ingersoll	W
96	JAREL SWB Scale	11.5	4.5		3	2		Y3	?	adults	USA	Hungelmann	P
97	New Spiritual Well-Being Scale	10.5	1		2	2.5		N	119	adults	Aus	Fraid	T
98	Spirituality and Well-Being	3.5			3	3.5	7	N	70	adult F	USA	Kennedy	P
98	Spiritual Wellness tool	10	5		0.5	1.5	1	?	?	church	USA	Hart	T
99	Revised Spiritual Well-being Scale	15.5	1.5		11	2		Y2/5?	150	adults	USA	Endyke	T
04	Spiritual Health Inventory (SHI)	15	2.5	3	5	2.5		Y3	243	jail/alc	USA	Korinek	P
04	Spirituality Index of Well-Being (SIWB)	12						Y2	523	out-pts	USA	Daaleman	P
07	Adapted Spiritual Well-Being Scale	17.5	0.5					N	10	hospice pts	USA	Wlodarczyk	P
07	Spiritual Health Locus of Control Scale	5			7.5		0.5	Y4	108	Afr-Am F	USA	Holt	P
08	Geriatric Spiritual Wellbeing Scale	4	8	1	2.5	0.5		Y4?	138	elderly	USA	Dunn	P
14	SHALOM-generic	**5**	**5**	**5**	**5**			Y4	453	adults	world	Fisher	P
14	Clergy Spiritual Well-Being Scale		1.5		7.5	1.5	1.5	Y2	1513	clergy	USA	Proeschold-Bell	P

(Continued)

Spirituality measures		SWB											
Yr	**Study/instrument**	**P**	**C**	**E**	**T**	**R**	**O**	**FA**	**N**	**type**	**place**	**author**	**S**
84	Spiritual Maturity Index	8	3		17	2		Y1?			USA	Ellison	H
88	Spiritual Orientation Inventory (SOI)	35.5	19.5	4.5	17.5	8		N	120	uni/adult	USA	Elkins	P
90	Index of Spiritual Orientation	3		1	4	4	7	Y3	313	pts/adult	USA	Glik	P
91	Human Spirituality Scale (HSS)	6.5	8.5	5				Y3	285	adults	USA	Wheat	T
Yr	**Study/instrument**	**P**	**C**	**E**	**T**	**R**	**O**	**FA**	**N**	**type**	**place**	**author**	**S**
91	Index of Core Spiritual Experience (INSPIRIT)	5	3	1	7	3		Y4	83	adult outpts	USA	Kass	P
93	Spirituality Assessment Scale (SAS)	18	5.5	3.5	1			Y4	189	adults	USA	Howden	T
93	Temperament & Character Inventory Self-transcendence (TCIS)							Y7?	300		USA	Cloninger	P
		4.5	3.5	4	3			N	2738	>50twins	Aus	Kirk 99	P
96	Orientation Toward R&S Index	5.5	3		1.5	2	6	Y3?	220	uni/pts	USA	Goldfarb	P
96	Spiritual Assessment Inventory (2)	11.5	16.5		20	8	16	N	56	church	USA	Cunyus	T
96	Spiritual Beliefs Scale	3.5	1		3.5			Y2	295	alcohol	USA	Schaler	P
97	Psychomatrix Spirituality Inventory (PSI)	23	12.5	3.5	9.5	13	18.5	Y7?	714	adults	USA	Wolman	P
97	Spiritual Experience Index-Revised	6	3	1	3	10		Y2	286	uni/adult	USA	Genia	P
98	Spiritual Beliefs Inventory (SBI-15R)	2	2.5		6	4.5		Y2	301	adults	USA	Holland	P
98	Spiritual Involvement and Beliefs Scale (SIBS)	14.5	4		4	2.5	1	Y4?	83	adults	USA	Hatch	P
99	Brief Multidimensional Measure of Religiousness/Spirituality	5.5	6.5	1	9.5	10.5		Y9	1445	adults	USA	Fetzer Idler 03/04	W P
Yr	**Study/instrument**	**P**	**C**	**E**	**T**	**R**	**O**	**FA**	**N**	**type**	**place**	**author**	**S**
99	Daily Spiritual Experiences Scale - 6	1.5		1	3	0.5		?		uni/adults	USA	Fetzer	W
99	Personal Experiences Scale (PES)	18.5	11	20	8	12.5	20	Y8	246	uni	USA	Perez	T

99	Spiritual Practices scale	14.5	8.5		9	27	3	N	88	uni	USA	Endyke Janzen	T
01	Royal Free Interview for R/S Beliefs RFIRSB –self-report version	0.5	0.5	0.5	4.5	4		N	297	adults	UK	King, M	P
01	Spiritual History Scale in Four Dimensions (SHS-4)	1	4		6.5	11.5		Y4	228	elderly	USA	Hays	P
01	Spiritual Needs (parent's perceptions)	8	12.5	2	10	9.5	1	Y2?	523	parents	USA	Smith JM	T
01	Spirituality/Religiosity Scale	0.5	0.5		5	3		Y1	41	black F	USA	Lukwago	T
02	Daily Spiritual Experiences Scale	2	2	1	9	2		Y2?	355	uni/adult	USA	Underwood	P
02	Independent Spirituality Assessment Scale	29	9		1			Y10	508	adults	USA	Rojas	T
02	Spiritual Transcendence Index (STI)	4			4			Y2	226	adults	USA	Seidlitz	P
03	CRRUCS/Gallup Spiritual Index	2	1		1	5		2?	1509	adults	USA	Gallup	W
03	Older Adult Spirituality Scale	6.5	1		2.5	1		N	320	elderly	USA	Eggers	P
Yr	**Study/instrument**	**P**	**C**	**E**	**T**	**R**	**O**	**FA**	**N**	**type**	**place**	**author**	**S**
03	Spiritual Beliefs Scale (2)					4		N	165	patients	USA	Kimmel	P
03	Spiritual Focus Questionnaire (SFQ)	7.5	3	3.5	4	2		Y5	456	F/pts	USA	Wikoff	T
04	ASPIRES- Spiritual Transcendence Scale-revised Short Form	1.5	5			1.5	1	Y3?	322	uni?	USA	Piedmont Smith, DJ06	P P
04	Christian Spiritual Participation Profile (CSPP)	8	14	2	13.5	12.5		Y4	1687	church	USA	Thayer	P
04	State-Trait Spirituality Inventory	6		1	4	1	1	Y2	141	church	USA	Harvey	T
05	Body-Mind-Spirit Well-Being – Spirituality scale	10.5	1	1	0.5			Y3	674	adults	Hong Kong	Ng	P
05	Embodied Spirituality Scale	0.5	1.5		5		2	N	267	church	USA	Horn	P
05	Expressions of Spirituality Index - Revised	12.5		7	5.5	4	1	Y4?	309	adults	USA	Clarke	T
05	Korean Spiritual Maturity Assessment	20	8.5		7	3.5	9	?	180	Christians	SKore	Jo	T
05	Religious & Spiritual variables	2	2		1.5	2.5		N	453	21-26yo	USA	Horosewski	T

(Continued)

Yr	Study/instrument	P	C	E	T	R	O	FA	N	type	place	author	S
05	Spiritual & Religious Dimension Scale	11		2.5	2	19.5		Y5	180	uni/adults	Aus	Nasel	P
05	Spiritual Leadership & Transformation (SLT)	15.5	13.5				4	Y7	370	army	USA	Fry	P
05	Spiritual Personality Questionnaire	17.5	11.5	2.5	0.5			?	?	adults	UK	MySkillsProf	W
Yr	**Study/instrument**	**P**	**C**	**E**	**T**	**R**	**O**	**FA**	**N**	**type**	**place**	**author**	**S**
05	Spirituelle Bedürfnisse krebskranker Menschen–Einstellung und Praxis (SpREUK-P1.1)	7	6	3	1	8		Y5	354	well/sick	Germany	Büssing	P
06	Exceptional Experiences Questionnaire	10	2	5	7	1		Y4	705	adults	Europe	Kohls	P
06	Integrating Spirituality in the Workplace Survey	15.5	1.5		2		2	Y3?	569	soc wkrs	USA	Chamiec-Case	T
06	Spirit at Work Scale (SAWS)	13	3		2			Y4	335	adults	Canada	Kinjerski	P
07	ASP Questionnaire (Expressions of spirituality)	21	6.5	1.5	6.5	4.5		Y7	488	adults	Europe	Büssing	P
07	Health Intelligence Questionnaire – Spirituality subscale	3	0.5		5	0.5		Y2	140	adults	USA	Rachelle	T
08	Spiritual Competencies Scale	3	2		1.5	9.5	12	Y6	602	uni	USA	Robertson	T
08	Spiritual Connection Questionnaire(SCQ14)	6.5	2.5	2	3			Y1?	420	uni/adults	UK	Wheeler	P
08	Spiritual Screening Tool for Older Adults	8.5	3.5	1	3.5	3.5		N	49	elderly	USA	Stranahan	P
11	Spirituality in the Workplace	1.5	6.5	4	4			Y3	2230	adults	USA	Liu	P
11	Women's Spirituality Instrument	1	2.5	1		8.5	2	Y1	366	women	USA	Yakushko	P
12	Spiritual Attitude & Involvement List (SAIL)	16	3.5	4	2.5	2	2	Y7	1035	uni/adults	N'lands	Meezenbroek	P
12	Spiritual Care Questionnaire	9	9			15		Y4	200	nurse stu	Iran	Iranmanesh	P
12	Spirituality Scale	1.5		2	1.5		3	N	1931	adults	Finland	Lindeman	P
14	Religious & Spiritual Struggle Scale	7	2		9	8		Y6	2024	adult/uni	USA	Exline	P
Related/partial spirituality measures		**SWB**											
Yr	**Study/instrument**	**P**	**C**	**E**	**T**	**R**	**O**	**FA**	**N**	**type**	**place**	**author**	**S**
64	Purpose in Life Test (PIL)	13		2			5	?			USA	Crumbaugh Leath 99	P W

67	Religious Orientation Scale	4	3		2	11		N	309	church	USA	Allport Valentine07	P T
73	Life Regard Index (LRI)	26.5		0.5			1	?			USA	Battista/Leath	W
79	East-West Questionnaire	11	4.5	7	1	2	8.5	N	329	uni/adult	USA	Gilgen	P
87	Health-Promoting Lifestyle profile (HPLP)	15.5	6.5	1	0.5	0.5	24	Y6	952	adults	USA	Walker, S	P
92	Quality of Life Index (QLI)	15	11	1	1		5	Y4	349	pts	USA	Ferrans	P
97	Scale of Resilience (SCOPE)	19	12.5	0.5				Y5?	283	parents	USA	Vestal	T
98	Brief RCOPE	4.5	4	1	10.5	1		Y2	1387	uni/adult	USA	Pargament	P
Yr	**Study/instrument**	**P**	**C**	**E**	**T**	**R**	**O**	**FA**	**N**	**type**	**place**	**author**	**S**
98	Personal Meaning Profile	29.5	17.5	1.5	5.5		2	Y7	?	?	USA?	Wong Leung 03	P T
99	Pargament's Meaning Scale	14		0.5	4.5	1		?		adults?	USA	Pargament	P
00	Africultural Coping Systems Inventory	3	7		2	7	11	Y4	220	Afr-Am	USA	Utsey	P
00	Francis-Louden Mystical Orientation Scale (FLMOS)	7		4.5	9.5			Y1?	?	priests	UK	Francis Edwards 08	P P
01	Life-Regard Index-Revised	28						Y2?	91	adults	USA	Harris, A	P
03	Adult Strengths	1			2	4	45	9?	369	adults	USA	Isaacowitz	P
03	Life Attitude Scale	17.5	6	1	3.5	1	3	Y5	183	adults	Canada	Leung	T
03	Salient Beliefs Review (SBR)	4.5	2.5					N	79	adults	USA	Bloch	P
04	Short Index of Mystical Orientation	0.5		5	3.5			N	1468	priests	UK	Francis	P
05	Existential Meaning Scale	10						Y1	150	adults	USA	Lyon	T
06	Beliefs and Values Scale	5		1	3	11		Y2	656	adult/pts	UK	King	P
06	Sources of Meaning & Meaningfulness Questionnaire (SoMe)	13.5	5.5	1	1	1	4	Y4	202	19-68yo	Germany	Schnell	P
08	Attitudes to Mysticism Scale	3	1		4	14	2	N	90	uni/adult	UK	Edwards	P
09	Meaningful Life Measure	23						Y5	200	uni/adult	UK	Morgan, J	P
09	Thai Healthy Aging Scale – sp hlth subscale	6.5	2.5		2	4	1	Y1/1	350	aged	Thailand	Thiamwong	P
09	Worldview Analysis Scale	5.5	9.5	5	2.5	8.5	14	Y7	816	uni	USA	Obasi	P

(Continued)

Yr	Study/instrument	P	C	E	T	R	O	FA	N	type	place	author	S
UNIVERSITY only													
SH/WB measures		**SWB**											
Yr	**Study/instrument**	**P**	**C**	**E**	**T**	**R**	**O**	**FA**	**N**	**type**	**place**	**author**	**S**
06	Spiritual Wellness Survey	10	4		1			N	303	uni	USA	Patneaude	T
07	Brief Spiritual Well-being Scale	3			3			N	150	grad stu	USA	Kroft	T
12	Multidimensional Inventory for Relig/Sp Well-Being (MI-RSWB-E)	14.5	11	1	6.5	6	9	Y6	400	uni	UK	Unterrainer	P
Spirituality measures		**SWB**											
Yr	**Study/instrument**	**P**	**C**	**E**	**T**	**R**	**O**	**FA**	**N**	**type**	**place**	**author**	**S**
85	Spirituality Scale	3.5	2	6.5	0.5	5	2.5	?	?	Afr-Am uni	USA	Jagers Smith T 99	T T
86	Spiritual Perspective Scale	5	2.5		2.5			?	?	?	USA	Reed Jesse 99	T
96	Spiritual Assessment Inventory (SAI)	3.5	2		37	0.5		Y5	449	uni	USA	Hall	P
Yr	**Study/instrument**	**P**	**C**	**E**	**T**	**R**	**O**	**FA**	**N**	**type**	**place**	**author**	**S**
96	Spiritual Maturity Index	3	1		8.5	0.5	2	N	100	uni	USA	Ashdown	T
97	Expressions of Spirituality Inventory(ESI)	43	5.5	18.5	10.5	12.5	8	Y5	938	uni	Canada	MacDonald	T
97	Spirituality Assessment Scale(2)	8.5	7		6.5	2	6	Y4?	332	grad stu	USA	Beazley	T
99	Cognitive-Behavioral Spirituality Scale	6			9			Y3?	103	uni	USA	Niederman	W
99	Multidimensional Spiritual Orientation Inventory (MSOI)	35	6		8	14		Y6	444	uni	USA	Morgan, D	T
99	Spiritual Transcendence Scale	9	10	2	1.5	1.5		Y3	735	uni	USA	Piedmont	P
00	Spirituality Questionnaire	21	3	1	13.5	9.5	2	N	674	uni	Canada	Fazakas-deHoog	T
02	Spiritual beliefs & religious particip	1.5	2.5		4	8		Y2	192	uni	USA	Walker, K	P
02	Spiritual Involvement Scale (SIS)	7	5		4.5	0.5	1	Y2	136	uni	USA	Fenzel	C

02	Spirituality Rating Scale	15?						Y5	385	uni	Japan	Hayato	P
03	Intrinsic Spirituality Scale	6?						Y	172	uni	USA	Hodge	P
03	Means-Ends Spirituality Qunaire	17.5	8	1	10	5.5		Y2	405	uni	USA	Ryan	P
04	Miller Measure of Spirituality (MMS)	12	4.5	2.5	7	1.5	3.5	Y2?	781	uni	USA	Miller	P
04	Spiritual Meaning Scale	10.5	1		2	0.5		Y1	465	uni	USA	Mascaro	P
Yr	**Study/instrument**	**P**	**C**	**E**	**T**	**R**	**O**	**FA**	**N**	**type**	**place**	**author**	**S**
04	Spiritual Transformation Inventory	8.5	13		20	2.5		Y19?	371	uni	USA	Hall	W
05	Inclusive Spirituality Index	24	13.5	7	0.5	1	1	Y6	251	uni	USA	Muse-Burk	T
05	Ryff's Scales of Psychological &spiritual wellbeing	8.5			1.5			Y2?	233	uni	Nland	van Dierendonck	P
05	Spiritual growth Survey	3.5	1		14.5	1		Y1	176	uni	USA	Hancock	P
05	Spiritual Support Scale (SSS)	4.5			4.5	3		Y1	453	uni	USA	Ai	P
05	Theistic Spiritual Outcome Survey	7.5	4.5	1	4			Y3	344	uni	USA	Richards	P
06	Spirituality, Religion & Life Satisfaction	2			1	2	2	N	522	uni	USA	Zullig	P
07	College Students Beliefs & Values (CSBV) Spirituality Factor Scale							Y12	14527	uni	USA	HERI, UCLA	W
	Spiritual Quest	9	1	3	1								
	Ethic of caring, compassionate self-concept	7	11				1						
	Global citizenship, personal God	0.5	6	1	5.5								
07	Fundamental Spiritual Profile (FSP)	21.5	14	4	6.5		7	Y10	1080	uni	USA	Del Rio	T
Yr	**Study/instrument**	**P**	**C**	**E**	**T**	**R**	**O**	**FA**	**N**	**type**	**place**	**author**	**S**
07	Spiritual Fitness Assessment	12	4.5		11.5	10		Y5?	196	Cath uni	USA	Fletcher Kassab 11	W P
07	Spirituality Scale (4)	9	1		2	1		N	221	uni	USA	Nelms	P
08	Spiritual Intelligence Self-Report Inventory SISRI-24	15	2.5	3.5	1		2	Y4	619	uni	Canada	King, D	T W
08	Wilderness Spirituality Scale	3.5	0.5	15	1		8	Y2?	608	uni	USA	Bloom	T
09	Similarity of Offender's Spirituality Scale	8				1		Y2	200	uni	USA	Davis	P
10	Community Spirituality Scale	0.5	3.5		1.5	1.5		Y1	198	theol stu	USA	Rovers	P
11	Spiritual Maturity Scale	5.5	1.5		2.5	10.5		Y2	541	uni	USA	Watson	T
14	RiTE Measure of Spirituality	5	4	1	6	13	1	Y3	1301	uni	USA	Webb	P

(Continued)

Related/partial spirituality measures		SWB											
Yr	Study/instrument	P	C	E	T	R	O	FA	N	type	place	author	S
75	Mysticism Scale	2		17	9		4	Y3	300	uni	USA	Hood	H
81	Life Attitude Profile	44						Y7	219	uni	USA	Reker	P
87	Word-Spirit Orientation Scale	4.5	1		1	9.5		?	?	Uni?	USA	Hsieh	P
89	Intrinsic/Extrinsic Measurement	3	3		2	6		Y3?	771	uni	USA	Gorsuch	P
Yr	**Study/instrument**	**P**	**C**	**E**	**T**	**R**	**O**	**FA**	**N**	**type**	**place**	**author**	**S**
91	Quest Scale	1.5		0.5	0.5	9.5		N	214	uni	USA	Batson	P
97	Santa Clara Strength of Religious FaithQuestionnaire (SCORF)	2.5	1		2	4.5		Y1	102	uni	USA	Plante/ Freiheit 06	P P
00	Religious Coping (RCOPE)	33.5	14.5		46.5	10.5		Y17	540	uni	USA	Pargament	P
01	Adolescent Lifestyle Profile	13	10		2	2	17	?	168	Afr-Am uni	USA	Hendricks Hendricks04	T
03	Affective Neuroscience Personality Scales	5	2	3		2	98	Y7	171	uni stu	USA	Davis, K	P
03	Personal Meanings of Spirituality	7.5	0.5	0.5	3.5	3.5	4.5	Y2	254	uni	USA	Graci	P
04	Life Attitude Profile-Revised (LAP-R)	48						Y6	524	uni	USA	Dennis	P
06	Body-Mind-Spirit Wellness Behavior & Characteristic Inventory (BMS-WBCI)	13.5	0.5			1	29	Y3	41	uni	USA	Hey	P
06	Meaning in Life Questionnaire (MLQ)	10						Y2	154	uni	USA	Steger	P
07	Mystical Experience Scale(MES)	7.5	4	3.5	4			Y1?	778	uni	Aus/ UK	Lange	P
SCHOOL													
SH/WB measures		**SWB**											
Yr	**Study/instrument**	**P**	**C**	**E**	**T**	**R**	**O**	**FA**	**N**	**type**	**place**	**author**	**S**
88	Spirituality Inventory	6.5	6		15	12.5		N	591	SDA adol	USA	Youlden	T

Yr	Study/instrument	P	C	E	T	R	O	FA	N	type	place	author	S
99	<u>S</u>piritual <u>**H**</u>ealth <u>**&**</u> <u>**L**</u>ife-<u>**O**</u>rientation <u>**M**</u>easure (SHALOM)	**5**	**5**	**5**	**5**		(5)	Y4	850	20 stu	Aus	Fisher	P
00	**Spiritual Health in** 4 **Domains** Index (SH4DI)	7	5.5	5	4	1. 5	1	Y4	311	10 teachrs	UK	Fisher	P
01	Level of <u>**SWB**</u> <u>in</u> <u>schools</u>	**8**	**8**	**8**	**8**			Y4	144	teachers	Aus	Fisher	P
03	Modified Spiritual Well-Being Scale	11.5			8.5			N	71	11-12yo	USA	Patrick	T
03	Spiritual **W**ell-**B**eing **Q**uestionnaire SWBQ	**5**	**5**	**5**	**5**			Y4	2071	20,uni,tr	Aus	Gomez/ Fisher	P
04	<u>Feeling</u> <u>**Good**/**L**iving</u> <u>**L**ife(FGLL)</u>	**4**	**4**	**4**	**4**			Y4	1080	10 student	Aus	Fisher	P
05	Urban Hope & Spiritual Health	6	9.5	4.5	2	3	3	N	23418	13-15yo	UK	Francis	P
07	SWBQ modified	4	5	7	5			N	1184	13-20yo	SAfr	Van Rooyen	T
07	Young People Putting Life Together Australian Youth Spirituality	36	54	5.5	6.5	31		N	4000	13-24yo	Aus	Hughes	P
13	SWBQ2	**5**	**5**	**5**	**5**			Y4	460	13-18yo	Aus	Fisher	P
Spirituality measures		**SWB**											
Yr	**Study/instrument**	**P**	**C**	**E**	**T**	**R**	**O**	**FA**	**N**	**type**	**place**	**author**	**S**
00	Adolescent Spirituality	4	18.5		5.5	19		N	141	11-25yo	USA	Holder	P
00	Smithline Spirituality Inventory for Teens (SSIT)	3	4.5		3.5	3	1	Y2?	196	hi schl	USA	Smithline	T
00	TestWell: Wellness Inventory- Spirituality & Values Section	2.5	2.5				45	?	?	high school	USA	National Wellness	W
01	Religion/Spirituality Survey	7.5	4		3.5	8		N	100	12-19yo Afr-Am	USA	Chase	T
02	WHOQOL-Spiritual, Religion & Personal Beliefs (SRPB) – Field test Instrument	22	1	3	2	4		Y6/ 8?	3636	16-90yo	world	WHOQOL SRPB gp	P
03	Sifers Childrens Spirituality Scale (SCSS)	6	5.5		7.5		1	N	175	7-14yo	USA	Sifers	C
04	Spirituality scale(3)	2	0.5		3	0.5	2	N	642	20 stu	USA	Ritt-Olson	P
05	Prague Spirituality Questionnaire	8.5	6.5	8	4	7	2	Y6	1088	hi schl	Czech Rep	Rican10	P
06	Generation Y study	2	1		10.5	11.5		N	1216	13-29yo	Aus	Mason	W
06	Spiritual Sensitivity Scale (SSS)	7	3	1				Y4?	496	stu/adults	Finland	Tirri	P

(Continued)

Yr	Study/instrument	P	C	E	T	R	O	FA	N	type	place	author	S
08	Search Institute Inventory of Youth Spiritual	59	32.5	12.5	17.	27.5	7	N	6853	12-25yo	8countries	Center for	C
10	Aspects of spirituality (ASP-S)	10	3.5	2	3	6.5		Y4	254	Adol.	WGerman	Büssing	P
10	Christian Inventory of Spirituality	17	10.5		15.	4	1	Y5	954	adults	drug/alc	Shorkey	P
14	Sp. Sensitivity Scale for Children	7	6.5	3.5			6	N	118	8-11yo	Aus	Stoyles	P
Related/partial spirituality measures		**SWB**											
Yr	**Study/instrument**	**P**	**C**	**E**	**T**	**R**	**O**	**FA**	**N**	**type**	**place**	**author**	**S**
nd	Child Health Questionnaire	7	3				77			10-18yo	USA	HealthAct	W
93	Faith Maturity Scale(FMS)	7.5	10	3	8.5	8	1	N	3986	yth/adult	USA	Benson	H
94	Multidimensional Life Satisfaction Scale for Children	7.5	13.5	3			16	Y5	725	1^0 school	USA	Huebner	P
94	Scale of Racial Socialisation for Adolescents	3	1		1.5	1.5	30	Y4	200	Af-Am yth	USA	Stevenson	P
98	Frameworks for Life Questionnaire	4	1		1	3.5	75.	N	144	15-16yo	Aus	Gehrig	T
98	Personal Inventory of Kid's Optimal Capacities (PIKOC)	8	14				70	Y3/ 4?	174	grade 3-5	USA	Ziegler	T
00	Children's Quality of life (C-QOL) Thai	3	7	4		3	45	N	35	5-8yo	Thailand	Jirojanakul	P
00	2Vécu et Santé Perçue de l'Adolescent (VSP-A)	15	12	2			11	Y6	2941	11-17yo	France	Simeoni	P
02	Quality Of Life Profile –Adolescent	8	8	3		1	17	Y8	899	12-16yo	UK	Bradford	P
04	S/R & Thriving in Adolescence	1	9.5			9.5	27	Y16	1000	9-15yo	USA	Dowling	P
07	Alcohol-related God Locus of Control Scale for Adolescents (AGLOC-A)				12			Y1	356	Afr-Am. youth	USA	Goggin	P
07	Benefit Finding Scale for Children (BFSC)	5	5					Y1	199	7-18yo	USA	Phipps	P
07	Chinese Positive Youth Development Scale	6.5		0.5			83	Y15	322	adol	HKong	Shek	P
HEALTH													
SH/WB measures		**SWB**											
Yr	**Study/instrument**	**P**	**C**	**E**	**T**	**R**	**O**	**FA**	**N**	**type**	**place**	**author**	**S**

Yr	Study/instrument	P	C	E	T	R	O	FA	N	type	place	author	S
92	Spiritual Health Inventory	14	5.5		3	1.5	7	?	23	ca pts	USA	Highfield	P
92	Spiritual Health Inventory	10	10		5	1	5	?	27	nurses	USA	Highfield	P
99	Spirit Core Scale	25	4		1	2		Y5	668	adolescent	USA	Johnson	T
03	End-Stage Renal Disease Spiritual Beliefs Scale		8			4		N	165	pts	USA	Kimmel	P
06	Spirituality Transcendence Measure	11	4.5			4.5	2	Y3	37	ca pts	Taiwan	Leung	T
09	Brief Serenity Scale	19	1					Y3	86	org t'plant	USA	Kreitzer	P
10	Spiritual Distress Scale	14.5	6		2	3.5	4	Y4	85	ca pts	Taiwan	Ku	P
11	Physician's spiritual well-being scale	10	4			1	5	Y4	177	physician	Taiwan	Fang	P
12	EORTC QLQ-SWB36	8.5	6		4	5.5	12	?	113	PC ca pts	world	Vivat	P
12	Spirit 8	7		1				Y1	285	pallcare	Africa	Selman	P
Spirituality measures		**SWB**											
Yr	**Study/instrument**	**P**	**C**	**E**	**T**	**R**	**O**	**FA**	**N**	**type**	**place**	**author**	**S**
84	Spirituality Self-Assessment Scale	20.5	9	0.5	3		1	N	?	alcs	USA	Whitfield	P
92	Spiritual Injury Scale	6			2			?	?	adults	USA	Berg	W
94	Nurses Spiritual Care Perspective Scale		1.5		3	5.5	2	N	244	pts/carers	USA	Taylor	P
95	Spiritual Beliefs Questionnaire	1.5			2	1.5	2	N	101	drug users	UK	Christo	P
97	Spiritual Needs Inventory	4.5	7.5	1	1	3		Y5	100	pts	USA	Hermann	P
00	Spirituality & Religion Survey	1.5	1.5		4.5	12	1.5	N	275	HIV pts	USA	Somlai	P
00	Spirituality at Work	20.5	7.5		2		3	Y7	696	hosp staff	USA	Ashmos	P
01	Spiritual Support for terminally ill – nurse assessment	3.5	2	1	3	7.5	4	N	328	nurses	Finland	Kuuppelo-mäki	P
02	Functional Assessment of Chronic Illness Therapy – SWBS (FACIT-Sp-12)	10.5				1.5		Y2?	1617	ca pts	USA	Peterman Canada 08	P P
02	Ironson-Woods Sp/Relig Index	7.5	6		5	6.5		Y4	279	HIV pts	USA	Ironson	P
02	Physicians' Spiritual Assessment Survey	3	2		2	1	18	N	38	psychol	USA	Milne	T
02	Spirituality & Sp. Care Rating Scale	7	5.5	0.5	1	3		Y4?	549	nurses	UK	McSherry	P
Yr	**Study/instrument**	**P**	**C**	**E**	**T**	**R**	**O**	**FA**	**N**	**type**	**place**	**author**	**S**
03	Spirituality Scale (SS) (2)	10	3	6	2.5	1.5		Y3	240	chronic pt	USA	Delaney	T
05	Spiritual Strategies Scale (SSS)	5	5.5		1.5	5	1	Y6	79	elderly	USA	Nelson-Becker	P

(Continued)

06	Higher Power Relationship Scale	8			8	1		Y1	350	subs use	USA	Rowan	P
06	Multidimensional Measurement of religiosity/Spirituality Instrument	24	4	2.5	15	13.5		Y5	515	Uni/alc	USA	Stewart	P
06	Spiritual Interests Related to Illness Tool (SpIRIT)	18.5	10.5		7.5	5.5		Y8	244	pts/carers	USA	Taylor	P
06	Spiritual Needs Assessment Scale (SNAS)	11	4.5	3.5	1.5	2.5		Y6?	683	pts	USA	Flannelly	P
07	Spirituality in hospice	17.5	0.5					N	10	pts	USA	Wlodarczyk	P
07	Spirituality Self-Rating Scale	1.5	1		1.5	2		N	791	uni, drugs	USA	Galanter	P
08	Multidimensional Measure of Spirituality-Religiosity	6.5	12		16	5.5		Y4	237	subs use	USA	Neff	P
08	Spiritual Needs Scale	10.5	4		2	5	4.5	Y5	257	ca pts	Korea	Yong	P
08	Spiritual Transformation Scale	23.5	8.5	1	4	3		Y2	253	ca pts	USA	Cole	P
08	Treatment Spirituality/Religiosity Scale				2	8		Y1	3347	pts/staff	USA	Lillis	P
09	Sexual-Spiritual Integration Scale	8.5			3	3.5	9	Y3	383	adults	USA	Wittstock	T

Yr	Study/instrument	P	C	E	T	R	O	FA	N	type	place	author	S
09	Spiritual Connection Scale		1.5		3	1.5		N	163	aged	USA	Leppert Krause 02	P
09	10 Spiritual Emergency Subscales	29.5	3	13.5	11	8	19	Y1	109	adults	Aust	Goretzki	P
10	Spiritual Needs Questionnaire	7	4.5	2	2.5	3		Y4	210	pain, ca pts	Europe	Büssing	P
11	Spiritual Care Inventory	11	4.5		0.5	1		Y3?	298	carers	USA	Burkhart	P
12	Spiritual Needs Assessment for Patients (SNAP)	9	6.5		1	6.5		3?	47	outpts	USA	Sharma	P
12	Spirituality in coping	7	16		8		1	Y8?	100	AfAm ca	USA	Holt	P
14	GES questionnaire	4.5	2.5		1			Y3	108	pallcare	Spain	Benito	P
14	Quality of Spiritual Care Scale	7	2		1			Y2	165	fam carer	USA	Daaleman	P

Related/partial spirituality measures		SWB											
Yr	**Study/instrument**	**P**	**C**	**E**	**T**	**R**	**O**	**FA**	**N**	**type**	**place**	**author**	**S**
86	Nowotny's Hope Scale	22	4		1	2		N?	306	adults+ca	USA	Nowotny	W
86	Self-Transcendence Scale	8	4			1	2	N	55	aged	USA	Reed	C
87	Meaning in Life Scale (1)	8	4		2	1		N	257	LT care	Canada	Warner	P
Yr	**Study/instrument**	**P**	**C**	**E**	**T**	**R**	**O**	**FA**	**N**	**type**	**place**	**author**	**S**
91	Brown-Peterson Recovery Progress Inventory	19	16		7	1	10		58	alcs	USA	Brown	P
95	Quality Of Life – Cancer Survivors	6				1	34	Y4	686	ca pts	USA	Ferrell	P
96	Life Evaluation Questionnaire (LEQ)	15	8			1	20	Y5	200	ca pts	UK	Salmon	P
96	Long-Term Quality of Life Instrument	4	2	1	1		26	Y4	188	F ca pts	USA	Wyatt	P
97	McGill Quality of Life Questionnaire MQOL	8	1	1			6	Y4?	120	ca pts	Canada	Cohen	P
98	Missoula-VITAS qol index	11	5		1		8	Y6?	257	PC pts	USA	Byock	P
98	Revised Hospice Quality of Life Index – Social/Spiritual WB	1.5	3.5	1	1		11	Y1/3	255	hospice pts	USA	McMillan	P
98	Skalen zur Erfassung von Lebensqualität bei Tumorkranken (SELT-M)+ spQL	8					16	N	89	ca pts	Swiss	van Wegberg	P
99	Perceived meanings of cancer pain inventory	5					22	Y6	200	ca pts	Taiwan	Chen	P
01	Quality Of Life –Cancer Survivors (2)	11	1			1	24	Y5/6?	177	adults	USA	Zebrack	P
01	Valuation of Life – swb subscale	7				1		N	319	aged	USA	Lawton 01 Dennis 05	P W
Yr	**Study/instrument**	**P**	**C**	**E**	**T**	**R**	**O**	**FA**	**N**	**type**	**place**	**author**	**S**
02	Existential Loneliness Questionnaire	9.5	11.5	1				N	47	HIV F	USA	Mayers	P
04	Benefit Finding Scale	10	8				2	Y3?	364	F ca pts	USA	Tomich	P
04	City of Hope QOL-Ostomy Questionnaire	5				5	13	Y4?	1513	pts	USA	Grant	P

(Continued)

04	Problems & Needs in Palliative Care (PNPC) questionnaire (sp subset)	2	1		1	1		N	64	ca pts	N'lands	Osse	P
04	Self-Perception & Relationships Tool (S- PRT)	7	14		14			Y5	136	patients	Canada	Atkinson	P
05	Missoula-VITAS Quality of Life Index – Revised (MVQOLI-R)	8.5	5.5	1			10	Y5	175	pts	USA	Schwartz	P
05	Palliative care Outcome Scale (POS)	2					8	N	471	pts	N'lands	Büssing	P
06	ALSSQOL	17.5	19	2	1	2.5	17	Y6	342	ALS pts	USA	Simmons	P
06	Meaning in Life Scale (2)	19.5				1.5		Y4	167	ca pts	USA	Jim	P
07	Chinese Cancer Coherence Scale	9	1		1			Y2	390	F ca pts	HK	Chan	P
Yr	**Study/instrument**	**P**	**C**	**E**	**T**	**R**	**O**	**FA**	**N**	**type**	**place**	**author**	**S**
07	QE Health Scale	12	1.5	1.5	3		10	Y6?	205	disabled	NZ	Faull	TP
07	Heart Failure Caregiver Quality of Life scale	6	2			1	7	Y1	100	carers	USA	Nauser	T
07	Personal Meaning Profile	23	9		4	3		Y5	294	ca pts	N'lan	Jaarsma	P
07	Systemic Lupus Erythematosus Needs Questionnaire (SLENQ)	14.5	1.5			1	66	Y7	386	SLE support	Aust	Moses	P
09	Cancer & Deity Questionnaire				12			Y2	52	ca pts	USA	Bowman	P
10	Health-Related Quality of Life in Stroke Patients HRQOLISP-40 sp subscale	1.5	0.5		5	4		Y2	353	pts	Nigeria Germany	Owolabi	P
11	Culturally appropriate Positive Mental Health Measure				5	2	41	Y6	404	adults	S'por	Vaingankar	P W
11	View of God Inventory	1			3	8		Y2	101	HIV pts	USA	Ironson	P

Conclusion

This chapter only lists the origin and composition of each quantitative spirituality/well-being and allied measure. It does not report all applications of each one. Nevertheless, it is hoped that the valuable information provided in this chapter will facilitate further research involving assessment of spirituality, spiritual well-being and related areas.

References

Ai, A.L., Tice, T.N., Peterson, C. & Huang, B. (2005). Prayers, spiritual support, and positive coping with the September 11 National Crisis. *Journal of Personality, 73*(3), 763-792.

Aird, R. (2007). *Religion, spirituality, and mental health and social behaviour in young adulthood: A longitudinal study.* PhD thesis. Retrieved 5 May, 2008, from: http://adt.library.uq.edu.au/public/adt-QU20071122.163803/

Allport, G.W. & Ross, J.M. (1967). Personal religious orientation and prejudice. *Journal of Personality and Social Psychology, 5*, 423-443.

Ark, P.D. (1997). *Health risk behaviors and coping strategies of African-American sixth graders.* PhD dissertation, University of Tennessee Health Science Center.

Ashdown, F.S. (1996). *Spiritual Maturity Index: A revision.* D Clin Psych dissertation, George Fox University, Newberg, OR.

Ashmos, D.P. & Duchon, D. (2000). Spirituality at work: A conceptualization and measure. *Journal of Management Inquiry, 9*(2), 134-145.

Atkinson, M.J., Wishart, P.M., Wasil, B.I. & Robinson, J.W. (2004). The Self-Perception and Relationships Tool (S-PRT): A novel approach to the measurement of subjective health-related quality of life. *Health and Quality of Life Outcomes, 2*, 36. 15 pages. doi:10.1186/1477-7525-2-36.

Awartani, M., Whitman, C.V. & Gordon, J. (2008). Developing instruments to capture young people's perceptions of how school as a learning environment affects their well-being. *European Journal of Education, 43*(1), 51-70.

Batson, C.D. & Schoenrade, P.A. (1991). Measuring religion as Quest: 2) reliability concerns. *Journal for the Scientific Study of Religion, 30*(4), 430-447.

Battista, J. & Almond, R. (1973). The development of meaning in life. *Psychiatry, 36*, 409-427.

Beazley, H. (1997). *Meaning and measurement in organizational settings: Development of a Spirituality Assessment Scale.* PhD dissertation, George Washington University, D.C.

Ben-Arieh, A. (2008). Indicators and indices of children's well-being: Towards a more policy-oriented perspective. *European Journal of Education, 43*(1), 37-50.

Benito, E., Oliver, A., Galiana, L., Barreto, P., Pascual, A., Gomis, C. & Barbero, J. (2014). Development and validation of a new tool for the assessment and spiritual care of palliative care patients. *Journal of Pain and Symptom Management, 47* (6), 1008-1018.e1. doi: 10.1016/j.jpainsymman.2013.06.018

Benson, P.L., Donahue, M.J. & Erickson, J.A. (1993). The Faith Maturity Scale: Conceptualization, measurement, and empirical validation. In M. Lynn & D.O. Moberg

(Eds.), *Research in the Social Scientific Study of Religion* (Vol. *5*, pp.1-26). Greenwich: JAI Press.

Berg, G.E. Living Water Computer Assessment Program. Accessed 14 March 2014 from http://www.spiritualassessment.com/Manual.html

Berry, D. (2005). Methodological pitfalls in the study of religiosity and spirituality. *Western Journal of Nursing Research, 27*(5), 628-647.

Bloch, D.P. (2003). *Salient Beliefs Review: Administrator's Guide.* Indianapolis, IN: JIST Publishing Inc.

Boero, M., Caviglia, M., Monteverdi, R., Braida, V., Fabello, M, & Zorzella, L. (2005). Spirituality of health workers: A descriptive study. *International Journal of Nursing Studies, 42*, 915-921.

Bowman, E.S., Beitman. J.A., Palesh, O., Pérez, J.E. & Koopman, C. (2009). The Cancer and Deity Questionnaire: A new religion and cancer measure. *Journal of Psychosocial Oncology, 27*, 435-453.

Bradford, R., Rutherford, D.L. & John, A. (2002). Quality of life in young people: Ratings and factor structure of the Quality of Life Profile – Adolescent version. *Journal of Adolescence, 25*, 261-274.

Brown, H.P. & Peterson, J.H. (2008). Assessing spirituality in addiction treatment and follow-up. *Alcoholism Treatment Quarterly, 8*(2), 21-50.

Buckey, J.W. (2007). *Factors affecting life-sustaining treatment decisions by health care surrogates and proxies*. PhD dissertation, Florida State University, College of Social Work.

Burkhart, L. Schmidt, L. & Hogan, N. (2011). Development and psychometric testing of the Spiritual Care Inventory instrument. *Journal of Advanced Nursing, 67*(11), 2463-2472.

Büssing, A., Balzat, H.-J., Heusser, P. (2010). Spiritual needs of patients with chronic pain disease and cancer – validation of the Spiritual Needs Questionnaire. *European Journal of Medical Research, 15,* 266-273.

Büssing, A., Föller-Mancini, A., Gidley, J. & Heusser, P. (2010). Aspects of spirituality in adolescents. *International Journal of Children's Spirituality, 15*(1), 25-44.

Büssing, A., Matthiessen, P.F. & Ostermann, T. (2005).Engagement of patients in religious and spiritual practices: Confirmatory results with the SpREUK-P 1.1 questionnaire as a tool of quality of life research. *Health and Quality of Life Outcomes, 3*, 53. 11 pages,

Büssing, A., Ostermann, T. & Matthiessen, P. (2007). Distinct expressions of vital spirituality: The ASP Questionnaire as an exploratory research tool. *Journal of Religion and Health, 46*(2), 267-286.

Byock, I.R. & Merriman, M.P. (1998). Measuring quality of life for patients with terminal illness: The Missoula-VITAS® quality of life index. *Palliative Medicine, 12*, 231-244.

Canada, A.L., Murphy, P.E., Fitchett, G., Peterman, A.H. & Shrover, L.R. (2008). A 3-factor model for the FACIT-Sp. *Psycho-Oncology, 17*, 908-916.

Center for Spiritual Development in Childhood & Adolescence) (2008). *Search Institute Inventory of Youth Spiritual Development.* This survey tool was used for the report *With Their Own Voices* Roehlkepartain et al. (Eds.) (2008), listed below.

Chamiec-Case, R.R. (2006). *Developing a tool to measure social workers' perceptions regarding the extent to which they integrate their spirituality in the workplace.* Doctor of Social Work dissertation, Fordham University Graduate School of Social Science.

Chan, T.H.Y., Ho, R.T.H. & Chan, C.L.W. (2007). Developing an outcome measurement for meaning-making intervention with Chinese cancer patients. *Psycho-Oncology, 16*(9), 843-850.

Chase, M.W. (2001). *Spirituality as a salutogenic factor in African American adolescents: Understanding the relationships among religion, health, and well-being*. PhD dissertation, California School of Professional Psychology – Berkeley/Alameda. ProQuest doc ID: 729036591.

Chen, M.-L. (1999). Validation of the structure of the perceived meanings of cancer pain inventory. *Journal of Advanced Nursing, 30*(2), 344-351.

Christo, G. & Franey, C. (1995). Drug users' spiritual beliefs, locus of control and the disease concept in relation to Narcotics Anonymous attendance and six0month outcomes. *Drug & Alcohol Dependence, 38,* 51-56.

Clarke, S. (2005). *Religiosity and spirituality in younger and older adults.* PhD dissertation, University of North Texas.

Cohen, S.R., Mount, B.M., Bruera, E., Provost, M., Rowe, J. & Tong, K. (1997). Validity of the McGill Quality of Life Questionnaire in the palliative care setting: a multi-centre Canadian study demonstrating the importance of the existential domain. *Palliative Medicine, 11*, 3-20.

Cole, B.S., Hopkins, C.M., Tisak, J., Steel, J.L. & Carr, B.I. (2008). Assessing spiritual growth and spiritual decline following a diagnosis of cancer: reliability and validity of the Spiritual Transformation Scale. *Psycho-Oncology, 17*, 112-121.

Crumbaugh, J.L. & Maholick, L.T. (1964). An experimental study in existentialism: The psychometric approach to Frankl's concept of noogenic neurosis. *Journal of Clinical Psychology, 20*, 200-207.

Cummins, R.A. (2008). *Australian Unity Wellbeing Index Survey 19.* Retrieved 16 October, 2008, from:http://www. deakin.edu.au/research/acqol/index_wellbeing/index.htm

Cunyus, J.G. (1996). *A Spiritual Assessment Inventory: An objective standard for an elusive reality*. Doctoral dissertation, Pacific Western University.

Daaleman, T.P. & Frey, B.B. (2004). The Spirituality Index of Well-Being: A new instrument for health-related quality of life research. *Annals of Family Medicine, 2*(5), 499-503.

Daaleman , T.P., Reed, D., Cohen, L.W. & Zimmerman, S. (2014). Development and preliminary testing of the Quality of Spiritual Care Scale. *Journal of Pain and Symptom Management, 47*(4), 793-800. doi: 10.1016/j.jpainsymman.2013.06.004

Davis, D.E., Worthington, E.L., Hook, J.N., Van Tongenen, D.R., Green, J.D. & Jennings, D.J.II. (2009). Relational spirituality and the development of the Similarity of the Offender's Spirituality Scale. *Psychology of Religion and Spirituality, 1*(4), 249-262.

Davis, K.D., Panksepp, J & Normansell, L. (2003). The Affective Neuroscience Personality Scales: Normative data and implications. *Neuro-Psychoanalysis, 5*(1), 57-69.

Delaney, C. (2003). *The spirituality scale: Development, refinement and psychometric testing of an instrument to assess the human spiritual dimension*. PhD dissertation, University of Connecticut. ProQuest doc ID: 765281331.

Del Rio, C.M. (2007). *Psychometric properties of the Spiritual Typology Inventory.* PhD dissertation, Southern Illinois University at Carbondale. ProQuest doc ID: 1456390391.

Dennis, D., Muller, S.M., Miller, K. & Banerjee, P. (2004). Spirituality among a college student cohort: A quantitative assessment. *American Journal of Health Education, 35*(4), 220-227.

Dennis, M.P., Gitlin, L.N., Winter, L. & Chee, Y.K. (2005). The role of spiritual well-being in moderating frail elders' affective response to functional difficulty. *Center for Applied Research on Aging and Health Research Papers.* Paper 7. http://jdc.jefferson.edu/carah_papers/7

Dowling, E.M., Gestsdottir, S., Anderson, P.M., von Eye, A., Almerigi, J. & Lerner, R.M. (2004). Structural relations among spirituality, religiosity, and thriving in adolescence. *Applied Developmental Science, 8*(1), 7-16.

Dunn, K.S. (2008). Development and psychometric testing of a new geriatric spiritual well-being scale. *International Journal of Older People Nursing, 3*, 161-169.

Edwards, A.C. & Lowis, M.J. (2008). Construction and validation of a scale to assess attitudes to mysticism: The need for a new scale for research in the psychology of religion. *Spirituality and Health International, 9*(1), 16-31.

Egbert, N., Mickley, J. & Coeling, H. (2004). A review and application of social scientific measures of religiosity and spirituality: Assessing a missing component in health communication research. *Health Communication, 16*(1), 7-27.

Eggers, S.J. (2003). Older adult spirituality: What is it? A factor analysis of three related instruments. *Journal of Religious Gerontology, 14*(4), 3-11.

Elkins, D., Hedstrom, L., Hughes, L., Leaf, J. & Saunders, C. (1988). Toward a humanistic-phenomenological spirituality. *Journal of Humanistic Psychology, 28*(4), 5-18. Retrieved Spiritual Orientation Inventory 11 October, 2007, from: http://cla.calpoly.edu/~bfiorito/soi.html.

Ellison, C. (1983). Spiritual well-being: Conceptualization and measurement. *Journal of Psychology and Theology, 11*(4), 330-340.

Ellison, C.W. (1984). *Personality, religious orientation, and spiritual well-being.* Unpublished manuscript, Alliance Theological Seminary, Nyack, NY. In P.C. Hill, & R.W. Hood, (Eds.) (1999). *Measures of Religiosity* (pp.210-204). Birmingham, Alabama: Religious Education Press.

Endyke, P.D. (1999). *A revision of the Spiritual Well-Being Scale. (ceiling effects).* PhD dissertation, George Fox University, USA.

Endyke, P., Bufford, R., Gathercoal, K . & Koch, C. (1999). Spiritual well-being: A proposed scale revision. Paper presented at the Meeting of the Christian Association for Psychological Studies, Western Regional Meeting, Newberg, Oregon. (see Janzen, D.M)

Exline, J.L., Pargament, K.I., Grubbs, J.B. & Yali, A.M. (2014). The Religious and Spiritual Struggles Scale: Development and initial validation. *Psychology of Religion & Spirituality, 6*(3), 208-222.

Fang, C.K., Li, P.Y., Lai, M.L., Lin, M.H., Bridge, D.T. & Chen, H.W. (2011). Establishing a 'physician's spiritual well-being scale' and testing its reliability and validity. *Journal of Medical Ethics, 37*, 6-12.

Faull, K. (2006). *Health and the spiritual self: Development and application of a theory and measure of the process of healthy change.* PhD thesis, University of Waikato.

Faull, K. & Hills, M.D. (2007). The QE Health Scale (QEHS): Assessment of the clinical reliability and validity of a spiritually based holistic health measure. *Disability & Rehabilitation, 29*(9), 701-716. (Also see 29(13), 999-1010).

Fazakas-deHoog, L.L. (2000). *The development of a multidimensional spirituality questionnaire and its relationship with quality of life.* MA dissertation, University of Western Ontario (Canada). ProQuest doc ID: 729262121.

Fenzel, L.M. (2002). The development of the Spiritual Involvement Scale: Examining the spiritual lives of late adolescents. Poster presented at the Biennial Conference of the Society for Research on Adolescence, New Orleans, April, 2002. Accessed 29 October, 2008, from: lfenzel@loyola.edu.

Ferrans, C.E. & Powers, M.J. (1992). Psychometric testing of the Quality of Life Index. *Research in Nursing and Health, 15*(1), 29-38. doi 10.1002/nur.4770150106.

Ferrell, B.R., Hassey Dow, K. & Grant, M. (1995). Measurement of the Quality Of Life in Cancer Survivors (QOL-CS). *Quality of Life Research, 4*, 523-531.

Fetzer Institute (1999). Brief Multidimensional Measure of Religiousness/Spirituality. Retrieved 21 May, 2007, from http://www.fetzer.org/PDF/Total_Fetzer_Book.pdf.

Fetzer Institute (1999). Daily Spiritual Experiences Scale (6 items). Retrieved 21 May, 2007, from: http://www.fetzer.org/PDF/Total_Fetzer_Book.pdf.

Fisher, J.W. (1998). *Spiritual health: Its nature and place in the school curriculum*. PhD thesis, University of Melbourne. Available from: https://minerva-access.unimelb. edu.au/handle/ 11343/39206

Fisher, J.W. (1999a). Helps to fostering students' spiritual health. *International Journal of Children's Spirituality, 4*(1), 29-49.

Fisher, John (1999b). *Developing a Spiritual Health And Life-Orientation Measure for secondary school students.* In Proceedings of University of Ballarat Annual Research Conference, 15 October, pp. 57-63.

Fisher, J.W. (2001). Comparing levels of spiritual well-being in state, Catholic and independent schools in Victoria, Australia. *Journal of Beliefs and Values, 22*(1), 99-105.

Fisher, John (2004). Feeling Good, Living Life: A spiritual health measure for young children. *Journal of Beliefs & Values, 25*(3), 307-315.

Fisher, J.W. (2009). Investigating Australian education students' views about spiritual well-being as compared with teachers in schools. *International Journal of Children's Spirituality, 14*(2), 151-167.

Fisher, J.W. (2013). Assessing spiritual well-being: Relating with God explains greatest variance in spiritual well-being among Australian youth. *International Journal of Children's Spirituality, 18*(4), 306-317.

Fisher, J.W. (2014). Comparing the influence of God and other Transcendents on spiritual well-being. *Religious Education Journal of Australia, 30*(2), 9-15.

Fisher, J.W., Francis, L.J. & Johnson, P. (2000). Assessing spiritual health via four domains of well-being: The SH4DI. *Pastoral Psychology, 49*(2), 133-145.

Flannelly, K.J., Galek, K. & Flannelly, L.T. (2006). A test of the factor structure of the Patient Spiritual Needs Assessment Scale. *Holistic Nursing Practice, 20*(4), 187-190.

Fletcher, D. (2007). *Spiritual Fitness Assessment.* http://www.faithandhealthConnection. org/wp-content/uploads/ 2007/11/spiritual_fitness-assessment_4_8_071.pdf (see Kassab & MacDonald, 2011)

Fluellen, S.J. (2007). *Development of the Spiritual and Religious Competency Assessment (SARCA): An instrument to measure competency in supervisees.* PhD dissertation, Oklahoma State University.

Fraid, R. (1997). *The impact of obesity on subjective quality of life.* Master of Clinical Psychology dissertation, Deakin University (Burwood) Victoria, Australia.

Francis, L.J. & Louden, S.H. (2000). The Francis-Louden Mystical Orientation Scale: A study among male Anglican priests. *Research in the Social Scientific Study of Religion, 11*, 99-116.

Francis, L.J. & Louden, S.H. (2004). A Short Index of Mystical Orientation (SIMO): A study among Roman Catholic priests. *Pastoral Psychology, 53*(1), 49-51.

Francis, L.J. & Robbins, M. (2005). *Urban Hope and Spiritual Health: The Adolescent Voice.* Peterborough, UK: Epworth.

Freiheit, S.R., Sonstegard, K., Schmitt, A. & Vye, C. (2006). Religiosity and spirituality: A psychometric evaluation of the Santa Clara Strength of Religious Faith Questionnaire. *Pastoral Psychology, 55*, 27-33. doi: 10.1007/s11089-006-0029-y.

Fry, L.W., Vitucci, S. & Cedillo, M. (2005). Spiritual leadership and army transformation: Theory, measurement, and establishing a baseline. *The Leadership Quarterly, 16,* 835-862.

Galanter, M., Dermatis, H., Bunt, G., Williams, C., Trujillo, M. & Steinke, P. (2007). Assessment of spirituality and its relevance to addiction treatment. *Journal of Substance Abuse Treatment, 33*(3), 257-264.

Gallup, G.H. & Johnson, B.R. (2003). New index tracks "Spiritual State of the Union." *The Gallup Organization, Gallup Poll Tuesday briefing 28 January.* http://www.gallup.com

Gehrig, S. (1998). *The spiritual health of sixteen year old Australians: A study of spiritual health and its relationship with health behaviours.* MEd thesis, University of Sydney.

Genia, V. (1997). The Spiritual Experience Index: Revision and reformulation. *Review of Religious Research, 38*(4), 344-361.

Gilgen, A.R. & Cho, J.H. (1979). Questionnaire to measure Eastern and Western thought. *Psychological Reports, 44,* 835-841.

Glik, D.C. (1990). Participation in spiritual healing, religiosity, and mental health. *Sociological Inquiry, 60*(2), 158-176.

Goggin, K., Murray, T.S., Malcarne, V.L., Brown, S.A. & Wallston, K.A. (2007). Do religious and control cognitions predict risky behavior? I. Development and validation of the Alcohol-related God Locus of Control Scale for Adolescents (AGLOC-A). *Cognitive Therapy Research, 31*, 111-122.

Goldfarb, L.M., Galanter, M., McDowell, D., Lifshutz. & Dermatis, H. (1996). *American Journal of Drug & Alcohol Abuse, 22*(4), 549-561.

Gomez, R. & Fisher, J.W. (2003). Domains of spiritual well-being and development and validation of the Spiritual Well-Being Questionnaire. *Personality and Individual Differences, 35*(8), 1975-1991.

Good, M. & Willoughby, T. (2006). The role of spirituality versus religiosity in adolescent psychosocial adjustment. *Journal of Youth and Adolescence, 35*(1), 41-55.

Goretzki. M., Thalbourne, M.A. & Storm, L. (2009). The questionnaire measurement of spiritual emergency. *The Journal of Transpersonal Psychology, 41*(1), 81-97.

Graci, G.M., O'Rourke, N. & Mahoney, M.J. (2003). Personal meanings of spirituality. *Constructivism in the Human Sciences, 8*(1), 47-56.

Grant, M., Ferrell, B., Dean, G., Uman, D., Chu, D. & Krouse, R. (2004). Revision and psychometric testing of the City of Hope Quality of Life-Ostomy Questionnaire. *Quality of Life Research, 13*, 1445-1457.

Gray, J. (2006). Measuring spirituality: Conceptual and methodological considerations. *The Journal of Theory Construction & Testing, 10*(2), 58-64.

Hall. T.W. (2004). Spiritual Transformation Inventory™, web-based inventory, available through Concentus Assessment Solutions.

Hall, T.W., Tisdale, T.C. & Brokaw, B.F. (1994). Assessment of religious dimensions in Christian clients: A review of instruments for research and clinical use. *Journal of Psychology and Theology, 22*, 133-140.

Hancock, T.E., Bufford, R.K., Lau, B. & Ninteman, N. (2005). Attempting valid assessment of Spiritual Growth: A survey of Christ-centered living. *Christian Education Journal, Series 3, vol 2*(1), 130-153.

Harris, A.H.S. (2001). Psychometric properties of the Life-Regard Index-Revised: A validation study of a measure of personal meaning. *Psychological Reports, 89*(3), 759-773.

Hart, M. (1998). *Utilizing a spiritual wellness tool to assist the pastoral caregiver in the dialogue of spirituality.* D Min. dissertation, Brite Divinity School, Texas Christian University.

Harvey, M. B. (2004). *Development and psychometric properties of the State-Trait Spirituality Inventory.* PhD dissertation, University of North Texas. ProQuest doc ID: 790293881.

Hatch, R.L., Burg, M.A., Naberhaus, D.S. & Hellmich, L.K. (1998). The Spiritual Involvement and Beliefs Scale: Development and testing of a new instrument. *Journal of Family Practice, 46*(6), 476-486.

Haugan, G et al. (2012). The Self-Transcendence Scale. *Journal of Holistic Nursing, 30*(3), 147-159.

Hayato, H. (2002). Development of Spirituality Rating Scale and study of its reliability and validity. *Journal of Japan Academy of Nursing Science, 22*(3), 29-38.

Hays, J.C., Meador, K.G., Branch, P.S. & George, L.K. (2001). The Spiritual History Scale in Four Dimensions (SHS-4): Validity and reliability. *The Gerontologist, 41*(2), 239-249.

Healthactchq (n.d.) CHQ: Child Health Questionnaire. Retrieved 14 December, 2007 from http://healthactchq.com/chq.html.

Hendricks, C., Pender, N. & Hendricks, D. (2001). *The Adolescent Lifestyle Profile*, copyrighted by the National Library of Congress (see Hendricks, D.L. below)

Hendricks, D.L. (2004). *The relationship of hope and self-efficacy to health-promoting behaviors among student-athletes attending historically black colleges and universities.* EdD dissertation, Auburn University, Alabama.

Hermann, C.P. (1997). *Spiritual needs of dying patients: A methodological study.* PhD dissertation, University of Kentucky, Lexington, Kentucky.

Hey, W.T., Calderon, K.S. & Carroll, H. (2006). Use of body-mind-spirit dimensions for the development of a Wellness Behaviour and Characteristic Inventory for college students. *Health Promotion Practice, 7,* 125-132.

Higher Education Research Institute (HERI) (2007) *2007 College Students' Beliefs and Values (CSBV) Factor Scales Table.* Retrieved 20 May, 2008, from: Spirituality in Higher Education, UCLA, http://www.spirituality.ucla.edu.

Highfield, M.F. (1992). Spiritual health of oncology patients: Nurse and patient perspectives. *Cancer Nursing, 15*(1), 1-8.

Hill, P.C. & Hood, R.W. (Eds.) (1999). *Measures of Religiosity.* Birmingham, Alabama: Religious Education Press.

Hill, P.C., Pargament, K.I., Hood, R.W., McCullough, J.P., Swyers, D.B., Larson, D.B. & Zinnbauer, B.J. (2000). Conceptualizing religion and spirituality: Points of commonality, points of departure. *Journal for the Theory of Social Behavior, 30*(1), 51-77.

Hill, P.C. & Pargament, K.I. (2003). Advances in the conceptualization and measurement of religion and spirituality. *American Psychologist, 58*(1), 64-74.

Hodge, D.R. (2003). The Intrinsic Spirituality Scale: A new six-item instrument for assessing the salience of spirituality as a motivational construct. *Journal of Social Science Research, 30*(1), 41-61.

Holder, D.W., Durant, R.H., Harris, T.L., Daniel, J.H., Obeidallah, D. & Goodman, E. (2000). The association between adolescent spirituality and voluntary sexual activity. *Society for Adolescent Medicine, 26*, 295-302.

Holland, J.C., Kash, K.M., Passik,S., Gronert, M.K., Sison, A., Lederberg, M., Russak, S.M., Bader, L. & Fox, B. (1998). A brief Spiritual Beliefs Inventory for use in quality of life research in life-threatening illness. *Psycho-Oncology, 7*, 460-469.

Holt, C.L., Clark, E. & Klem, P.R. (2007). Expansion and validation of the Spiritual Health Locus of Control Scale: Factorial analysis and predictive ability. *Journal of Health Psychology, 12*, 597-612.

Holt, C.L., Schultz, E., Caplan, L., Blake, V., Southward, V.L. & Buckner, A.V. (2012). Assessing the role of spirituality in coping among African Americans diagnosed with cancer. *Journal of Religion and Health, 51*(2), 507-521.

Hood, R.W. Jr (1975). The construction and preliminary validation of a measure of reported mystical experience. *Journal for the Scientific Study of Religion, 14*, 29-41.

Horn, M.J., Piedmont, R.L., Fialkowski, G.M., Wicks, R.J. & Hunt, M.E. (2005). Sexuality and spirituality. *Theology & Sexuality, 12*(1), 81-102.

Horosewski, M.L. (2005). *A synthesis of spirituality, mutuality, and sexuality: Toward an understanding of religious and spiritual variables in sexual health communication research.* PhD dissertation, University of Kentucky, Lexington.

Houscamp, B.M., Fisher, L.A. & Stuber, M.L. (2004). Spirituality in children and adolescents: Research findings and implications for clinicians and researchers. *Child and Adolescent Psychiatric Clinics of North America, 13*, 221-230.

Howden, J.W. (1993). Development and psychometric characteristics of the Spirituality Assessment Scale. PhD dissertation, Texas Women's University.

Hsieh, T.T. (1987). Heavenly-minded and earthly good: A study of social interest, ethical style, and Word-Spirit orientation among Christians. *Journal of Psychology & Theology, 15*(2), 141-147.

Huebner, E.S. (1994). Preliminary development and validation of a multidimensional Life Satisfaction Scale for Children. *Psychological Assessment, 6*(2), 149-158.

Hughes, P. (2007). *Putting Life Together: Findings from Australian Youth Spirituality Research.* Melbourne: CRA/Fairfield Press.

Hungelmann, J., Kenkel-Rossi, E., Klassen, L. & Stollenwerk, R. (1996). Focus on spiritual well-being: Harmonious interconnectedness of mind-body-spirit – Use of the JAREL Spiritual Well-Being Scale. *Geriatric Nursing, 17*(6), 262-266.

Idler, E.L., Musick, M.A., Ellison, C.G., George, L.K., Krause, N., Ory, M.G., Pargament, K.I., Powell, L.H., Underwood, L.G. & Williams, D.R. (2003). Measuring multiple dimensions of religion and spirituality for health research: Conceptual background and findings from the 1998 General Social Survey. *Research on Aging*, *25*(4), 327-365. (erratum, *26*(2), 284, March, 2004).

Ingersoll, R.E. (1995). *Construction and initial validation of the Spiritual Wellness Inventory.* Unpublished PhD dissertation, Kent State University. Retrieved 21 October 2008 from http://elloittingersoll.com/Spiritual_Wellness_Test.html.

Iranmanesh, S., Tirgari, B. & Cheraghi, M.A. (2012). Developing and testing a Spiritual Care Questionnaire in the Iranian context. *Journal of Religion & Health, 51*, 1104-1116.

Ironson, G., Solomon, G.F., Balbin, E.G., O'Cleirigh, C., George, A., Kumar, M., Larson, D. & Woods, T.E. (2002). The Ironson-Woods Spirituality/Religiousness Index is associated with long survival, health behaviors, less distress, and low cortisol in people with HIV/AIDS. *Annals of Behavioral Medicine, 24*(1), 34-48.

Ironson, G., Stuetzle, R., Ironson, D., Balbin, E., Kramer, H., George, A., Schneiderman, N. & Fletcher, M.A. (2011). View of God as benevolent and forgiving or punishing and judgmental predicts HIV disease progression. *Journal of Behavioural Medicine, 34,* 414-425.

Isaacowitz, D.M., Vaillant, G.E. & Seligman, M.E.P. (2003). Strengths and satisfaction across the adult lifespan. *International Journal of Aging and Human Development, 57*(2), 181-201.

Jaarsma, T.A., Pool, G., Ranchor, A.V. & Sanderman, R. (2007). The concept and measurement of meaning in life in Dutch cancer patients. *Psycho-Oncology, 16,* 241-248.

Jagers, R.J. (1985). *Spirituality: Towards an understanding of Afro-American religious expression.* Unpublished Master's thesis, Howard University, Washington, D.C.

Janzen, D.M. (2005). *A correlational study of anxiety level, spiritual practices, and spiritual well-being.* DPsy, dissertation, George Fox University, Oregon.

Jesse, D.E. (1999). *Holistic Obstetrical Problem Evaluation (HOPE): Testing a midwifery theory to predict maternal and perinatal health outcomes.* PhD dissertation, University of Tennessee.

Jim, H.S., Purnell, J.Q., Richardson, S.A., Golden-Kreutz, D. & Andersen, B.L. (2006). Measuring meaning in life following cancer. *Quality of Life Research, 15*, 1355-1371.

Jirojanakul, P. & Skevington, S. (2000). Developing a quality of life measure for children aged 5-8 years. *British Journal of Health Psychology, 5*, 299-321.

Jo, K. (2005). *A three-fold relational approach to spiritual maturity: An exploratory study of Korean evangelical spirituality.* PhD dissertation, School of Theology, Fuller Theological Seminary, Pasadena, CA.

Johnson, K.L. (1999). *Measuring the spirit and spiritual attributes of resiliency.* U Utah. Dissertation Abstracts International: Section B: The Sciences & Engineering, Vol 59(11-B), May, 1999.pp.6113.

Johnson, M.E., Piderman, K.M., Sloan, J.A., Huschka, M., Atherton, P.J., Hanson, J.M., Brown, P.D., Rummans, T.A., Clark, M.M. & Frost, M.H. (2007). Measuring Spiritual Quality of Life in Cancer Patients. *The Journal of Supportive Oncology, 5*(9), 437-442.

Kass, J.D., Friedman, R., Leserman, J., Zuttermeister, P.C. & Benson, H. (1991). Health outcomes and a new index of spiritual experience. *Journal for the Scientific Study of Religion, 30*(2), 203-211.

Kassab, V.A. & MacDonald, D.A. (2011). Examination of the psychometric properties of the Spiritual Fitness Assessment. *Journal of Religion & Health, 50*, 975-985.

Kelly, M.K. (1994). *A revision of the Spiritual Well-Being Scale.* PhD dissertation, University of Nebraska, Lincoln.

Kennedy, J.E., Davis, R.C. & Taylor, B.G. (1998). Changes in spirituality and well-being among victims of sexual assault. *Journal for the Scientific Study of Religion, 37*(2), 322-328.

Kimmel, P.L., Emont, S.L., Newmann, J.M., Danko, H. & Moss, A.H. (2003). ESRD Patient quality of life: Symptoms, spiritual beliefs, psychosocial factors, and ethnicity. *American Journal of Kidney Diseases, 42*(4), 713-721.

King, D.B. (2008). *Rethinking claims of spiritual intelligence: A definition, model, and measure.* Unpublished Master's thesis, Trent University, Peterborough, Ontario, Canada. Retrieved 21 October, 2008, from: http://dbking.net/spiritualintelligence/ model/htm.

King, J.E. & Crowther, M.R. (2004). The measurement of religiosity and spirituality: Examples and issues from psychology. *Journal of Organizational Change Management, 17*(1), 83-101.

King, M., Jones, L., Barnes, K., Low, J., Walker, C., Wilkinson, S., Mason, C, Sutherland, J. & Tookman, A. (2006). Measuring spiritual belief: Development and standardization of a Beliefs and Values Scale. *Psychological Medicine, 36*, 417-425.

King, M., Speck, P. & Thomas, A. (2001). The Royal Free Interview for Spiritual and Religious Beliefs: Development and validation of a self-report version. *Psychological Medicine, 31*, 1015-1023.

Kinjerski, V. & Skrypnek, B.J. (2006). *Measuring the intangible: Development of the Spirit at Work Scale.* Paper presented at the Sixty-fifth Annual Meeting of the Academy of Management, Atlanta, GA, 16 pages.

Kirk, K.M., Eaves, L.J. & Martin, N.G. (1999). Self-transcendence as a measure of spirituality in a sample of older Australian twins. *Twin Research, 2*, 81-87.

Koenig, H.G., McCullough, M.E. & Larson, D.B. (Eds.) (2001). *Handbook of Religion and Health.* Oxford: Oxford University Press.

Koenig, H.G., King, D.E. & Carson, V.B. (2011). *Handbook of Religion and Health.* Oxford: Oxford University Press. 2nd edn.

Kohls, N. & Walach, H. (2006). Exceptional experiences and spiritual practice: A new measurement approach. *Spirituality and Health International, 7*, 125-150.

Korinek, A.W. & Arredondo, R. (2004). The Spiritual Health Inventory (SHI): Assessment of an instrument for measuring spiritual health in a substance abusing population. *Alcoholism Treatment Quarterly, 22*(2), 55-66.

Krause, N. Church-based social support and health in old age: Exploring variations by age. *Journal of Gerontology: Social Sciences, 57B*(6), S332-S347.

Kreitzer, M.J. & Gross, C.R. (2009). The Brief Serenity Scale: A psychometric analysis of a measure of spirituality and well-being. *Journal of Holistic Nursing, 27*(1), 7-16.

Kroft, R. (2007). *A Brief Spiritual Well-Being Scale with Degree Completion Students.* Doctor of Education dissertation, George Fox University, Newberg, Oregon.

Ku, Y.-L., Kuo, S.-M., Yao, C.-Y. (2010). Establishing the validity of a spiritual distress scale for cancer patients hospitalized in southern Taiwan. *International Journal of Palliative Nursing, 16*(3), 133-137.

Kuuppelomäki, M. (2001). Spiritual support for terminally ill patients: Nursing staff assessments. *Journal of Clinical Nursing, 10*, 660-670.

Land, K.C., Lamb, V.L. & Mustillo, S.K. (2001). Child and youth well-being in the United States, 1975-1998: Some findings from a new index. *Social Indicators Research, 56*(3), 241-320.

Lange, R. & Thalbourne, M.A. (2007). The Rasch Scaling of mystical experiences: Construct validity and correlates of the Mystical Experience Scale (MES). *The International Journal for the Psychology of Religion, 17*(2), 121-140.

Lawton, M.P., Moss, M., Hoffman, C., Kleban, M.H., Ruckdeschel, K. & Winter, L. (2001). Valuation of life: A concept and scale. *Journal of Aging & Health, 13*(1), 3-31.

Leath, C. (1999). The experience of meaning in life from a psychological perspective. Psychology Honors Paper, U of W. Retrieved 21 October, 2008, from: http://ea.freehostia.com/ cleath/docs/meaning.htm

Leung, K.-K., Chiu, T.-Y. & Chen, C.-Y. (2006). The influence of awareness of terminal condition on spiritual well-being in terminal cancer patients. *Journal of Pain & Symptom Management, 31*(5), 449-456.

Leung, M., Steinfort,T. & Vroon, E.J. (2003). *Life Attitudes Scale: development and validation of a measurement of the construct of tragic optimism.* MA dissertation, Trinity Western University.

Lillis, J., Gifford, E., Humphreys, K. & Moos, R. (2008). Assessing spirituality/religiosity in the treatment environment: The Treatment Spirituality/Religiosity Scale. *Journal of Substance Abuse Treatment, 35,* 427-433.

Lindeman, M., Blomqvist, S. & Takada, M. (2012). Distinguishing spirituality from other constructs. *The Journal of Nervous & Mental Disease, 200*(2), 167-173.

Lindholm, J.A. & Astin, H.S. (2008). Spirituality and pedagogy: Faculty's spirituality and use of student-centered approaches to Undergraduate Teaching. *The Review of Higher Education, 31*(2), 185-207.

Liu, C.H. & Robertson, P.J. (2011). Spirituality in the workplace: Theory and measurement. *Journal of Management Inquiry, 20*(1), 35-50.

Lukwago, S.N. (2001). *Measurement and health-related correlates of collectivism, spirituality, racial pride and time orientation in urban black women.* PhD dissertation, Saint Louis University.

Lyon, D.E. & Younger, J. (2005). Development and preliminary evaluation of the Existential Meaning Scale. *Journal of Holistic Nursing, 23*(1), 54-65.

MacDonald, D.A. (1997). *The Development of a comprehensive factor analytically derived measure of spirituality and its relationship to psychological functioning.* PhD dissertation, University of Windsor, Ontario, Canada.

MacDonald, D.A. & Friedman, H.L. (2002). Assessment of humanistic, transpersonal, and spiritual constructs: State of the science. *Journal of Humanistic Psychology, 42,* 102-125.

McMillan, S.C. & Weitzner, M. (1998). Quality of life in cancer patients: Use of a Revised Hospice Index. *Cancer Practice, 6*(5), 282-288.

McSherry, W., Draper, P. & Kendrick, D. (2002). The construct validity of a rating scale designed to assess spirituality and spiritual care. *International Journal of Nursing Studies, 39*, 723-734.

Mascaro, N., Rosen, D.H. & Morey, L.C. (2004). The development and construct validity, and clinical utility of the Spiritual Meaning Scale. *Personality and Individual Differences, 37*(4), 845-860.

Mason, M., Webber, R., Singleton, A. & Hughes, P. (2006). *The Spirit of Generation Y. Summary of the final report of a three year study.* Retrieved 12 February, 2007, from: http://dlibrary.acu.edu.au/ research/ccls/spir/sppub/sppub.htm Subsequently published as: Mason. M., Singleton, A. & Webber, R. (2007). *The Spirit of Generation Y.* Melbourne: John Garratt. [AND Hughes, P. (2007) *Putting Life Together* (see above)].

Maton, K.I. (1989). The stress-buffering role of spiritual support: Cross-sectional and prospective investigations. *Journal for the Scientific Study of Religions, 28*(3), 310-323.

Mayer, T.A. (2005). *The efficacy of integrating mentoring and spiritual well-being services for adolescents receiving residential treatment services.* PhD Psychology dissertation, Walden University.

Mayers, A.M., Khoo, S-T. & Svartberg, M. (2002). The Existential Loneliness Questionnaire: Background, development, and preliminary findings. *Journal of Clinical Psychology, 58*(9), 1183-1193.

Meezenbroek, E. deJ., Garssen, B., van den Berg, M., Tuytel, G. et al. (2012). Measuring spirituality as a universal human experience: Development of the Spiritual Attitude and Involvement List (SAIL). *Journal of Psychosocial Oncology, 30*(2), 141-167.

Miller, E.D. (2004). The development and validation of a new measure of spirituality. *North American Journal of Psychology, 6*(3), 423-430.

Milne, J.M. (2002). *The spiritual well-being of health psychologists: Spiritual-care attitudes and practices.* PhD dissertation, Capella University.

Mission Australia (2007). *2007 National Survey of Young Australians.* Sydney: Author.

Moberg, D.O. (1984). Subjective measures of spiritual well-being. *Review of Religious Research, 25*(4), 351-364.

Morgan, D.T. (1999). *The initial development of the Multidimensional Spiritual Orientation Inventory.* PhD dissertation, Brigham Young University, Utah.

Morgan, J. & Farsides, T. (2009). Measuring Meaning in Life. *Journal of Happiness Studies, 10*(2), 197-214. doi: 10.1007/s10902-007-9075-0.

Moses, N., Wiggers, J., Nicholas, C. & Cockburn. J. (2007). Development and psychometric analysis of the systemic lupus erythematosus needs questionnaire (SLENQ). *Quality of Life Research, 16*, 461-466.

Muse-Burke, J.L. (2005). *Development and validation of the Inclusive Spirituality Index.* PhD dissertation, Lehigh University.

MySkillsProfile (2005). *Spiritual Personality Questionnaire.* Retrieved 20 March, 2014, from: MySkillsProfile.com

Nasel, D.D. & Haynes, W.D.G. (2005). Spiritual and Religious Dimensions Scale: Development and psychometric analysis. *Australian Journal of Psychology, 57*(1), 61-71.

National Wellness Institute (2000). TestWell: Wellness Inventory, High School Edition. Retrieved 27 October, 2008, from: http://www.nationalwellness.org/freepdf/assessments/ QsetTeen10.pdf.

Nauser, J.A. (2007). *Heart failure family caregivers: Psychometrics of a new quality of life scale and variables associated with caregiver outcomes.* PhD dissertation, Indiana University.

Neff, J.A. (2008). A new multidimensional measure of spirituality-religiosity for use in diverse substance abuse treatment populations. *Journal for the Scientific Study of Religion, 47*(3), 393-409.

Nelms, L.W., Hutchins, E., Hutchins, D. & Pursley, R.J. (2007). Spirituality and the health of college students. *Journal of Religion and Health, 46*(2), 249-265.

Nelson-Becker, H. (2005). Development of a Spiritual Support Scale for use with older adults. *Journal of Human Behavior in the Social Environment, 11*(3/4), 195-212.

Ng, S.M., Yau, J.K.Y., Chan, C.L.W., Chan, C.H.Y. & Ho, D.Y.F. (2005). The Measurement of body-mind-spirit well-being: Toward multidimensionality and transcultural applicability. *Social Work in Health Care, 41*(1), 33-52.

Niederman, R. (1999). The Cognitive-Behavioral Spirituality Scale. Retrieved 12 October, 2008, from: http://www.geocities. com/randynied/CBSSinfo.htm?200712. In, *The conceptualization of a model of spirituality*, unpublished doctoral dissertation, University of Georgia, Athens (Social Work).

Nowotny, M.L. (1989). Assessment of hope in patients with cancer: development of an instrument. *Oncology Nursing Forum, 16*(1), 57-61. Instrument downloaded on 30 January, 2014, from: http://www.outcomesdatabase.org/print/670

Obasi, E.M., Flores, L.Y. & James-Myers, L. (2009). Construction and initial validation of the Worldview Analysis Scale (WAS). *Journal of Black Studies, 39*(6), 937-961.

Osse, B.H.P., Vernooij, M.J.F. & Schadé, E. (2004). Towards a new clinical tool for needs assessment in the palliative care of cancer patients The PCNC instrument. *Journal of Pain and Symptom Management, 28*(4), 329-341.

Owolabi, M.O. (2010). Psychometric properties of the HRQOLISP-40: A novel, shortened multiculturally valid holistic stroke measure. *Neurorehabilitation and Neural Repair, 24*(9), 814-825.

Pargament, K.I. (1999). Pargament's Meaning Scale and factor loadings, In, Fetzer Institute/National Institute on Aging Working Group, *Multidimensional Measurements of Religiousness/ Spirituality for Use in Health Research,* (pp.21-22). Kalamazoo, MI: Fetzer Institute.

Pargament, K.I., Koenig, H.G. & Perez, L.M. (2000). The many methods of religious coping: Development and initial validation of the RCOPE. *Journal of Clinical Psychology, 56*(4), 519-543.

Pargament, K.I., Smith, B.W., Koenig, H.G. & Perez, L. (1998). Patterns of positive and negative religious coping with major life stressors. *Journal for the Scientific Study of Religion, 37*(4), 710-724.

Patneaude, A.B. (2006). *Spiritual wellness among undergraduate college students.* PhD dissertation, Colorado State University, Fort Collins, Colorado.

Patrick, S.K. (2003). *Children and spirituality: Exploring the relationships among spiritual well-being, religious participation, competence and behavior in 11 and 12 year-olds.* PhD dissertation, University of Northern Colorado, Greeley, Colorado.

Perez, S. Religious and non-religious aspects of spirituality and their relation to Myer-Briggs Personality Typology. Dissertation Abstracts International: Section B: The Sciences & Engineering. Vol. 59(9-B), Mar 1999, pp.5104. Downloaded on 7 February, 2007, from: http://gateway.ut.ovid.com/gw1/ovidweb.cgi

Peterman, A.H., Fitchett, G., Brady, M.J., Hernandez, L. & Cella, D. (2002). Measuring spiritual well-being in people with cancer: The Functional Assessment of Chronic Illness Therapy – Spiritual Well-Being Scale (FACIT-Sp). *Annals of Behavioral Medicine, 24*(1), 49-58.

Phipps, S., Long, A.M. & Ogden, J. (2007). Benefit Finding Scale for children: Preliminary findings from a childhood cancer population. *Journal of Pediatric Psychology, 32*(10), 1264-1271.

Piedmont, R.L. (1999). Does spirituality represent the sixth factor in personality? Spiritual transcendence and the Five Factor Model. *Journal of Personality, 67*(6), 985-1013.

Piedmont, R.L. (2004). *Assessment of Spirituality and Religious Sentiments (ASPIRES) Technical Manual.* In, D.J. Smith (2006). Rehabilitation counsellor willingness to integrate spirituality into client counselling sessions. *Journal of Rehabilitation, 72*(3), p.6.

Plante, T.G. & Boccaccini, M.T. (1997). The Santa Clara Strength of Religious Faith Questionnaire (SCORF). *Pastoral Psychology, 45*(5), 375-387.

Poston, D.J. & Turnbull, A.P. (2004). Role of spirituality and religion in family quality of life for families of children with disabilities. *Education and Training in Developmental Disabilities, 39*(2), 95-108.

Proeschold-Bell, R.J., Yang, C., Toth, M., Rivers, M.C. & Carder, K. (2014). Closeness to God among those doing God's work: A spiritual well-being measure for clergy. *Journal of Religion & Health 53*(3), 878-894. doi: 10.1007/s10943-013-9682-5

Rachelle, A. (2007). *Health Intelligence: Theory, model, validity of questionnaire and path to stress, spirituality, personality, psychological well being and health status.* PhD dissertation, Yeshiva University, New York.

Ratner, P.A., Johnson, J.L. & Jeffery, B. (1998). Examining emotional, physical, social, and spiritual health as determinants of self-rated health status. *American Journal of Health Promotion, 12*(4), 275-282.

Reed, P.G. (1986) *Spiritual Perspective Scale.* Unpublished instrument, Arizona State University.

Reed, P.G. (1991). Self-Transcendence and mental health in oldest-old adults. *Nursing Research, 40*(1), 5-11. Copy received on 19 May, 2014, from: *preed@arizona.edu*

Reker, G.T. & Peacock, E.J. (1981). The Life Attitude Profile (LAP): A multidimensional instrument for assessing attitudes toward life. *Canadian Journal of Behavioral Science, 13*(3), 264-273.

Rican, P. & Janosova, P. (2010). Spirituality as a basic aspect of personality: A cross-cultural verification of Piedmont's model. *International Journal for the Psychology of Religion, 20*(1), 2-13.

Rich, Y. & Cinamon, R.G. (2007). *Journal of Humanistic Psychology,47*(1), 7-29.

Richards, P.S., Smith, T.B., Schowalter, M., Richard, M., Berrett, M.E. & Hardman, R.K. (2005). Development and validation of the Theistic Spiritual Outcome Survey. *Psychotherapy Research, 15*(4), 457-469.

Ritt-Olson, A., Milam, J., Unger, J.B., Trinidad, D., Teran, L., Dent, C.W. & Sussman, S. (2004). The protective influence of spirituality and "Health-as-a-Value" against monthly substance use among adolescents varying at risk. *Journal of Adolescent Health, 34*, 192-199.

Robertson, L.A. (2008). *The Spiritual Competency Scale: A comparison to the Aservic Spiritual Competencies.* PhD dissertation, College of Education, University of Central Florida, Orlando, Florida.

Roehlkepartain, E.C., Benson, P.L., Scales, P.C., Kimball, L. & King, P.E. (2008). *With Their Own Voices: A global exploration of how today's young people experience and think about spiritual development.* Minneapolis, Minnesota, USA: Search Institute.

Rojas, R.R. (2002). *Management theory and spirituality: A framework and validation of the Independent Spirituality Assessment Scale.* Doctor of Business Administration dissertation, Argosy University, Sarasota.

Ross, L. (2006). Spiritual care in nursing: An overview of the research to date. *Journal of Clinical Nursing, 15*, 852-862.

Rovers, M. & Kocum, L. (2010). Development of a holistic model of spirituality. *Journal of Spirituality in Mental Health, 12*, 2-24.

Rowan, N.L., Faul, A.C., Cloud, R.N. & Huber, R. (2006). The Higher Power Relationship Scale: A validation. *Journal of Social Work Practice in the Addictions, 6*(3), 81-95.

Ryan, K. & Fiorito, B. (2003). Means-Ends Spirituality Questionnaire: Reliability, validity and relationship to psychological well-being. *Review of Religious Research, 45*(2), 130-154.

Salmon, P., Manzi, F. & Valori, R.M. (1996). Measuring the meaning of life for patients with incurable cancer: The Life Evaluation Questionnaire (LEQ). *European Journal of Cancer, 32A*(5), 755-760.

Schaler, J.A. (1996). Spiritual thinking in addiction-treatment providers: The Spiritual Belief Scale (SBS). *Alcoholism Treatment Quarterly, 14*(3), 7-33.

Schnell, T. & Becker, P. (2006). Personality and meaning in life. *Personality and Individual Differences, 41*, 117-129.

Schwartz, L.M. (2005). Spiritual struggles and student development. *Spirituality in Higher Education Newsletter,* IV(4). Retrieved 27 October, 2008 from: spiritualitynewsletter@gseis.ucla.edu

Seidlitz, L., Abernethy, A.A., Duberstein, P.R., Evinger, J.S., Chang, T.H. & Lewis, B.L. (2002). Development of the Spiritual Transcendence Index. *Journal for the Scientific Study of Religion, 41*(3), 439-453.

Selman, L., Siegert, R.J., Higginson, I.J., Agupio, G., et al. (2012). The 'Spirit 8' successfully captured spiritual well-being in African palliative care: factor and Rasch analysis. *Journal of Clinical Epidemiology, 65,* 434-443.

Sharma, R.K., Astrow, A.B., Texeira, K. & Sulmasy, D.P. (2012). The Spiritual Needs Assessment for Patients (SNAP): Development and validation of a comprehensive instrument to assess unmet spiritual needs. *Journal of Pain and Symptom Management, 44*(1), 44-51.

Shek, D.T.L., Siu, A.M.H. & Lee, T.K. (2007). The Chinese Positive Youth Development Scale: A validation study. *Research on Social Work Practice, 17,* 380-391.

Shorkey, C.T. & Windsor, L.C. (2010). Inventory of spirituality in alcohol/other drug research: Psychometric dimensions. *Alcoholism Treatment Quarterly, 28,* 17-37.

Sifers, S.K. & Warren, J.S. (2003). Measuring Spirituality in Children. Unpublished manuscript, retrieved 12 October, 2008, from: sarah.sifers@mnsu.edu.

Simeoni, M.C., Auquier, P., Antoniotti, S., Sapin, C. & San Marco, J.L. (2000). Validation of a French health-related quality of life instrument for adolescents: The VSP-A. *Quality of Life Research, 9*(4), 393-403.

Simmons, Z., Felgoise, S.H., Bremer, B.A., Walsh, S.M., et al. (2006). The ALSSQOL : Balancing physical and not physical factors in assessing quality of life in ALS. *Neurology, 67*(1), 1659-1664.

Sloan, J.A., Aaronson, N., Cappelleri, J.C., Fairclough, D.L., Varrichio, C. et al. (2002). Assessing the clinical significance of single items relative to summated scores. *Mayo Clinic Proceedings*, *77*, 479-487.

Smith, D.J. (2006). Rehabilitation counselor willingness to integrate spirituality into client counseling sessions. *Journal of Rehabilitation, 72*(3), 4-11.

Smith, J.M.W. (2001). *Parents' perceptions of the spiritual needs of their adult son or daughter with developmental disabilities.* D.N.Sc. dissertation, Rush University, College of Nursing.

Smithline, C.W. (2000). *Spirituality as a protective factor against adolescent substance abuse.* PhD dissertation, California School of Professional Psychology, Berkeley/Alameda.

Somlai, A.M. & Heckman, T.G. (2000). Correlates of spirituality and well-being in a community sample of people living with HIV disease. *Mental Health, Religion & Culture, 3*(1), 57-70.

Stanton, W.R., Willis, M. & Balanda, K.P. (2000). Development of an instrument for monitoring adolescent health issues. *Health Education Research – Theory & Practice, 15*(2), 181-190.

Steger, M.F., Frazier, P., Oishi, S. & Kaler, M. (2006). The Meaning in Life Questionnaire: Assessing the presence of and search for meaning in life. *Journal of Counseling Psychology, 53*(1), 80-93.

Stevenson, H.C. (1994). Validation of the Scale of Racial Socialization for African American Adolescents: Steps towards multidimensionality. *Journal of Black Psychology, 20,* 445-468.

Stewart, C. & Koeske, G.F. (2006). A preliminary construct validation of the Multidimensional Measurement of Religiousness/Spirituality Instrument: A study of Southern USA samples. *International Journal for the Psychology of Religion, 16*(3), 181-196.

Stoyles, G.J., Stanford, B., Caputi, P., Keating, A-l. & Hyde, B. (2012). A measure of spiritual sensitivity for children. *International Journal of Children's Spirituality, 17*(3), 203-215.

Stranahan, S. (2008). A spiritual screening tool for older adults. *Journal of Religion and Health, 47*(4), 491-503.

Taylor, E.J. (2006). Prevalence and associated factors of spiritual needs among patients with cancer and family caregivers. *Oncology Nursing Forum, 33*(4): 729-735.

Taylor, E., Highfield, M. & Amenta, M. (1994). Attitudes and beliefs regarding spiritual care. *Cancer Nursing, 17*(6), 479-487.

Thayer, O.J. (2004). Constructing a spirituality measure based on learning theory: The Christian Spiritual Participation Profile. *Journal of Psychology and Christianity, 23*(3), 195-207.

Thiamwong, L. Stewart, A.L. & Warahut, J. (2009). Development, reliability and validity of the Thai Healthy Aging Survey. *Walailak Journal of Science & Technology, 6*(2), 167-188.

Tirri, K., Nokelainen, P. & Ubani, M. (2006). Conceptual definition and empirical validation of the Spiritual Sensitivity Scale. *Journal of Empirical Theology, 19*(1), 37-62.

Tomich, P.L. & Helgeson, V.S. (2004). Is finding something good in the bad always good? Benefit finding among women with breast cancer. *Health Psychology, 23*(1), 16-23.

Underwood, L.G. & Teresi, J.A. (2002). The Daily Spiritual Experience Scale: Development, theoretical description, reliability, exploratory factor analysis, and preliminary construct validity using health-related data. *Annals of Behavioral Medicine, 24*(1), 22-33.

UNICEF (2007). *Child poverty in perspective: An overview of child well-being in rich countries.* Florence, Italy: UNICEF Innocenti Research Centre.

Unterrainer, H-F., Nelson, O., Collicutt, J. & Fink, A. (2012). The English version of the Multidimensional Inventory for Religious/Spiritual Well-Being (MI-RSWB-E): First results from British college students. *Religions, 3,* 588-599.

Utsey, S.O., Adams, E.P. & Bolden, M. (2000). Development and initial validation of the Africultural Coping Systems Inventory. *Journal of Black Psychology, 26,* 194-215.

Vaingankar, J.A.et al. (2011). The positive mental health instrument: Development and validation of a culturally relevant scale in a multi-ethnic Asian population. *Health and Quality of Life Outcomes, 9*, 92-109. From: http://www.hqlo.com/content/9/1/92

Valentine, S.L. (2007). *Measuring religiosity in non-biblical spiritual practices: A new perspective on I/E and Quest orientations.* MA thesis, University of Houston Clear Lake.

van Dierendonck, D. (2005). The construct validity of Ryff's Scales of psychological well-being and its extension to spiritual well-being. *Personality and Individual Differences, 36*, 629-643.

Van Rooyen, B.M. (2007). *Spiritual well-being in a group of South African adolescents.* PhD dissertation, University of the Free State, Bloemfontein.

van Wegberg, B., Bacchi, M., Heusser, P., Helwig, S. Schaad, R., von Rohr, E., Bernhard, J., Hürny, C., Castiglione, M. & Cerny, Th. (1998). The cognitive-spiritual dimension – an important addition to the assessment of quality of life: Validation of a questionnaire (SELT-M) in patients with advanced cancer. *Annals of Oncology, 9*, 1091-1096.

Vella-Brodrick, D.A. & Allen, F.C.L. (1995). Development and psychometric validation of the Mental, Physical, and Spiritual Well-Being Scale. *Psychological Reports,* 77, 659-674.

Vestal, J.E.C. (1997). *Development of the Scale of Resilience (SCORE).* PhD dissertation, Texas Women's University, Denton, Texas.

Vivat, B., Young, T., Efficace, F. et al. (2012). Cross-cultural development of the EORTC QLQ-SWB36: A stand-alone measure of spiritual well-being for palliative care patients with cancer. *Palliative Medicine, 27*(5), 457-469.

Walker, K.L. & Dixon, V. (2002). Spirituality and academic performance among African American college students. *Journal of Black Psychology, 28*(2), 107-121.

Walker, S.N., Sechrist, K.R. & Pender, N.J. (1987). The Health-Promoting Lifestyle Profile: Development and psychometric characteristics. *Nursing Research, 36*(2), 76-81.

Warner, S.C. & Williams, J.I. (1987). The Meaning In Life Scale: Determining the reliability and validity of a measure. *Journal of Chronic Disease, 40*(6), 503-512.

Watson, A. (2011). *A developmental approach to measuring spiritual maturity from a Christian perspective.* PhD dissertation, Oklahoma State University.

Webb, J.R., Toussaint, L. & Dula, C.S. (2014). Ritualistic, Theistic, and Existential Spirituality: Initial psychometric qualities of the RiTE Measure of Spirituality. *Journal of Religion & Health, 53,* 972-985.

Wheat, L.W. (1991). *Development of a scale for the measurement of human spirituality.* PhD dissertation, University of Maryland College Park.

Wheeler, P. & Hyland, M.E. (2008). The development of a scale to measure the experience of spiritual connection and the correlation between this experience and values. *Spirituality and Health International, 9*(4), 193-217. doi: 10.1002/shi.348.

Whitfield, C.L. (1984). Stress management and spirituality during recovery. *Alcoholism Treatment Quarterly, 1*(1), 3-54.

WHOQOL SRPB Group (2006). A cross-cultural study of spirituality, religion, and personal beliefs as components of quality of life. *Social Science and Medicine, 62*, 1486-1497.

Wills, E. (2009). Spirituality and subjective well-being: Evidences for a new domain in the Personal Well-Being Index. *Journal of Happiness Studies,* 10(1), 49-69.

Wittstock, J.S. (2009). *Further validation of the Sexual_Spiritual Integration Scale: Factor structure and relations to spirituality and psychological integration.* PhD dissertation, Department of Pastoral Counseling, Loyola College, Maryland.

Wlodarczyk, N. (2007). The effect of music therapy on the spirituality of persons in an in-patient hospice unit as measured by self-report. *Journal of Music Therapy, 44*(2), 113-122.

WHOQOL SRPB Group (2002). *WHOQOL Spirituality, Religiousness and Personal Beliefs (SRPB) Field test Instrument.* Geneva, Switzerland: WHO.

Wikoff, K.L. (2003). *Development and psychometric evaluation of the Wikoff Spiritual Focus Questionnaire.* PhD dissertation, University of San Diego.

Wolman, R. (1997). Spirituality: What does it mean to you? *New Age Journal, Sep/Oct pp.78-81.*

Wong, P.T.P. (1998) Meaning centered counseling. In P.T.P. Wong & P.S. Taylor (Eds.), *The Human Quest for Meaning: A handbook of psychological research and clinical application* (pp. 395-435). Mahwah, NJ: Erlbaum.

Wyatt, G., Kurtz, M.E., Friedman, L.L., Given, B. & Given, C.W. (1996). Preliminary testing of the Long-Term Quality of Life (LTQL) Instrument for female cancer survivors. *Journal of Nursing Measurement, 4*(2), 153-170.

Yakushko, O. (2011). Preliminary validation of the Women's Spirituality Instrument: Development of a measure to assess feminist religious and spiritual attitudes. *Psychology of Religion & Spirituality, 3*(3), 194-200.

Yong, J., Kim, J., Han, S-S. & Puchalski, C.M. (2008). Development and validation of a scale assessing spiritual needs for Korean patients with cancer. *Journal of Palliative Care, 24*(4), 240-246.

Youlden, B.R. (1988). *A study for educational administrators concerning the relationships between selected dimensions of Christian Education and student spirituality in Seventh-Day Adventist day academies in the United States of America.* PhD dissertation, School of Education, Andrews University.

Zebrack, B.J. & Chesler, M.A. (2001). A psychometric analysis of the Quality-Of-Life-Cancer Survivors (QOL-CS) in survivors of childhood cancer. *Quality of Life Research, 10*, 319-329.

Ziegler, D.L. (1998). *The validity and reliability of a self-report measure of health integrity, the Personal Inventory of Kid's Optimal Characteristics – The PIKOC*. PhD dissertation, University of Oregon.

Zullig, K.J., Ward, R.M. & Horn T. (2006). The association between perceived spirituality, religiosity, and life satisfaction: The mediating role of self-rated health. *Social Indicators Research, 79*, 255-274.

In: Spirituality
Editor: Edith C. Roberts

ISBN: 978-1-63482-370-8

Chapter 6

BELIEVERS, PROPHETS AND VISIONARIES: ATTACHMENT, SPIRITUALITY AND HEALTH

***Imre Lázár**, MD, PhD**
Semmelweis University, Institute of Behavioral Sciences, Budapest, Hungary

ABSTRACT

There is evidence that spiritual attachment may confer psychological benefits associated with secure interpersonal attachments. Spirituality, perceived relationships with God, meets all the defining criteria of attachment relationships. Religion itself may be seen as a dynamic attachment process. God or other supernatural beings may act so a to substitute the role of an attachment figure. In this healing relationship, God is the "*Secure base*" and the "*Safe Haven*, which may relieve the wounds of bereavement and other kinds of loss. Attachment to God may confer emotional benefits associated with secure interpersonal attachments.

This chapter offers both qualitative and quantitative insight to the issue of spiritual attachment. The results of an anthropological field work with charismatic religious visionares are presented in context of their confessed close and intimate spiritual attachment mirrored by their narratives, life stories, texts and sacred dialogues. The prominent role of attachment in sacral communication is demonstrated.

The health aspects of the spiritual attachment are explored by the results of two consecutive behavioral epidemiological studies called Hungarostudy. The health psychological significance of spirituality is summarized by comparing our results with the data of studies and metanalyses of this field. Regarding religious attitudes and adult attachment features the 2013 Hungarostudy data helped us uncover relationships between sociality, spirituality and the mental health gains. We found significant differences regarding avoidant, dismissive attachment between the religiously indifferent and those practicing their religion. Our findings proved that religiosity can be classified as a life - enhancing factor. The positive relationship between religiosity and health psychological indicators have gained broader multidimensional significance as we could demonstrate it.

* lazimre@net.sote.hu.

Health, Protective and Broken Bonds

Both attachment and spirituality have a complex relationship to personal health – this observation has been proven using epidemiological data. Attachment itself plays a central role in the psychological embodiment of emotional communion with a spiritual significant 'Other', The Divine Person to whom one directs one's prayers. The experience of ecclesiastical membership, with its attendant benefit of perceived social support, has a positive impact on health through its stress buffering impact.

The etymology of religion expresses the importance of connection; the bond is a central tenet of religious experience, be it social, communal or the deep personal experience of mystical union, even in the case of religions which favor emotional neutrality and detachment from the world.

The importance of attachment to health, spirituality and the sense of their connection may be deduced by observing what occurs when they are lacking: a social-physiological shock caused by a feeling of being radically detached or excluded. Sociocultural death, described first by Mauss (1927), or 'voodoo death', as reported on by Levi-Strauss in his "Tristes Tropiaues" and explained by Cannon (1942) in psychophysiological terms, shows the serious health/psychological impacts of broken social links which otherwise help secure ones' personal existence.

This trauma is based on enculturated expectations and attributes which are basically culture-bound, psychologically-meditated processes that depend on subjective perceptions that are framed by a given community. Just like a nocebo (a placebo with negative impacts) damages the health of a person via psychophysiological processes, having a feeling of security and trust in divine providence has beneficial impacts in terms of the support it gives to psychological and general health. Even the Latin term *religion/relegate* implies relatedness and 'attachment' as a kind of imaginary '*attachment ring'.* This psychic organization includes the perceived presence of the significant Divine Other and the Church as the mystic body of Christ and the religious community of Christians, offering social support and a sense of social embeddedness.

The Meaning of the Divine Bond

The letter written by St. John during his exile on the Island of Patmos reveals the very central element of the Logos, the primordial essence of Christian cosmology: He identifies the Lord with Love : "*The one who does not love does not know God, for God is love.*"(1John 4:9). This is more than a statement about moral conduct; it is the ἀγάπη, the agape, the Lord's unconditional love, as an almost cosmic essence of healing power, a drive, a motive and habitus for restituting harmony. This statement has antecedents such as the teachings of Plato who found Eros among the primordial Divinities in his Symposium. In his description of the fate of Atlantis Plato describes how the divine part of the soul of Atlantis' pristine citizens faded away, implying something close to the habitus organized by the agape, inside: "For many generations, as long as the divine nature lasted in them, they were obedient to the laws, and *well-affectioned towards the god, whose seed they were*; for they possessed true and in every way great spirits, *uniting gentleness with wisdom* in the various chances of life, and in their *intercourse with one another*. They despised everything but virtue, caring little for their present state of life, and thinking lightly of the possession of gold and other property, which seemed only a burden to them; neither were they intoxicated by luxury; nor did wealth deprive them of their self-control; but they were sober, and saw clearly that *all these goods are increased by virtue and friendship with one another*, whereas by too great regard and respect for them, they are lost and friendship with them, when the *divine portion began to fade away...." (Plato's Critias).*

This divine portion concerns the relation to the divine and to each other – this is love itself, and not the love of gold and other reified goods.

When exploring the biblical world of the Gospel one can find reasons to challenge the proposition that love is the fundamental basis. We are confronted by some counter-family statements in the Testaments. To leave ones' family of origin may be commanded. Leaving the family for a new one may be welcomed in everyday life. We have to keep in mind, however, that, although it is the will of God that parents should be respected, they are always ranked second in importance after God. It is important to see the difference between the Pagan and the Biblical Jewish social reality: that honoring parents after their death does not and must not mean venerating them as divine beings. This can help solve the love paradox – explaining why children have to leave their parents and follow Jesus.(Balla 2003). This Christian radicalism does not necessarily involve severing family relationships, although metanoia may indeed cause divisions in a family. The Pauline Epistles reflect the view of God's people as a "family". The Gospel calls for children to be highly respected too. This emotional turn relates to extending intensive interpersonal relations to include the personified and incarnate Divine as the Son, and the unincarnated as Father and Holy Church, and its members as family, as brothers and sisters, based on the command to love all human beings.

The importance of Family relationships is also reflected in Nativity scenes and the Flight to Egypt, where two dimensions of attachment become visible: obedience to the Lord and the messengers (the angels who mediated the message to Mary and to Joseph) and to the Family, thereby creating sacred bonds of relatedness to the Divine – and attachment to each other, during a strange, existential and marginalizing social moment, under threat of infanticide. Narrative analysis – from a structuralist perspective – allows a more personal interpretation: Mary's unskeptical obedience, based on her unconditional faith (the moment of AVE), helped create her relation to Christ, while offering unconditional approval of the given social pattern was the challenge for Joseph; the reward their tight, three dimensional relatedness.

ATTACHMENT TO THE DIVINE OTHER

It is worth examining the dynamics of the divine bond which arises and the attachment which occurs in the case of Saints, prophets, and visionaries. It usually goes well beyond what is scientifically explainable, as many of these holy people transcend ordinary human reality, receiving stigmata such as in the case of St. Francis or Padre Pio; their mortal remains are also beyond mundane reality, as in the case of the incorruptible bodies of Imelda of Bologna, Bernadette Subirous or Catharine Laboure.

Much may be said about that internal communicative and emotional register of sacred intimacy, the experience of which is not limited to those who lead an exceptional and sacred life, but may occur with believers who have a deeper personal relationship to the divine, to the Other person, and their own, deeper Self. Although those who lead a sacred life are sometimes really victims of early social or economic circumstances (perhaps they are just one child of many and receive less parental attention, or less understanding, or are victims of insecure secondary attachment organizations), after metanoia they may gain a new and infinite sense of security. Their relationship with the divine and their sacral communication becomes so intimate that formerly-closed channels become open; speaking in tongues occurs, altered acoustic and visual perception and inner hearing of sacred texts, dictated by the divine.

Our respondents too include some exceptional people who otherwise lead normal lives – mothers, or lonely, but socially accepted spiritual specialists such as psychics; mediators between souls and their relatives.

This paper does not seek to explore their activity or the messages they receive, but rather only one component of it: the rise and establishment of the relationship, the intimacy of connection, mediation and the spiritual relationship. In such cases the anthropologist must use an emic, charismatic Christian perspective to explore the web of meaning and the psychological phenomenology of mystic attachment.

THE PATH: THE CALL, THE OBSTACLES AND THE FIGHT

The first mystical experience of the seven years long process occurred to the female prophet during her adoration of the Lord in 2000. (Lázár 2014) She first heard an inner voice: "*I'm not taking you out of this world, but you're mine*" which she then started to transcribe in her diary. These documents reflect the inner dialogue after the prophetic call as a response, the faithful soul's devoted affirmation: "*Lord, I'd like to carry Your cross*! The divine reply to her response did not promise an easy journey: "*I have prepared your cross. Do not worry! All the pain which you bear with love for me will unite you with me on the cross*!" The message she was given included reference to millennial elements and content similar to other prophetic texts, especially the prophecies of the Second Coming by Maria Divine Mercy. "*You are my messenger! Thou apostolate my coming, you are My prophet! I am the Christ, Thy Lord*!" This message was not be adopted without uncertainty and suspicion according to the log entry: "*I said the glorious holy Rosary in my home, and I began to doubt whether my soul hear the voice of Christ, indeed*?" "*Honey, It is me, do not worry!*" There followed an important sentence in the sacred inner locution: "*Lord, I want to comfort you, I want to be the Tabernacle, I want to become your small Wafer, be distributed by your grace*"

In a theological regard, it is important to pay regard to the divine secret of love, registered in the diary on 18th January 2001: "*All I want to speak my word for is to love you, little children! Why do not you see how simple it is, what I want? Love one another at all times! Yes, my secret is Love, my daughter, with bottomless depth!*

My request to you is to be gentle and humble in heart!"

DUBITATION AND PSYCHOSOMATIC SYMPTOMS

The first steps along her sacred path was hindered by growing doubt and blocked by external pressure in January, 2001. This crisis was reflected also in the diary texts: "*You call the sacred name in vain if your heart does not respond to the prayer of mine, my daughter" "Lord, did I leave you? Am I not hearing you?"* "*Word of crying, why don't you listen to me? Why did you allow yourself to be troubled and why do you not open your heart to my voice?*" "*Lord, what do you mean? I stopped.*" "*Please, do not leave me alone in prayer, and please, feel free to write down what I tell you!*" "*Lord! I am deathly afraid that this is an error that was not according to his grace! Please, give me certainty because I am deathly afraid! If this is not your mercy, do not let me speak, and do not let me hear*!" "*I'm here, do not be afraid! I am constant in my affection and I will protect you because I am your teacher, Jesus Christ, the only begotten Son of God"* Elsewhere, March 23, 2001: "*Please, do not leave me! Stay with me, because there is not enough time and the curse has been threatening the world! You still need to communicate with me for seven years to understand me!"*

At this time of this prophetic journey (in the spring of 2001) an obstacle emerged in the form of a civilian leader of a Catholic charismatic community who was thought to have the "*charisma of distinguishing souls*": he questioned the authenticity of the message. Due to the crisis this perpetuated the woman experienced psychosomatic symptoms, and wrote: "*But my life from then began to lead to the Valley of Death! As my personal relationship with God loosened, deeper anxiety, listlessness, guilt and emptiness I felt. On the other hand, from the depths of my soul I wanted more of the Lord Jesus' loving presence and to experience His merciful goodness! My life has been filled with growing spiritual darkness. I was depressed, I often felt, my life was aimless, despite my seemingly complete and happy family life"*

Her doubts cleared away as she received support and conclusive evidence: "*Go home to a new life! Yes, the birth of a new child from your womb. He will be born to a new life, to my life!"* Indeed, her child was born in 2003, and after this she turned again towards God. After a short period when she experienced the dark night of the soul with associated psychosomatic complaints, she felt healed and again heard the voice in response to her glossolalia.

Comparing her sense of connectedness and relatedness to the content of the messages of Sister Divine Mercy, we find a similar register.(The Warning) In the first message of Sister Divine Mercy the intimate dialogue reflects also a deep internal intimacy, and a personal calling for spiritual agency on behalf of Holy Mary: *"My child, you have a responsible job to do, and you must not let anyone stop you. The Truth has to come out. You have been chosen to do this Work. My child, stay strong. Look to God above for guidance to do my Work."*

Christ's first words to Sister Divine Mercy were these:

"I Am distressed, and cry bitter tears of disappointment and sorrow at the way I have been rejected for the second time. *I urge My followers to gather together at this time of sorrow in the world. They must leave aside their indifference to pray and join with Me to help those whose souls have been stolen by the evil one.*

There is still time for sinners to repent. There is no easy way. It must be from the heart. Believers, do not be afraid to raise your voices in unison to declare the Love that I have for all."

It is worth examining the last message (December 28, 2014) to understand what kind of relatedness to God eme**rges *in the role of prophesying*** in the context of 'contra mundi' (and of course, pro mundi), similar to the narrative pattern in the metaphor of the 'flight to Egypt', when the power of the world turned to infanticide, wanting killing the Christ who dwelled inside, the prior connection to the Divine. The importance of internal attachment to the divine remains the most important support.

"My dearly beloved daughter, the greatest pain of the tribulation is that which exists within the Laws of your nations that oppose the laws of God in every way, both visible and invisible. ***For every Law of God broken by those who run your nations is now replaced by a silent killer of the soul. Every wrongdoing will be presented as being a good thing. The more wicked the act, the greater will it be applauded.***

The time has truly arrived for the Truth to be turned inside out and presented as a lie. The Word will now be deemed by the majority to be a work of fiction – a lie. God's Laws, however, are difficult to ignore and so it will be that when those who run your nations, when asked to answer for their wicked actions, will declare that the Word of God is flawed and outdated.

Sin is today embraced with relish and promoted as a civil right, and therefore you are expected to respect it. If you do not show respect towards sinful acts then you could find that you will be guilty of a crime. Your crime will be that you uphold the Word of God and for that you will be made to suffer."

The millennial and apocalyptic messages of Sister Divine Mercy also have love at their center.

"In the meantime, My Love will sustain the world and for every wrong-doing and act of evil perpetrated by My enemies, I will put an end to its source. The battle against evil will be won by the Love which I will instil in the hearts of good souls. This Love will enrapture all who come into contact with it, and the Fire of the Holy Spirit will fill the souls of all who are blessed with the Love of God."Rejoice, My beloved followers, because it is because of the Power of My Love that I will save the world and all of those who accept My Mercy. Go in My Love. Love one another as God loves you."

Ghostly Service and the Strains of Loss

The narratives of the Csángó psychic Ilona Jánó, - with whom I made these interviews in Eger, Hungary in 2007 - also represent visionary frames of divine connectedness. She was accepted as a spiritual specialist for a long time in her Village of Lészped (Romania) where she was brought up. Here we see that childhood events may determine spiritual attachment through their profound impact. Ilona was three when she had her first vision:

"My mother was suckling me when I saw the devil in the image of a dog coming close to me. I was crying, and kicking. Mummy took me up and said hush, hush, but the dog did not go away. They called the priest to say a prayer, to perform an exorcism. But the dog remained. When my mother came back, I heard shouting, what I saw was stars dancing around the ceiling, round and round, bigger and smaller like roses, they went around. And the picture of the Blessed Virgin Mary, the Holy Mother, the picture of her heart, came close to my head, it was close, I was shouting. Mummy asked, what did I see?...The heart of the Holy Mother. My mummy said hush, hush, caressed me and I showed her the picture on the wall, and Mother lifted me, I kissed the picture."

These events may be seen as a form of spiritual imprinting as Ilona developed a sense of protection against the devil from this early experience. She felt a sense of security based on her early intimate internal connectedness to the Blessed Virgin Mary in her early childhood.

Her calling happened when she was twelve:

"It started with the guardian angel... I saw it at a wayside cross, I was twelve, and Jesus was also twelve, he came and said, Ilona. Here, at the cross, there are so many. They come and go, and they don't greet me. I died for them, and do not hail me. People of the world in front of the Cross. Let's pray together, the Lord's Prayer. We knelt down in front of the Cross, close to the Cross and prayed together, the Lord's Prayer. Then he stood up and said, Ilona, I give you a cross to strengthen and enlighten and help you. He put it into my right hand. I have still to go, I will go to take it, and then he left me. Then my guardian angel appeared and said to me: Take the cross with your left hand, and give the right to me, I will guide you. This was the first occasion that I left my body...."

Since then she has experienced out of body sensations several times. During such events she has had visions of heaven and visited heaven and hell and witnessed all the sins. In this altered state of consciousness she was often asked to pray for the souls of those who had suddenly died. She was given the charisma to heal, too, and practiced as a mediator of holy help through her blessing, prayer and touch.

In the above text we may see the internally-focused intimacy of the relationship with the vision of the divine. It is not the 'tremendum' but the 'mysterium fascinans' which gives a framework to her relationship with the significant Other. In the case of Ilona Jánó we see the long-lasting power and shield-like protection of this relationship which helped her through numerous discriminative, social and institutional threats and occasions of persecution.

The above samples illustrate exceptional ways of becoming personally attached to the divine; attachments which detach a person from society as it is, and create a basis for transferring messages which could transform society. These events may reorganize the self around a renewed and stable relationship with all its beneficial consequences: a strengthened sense of coherence, a better perspective about losses and difficulties, a reinforced internal locus of control and commitment and a strengthened sense of identity, greater resistance to social harassment and economic and social deprivation.

Temporary or long-term detachment from this inner spiritual connectedness may cause symptoms. The re-attachment is healing.

Human Attachments, Sacred Bonds and Health

We can extend the meaning of the sacred bond – as Hanhardt did – to include developmental stages using a life span perspective, with the message that "*attachment is, from the beginning, spiritual*". His core statement is that attachment is a new word for love from God; non-attachment a state of vulnerability to the negative and evil forces in the world.

In his framework, the concept of attachment is divided into three components. The first phase is well-known, it is the concept used by Bowly and his followers (Ainsworth, Main, IJzendorn and many others): initial attachment to nurturing parents.

If we find parental love and attention to be insufficient (e.g. as babies we feel insecure) we may compensate for this relationship insecurity in two ways. The behavioral response with 'A-type' secondary attachment reveals itself as a *tendency for inhibited bonding* (Rudisch, Molnár 1991), a response to parental negligence. This results in so called anxious-avoidant secondary attachment organization. The determinative feature of these early psychosocial engrammes and the learnt model of relatedness to the Other is framed in the

Bowlbian concept of “internal working models” (IWMs) which are engraved in situations of attachment systems by repeated experiences with caregivers and which lead to working models of self and others. These models are both conscious and unconscious mental structures, or schemas, that inform the child of his or her self-worth.

When the mother expresses ambivalent behavior, the same insecurity without consequent negligence leads to so-called ‘C-type’ secondary attachment. In this case, the baby develops ambivalent, anxious attachments and shows high physiological arousal, inhibited aggression and low self-esteem.

These early psychosocial experiences with a *non-loving* psychological environment may have long-lasting embodied, neurobiological consequences. It is an evidence-based fact that early (emotional) abuse may lead to methylation of gene fragments, resulting in changes in hippocampal GR expression and enhanced vulnerability to stress (Szyf, McGowan and Meaney, 2008). In humans, prenatal exposure to depressed/anxious moods has also been associated with increased epigenetic changes in terms of increased DNA methylation at the glucocorticoid receptor gene with consequently increased HPA axis stress reactivity, reflected in the increased concentration of salivary cortisol in three month old infants (Oberlander et al, 2008). Deeper insight is gained from rodent experiments which have proved that high licking-grooming frequency due to decreased DNA methylation may increase access to the hippocampal glucocorticoid receptor genes in the offspring, leading to a decrease in the amount of cortisol that is released, while low amounts of licking-grooming and less parental care as seen in distorted attachment organizations results in increases in cortisol release. (Masterpasqua, 2009). Early stressful experiences (such as maternal abuse or neglect) induce hippocampal GR17 promoter methylation, leading to consequent depression of GR expression, and disturbed HPA cortisol feedback *(*Weaver et al 2004). Based on these findings of developmental neurogenomics, we may say that mothering can forestall the potential effects of genic activity. Psychoimmunological research and epigenetics together lead to insights about how disease can materialize disturbed bonds according to the different quality of nurturing.

Blatt explored polarization and the differing vulnerability of personality styles and their potential outcomes and took a differential clinical approach to immunology and cardiovascular diseases (Blatt 1993). Based on the long term influence of the internal working model and the epigenetic processes shaped by attachment organizations, we proposed developmental links between A and C type secondary attachment organizations and A and C type behavioral patterns (Lázár 1994, 2001,). The corresponding features of A-C type secondary attachment organizations and A-C type personality or ATBP/CTBP classifications induce us to propose a learning-based common framework with poles of “independence versus pathologic dependence”, “assertivity, aggressiveness versus inhibition of aggression”, and “expression of negative feelings, lack of empathy versus extreme need for affiliation, acceptance, exaggerated empathy” as consecutive representations of basic IWM with strong psycho-physiological correlations. We have proposed a polar model of A and C type risky behavioral patterns deduced from the developmental concept of A and C type secondary attachment organizations. (Lázár 2014)

In a large survey of the population (from ‘Hungarostudy’ research) we identified more than four hundred informants who reported having a tumor (from a total sample of more than twelve thousand informants). There was no significant difference in smoking habits between the tumor patients and the other informants, but in those DAS (Dysfunctional Attitude Scale) parameters which resemble semantically the features of the C type personality we found convincingly significant differences (Kaszab, Lázár, Szendi, Lőke, Szedmák & Kopp, 1998).

Accordingly, the cradle may become a source of personal destiny, where "*genetic propensity may lead to one outcome for one person and the opposite for another, based on the tending they received.*" (Taylor, 2002). The personality is the basis of human psychological transactions and the weaving of relationships, as well as the source of the traps and games that come with them.

When we explored adult attachment patterns in the sample of informants from the Hungarostudy 2013 (600 individuals of under age 35 from 2000 respondents), the four dimensional Bartholomew model offered considerable insight into the adult attachment profile, where self-presentation and the image of the significant other together shaped the character of the bonding. In the Hungarostudy 2013 survey we scaled the values of independence and preoccupation as features of adult attachment tendencies using Griffin and Bartholomew's framework (Csóka, Lázár, 2013). Our findings about attachment characteristics of the population were presented in relation to the following four broader themes; sex differences and age characteristics, health status and bonding style. As there is a state of serious marital crises in Hungary, expressed in the reduction in the number of marriages and the fact that more than half of all adult women of child-bearing age live alone, we also explored attachment tendencies related to data about marriages. Finally, we looked at the quality of attachment and childbearing. Based on the typically conservative value system of Hungarians regarding the institution of marriage, one could expect that the whole sample from the Hungarostudy 2013 survey would be dominated by a secure attachment pattern. In spite of these expectations, we found that secure bonding was only present for 34.4% of the sample under analysis, while the *independent, avoidant* tendency showed up at a surprisingly high rate. The 'dismissive' pattern occurred at 37.9%, the 'preoccupied' pattern amounted to 10.3%, while the proportion of 'fearful' bonding was as high as 20.4%. 58% of the representative sample studied could be characterized by their high values of *independence*, while along the axis of *anxiety* we found informants with preoccupied and fearful attachment patterns in as many as *42%* of all cases. (Csóka, Lázár, 2013). We can imagine how labyrinthine hindrances arise from the personal handicaps of those whose ability to love has been damaged. The scripts people live and the games people play are all 'internal working model'-based narratives, as in the TA concept of Harris, and the variations in the evaluation of the Self and the Other may generate the same bipolar frames: avoidant, independent (I am O.K., you are not O.K.) preoccupied or anxious and worried (I am not O.K., you are O.K.) and trustful, secure (I am O.K., you are O.K.). We can add a fourth, the fearful type (I am not O.K. you are not O.K.) to the avoidant group, to represent a distinctly worried outlook.

Internal (personal-psychological, psychobiological) personal risks are realized as ill-health and psychosomatic diseases or other behavioral medical consequences in the interpersonal space of human relatedness, be it personal social support, or socio-cultural and institutional. In turn, culture and institutions may be also influenced by these early experiences of the presence or absence of maternal love. (Lázár 2000)

According to John L. Weil's studies (1992), low empathy childcare is a frequent occurrence in the childhoods of people who later become psychopaths, drug abusers and addicts, etc. We may consider drug and alcohol abuse to be surrogates for maternal acceptance and support, and must bear in mind that A type secondary attachments and A type personalities tend to develop cardiovascular diseases and suffer myocardial infarctions.

Rohner and Britner (2002) have also provided well-supported evidence about the globally-visible correlation between parental acceptance-rejection and other mental health issues such as depression and a depressed affect, behavioral problems, including conduct disorders, externalizing behaviors, and substance abuse. Their cross-cultural work using parental acceptance-rejection theory also showed that societies that can be identified by warm and accepting parenting tended to construct deities with analogous qualities, whereas societies in which parenting was typically of a 'rejecting' nature had constructed more distant and interfering deities.

This evidence explains why a problematic period of motherhood that results in a distorted mother-and child attachment relationship may be a source of illness, disease and sickness. (Lázár 2014) Hanhardt inserted a sacred element into the concept of adult romantic attachment which replaces attachment towards nurturing parents. According to him, the reversal of attachment to parents is deeper attachment to God and a soul mate in adolescence and young adulthood. On the other hand, his concept is close to that of the Kirkpatrickian concept of God playing the role of an attachment figure. According to Kirkpatrick, an attachment system is a fundamental component of thinking, believing and reasoning about God and an individual's relationship to God. Hanhardt uses an "and" between adult attachment *and* attachment to God, just as Simon and Low (2003) also distinguish between adult attachments *and* attachment to God, seeing them as fundamentally distinct phenomena. But Hanhardt's developmental frame of detachment/spiritual attachment transitions can be compared to Hazan and Zeifman's model (1999) which connects particular life periods, characterized by religious transitions and important maturational processes in adolescence and early adulthood, with attachment, implying the relocation of attachment figures in an individual's life.

This phenomena of religious attachment through prayer, meditation and other rituals and internal communication resemble social referencing in young children, the occasional checks on the availability of the caregiver, the experience of a safe haven. Religious individuals are used to turning to God frequently in situations of distress, especially in during periods of severe stress, accidents, illness, the death of close relatives or divorce (Granqvist & Hagekull, 2000, 2002; Loveland, 1968; Parkes, 1982). The notion of God's omnipresence reassures the believer about the proximity of the divine "attachment figure".

Spiritual attachment serves as a form of religious coping and support-seeking behavior in the case of (or fear of) serious illnesses (Johnson & Spilka, 1991; O'Brien, 1982), relationship problems (Ullman, 1982), losses such as the death of a loved one (Bjorck & Cohen, 1993; McCrae, 1984) and negative life events (Hood et al., 1996) because such events are thought to activate an individual's attachment system (Bowlby, 1969). It is interesting to note that in situations such as these private prayer may function as a religious analogue to attachment behaviors (see Kirkpatrick, 1999). The forms that God takes may be diverse, and the safe haven metaphor requires an always-available, loving, personal, good God who offers providence. The Totaliter Aliter, distant, impersonal, tremendous and vindictive God of fear does not offer a safe haven in human relations, either in times of harmony nor situations of severe psychosocial crisis. Benson and Spilka (1973) have found through their research that having a loving, as opposed to distant, image of God is linked to higher self-esteem. In the Protestant tradition, closeness to Christ through prayer offers attachment-like psychological support and security, while in Catholicism the role is played by the Holy Mary too, who represents the "maternal functions" related to attachment. Religion itself may be seen as a dynamic attachment process. On the other hand, to be far away, or separated from God, as in the case of apostasy or deconversion, can result in real psychological hell for a believer.

Distortion of the early mother-child relationship may affect spiritual openness and religiosity as well. On the one hand, spiritual attachment may be fragile in certain circumstances, and when believers are unable to experience God as they did at some point in their life, the separation from God becomes a serious, hell-like experience, with emerging psychosomatic symptoms such as those we cited from the diary of our charismatic informant. The same narrative provided a clear picture about how return to the divine significant Other, and how restitution of spiritual attachment brings a healing change which diminishes psychological and psychosomatic disturbances. In this healing relationship, God is again the "*Secure base*" and the "*Haven of Safety*". Attachment to God may confer emotional benefits that are typically associated with secure interpersonal attachments. The secularist, atheist or nonspiritual cultural impact of materialism and consumerism inhibit this healing potential.

So-called B type, harmonic attachment displays may also be a perfect niche for spirituality, representing unity, compassion and attachment to others and to Nature and to God. The *correspondence hypothesis*, offered by Granqvist (2002; Granqvist & Hagekull, 1999), constitutes a model whereby an early experience of a secure childhood attachment establishes the basis for a correspondingly secure relationship with God. (IWM correspondence; see also Kirkpatrick, 1992) The secure attachment establishes the basis for better socialization which leads to the adoption of the attachment figure's religious or nonreligious standards (socialized correspondence; Granqvist & Hagekull, 1999). The implication of these findings is that apostasy is not necessarily a normative adolescent phenomenon.

According to the *compensation hypothesis,* individuals with insecure childhood attachment relationships may be helped through *the compensatory role of spiritual attachment* to cope with distress. Jesus Christ and the Blessed Virgin Mary may be experienced as such surrogate attachment figures. This concept has received support, for example, in findings showing that distress-driven religious changes and conversions are linked to attachment insecurity. In the case of the insecure attachment-based internal working model, the person's spirituality may be thought of as a stress-provoked distress regulation strategy in which the personal notion of God substitutes the missing significant Other. It is associated rather with insecure attachment characteristics and the forming and breaking of other affective bonds. Here we can recall anthropological efforts that have been undertaken to understand the relationship between personal suffering, psychological handicaps and alternative types of spiritualism. Mullholland (2007) offers such explanation of this hypothesized relationship to connect the New Age Movement, Bowlbian attachment and the mentalization framework of Fonagy. His approach differs from the concept of Kirkpatrick or Granquist as he has chosen the mentalization framework to explain the complex ways in which…"*psychological and religious development can be fostered or stymied by variations in and deviations from culturally valorised socialization processes and the historical and class-related socio-economic forces that shape them.*"

He seeks an explanation for the deviant particularism of personal religious cosmologies and strategies and tries to uncover how the Puritanical, legalistic-orthodox Church practice has influenced relational culture and skills, and tries to identify what answers can be found in Millennial spiritualism, the New Age Movement and New Religious Movements for those who have suffered from personal psychosocial burdens, early traumatization, maternal neglect and its developmental psychological consequences. He applies the mentalization theory as an explanatory model which connects attachment difficulties and the development of narcissistic tendencies to the 'own-way' spiritualism of the New Age Movement.

Attachment studies should be conducted outside of the Western world to examine the cross-cultural validity of the attachment framework as it is applied to religion and spirituality. Such research would be entirely relevant to attachment theory insofar as the behavior (e.g., praying) of individuals in a given religious tradition is directed to some external supernatural figure.

RELIGIOUS HABITUS AND HEALTH

In the list of health psychological factors which prove to be positively correlated with immunological factors in a psychoimmunological frame of reference, we find factors which may be connected to the embodied ecclesiastic security which may shape religious habitus; i.e. behavioral phenomena which have a positive outwards influence on human transactions, breaking the reciprocity of aggression, building positive emotional milieu filled with love, hope and trust and the inner impact of positive psychosomatic patterns. The positive psychoimmunological effects of optimism, hope, a sense of coherence and social support, or the hardiness that comes from ecclesiastical commitment and a religious sense of security on cellular immunity are supported by research (Koenig 2001). The same relationship is true of laughter, serenity and having a positive mood and a sense of perceived control. The religious habitus refers to a typical condition or state, a durable and transposable system of schemata of perception, appreciation and action that results from the institution of the social in the body, constituting a personally meaningful world endowed with sense and value (after Bourdieu and Wacquant, 1992). The Christian religious habitus exists as sum of behavioral manners and is manifested through its effects in the context of embodied social relationships and emotional and affective experiences, where interpersonal relationships tend to confirm or challenge this habitus as '*the generative principle of regulated improvisations*' with their focus on loving relatedness. This habitus is deeply influenced by the early, imprinted internal working model which is in turn affected by the quality of attachment and parental bonding.

Warren S Brown uses the term 'soulish' to describe our polyvalent human relation to other individuals and to God which may modulate the activation of our immune systems and influence our health. In the Western religions, based on this three dimensional model of personal *relatedness* are included the *subjective processes of self-relatedness and self-representation*, "*inter-individual relatedness*", and *relatedness to God.* PNI research has proven the significant positive impact of interpersonal relatedness and its support of the immune system.

Spiritual attachment to the significant Other in Western religious traditions requires the stable belief in the existence of a communicative, "*personal*" God who listens to one's prayers and actively intervenes in one's affairs. This sacral communication and connectedness are enhanced by the images of Jesus, Mary, and the saints; and the use of incense and other sacred objects, rituals, or texts, while the Protestants' experience is based on the spiritual indwelling of the Holy Spirit that is continually in and around one's life (Haskins, 1991). The difference between the health of regular Church-goers and the 'religious in their own way' group was shown in the Hungarostudy 2006 and 2013 (Székely and Lázár 2013), similarly to Gardner and Lyon's findings about the increased longevity of Mormons who are conscientious adherents to the stricter religious traditions compared to those who are tied more loosely to the same groups (Gardner and Lyon, 1982). This is an old topos of psychology of religion – James distinguished between the first-born religiosity of healthy minded individuals and the twice-born religiosity of sick souls as far back as 1902.

This intimate and protective relatedness evolves through a process of social learning of religion that creates the religious habitus, and whereby offspring with high quality parental relationships adopt their parents' religious standards more easily than those whose relationships have been less favorable. Parental sensitivity promotes compliance and the internalization of parental values with deeper identification (Richters & Waters, 1991). Along the same lines, disciplined health-promoting behavior may be due to compliance and identification with ethical and health-promoting values as well. Strawbridge and colleagues (1997) proved that those who more frequently attended religious institutions enjoyed better health and a longer life because of their religious commitment and practice (beyond that which would be expected from their superior health-related behaviors, increased numbers of social contacts and more stable marriages which also occurred in conjunction with attendance). In another study Hummer and colleagues (1999) found a 7-year difference in life expectancy at age 20 between those who never attend church and those who attend more than once a week, while research by Oman and Reed (1998) indicated that mortality was 24% lower among frequent religious service attenders than non-attenders.

Summing up the results of such surveys from the past decades, the indication is that people who belong to behaviorally strict denominations have a lower risk of mortality than people who belong to less strict religious groups, or who have no religious affiliation at all (Dwyer et al., 1990; Kark et al., 1996; Lyon et al., 1976; Phillips et al., 1980) Beyond the positive general health/psychological outcomes there are also observations of clinical benefit. Townsend et al (2002) verified that religious beliefs and regular church attendance are beneficial to the immune system, can significantly lower blood pressure and reduce the risks of coronary heart disease and suicide.

Health benefits that are shaped, buffered and/or counter indicated by spiritual habitus and dispositions may offer a plausible explanation for these findings. The protective role of religiosity was demonstrated in a mental health context in our earlier Hungarostudy research which found fewer sick days being taken from work and spiritual / psychological protection against addiction, smoking and alcoholism. The above figures are results of Hungarostudy 2006 of the national representative sample of 12000 informants, led by Prof. Maria Kopp at the Semmelweis University Institute of Behavioral Sciences.

The religious respondents of the Hungarostudy 2006 survey who practice their religion in an ordered, regular and complete manner proved to be less depressed, less hostile and more cooperative; moreover, having better coping methods they reported to benefitting from more social support (Kopp, Szekely, Skrabski 2006).

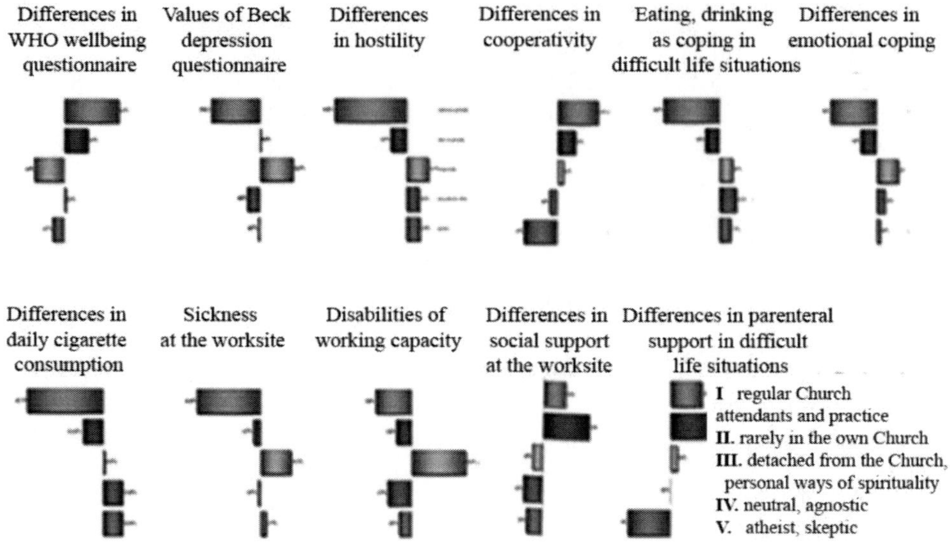

Figure 1. Religion and health in the Hungarostudy 2006.

Moreira– Almeida, Neto and Koenig (2006) in their meta-analysis affirmed that religious practice is positively correlated with psychological well-being indicators (such as satisfaction, happiness, positive emotional attitudes and morality), and has an inverse relationship with depression, suicidal inclination, drug abuse, and alcohol addiction. Research by Zonda and Paks (2006) found a significantly lower number of drinkers and smokers and higher level of refusal to contemplate suicide among religious respondents.

These considerations do not exclude the opposite perspective; that Eastern religious praxis (such as Buddhism and Hinduism) may also sustain health through their philosophy of detachment from mundane influence and discouragement of attachment to physical health and the use of religious practices for material gain (Littleton, 1996). But even these religions may offer samples of attachment such as spiritual relationships, as Kirkpatrick (1995) showed in the case of Mahayana Buddhists' devotion to ancestral spirits. If religious habitus depends on soulishness, this concerns three dimensional relatedness. Disturbances in a person's ability to attach, shaped by early internal working models, may distort this, which may further weaken the gains that traditional religious habitus as the embodied cultural heritage of a traditional, pre-secular society offers in a health context.

A significant difference in health indices and risk status can be identified from the Hungarostudy data (as shown in the figure) between those who regularly attend Church in their community and the growing numbers of those who practice religion in their own way (mostly in a syncretic, eclectic, frequently New Age way). The "compensative versus correspondence" model may help in understanding the better health status of regular church attendants. The *correspondence hypothesis* proposes that a secure attachment system helps with developing better socialization-incorporating religious habitus. Granqvist (2002) reported a significant correlation between secure attachment characteristics and scores on a socialization-based religiosity scale (Granqvist & Hagekull, 1999).

Those with "attachment scars" in their souls, using James' words for the twice-born religiosity of sick souls, might have health handicaps for several reasons. Distortion of early attachment itself may be a harmful factor with life-long consequences via epigenetic mechanisms. Behavioral epigenetics have proven that early traumatic experiences and disturbed attachment can lead to increased sensitivity to stress due to disturbances in the glucocorticoid feedback mechanisms induced by the methylation of the responsible genetic frequencies. The consequent disturbed personality traits that become rooted in the secondary attachment organizations of anxious, independent or anxious, ambivalent types that determine their internal working models might create a social logic that works against interpersonal relatedness, generating games and scripts for transactive patterns and patterns of adult attachment, too.

The gloomier health indexes of the 'own-way spiritualist' group may be hypothetically associated with their distorted attachment background.

According to the *compensation hypothesis,* individuals who had insecure childhood attachment relationships may be helped by *the compensatory role of spiritual attachment* to adjust to distress, as we mentioned above. Granquist has demonstrated, in the case of adults who practice a non-organized form of spirituality by adopting a new age orientation, some proof that supports the compensation hypothesis. (Granqvist & Hagekull, 2001). Mullholland's explanation also supports the existence of the hypothesized relationships based on Fonagy's mentalization framework, as described earlier.

Between 1995 and 2006 the demand for transcendence in society steadily increased and the proportion of those who claim to be religious in their own way doubled (32 percent) but the proportion of regular church-goers declined to 13 percent. However, between 2006 and 2013 the rate of decline in religious practice in favor of non-believers and the non-practicing reflects growing secularization, and the rate of regular church -goers diminished further to 7 % in 2013. These features of religiosity can also be compared to rates and composition of attachment styles. The trends are clear: there has been significant growth in the number of those who practice religion according to their individual styles, and a slight but definite decline in conventional religious behavior. In Budapest the proportion of non-believers has reached 43 per cent, according to the representative sample of Hungarostudy 2013. However, religion remains a proven, detectable, protective factor in health and general well-being and supports confidence in having a meaningful life of faith while reducing the incidence of depression, anxiety, relationship stress and even offending behavior. The coherence index reflects how we make sense or meaning of life, which is closely related to both religious indices for all age groups. The WHO Well-Being Index also proved the importance of religion for the elderly; a significant positive correlation was found. Depression is the most important mediating factor between psychosocial stressors and physical symptoms (Kopp et al. 2004). It is crucial to realize that religion is also protective factor in this field. In our analysis, we used the Beck Depression Inventory (BDI), a 9 element array, from the Hungarostudy 2013. We found a significant relationship between depression and religiosity. The highest Beck indices were found among non-believers (9.66), while those who were religious in their own way had a moderate (6.08) Beck Index and the lowest (i.e. healthiest) Beck values were found among those who regularly worship (5.10).

According to the survey (based on the Bartholomew questionnaire), we found high independent attachment tendencies and respondents. The secure group amounted to 31.4 %, and preoccupied informants 10.3%.

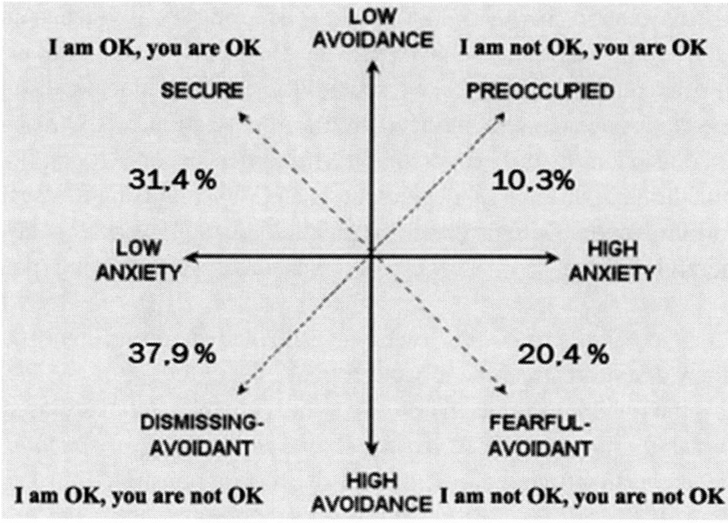

Figure 2. Adult attachment patterns based on the research results of Hungarostudy 2103 (after Csóka, Lázár 2013).

Our recent research that used the data from the 2013 Hungarostudy regarding religious attitudes and adult attachment features uncovered similar relationships of religious habitus in terms of sociality, spirituality and the mental health gains compared to the earlier survey. We found significant differences as regards avoidant and dismissive attachment between the religiously indifferent group and those who practice their religion. Examining the importance of religion also leads to the finding that there is a significant difference in the above 35 year old age group as concerns avoidant, independent adult attachment between experienced religiosity and superficial religiosity. Data about preoccupied adult attachment showed significant differences in the range of values according to the context of religious practice, and the difference was also significant for the age group under 35 years too. This may indicate that among those who undertake regular religious practice and those who have deeper religious experience, young people have a significantly higher tendency towards preoccupied adult attachment. This may be compensatory in nature, or part of spiritual-religious "empowerment". However, it cannot be ruled out that pervasive religious experiences based on the concept of original sin have generated a sense of imperfection and a submissive attitude towards the Divine significant other. In this sense, spiritual attachment may represent another type of corresponding spiritual attachment.

It is therefore worth considering what relationships were found between the values for religiosity and the indices gained from the attachment questionnaire of Bartholomew. The *preoccupied, anxious attachment* pattern was significant, which may indicate that the correspondence hypothesis works not only in the case of secure attachment, but also when the preoccupied, anxious attachment creates an analogous attachment situation with the notion of a secure Other (i.e. One is imperfect but the perfect Significant Other will provide security, if one meets Him). This may be doubly important as the mental health supporting ability of religion may work at the level of disturbed attachment in both compensative and corresponding ways. It can buffer the risks of damage to health caused by a disturbed attachment style and the internal working model that is associated with a predisposition to increased morbidity (Lazar 2001). We also revealed a strong trend towards secularization.

Both attachment styles and the religiosity have importance for psychological health. (Székely, Lázár 2013) Our findings are consistent with the metanalysis of 1200 studies from 400 research reports examined by Koenig et al., in which the role of religion proved to be a protective factor against depression and marital anxiety, which analysis confirmed the protective role of religion. (Koenig 2001)

CONCLUSION

There is evidence that spiritual attachment may confer psychological benefits that are associated with secure interpersonal attachments through a healing relationship. Spirituality and a perceived relationship with God match the defining criteria for attachment relationships. Religion itself may be seen as a dynamic attachment process. God or other supernatural beings may act so as to substitute the role of attachment figures. We can see that prophets and psychics develop very strong internal commitment and relatedness to the divine significant Other, who becomes the closest Person in their life, a secure haven and firm shield even in the case of loss, threats and persecution. The loss or damaging of this bond endangers their psyche and somatic health. After reviewing the data from the literature about the protective role of religiosity, we can contribute our findings from the Hungarostudy 2006 and 2013 which strongly support this proposition and show the health-related risks of adopting an eclectic, independent personal form of spirituality that is strongly influenced by 'New Age' ideas (Figure 1). The impact of such ideas may be explained through reference to the ritual return of "sick souls" with their scars of distorted attachment relationships. We revealed that the avoidant adult attachment style is becoming dominant in the representative Hungarostudy sample. This partly correlates to the tendency towards secularization and the compensatory spiritual attachment figures of a growing number of people who are religious in their own way. This chapter offers both qualitative and quantitative insight into the issue of spiritual attachment. In the paper the results of anthropological field work with charismatic religious visionaries were presented in the context of their confessed close and intimate spiritual attachment which is mirrored in their narratives, life stories, texts and sacred dialogues. The prominent role of attachment in sacral communication is demonstrated to be central. The health/psychological significance of spirituality was summed up by comparing research findings with data from other studies and metanalysis from this field. Regarding religious attitudes and adult attachment features, the 2013 Hungarostudy data helped us uncover the relationships which exist between sociality, spirituality and mental health. We found significant differences in avoidant, dismissive attachment between religiously indifferent respondents and those who practice their religion. Our findings proved that religiosity should be classified as a life-enhancing factor. The positive relationship between religiosity and health/psychological indicators has gained broader multidimensional significance through the demonstration if its protective role among those who have a disturbed attachment style and suffer high risks to health.

REFERENCES

Balla, P. (2003) *The Child-Parent Realtionship in the New Testament and Its Environment* Tübingen Mohr Siebeck

Benson, P. & Spilka, B. (1973). God image as a function of self-esteem and locus of control. *Journal for the Scientific Study of Religion,* 12, 297-310.

Blatt, SJ., Cornell, CE., & Eshkol, E. (1993). Personality style, differential vulnerability, and clinical course in immunological and cardiovascular disease. *Clinical Psychology Review, 13,* 421-450.

Bjorck, J.P., & Cohen, L.H. (1993). Coping with threats, losses, and challenges. *Journal of Social and Clinical Psychology,* 12, 56-72

Bourdieu, Pierre and Loïc Wacquant. 1992. *An Invitation to Reflexive Sociology* Chicago: The University of Chicago Press.

Cannon WB. (1942) Voodoo" death. *American Antropologist.* 1942; 44 (new series):169-181.

Csóka, Sz., Lázár I. (2013) Features of the attachment in the Hungarian population: secure attachment as potential protective factor (Kötődési jellemzők a mai magyar népesség körében; a kötődési biztonság mint potenciális védőfaktor) eds.: Susánszky É., Szántó Zs. *Magyar lelkiállapot 2013* Budapest: Semmelweis, 2013. pp. 187-199.

Dwyer, J. W., Clarke, L. L., & Miller, M. K. 1990. The effect of religious concentration and affiliation on county cancer mortality rates. *Journal of Health and Social Behavior* 31, 185–202

Francis D, Diorio J, LaPlante P, Weaver S., Seckl JR, Meaney MJ(1996) The role of early environmental events in regulating neuroendocrine development. Moms, pups, stress and glucocorticoid receptors *Ann N.Y. Acad.Sci.* 794:136-52.

Gardner, J. W., & Lyon, J. L. (1982). Cancer in Utah Mormon men by lay priesthood level. *American Journal of Epidemiology* 116, 243–257.

Granqvist P. and Hagekull B. (1999). *Religiousness and perceived childhood attachment: Profiling socialized correspondence and emotional compensation Journal for the Scientific Study of Religion* vol. 38 pp. 254–273

Granqvist, P., & Hagekull, B. (2000). Religiosity, adult attachment, and why "singles" are more religious. *The International Journal for the Psychology of Religion,* 10,111-123

Granqvist P. and Hagekull B. (2001) *Seeking security in the new age: On attachment and emotional compensation Journal for the Scientific Study of Religion* vol. 40 pp. 529-547

Hanhardt RW (2012) *Sacred Bond: A Model of Spiritual Transformation for Therapists, Clients, and Seekers* WestBowPress,

Haskins, J. (1991). *Religions of the world,* rev. ed. New York: Hippocrene

Hazan, C., & Zeifman, D. (1999). Pair bonds as attachments: Evaluating the evidence. In J. Cassidy & P.R. Shaver (Eds.*), Handbook of attachment: Theory, research, and clinical applications* (pp. 336-355). NY: Guilford.

Hood, R.W., Jr., Spilka, B., Hunsberger, B., & Gorsuch, R.L. (1996). *The Psychology of religion: An empirical approach* (2 nd ed.). NY: Guilford.

Hummer, RA., Rogers, RG. Nam ChB, and Ellison ChG.(1999) "Religious Participation and U.S. Adult Mortality." *Demography.* 36(2):273-285.

James, W. (1902). *Varieties of religious experience* . NY: Longmans, Green.

Johnson, P., & Spilka, B. (1991). Religion and the breast cancer patient: The roles of clergy and faith. *Journal of Religion & Health*, 31, 21-33.

Kark, J. D., Shemi, G., Friedlander, Y., Martin, O., Manor, O., & Blondheim, S. H. (1996). Does religious observance promote health? Mortality in secular vs. religious kibbutz in Israel. *American Journal of Public Health* 86, 341–346.

Kaszab Z, Lazar I, Szendi G, Szedmak S, Loke J,& Kopp M (1997). Quality of life and psychosocial characteristics of cancer patients *Quality of Life Research,* 6,(7-8) *p. 184.*

Kirkpatrick LA. (1992) *An attachment theory approach to the psychology of religion International Journal for the Psychology of Religion* vol. 2 pp. 3-28

Kirkpatrick, LA. (1995). *Attachment theory and religious experience.* In R. W. Hood Jr. (Ed.), *Handbook of religious experience* (pp. pp. 446–475). Birmingham, AL: Religious Education

Koenig HG, Cohen HJ (eds) (2002).*The Link between Religion and Health: Psychoneuroimmunology and the Faith Factor* Oxford University Press

Kopp MS, Réthelyi J (2004) Where psychology meets physiology: chronic stress and premature mortality--the Central-Eastern European health paradox. *Brain Res Bull.* 2004 Feb 1;62(5):351-67.

Kopp MS., Székely A., Skrabski Á. (2006): Vallásosság és életminőség az átalakuló társadalomban. In Kopp M., Kovács M. E.: *A magyar népesség életminősége az ezredfordulón.* Semmelweis Kiadó, Budapest, 156-166.

Lázár I. (1994) *Social-psychoimmunology* PNI Explanatory Models in Medical Anthropology PhD Dissertation (in Hungarian) Hungarian Academy of Sciences

Lázár I. (2000): Mothers and Mother Nature: Attachment, Detachment and Human Ecological Integrity. In: Crabbé, P. et al eds.: *Implementing Ecological Integrity. Restoring Regional and Global Environmental and Human Health* (NATO Science Series: IV. Earth and Environmental Sciences) Kluwer Academic, Dordrecht. 249-260.

Lázár I. (2001) Social-psychoimmunology (Szociálpszichoimmunológia) in Kopp M. Buda B., Nagy E. *Behavioral Sciences (Magatartástudományok)* (in Hungarian) Budapest, Medicina kiadó *pp. 227-266.*)

Lázár I. (2014) At the Cradle of Psychobiological Risks: Distorted Attachment Organizations in Human Ecological and Evolutionary Context in : *Social Behavior: Evolutionary Pathways, Environmental Influences and Impairments Nova Science Publisher*

Lázár I. (2014) Az áldozat rózsafüzére (Rosary of Sacrifice) in *A spirituális közvetítő* eds. Miklós Vassányi, Enikő Sepsi, Vilmos Voigt Budapest L'Harmattan

Littleton CS (1996) *Eastern wisdom* N.Y. Henry Holt

Loveland, G.G. (1968). The effects of bereavement on certain religious attitudes. *Sociological Symposium,* 1 , 17-27.

Lyon, J. L., Klauber, M. R., Gardner, J. W., & Smart, C. R. (1976). Cancer incidence in Mormons and non-Mormons in Utah, 1966–1970. *New England Journal of Medicine* 294, 129–133.

Mauss M. (2004) *Szociológia és antropológia* (Sociology and Anthropology) Bp.Osiris kiadó

Masterpasqua F. (2008) Psychology and Epigenetics *Review of General Psychology* 2009, Vol 13, No.3,194-201

McCrae, R.R. (1984). Situational determinants of coping responses: Loss, threat, and challenge. Journal of Personality and Social Psychology, 46, 919-928

Moreira-Almeida A, Neto FL, Koenig HG. (2006) Religiousness and mental health: a review. *Rev Bras Psiquiatr.* 28(3):242-50.

Mullholland P. (2007) Anthropology and Attachment. *Irish Journal of Anthropology*. Vol. 10 (1), 2007. 9

Oberlander TF, Weinberg J, Papsdorf M, Grunau R, Misri S, Devlin AM. (2008) Prenatal exposure to maternal depression, neonatal methylation of human glucocorticoid receptor gene (NR3C1) and infant cortisol stress responses. *Epigenetics.* 2008 Mar-Apr;3(2):97-106.

O΄Brien, M.E. (1982). Religious faith and adjustment to long-term hemodyalisis. *Journal of Religion and Health*, 21 , 68-80

Oman, D., & Reed, D. (1998). Religion and mortality among the communitydwelling elderly. *American Journal of Public Health* 88, 1469–1475.

Parkes, C.M. (1972). *Bereavement: Studies of grief in later life.* NY: International Universities Press.

Phillips, R. L., Kuzma, J. W., Benson, W. L., & Lotz, T. (1980). Influence of selection versus lifestyle on risk of fatal cancer and cardiovascular disease among Seventh-Day Adventist men. *Journal of the American Medical Association* 198, 137–146.

Richters, JE., & Waters, E. (1991). Attachment and socialization: The positive side of social influence. In M. Lewis & S. Feinman et al. (Eds.), Social influences and socialization in infancy, Genesis of Behavior Series (Vol. 6, pp 185-213). NY:Plenum

Rohner RP, Britner PA (2002) Worldwide Mental Health Correlates of Parental Acceptance-Rejection: Review of Cross-Cultural an Intracultural Evidence *Cross-Cultural Research* 36; 16

Rudisch T. Molnár P (1991) Adult consequences of infantile bonding dysfunctions (on the genesis of psychopatic condition). *International Journal of Psychophysiology*, Volume 11, Issue 1, page 71, Jul.1991.

Strawbridge WJ, Cohen RD, Shema SJ, Kaplan GA. (1997) Frequent attendance at religious services and mortality over 28 years. *Am J Public Health.*;87:957–961

Székely A. Lázár I. (2013) Religiosity and Attachment (Vallásosság és kötődés) eds Susánszky É., Szántó Zs. *Magyar lelkiállapot 2013* Budapest: Semmelweis, 2013. pp. 63-77

Szyf M, McGowan P, Meaney MJ. (2008) The social environment and the epigenome. *Environ Mol Mutagen.* 2008 Jan; 49(1):46-60.

Taylor Sh. (2002) *The Tending Instinct Women, Men, and the Biology of Nurturing* Times Books

Townsend M, Kladder V, Ayele H, Mulligan T. (2002) Systematic review of clinical trials examining the effects of religion on health. *South Med J.* 2002 Dec;95(12):1429-34.

Ullman, C. (1982). Cognitive and emotional antecedents of religious conversion. *Journal of Personality and Social Psychology*, 43, 183-192.

The Warning (2014) http://www.thewarningsecondcoming.com/category /latest-messages/page/125/

Weaver JCG, Cervoni N, Champagne FA, D'Alessio AC, Sharma S, Seckl JR, Dymov S, Szyf M Meaney MJ (2004) Epigenetic programming by maternal behavior *Nature Neuroscience* 7, 847 - 854

Weil John L. (1992) *Early Deprivation of Empathic Care International* University Press, Madison

Zonda T., Paksi B. (2006): Data supporting the protective role of religiosity in the mental and somatic health (Adatok a vallásosság protektív szerepéhez a testi és lelki egészségben). *Mentálhigiéné és Pszichoszomatika* 7. 1, 1-13

In: Spirituality
Editor: Edith C. Roberts

ISBN: 978-1-63482-370-8

Chapter 7

FROM THE BEGINNING TO SPIRITUAL WELL-BEING

Dr. John W. Fisher [*]
Adjunct Associate Professor, Education & Arts
Federation University Australia
Hon. Senior Fellow, Faculty of Medicine, University of Melbourne
Hon. Senior Research Fellow, CRSE, Hong Kong Institue of Education
Visiting Professor, IHMSS, University of Glyndŵr, Wales, UK

ABSTRACT

This chapter outlines potential interactions of God with humanity from the dawn of time through to attaining spiritual well-being. It briefly mentions alternative theories of origin, which connect to questions of ultimate reality, origin of human beings and our spiritual well-being.

The nature of spirit and its relationship with soul and mind is then canvassed, followed by an account of historical developments in 'spirituality'. The author's Four Domains Model posits that Spiritual Health/Well-Being is reflected in the quality of relationships that each person has in up to four areas, namely with themselves, with others, with nature and/or with a Transcendent Other (commonly referred to as God). A critique of available measures of spirituality and spiritual well-being reveals a decline in the number of instruments assessing human relationships with God from earlier to more recent times.

In contrast to this current trend of researchers selecting more humanistic emphases in spirituality/well-being in their research instruments, evidence is provided from recent findings that show that relating with God is the most important of the four sets of relationships for spiritual well-being. Further evidence is provided that God is the most influential Transcendent to enhance people's relationships with themselves and others. Although researchers are free to choose the nature of questions raised in their projects, findings presented here clearly show that any research that cuts God out of the equation is excising the foundation of spirituality/well-being.

[*] Email: j.fisher@federation.edu.au.

1.1. In the Beginning

'In the beginning, God created the heavens and the earth' are the opening words of the most published book, The Bible (Genesis 1:1). These words form the foundation of a Judaeo-Christian worldview that places God as the First Cause of everything we know and experience. This belief is said to derive from supernatural revelation from God to humankind. The beginning of the universe is connected to questions of ultimate reality. Cosmologists cannot agree on the origin of the universe (Chown, 2012). However, according to Lennox, science has shown that the hypothesis of Creation is testable. The universe is mathematically extremely well organised, which provides an overwhelming indication of its 'design' by a 'mind that was responsible for both the universe and for our minds' (Lennox, 2009, p.207). Lennox claims, 'what lies behind the universe is much more than a rational principle; it is God, the Creator, Himself' (ibid.), not just an abstraction or impersonal force. This chapter investigates the importance of relating with God (or other Transcendents) for spiritual well-being.

Belief in God is at one end of a spectrum of worldviews held by people. In fact it was a, or the, dominant worldview in Western civilisation until the 1800s. Slightly before this time, Rene Descartes (in 1637) penned the phrase, '*Cogito ergo sum* (I think, therefore I am) (Encyclopaedia Brittanica, 2013), which was built on by Rationalists, who hold reason, not revelation, as the chief source and test of knowledge. A rival of Rationalism is Empiricism, which holds that knowledge comes from, and must be tested by, sense experience. Many atheists believe that empirical science is the true path to understanding. The reason for saying many, rather than all, is that variations exist among people who claim each worldview. (For a useful exposition of many worldviews, see Sire 2009). The very idea of 'empiricism' itself was not derived from scientific experimentation, so, it can therefore be considered a faith statement – considering something that is not visible as true. Ideas are not visible. Empiricism is an idea; therefore it requires faith to believe, but just not in God (Geisler & Turek, 2004).

The answer to the existential question, 'Where did we come from?' has a major influence on one's quality of life and spiritual well-being. Believing in God and His Creation requires faith, as does belief in whatever permutation of the Big Bang or any other Theory that presumably explains how matter and energy arose from nothing to constitute our physical universe in four dimensions of space-time. Although Genesis starts, 'In the beginning,' this does not mean that nothing existed before Creation. Jesus claimed that God the Father loved Him before the foundation of the world (John 17:24), and that they shared glory before the world came into existence (John 17:5) (Schaeffer, 1972, p. 17). Two extreme worldviews posit 'man' [sic] being made in the image of God through Creation (Genesis 1:27), as opposed to inanimate matter yielding elemental life forms which subsequently evolved into human beings, without apparent causation. Both views are statements of faith. Neither of these worldviews on the origin of 'man' can be validated scientifically. As valuable as science is, it is a limited way of knowing, or attempting to explain, what happened, how and possibly where and when. It does not recognise revelation as a valid source of knowledge. But, science can never answer the question, 'Why?' This question, however, is critically important for spiritual well-being because it relates to meaning and purpose in life. According to theistic worldviews, God made man for a purpose – to commune with Him. Conversely, no matter how one tries to anthropomorphise it, Mother Nature, Father Time and Lady Luck could not have made life, nor given it purpose.

1.2. Nature of Spirit

Some Empiricists claim that spirit does not exist because it cannot be gauged/measured directly by human senses or the machines we have made. The same could be said of beauty and love, even mind, conscience and intelligence, but Empiricists most likely believe in them, and deal with these matters as if they are real. Moberg clearly attests, just because many scientists' opinions overstep the limitations of science by rejecting spirituality and the Bible as possible aspects of reality, is no reason for denying them. The fact of the existence of a spiritual dimension or of an intelligent Creator is outside the sphere of scientific examination per se. What is obvious in everyday experience need not be overlooked just because it cannot be measured. (2010, p. 106).

The first obvious recorded mention of 'spirit' in the Bible was attributed to Moses writing some time before 1100 BC (Morris, 1984). Moses may have recorded the stories handed down orally by generations of Jews, or some even suggest there could have been a written record made by Adam, following his conversations with his Creator in the Garden of Eden. But, evidence for this is disputed (Jewish Encyclopedia, 2002). Whatever the source, Moses was inspired by God to write the book of Genesis, as all scripture is inspired by God (2 Timothy 3:16). Genesis 2:7 states, 'The Lord God formed man from the dust of the ground and breathed into his nostrils the breath or spirit of life, and man became a living being'.

According to Moberg (2010), the Hebrew word *ruah,* referred to 378 times in the Old Testament, and the Greek word *pneuma*, referenced 146 times in the New Testament, describe human beings as *spirit*. The word 'breath' is derived from *spiritus*, Latin for 'that which gives life or vitality' (ibid.). It is interesting to note that scriptural references posit this expression (life is in the breath) only applying to humans and not the other organisms that appeared on Earth before them. Human spirit is eternal, like angelic and demonic spirits, as well as God Himself, whereas the spirit of animals ceases to exist when animals die (according to Ecclesiastes 3:21) (Morris, 1984, p. 74). This statement challenges re-incarnation into or from lower forms of life associated with some worldviews that are distinct from the Judaeo-Christian. With spirit, humans were given moral consciousness, capacity for abstract thinking, appreciation of beauty and emotions, and the capacity to worship and love God (ibid.).

Alternative views on nature of spirit include: New Physics, which is spawning some fascinating ideas, such as '*The Spiritual Genome*' in which it is postulated, 'the DNA of all living creatures (including plants) is connected in the quantum substratum, and that it is this networked intelligence which constitutes the essential oneness from which springs all the diversity of life we see around us' (Bartholomew, 2014). Simply put, this DNA-based supercomputer is supposedly 'the ultimate source of life' (ibid.). Bartholomew, who is heavily influenced by Hinduism, at least asks the reader to 'take a leap of faith', regarding his proposition. In similar vein, many ideas and philosophies, some having a form of god, are espoused in relation to 'spiritual evolution', without offering any alternative source of spirit, apart from God (Wikipedia, 6/5/14).

1.3. SPIRIT, SOUL AND MIND

Many believe humans are spirit, have a soul, and live in a body (e.g., Hagin, undated; Moberg, 2011). The supposed tri-partite nature of man is illustrated in the Bible quotation, 'And the God of peace Himself sanctify you completely, and your whole [being]; the spirit and the soul and the body be kept blameless in the presence of our Lord Jesus Christ' (1 Thess. 5:23). However, spirit and soul are often conflated, with both being claimed as the essence of life, or the immaterial part of 'man', which survives death (in Oxford and Webster Dictionaries). For example, according to Moberg, 'Spirit and its overlapping concept of soul refer primarily to the whole person…that can be interpreted as consisting of body, mind, and spirit or soul' (2011). Some even conflate spirit with mind (Helminiak, 1996; Newberg et al., 2001; Seybold, 2005). It appears that the spirit can impact the mind, or at least the brain, as 'different aspects of spirituality may be mapped in different neural regions' (Urgesi et al., 2010). Pandya's review of brain, mind and soul concludes, 'The mind and soul remain fascinating enigmas. Whilst we have made some progress in our understanding of these two hazy constituents of life, much is yet poorly understood' (2011). Going one step further, 'A growing body of empirical evidence suggests that human consciousness…is not confined to specific points in space, such as brains and bodies [and that] nonlocal consciousness and spirituality are seen as a complementary dyad' (Dossey, 2014).

Although it is difficult for some people to distinguish between spirit and soul, one Christian model proposes that soul (the seat of human personality) comprises conscious mind (thinking and reasoning), unconscious mind (will and emotions) together with beliefs, attitudes, feelings and memories (Copeland, undated). Hebrews 4:12 states that spirit and soul can be separated or divided as they are separate entities (Word of God …dividing…soul and spirit) (Hagin, undated). Although these scriptures identify separate aspects of our human being we are integrated wholes, made complete in Christ (Colossians 2:10) from a Christian perspective.

What does the spirit influence first – the *heart* (spirit) or the head (mind)? Berryman (1990) provided a thought-provoking view to help answer this question: When people have a tangible spiritual experience, words often fail them, as they just sense 'the larger presence to our being and knowing' (e.g., John Wesley's heart strangely warmed (Graves, undated) which 'causes us to draw in our breath' (Berryman, 1990). The experience causes a silent inspiration, followed by the response, a 'sigh of ecstasy ('AHH!')…which helps us uncover the deepest integration of self' (ibid. p. 531). Following this sigh, 'a sense of discovery ('AHA!') introduces us to the possibility of reflection on the experience' (ibid.). This could lead to a narrative or 'master story'. The accompanying sense of knowing, which comes from inspiration, is etched at the very core (French '*coeur*'), or heart of our being. Such a connection with God can lead to 'cosmic laughter' ('HAHA!') which 'marks awareness of a paradox, which stimulates the imagination to recover what is no longer present to it in experience' (ibid.). Berryman's narrative posits mental understanding as the rear guard, or interpreter of the event, rather than the instigator. As such, the language used to describe outcomes of spiritual, with subsequent mental, experiences should be moderated in recognition that human beings are integrated wholes, not compartmentalised or fragmented parts. Mind is the last place to recognise and interpret the impact of spirit on humans. As we are holistic beings, spirit and soul (thus mind) interact with each other and the body. Eastern philosophies take this holistic notion of human beings further by considering relationship with their environment (Chan et al., 2001).

There appears to be a heightening in the battle for hearts (spirits) and minds of the populace, between two extremes. The battle lines are not clearly divided by religion and science. Rather, it is discussion of contrasting views of theism and atheism (naturalism), which has been the subject of many books over the last two centuries (more recently by Dawkins, 2006; McGrath, 2007; Hawking & Mlodinow, 2010; Lennox, 2011). Theism goes beyond science to explain how perceived order is possible in the universe. Theism states that the universe is not self-generating, causing its own effect (Lennox, 2009, pp.63-4); it was made by a pre-existent, personal God, not some impersonal force that condensed itself into matter. Naturalists have their theories and laws, which by themselves cannot bring anything into existence. People believe what they want to believe, and this has consequences for their actions (York, 2012). Many people try to sit on the fence between theism and atheism, but that position becomes rather untenable. The New Atheists, such as Dawkins and Hitchens, not only want to deny that God exists, they want to eradicate any mention of, or allegiance to, Him (Lennox, 2009). So, they should really be called anti-theists.

One psychologist proposes that transcendence, going beyond the rational, is an ego experience rather than a metaphysical statement (Mirman, 2012). Countering this position, Hanfstingl (2013) argues that ego-transcendence is a kind of spiritual experience that contrasts with mystical experience, which itself involves spiritual transcendence and perception of divinity. Others are more subtly attempting to 'bracket out God' from psychology of spirituality by seeking removal of 'God and other non-falsifiable meta-physical entities or constructs from 'truly scientific study' (Helminiak, 2008). But, science is not the arbiter of truth. However, psychologists find ways of studying intelligence and personality, which are reflections of underlying states of humanity, not directly observable entities. In like manner, spirituality can be studied by its outcomes or effects on people. Some researchers are investigating a theistic approach to psychology to complement the more traditional secular approaches normally undertaken, in recognition that 'theists make up the vast majority of psychology's clientele', at least in the USA (Slife et al., 2012). In summary, then, science explains to a limited extent. To think not constitutes 'scientism' or absolute *faith* in science. Science cannot explain why anything happens, but, God explains why science explains. 'God is not an alternative to science as an explanation....He is the ground of all explanation ... whether scientific, or not' (Lennox, 2009, p. 48).

New Physics seems to be presenting a challenge to God, although not front-on. Shelton proposes, 'Quantum Skills are premised on the assumption that the quantum realm of energy is primary or causal and the material world is secondary' (2010, p. 165). These quantum skills supposedly provide humans with the ability to see intentionally, to think paradoxically, to feel vitally alive, to know intuitively, to act responsibly, to trust life's processes, and to be in relationship. However, no source of these skills is stated. Further detail in Shelton's paper concurs with recent thoughts by positive psychologist, Seligman, who effectively suggested that we make ourselves like god by use of our minds (2014). Some Transhumanists have a similar goal of transforming humans, but by use of technology and genetic manipulation, to attain immortality (Wikipedia, 12/05/14). However, Christians already have the promise of immortality. John 3:16 (NIV) states, 'For God so loved the world that He gave His one and only Son, that whoever believes in Him, shall not perish but have *eternal life'* [italics added for emphasis]. The battle for hearts and heads continues.

1.4. Spirituality

Considerable debate about the nature of spirituality has taken place for centuries. However, writers have had difficulty defining the concept (Goodloe & Arreola, 1992; Diaz, 1993; Seaward, 2001; Moberg, 2010). A conciliatory approach claims that agnostics and atheists can express a form of spirituality without God (Mohr, 2006). In contrast to this and the above views of New Physics, positive psychology and Transhumanism, Waaijman contends, 'spirituality appears as a complex whole, constructed out of elements which are complementarily interrelated. Spirituality is a relational process which constitutes an original whole in which God and man [who was made by God in His image] are reciprocally related' (2006, p.14). However, not all people agree with Waaijman that God is essentially involved in spirituality. Views have changed over time.

According to Principe (1983), historically speaking, spirituality was based on the Latin concept of '*spiritualitas*', which was not found in literature earlier than the fifth Century (C5th). Early comments on the Apostle Paul's writings posit the spiritual nature of a person being ordered, led and influenced by the Spirit of God. For Paul, being spiritual meant following the ways of Christ rather than the ways of man. Paul's ideas on spirituality held sway within Christian belief until around C12th, when there was a change in its meaning from a moral sense to an entitative-psychological sense, in which people began to despise the body. By C17th the word *spiritualité* (French) had been taken over by the Catholic Church and used as ecclesiastical property in the religious sense of a 'devout life', in contrast to physical property of the monarch, which was regarded as *temporalitas* (of this world, secular). In France, during the latter C18th and C19th, as the word 'spirituality' was used pejoratively, it fell into disuse until the early C20th, when it became frequently used once again, being linked to the soul in opposition to the body, in a bi-partite view of man. In English, a religious or devotional sense of 'spirituality' continued until the early C20th, when the term was appropriated by Hinduism to illustrate the superiority of Indian religion over Western 'materialism'. Thus, from a Western perspective, the original usage of the term spirituality was steeped in religion.

With increasing secularisation of the West, significant changes since the 1960s have seen 'spirituality acquire more distinct meanings [being seen as] separate from religion' (Turner et al., 1995). With attendant 'increasing individualism in American religious culture…new spiritual practices are evolving' (Zinnbauer et al., 1999). A diversity of different forms of spirituality that are arising is not often encountered in an explicitly religious domain, but rather in a secular context (Heelas & Woodhead, 2005).

A variety of opinion currently prevails on the nature of any relationship between spirituality and religion. Some people equate 'spirituality' with 'religious activity', or use these words interchangeably (Piedmont, 2001; Gorsuch & Walker, 2006), whereas others believe this stance is not valid (Banks et al., 1984; Scott, 2006). Some people discuss commonalities between spirituality and religion, as well as differences (Hill et al., 2000). Although spirituality and religiosity are often used interchangeably, they are distinct, yet overlapping, constructs. Three polarising views are held by some behavioural scientists, differentiating spirituality and religion (Zinnbauer et al., 1999). Some social scientists argue that spirituality is subsumed by religion (Hill et al., 2000), whereas others see religion as one dimension of spirituality (Nolan & Crawford, 1997). The view that 'religiosity can but does not necessarily include spirituality' (Gough et al., 2010) is countered by one that claims, 'Outstanding spiritual leaders developed most religions' (Hay et al., 2006). Rather simplistically speaking, Horsburgh (1997) maintains that religion focuses on ideology and rules of faith and belief systems, whereas spirituality focuses on experience and relationships which go beyond religion (Lukoff et al., 1992). This simplistic view is rejected by many (Martsolf & Mickley, 1998; Benson, 2004; Hay et al., 2006). In a recent study 'using a large sample of American adults, analyses demonstrate that subjective spirituality and tradition-oriented religiousness are empirically highly independent' (Saucier et al., 2006), suggesting divergence between the two constructs. A close inspection of the instruments used in that study is warranted to see how much confidence can be placed in the findings. In contrast to this view of divergence, Schneiders (2003) contends, 'some see religion and spirituality as two dimensions of a single enterprise…often in tension but are essential to each other and constitute, together, a single reality….as partners in the search for God.'

'A relationship [of people] to the sacred *or* transcendent' [my italics] is included in many definitions of spirituality (Sinnott, 2001; Hyman & Handal, 2006). Taking this broader view, Seaward asserts that spirituality involves 'connection to a divine source whatever we call it' (2001). But, spirituality does not have to include 'God-talk' according to Jose and Taylor (1986). A number of authors have followed this latter, humanistic line of thinking by attempting to define secular spirituality as a spirituality without any need for a religious/God component (Harvey, 1996; Newby, 1996). Understandably, many Christian writers raise arguments against removing religion and God from discussions of spirituality (Smith, 2000; Wright, 2000).

Abraham Maslow, claimed by many to be the father of humanistic psychology, and John Dewey, a founder of the philosophical school of Pragmatism, both consider spirituality to be part of a person's being, and therefore prior to and different from religiosity (Fahlberg & Fahlberg, 1991). Many supporters of the notion of evolutionary psychology fail to distinguish between 'spiritual awareness as a natural phenomenon [i.e., innate] and religion as a belief system', which is enculturated through family, education and community (Brown, 1978).

A wide range of descriptions and classifications of spirituality can be found in relevant literature. From his review of literature, Spilka (1993) proposed three categories of spirituality oriented towards (i) God, (ii) the world, or (iii) people. Marty (1997) reduced this classification even further by naming two prominent orientations of spiritual wellness as (i) theocentric (God-centred), and (ii) nontheocentric. According to Cohen et al. (2012), Larson and colleagues (1998) identified 10 general domains of religion and spirituality. Zinnbauer, Pargament and Scott (1999) conducted content analysis of 40 definitions of spirituality and 31 of religiousness, which yielded 9 content categories. Hill and Hood (1999) reviewed 125 measures of religion and spirituality which they placed in 17 different categories. Moberg (2010) reported that eight of these measures included 'spiritual' in their titles, and others would now be considered as measures of spirituality. Koenig et al. (2001) proposed five types of spirituality, (i) humanistic, with no reference to any higher power, (ii) unmoored, with focus on energy, connection, nature; and moored spirituality, (iii) Eastern, or Western, (iv) evangelical or (v) conservative. From a casual survey of literature, Moberg (2011) listed more than 20 'subcategories and types of spirituality, each reflecting a specialized range of perspectives'.

Therefore, it is not surprising to note that nearly every paper on spirituality/spiritual well-being states there is no agreed definition of these terms. Although that is so, and spirituality/spiritual well-being cannot be observed directly, most are agreed that they involve relationships. Many have mentioned a number of commonalities or potential areas of focus for these relationships, which, when present, illustrate or reflect healthy spirituality or spiritual well-being (Hyland, Wheeler, Kamble & Masters, 2010).

1.5. Spiritual Well-Being

The term 'spiritual well-being' (SWB) appears to have first been mentioned at the 1971 White House Conference on Aging (Moberg, 2010). Subsequent establishment of the National Interfaith Coalition on Aging (NICA) led to its 'working definition', namely that, 'Spiritual well-being is the affirmation of life in relationship with God, self, community and environment that nurtures and celebrates wholeness' (NICA, 1975). Many subsequent descriptions of SWB have consistently referred to these four notions. For example, in highlighting the centrality of relationships in these four areas, Waaijman states, 'Spirituality unfolds itself as the unity of the divine-human, interhuman, human-cosmic, and intrahuman relationships' (2007). However, not all researchers address all four areas. For example, Rovers and Kocum's (2010) definition of spirituality as 'Faith, hope and love' excluded mention of nature/environment, thus denying, or at least diminishing, spiritual reality for many indigenous peoples and most people with Eastern philosophies or environmental sensitivities.

Although 'spiritual well-being' was only proposed as a concept 40 years ago, the influence of spirit on health has been discussed from at least Hippocrates' time, around 400BC (Adams, 1939), as well as in Chinese medicine. In a similar vein, psychology, as a study of mind and behaviour, dates back to Ancient Greece, but psychology, as an independent scientific discipline only originated in the 1870s. A German, Johann Christian Reil, is reported to be the first person to use the term Psychiatry, derived from psych- and -iatry, to mean 'medical treatment of the soul', in 1808 (Wikipedia, 12/5/14). Therefore, close relationships between spiritual and mental aspects of health have been known for a considerable time. An American psychiatrist, Harold Koenig, has made comments to the effect that the concept of spiritual well-being has *contaminated* current research into relationships between mental and physical health (2008, 2012). Such comments should be ameliorated in light of the historical connections between psychology, psychiatry and spirituality mentioned. A focus on holistic well-being could be said to comprise spiritual-psycho-social-biophysical aspects of people as integrated wholes, not fragmented parts. I have deliberately re-ordered the components to challenge thinking about the relative importance of each factor of health, in contrast to the standard view which places the biophysical before the psycho-social, with spiritual being considered in last place, if at all (e.g., Sulmasy, 2002).

A conception of spiritual health posits that it is 'a, if not *the*, fundamental dimension of people's overall health and well-being, permeating and integrating all the other dimensions of health (i.e., physical, mental, emotional, social and vocational). Spiritual health is a dynamic state of being, shown by the extent to which people live in harmony within relationships in up to four domains of spiritual well-being' (from Fisher, 1998, p. 181), namely with themselves in the Personal domain, with other people in the Communal domain, with nature in the

Environmental domain, and/or with something or some-One beyond the human and natural world, in the Transcendental domain.

This working definition laid the foundation for the development of the Four Domains Model of Spiritual Health/Well-Being. In this model, nearly all descriptors that refer to self and to others are clearly stated, whereas the words 'environment' and 'nature' are used interchangeably. The fourth area, relationship with a Transcendent (commonly called God) is the one in which researchers use a diversity of terms depending on their worldviews. This model delves beneath the surface of labels to interrogate the structure of four domains shown in literature to be key components of spiritual health/well-being. This model can be represented pictorially as, shown in Figure 1.

	FOUR DOMAINS OF SPIRITUAL WELL-BEING			
	PERSONAL	COMMUNAL	ENVIRONMENTAL	TRANSCENDENTAL
Knowledge component - filtered by beliefs *Inspirational component - essence & motivation* - filtered by worldview	meaning, purpose, and values - human spirit creates - *self-awareness*	morality, culture (and religion) - *in-depth inter-personal relations* - reaching the heart of humanity	care, nurture and stewardship of the physical, eco-political and social environment *connectedness with Nature*/Creation	Transcendent Other - ultimate concern Tillich - cosmic force New Age - God, for theists *Faith*
Expressed as	- joy, - peace, - patience - identity, - self-worth	- love - forgiveness - justice - hope & faith in humanity - trust	- sense of awe and wonder - valuing Nature/ Creation	adoration & worship, being: - at one with Creator - in tune with God

Figure 1. Four Domains Model of Spiritual Health & Well-being.

The more I read, the more I find this model captures the views expressed by authors on spirituality and well-being.

For example, the claim that the *Inspirational component* of each domain, which can be considered as small t transcendent *essence* and *motivation* that can be experienced by people, is filtered by worldview, concurs with a statement by Sire, 'A worldview is a commitment, a fundamental orientation of the heart, that can be expressed as a story or in a set of presuppositions that we hold about the basic constitution of reality, and that provides the foundation on which we live and move and have our being' (2009, p.20).

Waaijman expresses a similar sentiment in a quote from philosopher Theo de Boer, 'One of the four pillars of scholarly research is inspiration: what animates and orientates human thought? Imagination, reasoning, and experience are not enough.

A truth-loving mind is not content with the so called 'reality' or 'horizons' or 'categories'.

The ultimate question is: what is this really? To what is this leading? What gives direction to these perceptions, constructions and argumentations?' (2007, p. 105).

There does not appear to be any expression of a worldview that does not fit the four domains model. Put more positively, this model of spiritual health/well-being appears to encompass the vast majority of, if not all, worldviews.

The two components of each of the four domains in Figure 1 work synergistically, relating to, while building up, each other. Neither knowledge, as cognitive construct, nor inspiration, as essence and motivation, can be seen or measured directly. However, expressions of their effect can be measured. This four domains model provided the solid theoretical framework upon which the Spiritual Health And Life-Orientation Measure (SHALOM) was built (Fisher, 1998).

A selection of 48 items was made from the model depicted in Figure 1. Exploratory Factor Analyses were used to select the best five items for each of the four domains.

The resultant items in the four *domains* of SWB in SHALOM relate to developing: 'sense of identity, self-awareness, joy in life, inner peace and meaning in life' for *Personal* SWB; 'love of other people, forgiveness toward others, trust between individuals, respect for others, kindness toward others' for *Communal* SWB; 'connection with nature, awe at a breathtaking view, oneness with nature, harmony with the environment and a sense of 'magic' in the environment' for *Environmental* SWB; relationship with the Divine/God, worship of the Creator, oneness with God, peace with God and prayer life' for *Transcendental* SWB.

Some studies, other than those using SHALOM, have also employed this model as the basis for research in spirituality (Francis & Robbins, 2005; 2012; Hughes, 2007).

1.6. Spirituality/Well-Being Measures

Publications abound with authors' personal beliefs about the relevance of God to spiritual well-being (see above), but very little hard evidence has been systematically supplied to support the plethora of divergent views. From a Western historical perspective, the term 'spirituality' was embedded in the confines of religion up to the start of the 20th Century, but now applies to broad contemporary views within and without religion. Compendiums of religiosity measures have been compiled by Hill and Hood (1999) and Koenig et al. (2001; 2011). However, only instruments that focussed on spirituality have been included in this chapter. Those with a focus on religion were excluded because the thrust of my research is on the importance of relating with God for *spiritual* well-being, not *religious* well-being. As most instruments which clearly focus on religion would be expected to show some concern about relating with God, this would skew the results of my studies.

Authors' views on what they consider important for spirituality/well-being are reflected in their choice of items included in any instrument or measure that they develop (Moberg, 2002). Three types of spirituality measures are found in literature:

- Those that focus on spiritual health, wellbeing or wellness (SH/WB)
- Those with specific mention of spirituality, and
- Related/partial spirituality measures (reflecting key aspects of the four domains model of SH/WB. These measures do not often employ a 'spirituality' label).

It is not possible for measures with only one, or even up to four, items to comprehensively cover four domains of spiritual health and well-being. In line with comments by Sloan et al. (2002), I decided that this multifaceted construct would best be measured with multidimensional, multi-item instruments. In my previous work, 169 multidimensional measures were described (Fisher, 2009, chapter 3). Further data-mining using 'spiritual*' with 'measure' and 'assess*' has revealed another 91 instruments that fit similar criteria. There are probably more measures available in literature worldwide, but these are the only ones that were readily accessible to me.

Table 1. Percentage composition of instruments in four domains of spirituality/ well-being

Instrument type	year	No.	Per wb	Com swb	Env swb	Tra swb	Relig.
Spiritual/	<2000	15	100	67	13	73	27
Health/	2000-5	8	100	63	75	75	17
Well-being	2006+	16	94	63	25	50	31
	total	39	97	64	28	64	26
	<2000	32	88	66	25	72	47
Spirituality	2000-5	55	76	49	11	55	49
	2006+	50	80	54	22	48	44
	total	136	80	55	18	56	46
Related/	<2000	32	91	56	13	19	22
Partial swb	2000-5	27	78	44	19	22	30
	2006+	23	78	26	9	39	35
	total	82	83	44	13	26	27
	<2000	79	91	62	19	51	33
ALL	2000-5	90	91	49	21	47	39
	2006+	89	82	49	18	46	38
	TOTAL	258*	88	53	18	47	37

NB * 2 undated, Per = Personal, Com = Communal, Env = Environmental, Tra = Transcendental spiritual well-being Relig = religious items.

A total of 260 multi-item spirituality/well-being measures are reported elsewhere in this book (chapter by author). These have been roughly divided into three groups in order to ascertain if any change in emphasis is present in the spirituality instruments developed over time. By the end of the 20th century, 79 pertinent measures had been reported. In the first five years of the 21st century, increasing interest in spirituality saw a further 90 instruments developed. Literature searches from 2006 to 2014 revealed another 86 newly-reported spirituality measures.

The percentage of instruments with three or more items per domain is shown in Table 1, for the three types of spirituality/well-being measures described above. Particular emphasis will be given here to the Transcendental domain, with cursory comments on religious items. Items in the instruments that referred to beliefs were categorised as either 'religious' or 'other'. Spirituality is taken to be reflected in respondents' quality of relationships, so an assessment of their lived experience is required, not just their beliefs. For example, belief in

God is a religious attitude, that may or may not result in any form of relationship with God, as even the devil 'believes' in God.

Some interesting trends were noted over time:

Personal SWB - Bregman claimed, 'The individual in his/her freedom and quest for meaning is now the *whole* focus of the concept of 'spirituality'' [my italics] (2012).

However, focus on the Personal domain of spiritual well-being for the range of instruments has dropped slightly over time, but it is still greater than for the other three domains of Communal, Environmental and Transcendental spiritual well-being.

Communal SWB – A similar percentage of Communal and Transcendental spiritual well-being factors are present over time in the spirituality/well-being measures.

Environmental SWB – apart from an influx of instruments based on the four domains model, reported in 2000-05, only one in five instruments address environmental issues for spiritual well-being. Transcendental SWB – Spiritual health/well-being measures developed since 2006 show a marked decline in percentage of instruments assessing relationship with a Transcendent (e.g., God); a drop from three quarters to half. This reducing trend had been noticed by Chiu et al. (2004). A decline of similar magnitude has taken place in spirituality measures from 2000 to the present time. Counter to this downward trend, related /partial measures of spirituality revealed an increase in assessment of relationships with a Transcendent over the last 40 years. However, even now, less than half of these instruments contain assessments of relationship with a Transcendent.

1.7. Importance of Relating with God for Spiritual Well-Being

The above trends in spirituality/well-being are of particular interest as they highlight the variations among researchers who are developing new scales. These trends raise questions as to whether researchers in spirituality are building on their own worldviews or focussing on the perceived needs or lived experiences of people being studied by means of their instruments. The marked divergence of worldviews and noticeable variations in measures of spirituality/well-being identified here lays the foundation for a primary research question which investigated, 'How important is relating with God (or Transcendent) for spiritual well-being?' Meta-analyses of 32 studies with approximately 15000 people revealed that, of the four sets of relationships assessed using SHALOM, relating with God is most important for spiritual well-being (Fisher, 2012). More recent analyses of 52 studies with 41686 people from 27 countries have reinforced this finding (Fisher, 2014a). Investigations with SHALOM and another measure of spiritual well-being, developed with a broad range of Australian students, also showed that relating with God is the most influential of four relationships which reflect SWB (Fisher, 2013a). Evidence presented from a study with a generic form of SHALOM revealed that it looks like you can't beat relating with God for spiritual well-being (Fisher, 2013b). 'Those who claim non-theistic Transcendents, such as fate, higher self and higher power, as their motivating forces in life show…less spiritual well-being' compared with those who relate with God (Fisher 2014b). This study also reported that relating with God helps people relate better with themselves and others, compared with the influence of other Transcendents.

CONCLUSION

Alternative worldviews are generally closely held truth claims, beliefs or opinions. No empirical studies had been identified that reported evidence comparing the importance of relating with God, with that of another three sets of relationships, for spiritual well-being until the recent study reported above (ibid.). Relating with God facilitates relationship with self and others to a significant extent, which relating with other Transcendents fails to do. These results indicate that, although each person has the right to choose what seems important to them, not all views are of equal value in practice. Therefore, contrary to the declining inclusion of God in studies of spirituality/well-being, relating with God must be included as an option in all future studies, otherwise the key component thereof is excluded.

REFERENCES

Adams, F. (1939). *The Genuine Works of Hippocrates*, trans. from the Greek (Aphorisms, I.1). London, UK: Bailliere, Tindall & Cox, p. 299.

Banks, R., Poehler, D. & Russell, R. (1984). Spirit and human-spiritual interaction as a factor in health and health education. *Health Education, 15*(5), 16-19.

Bartholomew, B. (2014). *The Spiritual Genome.* North Hollywood, CA.: Timeline Publishing Inc.

Benson, P.L. (2004) Emerging themes in research on adolescent spiritual and religious development. *Applied Developmental Science, 8,* 47-50.

Berryman, J.W. (1990). Teaching as presence and the existential curriculum. *Religious Education, 85*(4), 509-534.

Bregman, L. (2012). Spirituality definitions: A moving target. In *Spirituality: Theory Praxis and Pedagogy.* Edited by Martin Fowler, John D. Martin III, and John L. Hochheimer. Oxford, UK: Inter-Disciplinary Press, pp. 4–10.

Brown, I. (1978). Exploring the spiritual dimension of school health education. *Eta Sigma Gamman, 10,* 12-16.

Chan, C., Ho, Petula S.Y. & Chow, E. (2001). A Body-Mind-Spirit Model in health: An eastern approach. *Social Work Health and Mental Health, 34*(3 /4), 261-282.

Chiu, L. Emblen, J. D.,Van Hofwegen, L., Sawatzky, R. & Meyerhoff, H. (2004). An integrative review of the concept of spirituality in the health sciences. *Western Journal of Nursing Research, 26*, 405-428.

Chown, M. (2012). In the beginning. *New Scientist* 216, Issue 2893, 02624079, 12/1/2012.

Cohen, M. Z., Holley, L. M., Wengel, S.P. & Katzman. M. (2012). A platform for nursing research on spirituality and religiosity: Definitions and measures. *Western Journal of Nursing Research, 34*(6), 795-817.

Copeland, K. (undated). Kenneth Copeland Ministries. Understanding the Soul. Retrieved on 15 April 2014 from http://www.kcm.org/print/real-help/article/understanding-soul

Dawkins, R. (2006). *The God Delusion.* New York: Houghton Mifflin.

Diaz, D.P. (1993). Foundations for spirituality: Establishing the viability of spirituality within the health disciplines. *Journal of Health Education, 24,* 324-326.

Dossey, L. (2014). Spirituality and nonlocal mind: A necessary dyad. *Spirituality in Clinical Practice, 1*(1), 29-42.

Encyclopaedia Britannica. (2013). Retrieved on 10 June 2014 from http://www.britannica.com/EBcheckedtopic/124443/cogito-ergo-sum

Fahlberg, L. L., & Fahlberg, L.A. (1991). Exploring spirituality and consciousness with an expanded science: Beyond the ego with empiricism, phenomenology, and contemplation. *American Journal of Health Promotion*, *5*(4), 273-281.

Fisher, J. W. (1998). *Spiritual health: Its nature and place in the school curriculum.* PhD thesis, University of Melbourne. Available online https://minerva-access.unimelb.edu.au/handle/11343/39206

Fisher, J. W. (2009). *Reaching the heart: Assessing and nurturing spiritual well-being via education.* EdD dissertation, University of Ballarat, Victoria, Australia. Available online http://researchonline.federation.edu.au:8080/vital/ access/HandleResolver/1959.17/42221

Fisher, J.W. (2012) The importance of relating with God for spiritual well-being. In *Spirituality: New Reflections on Theory Praxis and Pedagogy.* Edited by Martin Fowler, Michael Weiss, and John L. Hochheimer. Oxford, UK: Inter-Disciplinary Press, pp. 147-161.

Fisher, J. W. (2013a). Assessing spiritual well-being: Relating with God explains greatest variance in spiritual well-being among Australian youth. *International Journal of Children's Spirituality, 18*(4), 306-317.

Fisher, J. W. (2013b) You can't beat relating with God for spiritual well-being: Comparing a generic version with the original spiritual well-being questionnaire called SHALOM. *Religions, 4*(3), 325-335.

Fisher, J. W. (2014a). *Importance of relating with God for spiritual well-being.* PhD dissertation, Federation University Australia. Available from:http://researchonline.federation.edu.au:8080/vital/access/HandleResolver/1959.17/73747

Fisher, J. W. (2014b). Comparing the influence of God and other Transcendents on spiritual well-being. *Religious Education Journal of Australia, 30*(2), 9-15.

Francis, L. J. & Robbins, M. (2005). *Urban Hope and Spiritual Health: The Adolescent Voice.* Peterborough, UK: Epworth.

Francis, L. J., Penny, G. & Baker, S. (2012). Defining and assessing spiritual health: A comparative study among 13- to 15-year old pupils attending secular schools, Anglican schools, and private Christian schools in England and Wales. *Peabody Journal of Education, 87*(3), 351-367.

Geisler, N. & Turek, F. (2004). *I Don't Have Enough Faith to be an Atheist.* Wheaton, IL: Crossway Books.

Goodloe, R. & Arreola, P. (1992). Spiritual health: Out of the closet. *Health Education, 23*, 221-226.

Gorsuch, R. L. & Walker, S.E. (2006). Measurement and research design in studying spiritual development. In *Handbook of Spiritual Development in Childhood and Adolescence.* Edited by E.C. Roehlkepartain, P.E. King, L.M. Wagener & P.L. Benson. Thousand Oaks, CA: Sage Publications, pp. 92-103.

Gough, H. R., Wilks, S.E. & Prattini, R.J. (2010). Spirituality among Alzheimer's caregivers: Psychometric reevaluation of the Intrinsic Spirituality Scale. *Journal of Social Science Research, 36*, 278-288.

Graves, D. (undated). John Wesley's heart strangely warmed. Retrieved on 7 May 2014 from http://christianity.com/church/church-history/timeline/1701-1800/john-wesleys-heart-strangely-warmed

Hagin, K. W. (undated). The dividing of soul and spirit. Retrieved on 15 April 2014 from http://www.rhema.org/index.php?option_content&view=article &id=274:the-dividing-of-soul-and-spirit

Hanfstingl, B. (2013). Ego and Spiritual Transcendence: Relevance to psychological resilience and the role of age. *Evidence-Based Complementary and Alternative Medicine* 2013, article ID 949838. http://dx.doi.org/10.1155/2013/949838

Harvey, C. L. (1996). *The role of the soul.* A paper presented at 'Whose Values?', the Third Annual Conference on "Education, Spirituality and the Whole Child", Roehampton Institute, London, June.

Hawking, S. & Mlodinow, L. (2010). *The Grand Design.* London: Bantam Press.

Hay, D., Reich, K.H. & Utsch, M. (2006). Spiritual development: Intersections and divergence with religious development. In *The Handbook of Spiritual Development in Childhood and Adolescence.* Edited by E.C. Roehlkepartain, P.E. King, L.M. Wagener & P.L. Benson. Thousand Oaks, CA, USA: Sage Publications, pp. 46-59.

Heelas, P. & Woodhead, L. (2005). *The Spiritual Revolution: Why religion is giving way to spirituality.* Oxford, UK: Blackwell.

Helminiak, D. (1996). *The Human Core of Spirituality: Mind as Psyche and Spirit.* Albany, NY: State University of New York Press.

Helminiak, D. A. (2008). Confounding the Divine and the Spiritual: Challenges to a Psychology of Spirituality. *Pastoral Psychology, 57*, 161-182.

Hill, P. C. & Hood, R.W. (Eds.) (1999). *Measures of Religiosity.* Birmingham, Alabama: Religious Education Press.

Hill, P.C., Pargament, K.I., Hood, R.W., McCullough, J.P., Swyers, D.B., Larson, D.B. & Zinnbauer, B.J. (2000). Conceptualizing religion and spirituality: Points of commonality, points of departure. *Journal for the Theory of Social Behavior, 30*(1), 51-77.

Horsburgh, M. (1997). Towards an inclusive spirituality: Wholeness, interdependence and waiting. *Disability and Rehabilitation, 19*(10), 398-406.

Hughes, P. (2007). *Putting Life Together: Findings from Australian Youth Spirituality Research.* Melbourne: CRA/Fairfield Press.

Hyland, M.E., Wheeler, P., Kamble, S. & Masters K.S. (2010). A sense of 'Special Connection', self-transcendent values and a common factor for religious and non-religious spirituality. *Archive for the Psychology of Religion, 32*, 293-326.

Hyman, C. & Handal, P.J. (2006). Definitions and evaluation of religion and spirituality by religious professionals: A pilot study. *Journal of Religion and Health, 45*(2), 264-282.

Jewish Encyclopedia. (2002). Book of Adam. Retrieved on 30 May 2014 from http://www.jewishencyclopedia.com/articles/759-adam-book-of

Jo, K. (2005). *A threefold relational approach to spiritual maturity: An exploratory study of Korean evangelical spirituality.* Dissertation Abstracts International, Section B: Hum. Soc Sci Vol 66(3-A), p.1042.

Jose, N. & Taylor, E. (1986). Spiritual health: A look at barriers to its inclusion in the health education curriculum. *The Eta Sigma Gamman, 18*(2), 16-19.

Koenig, H. G. (2008). Concerns about measuring "Spirituality" in research. *The Journal of Nervous and Mental Disease, 196*(5), 349-355.

Koenig, H. G. (2011). *Spirituality & Health Research: Methods, measurement, statistics and resources.* West Conshohocken, PA, USA: Templeton Press.

Koenig, H. G., McCullough, M.E. & Larson, D.B. (Eds.) (2001). *Handbook of Religion and Health.* Oxford: Oxford University Press.

Koenig, H. G., King, D. A. & Carson, V.B. (2012). *Handbook of Religion and Health.* 2nd ed. New York: Oxford University Press.

Larson, D. B., Swyers, J.P. & McCullough, M.E. (Eds). (1998). *Scientific research on spirituality and health: A consensus report.* Rockville, MD: National Institute for Healthcare Research.

Lennox, J.C. (2009). *God's Undertaker: Has science buried God?* rev. ed. Oxford, UK: Lion Books.

Lennox, J.C. (2011). God and Stephen Hawking: Whose design is it anyway? Oxford, UK: Lion Books.

Lukoff, D., Lu, F., Turner, R. (1992). Toward a more culturally sensitive DSM-IV. Psychoreligious and psychospiritual problems. *The Journal of Nervous and Mental Disease, 180*(11), 673-682.

McGrath, A. (2007). *The Dawkins Delusion?* London: SPCK Publishing.

Martsolf, D. S. & Mickley, J. R. (1998). The concept of spirituality in nursing theories: Differing world-views and extent of focus. *Journal of Advanced Nursing, 27,* 294-303.

Marty, M. (1997). Designed to be imprecise. *Aging and Spirituality, 9*(1), 3.

Mirman, M. C. (2012). An atheist's guide to the divine: Throwing out the bathwater but keeping the baby. *Research in the Social Scientific Study of Religion, 23*, 171-189.

Moberg, D. O. (2002). Assessing and measuring spirituality: Confronting dilemmas of universal and particular evaluative criteria. *Journal of Adult Development, 9*(1), 47-60.

Moberg, D. O. (2010). Spirituality research: Measuring the immeasurable? *Perspectives on Science and Christian Faith, 62*(2), 99-114.

Moberg, D. O. (2011). Expanding horizons for spirituality research. Retrieved on 15 October 2013 from http://hirr.hartsem.edu/sociology/spirituality-research.html

Mohr, W. K. (2006). Spiritual issues in Psychiatric Care. *Perspectives in Psychiatric Care, 42*(3), 174-183.

Morris H.M. (1984). *The Genesis Record: A scientific and devotional commentary on the book of beginnings*. Grand Rapids, MI: Baker House Books.

National Interfaith Coalition on Aging (NICA) (1975). *Spiritual well-being: A definition.* Athens, Georgia: Author. *Biology of Belief.* New York: Ballantine Books.

Newby, M. (1996). Towards a secular concept of spiritual maturity. In *Education, Spirituality and the Whole Child.* Edited by Ron Best. London: Cassell, pp. 99-107.

Nolan, P. & Crawford. P. (1997). Towards a rhetoric of spirituality in mental health care. *Journal of Advanced Nursing, 26*, 289-294.

Pandya, S. K. (2011). Understanding brain, mind and soul: Contributions from neurology and neurosurgery. *Mens Sana Monographs* 9(1) 129-149. Retrieved on 15 April 2014 from http://www.ncbi.nlm.nih.gov/pmc/articles/PMC3115284/

Piedmont, R. L. (2001). Spiritual transcendence and scientific study of spirituality. *Journal of Rehabilitation, 67*(1), 4-14.

Principe, W. (1983). Toward defining *spirituality. Studies in Religion, 12,* 127–41.

Rovers, M. & Kocum, L. (2010). Development of a Holistic Model of Spirituality. *Journal of Spirituality in Mental Health, 12*(1), 2-24.

Saucier, G. & Skrzypińska, K. (2006). Spiritual but not religious? Evidence for two independent dispositions. *Journal of Personality*, *74*(5), 1257-1292.

Schaeffer, F. (1972). *Genesis in Space and Time: The flow of Biblical History.* Downers Grove, IL: InterVarsity Press.

Schneiders, S. M. (2003). Religion vs. Spirituality: A contemporary conundrum. *Spiritus, 3,* 163-185.

Scott, D. G. (2006). Spirituality and identity within/without religion. In *International Handbook of the Religious, Moral and Spiritual Dimensions in Education.* Edited by Marian de Souza et al. Dordrecht, The Netherlands: Springer, pp. 1111-1125.

Seaward, B. L. (2001). *Health of the Human Spirit: Spiritual Dimensions for Personal Health.* Boston: Allyn and Bacon.

Seligman, M. (2014). God comes at the end. *Spirituality in Clinical Practice, 1*(1), 67-70.

Seybold, K. S. (2005). God and the brain: Neuroscience looks at religion. *Journal of Psychology and Religion, 24*(2), 122-129.

Shelton, S. (2010). Spirituality, mental health and the new physics. *International Journal of Applied Psychoanalytic Studies, 7*(2), 161-171.

Sinnott, J. D. (2001). Introduction: Special Issue on Spirituality and Adult Development, Part 1. *Journal of Adult Development, 8*(4), 199-200.

Sire, J. W. (2009). *The universe next door: A basic worldview catalog 5th ed.* Downers Grove, IL, USA: InterVarsity Press.

Slife, B. D., Reber, J.S. & Lefevor, G.T. (2012). When God truly matters: A theistic approach to psychology. *Research in the Social Scientific Study of Religion 23*, 213-236.

Sloan, J. A., Aaronson, N., Cappelleri, J.C., Fairclough, D.L., Varrichio, C. et al. (2002). Assessing the clinical significance of single items relative to summated scores. *Mayo Clinic Proceedings*, *77*, 479-487.

Smith, D. (2000). Secularism, religion and spiritual development. *Journal of Beliefs & Values, 21*(1), 27-38.

Spilka, B. (1993). Spirituality: Problems and directions in operationalizing a fuzzy concept. Paper presented at the meeting of the American Psychological Association, Toronto, August.

Sulmasy, D. P. (2002). A Biopsychosocial-Spiritual Model for the care of patients at the end of life. *The Gerontologist, 42*(special issue III), 24-33.

Turner, R. P., Lukoff, D., Barnhouse, R.T. & Lu, F.G. (1995). Religious or spiritual problem: A culturally sensitive diagnostic category in the DSM-IV. *Journal of Nervous and Mental Disease, 183,* 435-444.

Urgesi, C., Aglioti, S.M., Skrap, M. & Fabbro, F. (2010). The spiritual brain: Selective cortical lesions modulate human self-transcendence. *Neuron 65*, 309-319.

Waaijman, K. (2006). What is spirituality? *Acta Theologica Supplementum, 8*, 1-18.

Waaijman, K. (2007). Spirituality – A multifaceted phenomenon. *Studies in Spirituality, 17,* 1-113. doi:10.2143/SIS17.0.2024643

Wikipedia. Spiritual evolution. Retrieved on 5 May 2014 from: http://en.wikipedia.org/wiki/Spiritual_evolution

Wikipedia. Timeline of psychiatry. Retrieved on 12 May 2014 from http://en.wikipedia.org/wiki/Timeline_of_psychiatry

Wikipedia. Transhumanism. Retrieved on 12 May 2014 from http://en.wikipedia.org/wiki/Transhumanism

Wright, A. (2000). *Spirituality & Education.* Florence, KY, USA: Taylor & Francis.

York R. H. (2012). The concepts of the indwelling spirit and the self-critic in theistic theory and research. *Research in the Social Scientific Study of Religion 23*, 151-170.

Zinnbauer, B. J., Pargament, K. I. & Scott, A.B. (1999). The emerging meanings of religiousness and spirituality: Problems and prospects. *Journal of Personality, 67*(6), 889-919.

In: Spirituality
Editor: Edith C. Roberts

ISBN: 978-1-63482-370-8

Chapter 8

SPIRITUAL ADVOCACY IN ENGLAND? HOW THE OVERLAPPING ROLES OF CHAPLAINS AND INDEPENDENT ADVOCATES BENEFIT THE MOST VULNERABLE IN SOCIETY

Geoff Morgan*
Imperial College Healthcare NHS Trust, London, UK

ABSTRACT

Against a background of the relative numbers of advocates and chaplains in England, the nature of advocacy practice is considered. Changes in the law through the Mental Capacity Act (2005) (MCA) and the amendments to the Mental Health Act (1983) in 2007- which came into effect respectively in 2007 and 2009- made it a statutory duty in England and Wales for the National Health Service (NHS) and local authorities to refer to advocacy services, both Independent Mental Capacity Advocates (IMCAs) and Independent Mental Health Advocates (IMHAs). The MCA specifically facilitated the involvement of IMCAs in safeguarding adults' procedures and alongside other vulnerable groups, and in relation to Deprivation of Liberty Safeguards matters (DoLS). Both independent advocates and chaplains use advocacy skills, and for IMCAs, social, cultural and spiritual factors are influential. In combining interviews with over 40 advocates, chaplains and service users, and by comparing numbers in the field, I argue that emotion and spirituality should be considered more by advocates as part of their analytical process-audit role. This is also the case for those who are non-standard practitioners of advocacy, and may therefore have an impact in the community. The growth in advocacy coincided with an increase in literature on mental health and spirituality, of which a refreshed faith-based social conscience will want to be aware; the 'rediscovery of the spiritual dimension in health and social care' thus highlighted some shortcomings in the professionalisation of advocacy in relation to these areas, and possible advantages in a conversation between faith activists and advocacy practitioners. The question is left open as to whether such a fresh synthesis of knowledge and skills could be useful in improved safeguards for the most vulnerable in society.

* geoff.morgan@imperial.nhs.uk

Keywords: Independent advocacy; practical theology; spiritual care; well-being; professional studies; training; safeguarding vulnerable adults

INTRODUCTION

In this chapter I aim to present an integrated model of advocacy practice for the hospital and the community, based on spiritual and cultural aspects of a qualitative study on which it is based. A comparison between groups (between independent advocates and service users, and especially between hospital chaplains and advocates) could highlight aspects of the broad advocacy role and how attitudes to the practice complement each other. Although the large study in principle involves qualitative research, contrasts between spiritual care coordinators or chaplains and advocates may be enhanced by some relevant figures. In relation to numbers of full-time equivalent (FTE) chaplains, figures showed that at the beginning of 2010 there were around 425 full time, and approximately 3000 part time chaplains employed by the National Health Service (NHS). In addition there were 'numerous volunteer chaplains of all denominations and faiths' (Hospital-Chaplaincies-Council, 2010, p.5)

Against this, it was more difficult to discover numbers of FTE advocates because of the problem of knowing how many services there were nationally. This, according to Martin Coyle, former Head of Quality and Development at the now defunct Action for Advocacy, was because there was 'no obligation for groups to record or report this data', which would have included the number of volunteer and of part-time advocates. Also, there were a number of groups who said their work included advocacy where the services listed did not appear to reflect this appropriately, and vice versa, a few who may be providing advocacy without describing it as such. However, on the basis that every local authority in England (and Wales) must provide the statutory services of IMCAs and IMHAs and an aggregation of numbers of advocates depending on known provider organisations, the following figures emerged.

With approximately 600-800 advocacy organisations in the country, an educated estimate would give an average of 8 advocates per group, which would mean the total number would be in the range of 4800- 6400. It was also unclear what effect the variable of volunteer advocates would have on this number, in the same way as it was for chaplains.

There was not a definitive list of trained IMHAs or IMCAs- which must be provided in every Local Authority, but estimates of the number of trained IMCAs tended to be around 500. It would be reasonable to assume a similar number for IMHAs, according to Coyle (2010) although commissioning patterns across the country makes this assumption unclear. (Coyle, 2010). Therefore it was possible to view the number of 425 full-time and 3000 part-time paid chaplains alongside at least 4800 full-time paid advocates, with the possibility that there may be up to 1000 more, when IMCA and IMHA numbers are taken into account.

On this basis of a possible greater number of advocates than spiritual care practitioners, it is at least interesting- and in the light of funding and other pressures on chaplaincy and advocacy- to note the minimal spiritual or possibly 'pastoral' functions ('beliefs and values') which the Department of Health has now ascribed to the role of the IMCA, as we shall see below.

In the light of a possible new paradigm in pastoral care, the theme of a renewed social conscience and a religious or spiritual reshaping of the social sciences will also frame the fruits of the research I am sharing here. I will seek to set 'independent advocacy' and 'spiritual care' alongside one another, conceding that this is not an obvious pairing. But I want to argue- alongside the rising numbers of advocates, and the call for their further increase following a judgement in March 2014 in respect of the Deprivation of Liberty Safeguards role which IMCAs exercise, compared with chaplaincy provision in England- that the interface with spiritual carers could be enriching for both disciplines, and that it could provide a framework for the mutual recognition of secular and religious parties, whether volunteers or professionals, in a common response to the needs of the most socially vulnerable. (Miles, 2014)

But let me now turn to independent advocacy in more detail. Amongst the diversity of roles which it embraces, the requirement for Independent Mental Capacity Advocates (IMCAs) and Independent Mental Health Advocates (IMHAs), which passed into English and Welsh law in 2007 and 2009, underlined the growing significance of advocacy in health and social care and the emergence of these particular roles as occupations undergoing professionalisation. Growing out of the 'Patients' Rights' advocates' and the consumer and civil rights movements in the US of the 1970s (Mallik & Rafferty, 2000), advocacy in health and social care sparked a debate about whether nurses could effectively advocate for their patients, or whether greater independence from the employing health provider was desirable. (Bateman, 2000; Llewellyn & Northway, 2007; Ravich & Schmolka, 1996). There was evidence that social workers and other practitioners were in a good position to 'advocate' for their clients (Mallik, 1998); however advocacy was seen as a 'risky role to adopt' for nurses and not one which their career should embrace (Mallik, 1997 pp.130, 135). And if the 'central tenet of independence is missing from an advocacy relationship in which the advocate is also acting as a professional…' (Forbat & Atkinson, 2005, p.331), for a social worker it could also be problematic or bring them into conflict with their employers (Faust, 2008, pp.295-6; Gilbert, 2010).

Atkinson stated that the rejection of the professionalisation of the role of nurse-advocate by the nursing élite left a gap needing to be filled (Atkinson, 1999). This was the gap which voluntary sector organisations, funded increasingly by central government, were to fill. Thus independent advocacy came to be separated from 'the system' in order to be better able to support and represent clients, patients or service users. The Department of Health described IMCA- a service for the 'un-befriended'- as the creation of 'a new form of advocacy, a new profession and a new safeguard'. (Dept.-of-Health, 2008). Specifically in respect of safeguarding adults, there was a wider role for IMCAs since 'those who lack capacity who have family and friends can still have an IMCA… in… adult protection procedures,' (Dept.-for-Constitutional-Affairs, 2006b, p.198; see also Redley, Platten, Clare, & Holland, 2008), and additionally in Deprivation of Liberty Safeguards procedures. So far, so independent. But how to define advocacy?

ADVOCACY: VOICES TO RAISE, RIGHTS TO KNOW, CHOICES TO FACE

Clearly there could be much to say in terms of legal and theological definitions of advocacy, e.g. 'one who pleads or speaks for another': interestingly the Shorter Oxford

Dictionary refers to the 'person of Christ' in this context (Little, Fowler, Coulson, Onions, & Friedrichsen, 1983). Rather, a pragmatic approach is taken below. The wide range of advocacy roles- from mental health to children's advocacy and other varied forms, which I cannot develop in detail here, whether citizen advocacy which is mostly performed by volunteers, or professional advocacy done by paid staff- this range calls for some kind of comprehensive definition, bearing in mind that nuances will depend on the field and style of the expression. Atkinson (1999) has described it as 'speaking up', and writes that 'everyone, sooner or later, needs help in making their voice heard – and advocates are people who can provide the time and support to enable this to happen.' (Atkinson, 1999, pp.5-9; Henderson, 2005, p.206). This help is provided through different styles: either instructed or non-instructed advocacy. 'Instructed advocacy' describes activities which support those who can request or direct that support, or exercise choices in order to be able to 'speak up' for themselves. By contrast, 'non-instructed advocacy' focuses on individuals with disabilities or mental health issues, who are vulnerable or have been deemed to lack specific capacity and who therefore need specialist support (such as IMCA) in decision-making in their 'best interests.' In summary, independent advocacy happens when practitioners or volunteers are commissioned to support individuals to make choices, take decisions and secure rights and safeguards in relation to health, social care and housing, either on an instructed or non-instructed basis, as previously stated.

Advocacy As Cultural and Spiritual Support

The Department of Health's asserted 'new profession' of IMCA advocates (Dept.-of-Health, 2008) also included the statutory responsibility to take into account 'any beliefs and values (e.g. religious, cultural, moral or political) that would be likely to influence the decision in question' (Dept.-for-Constitutional-Affairs, 2006b, pp.20, 65), in accordance with the 'best interests' of a client. The Human Rights Act framework (specifically, Article Nine: Freedom of Conscience [Thought and Religion]) and the fact that public authorities uphold rights to 'manifest one's religion and beliefs'(Dept.-for-Constitutional-Affairs, 2006a) both locate a conduit for these principles to apply to independent advocacy.

This chapter derives from a larger study in which advocacy and spirituality were analysed, including a spiritual history of advocacy (Morgan 2014). Indeed there are distinctive views about the inception of advocacy: on the one hand it can be seen as arising in the 1970s, and in the post-modern context of de-institutionalisation, social rights and political activism (Thompson, 2008; Traustadóttir, 2006).

A longer view, as argued elsewhere (Morgan, 2010), could take in the spiritual concerns of early mental health reformers such as Pinel and Perceval and apply this to a history of independent advocacy in terms- to use a theological model- of a 'preferential option' for the oppressed, if not for the poor (Pattison, 1994). Moving forward and with reference to my research, I will now consider how the voices of non-standard advocates demonstrate skills in the area of independent advocacy, and how that develops the potency of advocacy as a skilled intervention across disciplines.

'You Are Not Restricted by Being Part of That System': (Olive)

In this section I will analyse two interviews to compare how advocacy outsiders, a chaplain and a self-advocacy worker saw their respective roles and how they used advocacy skills outside the territory of statutory advocates. I wanted to show how a close textual analysis revealed aspects of thinking on the experience of the provision of advocacy from participants who were not in the mainstream of advocacy practice.

In relation to my transcriptions, the word *'system'* was used 28 times over seven interviews and (from the Nvivo software tool) acquired *'In vivo'* or live status in this way. In my doctoral study I adopted a case study approach but used a grounded theory-type approach in the very initial stages of data analysis. In the texts of the participants which I scrutinised, I also used the model of 'interaction order' to understand them, which I explain further in footnote 1 below. *'System'* occurred 7 and 8 times respectively and caught my attention. I will therefore compare two longer sections of text **(i)** and **(ii)**, to elucidate the nature of a *'bounded social setting'* in which two non-advocates exercised advocacy skills, and I will elicit spiritual and theological analysis from their contributions. Bernard took up the story.

(F. = Facilitator [the researcher])

(i) First Extract...B: *the balance of power about the psychiatric system... is interesting... one service user said, 'Chaplains are like patients... they're dismissed and seen as not important', but I think that can be our attraction because we don't have...*

F: Was that comment specifically about cutbacks?

B: I think it was to the senior manager when he visited and asked, 'Where do you see chaplains fitting into the system?' and he said, 'I think they are regarded in the system as completely useless...' But what he described is that we are actually in a strange position, sometimes... I mean, some people will say, 'You must speak to my psychiatrist and tell them there is nothing wrong with me.' And I say, 'I can't do that' but I can help you if you want to further some complaint, or something...

F:... encourage that person to question it themselves?...

...as IMCAs can ask for a diagnosis to be reviewed

B: That would be very difficult...

B: I want to say to my supervisor who is head of the ... department, it's rather like John's gospel, in the system but not of it, and she says, 'You can't do that because you're in the system!' But sometimes we have to work in a way which makes us trusted and acceptable so you have to choose the moment when you challenge something...

(Bernard, 2008, August 19)

(ii.) Second Extract... F: ... *what (do) you think is happening within yourself when you are advocating for someone... how has being a self-advocate (self-advocacy group coordinator) helped you?*

O: I think one of them is a greater sense of the reward than I had when I was in the system, when I was part of the residential system because in many ways that is still stacked in favour of the system and the staff. The staff has union reps and contracts, and many other things that the people they are there to support don't have. So actually being out of that system and being on the side of advocacy is quite empowering, kind of liberating because you are not restricted by being part of that system.

F: You have a union that you could join and a contract though...

O: Yes, you do have that, but- I haven't made that clear- in terms of working as part of a care provider, if there was an allegation of neglect or abuse or wrongdoing about someone in the system, that member of staff has got the advantage of having a contract, having a union rep and all these things that a service user doesn't have, um, so, in trying to deal with things for the service user, to get a resolution and get new staff and get bad staff to move on is not as easy even when you are in the system, and when you are a manager in the system because you can't be seen to be discriminatory against the staff, and ask staff to do something that they don't think is in their contract and all this kind of stuff...

(Olive, 2007, November 7)

In the first section, Bernard noted the attribution of powerlessness by a service user to a chaplain as a way of reflecting on his own situation in the system. Both the religious professional and service user felt disenfranchised, the service user blamed the chaplain for being *'useless'* in not taking a more pro-active or advocating role; but Bernard saw his role as aiming to be *'trusted and accepted'* across the board. I referred to *'trust'* as a perceived core condition in advocacy practice. The sense from the service user that chaplains do not have a role to play is double-edged: on the one hand, for the service user, it could enhance in her eyes, the empathic, pastoral role of the chaplain; for the chaplain, this devaluing talk could reflect a difficulty in being taken seriously by a health decision-maker, and consequently hamper the chaplain in playing the role of an advocate to make a difference for the service user.

This sense of spiritual frustration was brought home by the later comment regarding Bernard's articulated reflection on his place in the system, quoting from John's Gospel. (Bible: John 17:11). Bernard was reminded by his supervisor that he was indeed 'in' and 'of' the system, and in one sense- that the NHS (the state-funded National Health Service in the UK) is the paymaster of chaplains- that is correct. This was underlined when I probed about whether Bernard could ask for a second opinion (*'That would be very difficult'*) which demonstrates the limitation of the role of a NHS-employed chaplain as against that of the independent statutory advocate. It would be interesting to know this service user's views of mental health advocates. However, there was evidence from other chaplains that being funded by the NHS did not prevent service users from seeing spiritual care coordinators as independent:

N: …they see the chaplaincy as independent… they regard it as…

C: Part of the humbling experience of being a chaplain is that there is an automatic assumption that we are really on their side; they never ask who pays you; and I think that makes our task a bit more complex but brings up the issue of the prophetic in the world

(Norman & Colin, 2008, September 11)

In the second section, Olive was a former health professional turned advocate; she was analysing her recent transformation of roles, or, more precisely, the difference she felt she could make as an advocate working to support people to self-advocate, which she did not feel she could make *'within the system.'* The repetition, anaphora almost, of the term *'system'* pinpointed a sense of dissatisfaction on the part of Olive when an alienating structure, and the use of the epithets *'empowering'* and *'liberating'* connoted the sense of release, which a new

to engage more fully with, for example, virtue ethics and practical theology and to allow my data to interact with these areas more richly in order to establish my thesis. (Morgan, 2014).

Finally, in relation to whether independent advocacy or spiritual care initiatives could in themselves meet the needs of those who are 'un-befriended', or desperately need support in a period of economic austerity, it is doubtful. But a society, which upholds tangible safeguards, including expressions of independent advocacy flowing from the Mental Health and Mental Capacity Acts in England, redounds to the public good and is more socially integrated, I argue. And alongside similar services, such as funded chaplaincy, which view the individual not only holistically, but also in spiritual terms, together all must find new, efficient and practical ways to keep faith with the most vulnerable individuals and groups in that society.

Note: Some of the above text was previously published as *Spiritual Advocacy in England?* in Catholic Social Conscience, Reflection and Action on Catholic Social Teaching, edited by Keith Chappell and Francis Davis, Gracewing, 2011.

About the Author

Revd. Dr. Geoff Morgan received his doctorate from King's College London. He was employed as an independent advocate in London and worked in the voluntary sector for 7 years. He has also published on African theology and is a licensed Anglican priest. Since June 2013 he has led the Spiritual and Pastoral Care (chaplaincy) team at Imperial College Healthcare NHS Trust, serving 11 London hospitals.

References

Atkinson, D. (1999). *Advocacy- a Review*. London: Pavilion/Joseph Rowntree.

Bateman, N. (2000). *Advocacy Skills for Health and Social Care Professionals*. London; Philadelphia: J. Kingsley.

BBC-News. (2011). Fiona Pilkington officers face misconduct proceedings [Electronic Version]. Retrieved 30th September 2012 from http://www.bbc.co.uk/news/uk-england-leicestershire-13504618.

Bernard, A. (2008, August 19). Interviewer: G.Morgan, Advocacy interviews, Ivs-BA London.

Carver, N., & Morrison, J. (2005). Advocacy in practice: the experiences of independent advocates on UK mental health wards. *Journal of Psychiatric & Mental Health Nursing, 12*(1), 75-84.

Cornah, D. (2006). *The Impact of Spirituality on Mental Health. A Literature Review*. London: Mental Health Foundation.

Cox, J., Campbell, A. V., & Fulford, K. W. M. (Eds.). (2007). *Medicine of the Person : Faith, Science and Values in health care provision*. London: Jessica Kingsley.

Coyle, M. (2008). *Here for good? A snapshot of the advocacy workforce*. London: Action-for-Advocacy.

Coyle, M. (2010). Email. In G. Morgan (Ed.). Leeds.

Coyte, M. E., Gilbert, P., & Nicholls, V. (Eds.). (2008). *Spirituality, Values, and Mental Health :Jewels for the Journey* London ; Philadelphia: Jessica Kingsley Publishers.

Dept.-for-Constitutional-Affairs. (2006a). *Human rights : human lives : a handbook for public authorities*. [London]: Department for Constitutional Affairs.

Dept.-for-Constitutional-Affairs. (2006b). *Mental Capacity Act code of practice*. London: Department for Constitutional Affairs.

Dept.-of-Health. (2008). *The first annual report of the Independent Mental Capacity Advocacy Service. Year 1, April 2007 - March 2008*. London: Crown.

Faust, J. (2008). Clinical Social Worker as Patient Advocate in a Community Mental Health Center. *Clinical Social Work Journal, 36*(3), 293-300.

Foley, R., & Platzer, H. (2007). Place and provision: Mapping mental health advocacy services in London. *Social Science & Medicine, 64*(3), 617-632.

Forbat, L., & Atkinson, D. (2005). Advocacy in Practice: The Troubled Position of Advocates in Adult Services. *Br J Soc Work, 35*(3), 321-335.

Foskett, J. (2004). Editorial. *Mental Health, Religion & Culture, 7*(1), 1 - 3.

Fulford, K., Ersser, S., & Hope, T. (Eds.). (1996). *Essential Practice in Patient-Centred Care*. Oxford: Blackwell Science.

Gilbert, P. (2008). Nurturing a new discourse: mental health and spirituality. *Spirituality and Health International*, n/a.

Gilbert, P. (2010). Seeking inspiration: the rediscovery of the spiritual dimension in health and social care in England. *Mental Health, Religion & Culture, 13*(1), 1-14.

Goffman, E. (1981). *Forms of talk*. Philadelphia: University of Pennsylvania Press.

Goffman, E. (1983). The Interaction Order: American Sociological Association, 1982 Presidential Address. *American Sociological Review, 48*(1), 1-17.

Henderson, R. (2005). Mental Health Advocacy and Empowerment in Focus. In T. Ryan, J. Pritchard, et al. (Ed.), *Good Practice in Adult Mental Health* (pp. 202-215). London; Philadelphia: Jessica Kingsley Publishers.

Hospital-Chaplaincies-Council. (2010). *Health Care Chaplaincy and The Church of England, A Review of the work of the Hospital Chaplaincies Council*. London: Church of England.

Little, W., Fowler, H. W., Coulson, J., Onions, C. T., & Friedrichsen, G. W. S. (1983). *The shorter Oxford English dictionary on historical principles*. London: Book Club Associates.

Llewellyn, P., & Northway, R. (2007). The views and experiences of learning disability nurses concerning their advocacy education. *Nurse Education Today, 27*(8), 955-963.

Mallik, M. (1997). Advocacy in nursing - a review of the literature. *Journal of Advanced Nursing, 25*(1), 130-138.

Mallik, M. (1998). Advocacy in nursing: perceptions and attitudes of the nursing elite in the United Kingdom. *Journal of Advanced Nursing, 28*(5), 1001-1011.

Mallik, M., & Rafferty, A. M. (2000). Diffusion of the Concept of Patient Advocacy. *Journal of Nursing Scholarship, 32*(4), 399-404.

Maltby, J., Lewis, C. A., & Day, L. (2008). Prayer and subjective well-being: The application of a cognitive-behavioural framework. *Mental Health, Religion & Culture, 11*(1), 119 - 129.

Miles, S. (2014). Cheshire West and its impact on Mental Health and Mental Capacity Lawyers [Electronic Version]. *Mental Health Lawyers Association website*. Retrieved

26th December 2014 from http://www.mhla.co.uk/news/cheshire-west-and-its-impact-on-mental-health-and-mental-capacity-lawyers/

Morgan, G. (2010). Independent advocacy and the "rise of spirituality": Views from advocates, service users and chaplains. *Mental Health, Religion & Culture, 13*(6), 623-636.

Morgan, G. (2014). *Spirit of Advocacy. Theory and practice in independent advocacy: an historical and qualitative analysis using Practical Theology.*, King's College London, London.

Norman, A., & Colin, B. (2008, September 11). Interviewer: G.Morgan, Advocacy interviews, Ivs-NA/CB. London.

Olive, P. (2007, November 7). Interviewer: G.Morgan, Advocacy interviews, Ivs-OP. London.

Pattison, S. (Ed.). (1994). *Pastoral Care and Liberation Theology.* Cambridge: Cambridge University Press.

Prigg, M. (2010, 24th February 2010). Google bosses convicted over abuse video of Down's syndrome boy. *Evening Standard.*

Rampton, B. (2008). Handout: Some Key Concepts in Erving Goffman's Exploration of the Interaction Order. King's College London.

Ravich, R., & Schmolka, L. (1996). Patient Representation: A Patient-centred approach to the provision of health services. In K. Fulford, S. Ersser & T. Hope (Eds.), *Essential Practice in Patient-Centred Care* (pp. 68-85). Oxford: Blackwell.

RCPsych. (2008). http://www.rcpsych.ac.uk/college/specialinterestgroups/spirituality.aspx (Publication. Retrieved 2nd June 2008, from Royal College of Psychiatrists:

Redley, M., Platten, M., Clare, I., & Holland, A. (2008). *The Involvement of Independent Mental Capacity Advocates (IMCAs) in Adult Protection Procedures in England:1st April 2007 – 31st March 2008* Cambridge Department of Psychiatry (Section of Developmental Psychiatry) University of Cambridge.

Riches, C. (2010, March 12). A 'true gent' tormented to death by gang of yobs *Daily Express.*

Swinton, J. (2001). Spirituality and the lives of people with Learning Disabilities. *Updates: Spirituality and Learning Disabilities 3*(6).

Swinton, J., Mowat, H., & Baines, S. (2011). Whose Story Am I? Redescribing Profound Intellectual Disability in the Kingdom of God. *J. Relig. Disabil. Health Journal of Religion, Disability and Health, 15*(1), 5-19.

Tew, J. (2003). Emancipatory Research in mental health. In S. Cochrane (Ed.), *SPN Paper 4: Where you stand affects your point of view. Emancipatory approaches to mental health research Notes from SPN Study Day: 12 June 2003* (pp. 24-27). London: Social Perspectives Network.

Thompson, D. (2008). Advocating beyond the institution. *Learning Disability Today, 8*(1), 16-21.

Traustadóttir, R. (2006). Learning about self-advocacy from life history: a case study from the United States. *British Journal of Learning Disabilities, 34*(3), 175-180.

Wallcraft, J. (2003). User Focused Research. In S. Cochrane (Ed.), *SPN Paper 4: Where you stand affects your point of view. Emancipatory approaches to mental health research Notes from SPN Study Day: 12 June 2003.* London: Social Perspectives Network.

Williams, R. (2010, 14th September 2010). 'Mate crime' fears for people with learning disabilities. Learning disabled people living in the community are increasingly finding themselves the victims of so-called mate crime. *The Guardian*.

In: Spirituality
Editor: Edith C. Roberts

ISBN: 978-1-63482-370-8

Chapter 9

THE MAPIMAÍ RITUAL IN THE PROCESS OF CONSTRUCTION TERRITORIALITY PAITER SURUI

Adnilson de Almeida Silva,[1*] ***Carlandio Alves da Silva,***[2†]
Sheila Castro dos Santos,[3‡] ***Adriana Francisca de Medeiros***[4#]
and Almir Narayamoga Suruí[5‖]

[1]Professor of Department of Geography and Program Master in Geography (PPGG) and Masters and Doctored in Regional Development and Environment (PGDRA) of the Federal University of Rondônia (UNIR), Brazil
[2]Bachelor's degree in Geography, UNIR, Brasil
[3]Ph.d. student in Geography – Federal University of Paraná (UFPR), Brasil
[4]Ph.d. student in Regional Development and Environment, UNIR, Brasil
[5]Doctor Honoris Causa in Geography, UNIR, Brasil

ABSTRACT

The article seeks to present how the universe of the Paiter Suruí is conceived and organized by this ethnic group. The construction follows the arrests and experiences of the action space of this ethnicity who inhabiting the States of Mato Grosso and Rondônia, which during the ritual Mapimaí – "the creation of the world" - in phenomena and symbolic representations meeting their identities, so that in the event becomes more noticeable the spirituality, of which the territoriality is integral, and therefore materialized. The design of this study is empirical basis (experience in Mapimaí) and theoretical frameworks that discuss the indigenous question. It is noteworthy that the ritual as representation and cultural event, due to factors external to ethnicity has been "dormant" for several years and was taken over since the understanding of Paiter Suruí strengthens its identity as a people and it provides spiritual and affective ties

[*] adnilsonn@gmail.com.
[†] carlandioalvesdasilva@gmail.com.
[‡] sheila1705@gmail.com.
[#] afdemedeiros@gmail.com.
[‖] almirsurui@gmail.com.

strengthening, which allows ensuring the territoriality, considering the constant threats to Indigenous Land Paiterey Garah (Setember Seven).

Keywords: Amazon; Mapimaí; Territorial Markers; Memory; Paiter Suruí

I. Inicitial Considerations

The issues about territory, territoriality and indigenous identity, related to the expropriation of territory, they have been originated from many contemporary discussions. However these matters are seen as "encounters of societies", but the essence of the problem would be focalized by the enunciation of cosmogonic representations – which it is the possible explanation in order to understand the indigenous universe.

Then we consider that in order to apprehend and pointed this cosmogonic indigenous universe we must support in theories and methods that subsidize our field (the empiric field – because we were invited to take part in the Mapimaí ritual with the Paiter Suruí too). Thereby it was possible understand the organization and reorganization from the own natives, though this dynamics had constantly been altered and is altered by the contact with the surrounding society, interfering by this way in the transmission of the culture to the new generations.

From this maxim we perceive that some scholars of social sciences assigned new understanding models for comprehension of the diverse forms of representations, signs and significations of the ethnicities, conferring meanings that deviate from the indigenous logic of world "vision" and "experience".

Considering about the indigenous role at present society and the relations that are established inside their populations, it may observe that exits a necessity for information must be registered and divulged in order to enable the knowledge of their life manner.

II. Theoretycal and Methodological Routes

With the need of understand the memory that is evoked at Mapimaí, we applied a flexible methodology for each activity, that is, by bibliographic review, testimonies, interviews, meetings and experiences with the Paiter Suruí.

At that point, to understand the question of memory and experience of the Pater Suruí, we used as support the Bosi's studies (2005) related to the habitual knowledge, this pointed by the continuity of learning, thus flowing in each individual through that was teach them, because

> [...] habit-memory is acquired by the effort of attention and by repetition of gestures or words. It is – although Bérgson does not address explicitly with this factor – a process that occurs by exigencies of socialization. It is an exercise that retaken until fixation transforms itself in habit, is a service for daily living. It is thanks to memory that we know by heart the motions that are required, for example, eating in accordance to the rules of etiquette, writing or speaking a foreign language, driving a car, sewing, typewriting etc. Habit-memory is a part of all our cultural training (Bosi, 2005: 49).

Quoting this authoress we remember the Mapimaí was recently resumed as a ritual used to identify and territorialize the clan members, by this way to give meaning and to constitute the daily life of ethnicity.

One of the particularities of this study was to deepen the research starting from the concepts present in the phenomenological method, having as scope the "territorial markers" foundation described by Almeida Silva (2010), concepts that present themselves as a contribution for understanding the indigenous territoriality.

In our work we also used as theoretical contribution some authors that formed links and aided us in the exposed reflections, among them Brandão (1982), who shows us that for a long time the social sciences (Geography seen as social science) cherished the dream and illusion of studying the society as the same manner as natural sciences studied the Nature, knowing the phenomena, ultimately to be capable of to foresee them and to describe their action, quantify them and which were the target to reach and the parameters of a truly scientific activity. However the studied problems are never those experienced and felt by population. At Brandão's conception (1981: 43):

> First of all, we should not be doing a fetish from science, as it were an entity with own life able to rule the universe and determine form and context of our society, both now as future. We must bear in mind that, far away from being so awful agent, science is only a cultural product of human intellect that responds to specific collective necessities – including those artistic considerations, supernatural and extra scientific – and also in precise historical periods.

By this way, we must recognize that nowadays the skilled community of scientists trend to monopolize the definition of sciences and to decide what is and what is not scientific. Under these conditions evidently the knowledge production, at such level, is orientated towards the preservation and crystallization of the system with a *status quo* of refusal thereof that is not measured statistically.

Following the research perspective we still lean on the concept of territory and territoriality advocated by Ávila (2008). According to this theoretician territory is not a concept that had been coupled up to the modern State exclusively:

> [...] this is because it is also not the hegelian ending of contradictions, quite the contrary, it is a representation of will and power from one class which maintains its hegemony from space (Ávila, 2008: 24).

Our research has a cultural feature which is supported in Claval (2007), who expounds a broad panorama of geographical studies where culture is the most important component in the relations between human being, environment and social relationships.

> Culture is a sum of behaviors, knowledge, techniques and values accumulated by individuals during their lives and, in other scale, by all the groups that participate in it. Culture is a heritage transmitted from one generation to another. It has its roots in a distant past which immerses in the territory where their deaths were buried and where their gods manifested themselves (Claval, 2007:63).

In this way our research was consolidated with the phenomenological contribution, without leave to use the results of skilled sciences, which have knowledge of admirable extent. With this we found at philosophy of symbolic forms and phenomenology of knowledge, both proposed by Cassirer, one of the paths of scientific construction without abdicate of Paiter Suruí's knowledge.

> From this point of view myth, art, language and science appear as symbols: not simply in the sense that they designate in image form, in indicating and explainer allegory, a real existing, but rather in the sense that each one of them generates and calves its own meaningful world. In this field, this auto deployment of spirit shows itself by virtue of which it only exists one "reality", an organized and definite being. Consequently, the special symbolic forms are not imitations, but yet, organs of that reality because it is only through them that real can become in the visible for us (Cassirer, 1992: 22).

Starting from this enunciation, we understand the Mapimaí as Paiter Suruí's "territorial marker" which it is of the most relevant importance for our debate about rituals that are reintroduced into ethnicity with their symbolic and representative value for their permanency as territorial aggregator.

Thus, the reflection on Mapimaí's construction and experience implies the (re)cognition of its culture and inward/outward relationships, that is, of their world interpretation way. In this sense it is necessary to comprehend the importance and role of the myth for the most different cultures.

In the comprehension about how myth is built it verifies that it is about inwardness of human cultures, what can be characterized as way of life or better, how world is experienced and interpreted by the Other, who has different knowledge from our own, according Rocha (1996: 7; 9; 12) affirms:

> [...] myth is a narrative. It is a discourse, a speech. It is a form of societies reflect their contradictions, express their paradoxes, doubts and disquiets. It can see as a possibility of meditating about existence, cosmos, situations of "being in the world" or social relationships. [...] Myth situates itself as a very ancient fact or passage. As something that happened in times of "dawn" of human being, in "fabulous times". It even says that behind myth exits a tradition. Or better, it is itself a tradition. Myth would have an allegoric form that "permits glimpsing a natural, historical or philosophical fact". [...] Myth can, then, reveal the thought of a society, its conception of existence and relationships that human beings must keep in between themselves and the world around them. This is possible to be investigated both the analysis of a single myth and a set of myths and even of the complete mythology of a society.

Under such point of view myth inserts itself as one of the "territorial markers" since this latter is understood from the symbols and representations that occur at space of action, which it defines territorialities linked to cosmogony and sociospacial experiences and it enables the formation of cultural identities and identitarian belonging (Almeida Silva, 2010).

Spatiality and territoriality, preceding to territory, are considered as human act on space since both reveal the physical approximation and, above all, sentiments, values about ways of construing, understanding, experiencing and seeing the world. Thus they are made by symbols, signs, signifies and representations that permit human being realizes himself in the world.

Almeida Silva (2010; 2013) notices that "territorial markers" are bonded to mental making, in which human beings are forced to fulfill the tasks concerning material and spiritual feeding, in which symbolic representations and presentifications, as phenomena, constitute the psycho-spiritual basis of their resistances, whereupon it cannot put aside the myths, ethical values in which they develop themselves as a culture.

In this sense, Rocha (1996) proposes a reflection about the understanding on what is that it conducts a community/ethnicity to believing, valorizing and to worshiping what presents itself as the "most important" rather than simply to searching the truth as form of life reality, because

> It is the effectiveness of the myth and not the truth that it must be the criterion for thinking it. Myth can be effective and, so, true as a powerful stimulus for leading both thought and behavior of human being when dealing with important existential realities. Ultimately, the very idea of truth is not an arguable concept. Many thinkers believe that it does not exist and what we call truth it is only a successful version on determinate event. In this sense, to find out if myth says strictly the truth it becomes, at best, a useless task (Rocha, 1996: 14).

Both authors look for to point the representative elements of indigenous everydayness, for example the *maloca* (longhouse, a kind of central village hut), the hammock, their amusement artifact, war weapons and other symbolic forms. In this case, the way how human being understands the world is derived from his/her integration to the group, which it is installed in a own territory, and it is defined not only by its specific structure but by difference that discerns himself/herself from other in his/her space of action.

Thus "territorial marks" are organized by the relation that human being maintains between human/territory/symbolic and his history, which it express itself not only by the presence of spirits of their forefathers but by the accumulation of signs, some of them created by nature and reinterpreted by human being, other from the "imaginary" and representations of the "dividuals" and their collectivity. Family, myths, collective memory are meaningful elements, in which each artefact has a significance and place for the group and supports the communal property idea.

These representations are materially constructed and they are seen not only by their material side but spiritual too. In those representations spirits reflect the connection between the alive and the dead frequently as a memorial valorization of their forefathers, and by this way they ensure the permanency of their identity and the historical construction of their collectivity. The use of representations has not an economic value idea, since its representative meaning pervades the own materialness.

According with Almeida Silva (2010) territorial "demarcations" and "markers" are placed in concepts which have very different meanings, representations and forms. Demarcations point a construction action – a constituent power – that demarcate and determine borderlands; markers are related to the cosmogonic and symbolic form which it marks the territory to distinguish it from another human collective, it is a construction action full of representations.

To this author "territorial markers" are not physical and natural features merely but a group of symbolic relationships linked to the beings and not-beings. This is what characterizes territoriality and spatiality notions which are measured by the constructed symbology and its values, affinities, meanings and other manifestations that are consolidated as symbolic forms and presentifications in the human collectives.

Bonnemaison (2002) points the ethnicity concept further on consanguinity theory since the links that preserve an ethnicity united pervade and transcend the blood relationship, because:

> An ethnicity exists, first of all, by the consciousness that has of itself and by the culture that produces. It is in its bosom that it elaborates and perpetuates the sum of beliefs, rituals and practices that found the culture and permit the reproduction of the groups. In other words, ethnicity is what in other places is denominated of cultural group, but whose outlines are strong in the traditional civilizations because they are frequently linked to a geographical political expression – circumscriptions of tribal chiefs, kingdoms, eventually nations -, that is, a territory, or at least a certain area of spatial occurrence. [...] Without a lineate ethnicity, it cannot exist culture neither cultural vision. Ethnicity elaborates a culture and, reciprocally, the existence of culture founds the identity of the ethnicity. In this sense, we can talk of ethnicity for every human group whose social function, or the mere geographical existence, conducts to a cultural specificity (Bonnemaison, 2002: 93-94).

The theoretical contextualization about ethnicity supplies elements and phenomena that are necessary for comprehending and apprehending the culture as well as the result of human experiences enables us understanding changes and permanencies, that is, the appreciation of ethnoknowledge and the acquisition of new representations that are consequence of the encounters of different cultures.

This qualification conducts us to the comprehension whereof cosmogonic phenomena act and inside them the natives organize themselves, build the historical process and grant new meanings and representations from the relations with the surrounding society, including the "appropriation" of other cultural and social values.

Thus, as consequence of the historical process of colonization effected by State and surrounding society, the natives had their territory fragmented/diminished/expropriated – by reason of the used means. In this way their ancestral territories went through of new ressignifications and new representations that intervene directly in their culture and way of life as consequence of the reduction of those territorialities.

In the specific case of Amazonia, it is important to point that the Brazilian State was the propelling of occupation of natives' lands and it adopted as "reparation" or "compensation" for these damages to the natives the demarcation of their lands. This event mitigated part of the problems and "contributed" for the amortization of historical debt. At the same time this compensation aimed to preserve the diversity of Brazilian culture that outlives nowadays. However this "reparation" does not attend to the demands of the ethnicities nor gives the complete guarantee for the rights of the native people.

On the one hand these conditions promote the necessity observed in indigenous discourses about to keep their culture as resistance way, and on the other hand they allow us to understand transformations or changes that happened after the encounter with the surrounding society.

This is observed in the dialogues that the Paiter Suruí set up as a part of the process by which they are going by, that is, these dialogues reinforce the cosmogonic values and apprehend new representations as condition of their existence. In this case the strategy adopted for territoriality and identity it is in agreement with the concepts of "change and permanency" defended by Sahlins (1997, 1997a, 2003 [1985]) and "encounter of societies" (Galvão, 1979).

The symbolic field pointed trough lived experience in each ethnicity (among them the Paiter Suruí) it is consubstantiated in the relationship between material and symbolic, since the "things of the world, that exist in the world as apparent, as phenomenon, as how they present themselves" are endued of signifies by us, human beings, and used for purposes often settled before their confection (Cassirer, 1994: 81-96 [1944]).

III. Paiter Surui and Post-Contact Territory

The indigenous lands identified at Brazilian Amazon occupy significant 20 % of the total area of Legal Amazon, according to official data of the National Indian Foundation (Fundação Nacional do Índio – Funai). Though these lands are constitutional and juridical protected the natives had seen the intervention of surrounding society and even national State in their culture, and their zones of ancestral occupation had been brutally and illegally invaded, and oftentimes they had been pushed to other zones – which generated ethnic tensions and conflicts. What we can see clearly are diminished territories, which preclude the survival of the natives, due to scarcity of food, especially hunting and fishing.

It was not different with the Paiter Suruí (True People – in Tupi Mondé language), since portion of their territory was invaded by settlers and colonizing companies at contact period in the final of sixties. Even a portion of their territory was cut by 364 BR.

The ethnicity has its social organization based in clans, which are Gameb (Black Wasps), Gamir (Yellow Wasps), Makor (a kind of Amazon bamboo), Kaban (a regional fruit).

Kaban clan has that denomination because their skin is similar with a regional fruit which is yellowish and the taste is sour. According to the Paiter Suruí's saying the origin of this clan happened when they were in war against the Cinta Larga – in consequence of colonization of Amazon – and a Paiter Suruí man took a Cinta Larga women as wife, creating one of the most bigger clans nowadays which corresponds to half of the population.

Other big clans are Gameb and Gamebey which always were involved in the organization of fests, wars, meetings and other manifestations. They always leadered the Paiter Suruí and they have good relations with the other clans trough confidence and ethnic respect, according to the decisions and operation as form of support.

Clans are organized in foundations of political governance system, which it is chosen by parentage system, which social organization is patrilinear and prescribes the clannish exogamy, in which marriages are permitted only between different clans.

Man gets married with his sister's daughter because according with his cosmogonic conception that women is not a close relative because she is from another clan, culminating in marriages between cross cousins, and thus the patrilinear clannish outbreeding is sustained.

The Paiter Suruí inhabit 25 villages spread over Paiterey Garah Indigenous Land – known nationally as "7 September Indigenous Land" (Terra Indígena Sete de Setembro), by 88.867 Decree of Oct. 18, 1983 – located in Rondônia (municipality of Cacoal) and Matto Grosso (Rondolândia) in an area of 248.147 hectares, where the official contact happened on September 7 of 1969, at *Nabekó Dabalaquibá* Village (Hunging Machete Village).

Their *Labiway Esaga* (head leader) Almir Narayamoga Suruí says that if "Brazil commemorates its independence from Portugal on September 7, for us natives it is the date in which we became dependent of Brazilian State". This assertion reveals a common problematic to other Brazilian indigenous ethnicities that in addition to dependency they have to live together with invisibility and society's prejudice that establishes value judgments which conflict with ways of life that are different from theirs.

Previously official contact the Paiter Suruí maintained sporadic relationships with other ethnicities, some of them bitter, as rubber tappers and telegraphers of Rondon Commission, in the early decades of 20th century. This official contact between Brazilian State and the Paiter Suruí "coincided" with the expansion of economic frontiers in the Amazon region, especially with the setting of BR-364, which it is the attraction way for a thousands of migrants.

It is necessary to point that the arrival of migrants to Amazon complied with geopolitical reasons as strategy of minimizing social and economic problems from other regions of the country, having as motto the occupancy of Amazon frontiers whilst permitting the access and insertion of the official economic model into the region.

In the seventies half of the Paiter Suruí died from diseases tranmitted by migrants, according to Paiter Suruí people. In the early 1980s, the indigenous population had been dramatically reduced, and today their population has 1.172 members (Funasa, 2010)[1], which is a long way from quantify verified when the official contact began.

According to the Paiter Suruí, when the first contact happened there were approximately 5000 persons of the ethinicity, but today they are just the half in spite of the demographic growth.

The Paiter Suruí relate that the endemic diseases originated from this contact were one of the main causes of the drastic reduction of their population, since their immunity system was not enable to face against virus and bacteria at that time unknown, especially measles, tuberculosis, grippe and pneumonia. This event is similar to the history of other indigenous ethnicities.

They also claim that it was not possible to register the number of deaths because sick persons escaped to other villages, and for this way these persons infected others whom have not any immune defenses, to such a degree that they did not have the time to bury the deaths.

The adopted policy by the Integration Program for Development of Northwest Brazil (Programa Integrado de Desenvolvimento do Noroeste do Brasil – POLONOROESTE) in the 1980s, with resources of Brazilian government and the International Bank for Reconstruction and Development – (BIRD in Portuguese), provided the basis for administrative, political territoriality arrangements in such a way that even today it expresses the territorial configurations in Rondônia, whether in the implementation of municipalities as in the definition of rural properties, conservation units, indigenous lands and mass transit lines.

The Polonoroeste had as aims: 1) national integration of this Amazon region; 2) occupation of northwest Brazil region, through of absorption of populations economically

[1] Data obtained in http://pib.socioambiental.org/pt/povo/surui-paiter/1763.

marginalized from other regions, enabling the improvement of quality of life; 3) to increase the regional production and to improve the income of the population; 4) reduction of the rates of regional and national inequalities; 5) to ensure the productive growth in harmony with the environment and protection of indigenous communities.

This program came under heavy criticism inside and outside the country by its social and environmental impacts, that is, there was inertness for protection the forest against deforestation. In that sense, Almeida Silva (2012: 11) emphasizes that

> In fact this latter objective was the one which had least relevance in meeting the target, since under the POLONOROESTE program the BR 364 highway was paved and with it the arrival of a migration which results are measured as the increased deforestation and the pressure on forests causing the deforestation and consequently on indigenous peoples.

At the end of the program it was implemented its substitute, the PLANAFORO (Plano Agropecuário e Florestal de Rondônia), also funded by the International Bank and the Government of Brazil, with the aim of to correct the mistakes originated by the POLONOROESTE, especially those related to the environmental problematic.

Thus we can see that the contact generated deep changes for the natives and in the case of the Paiter Suruí it was not different, even because their lands are close to the BR 364 highway and nearby cities (Cacoal, Pimenta Bueno, Espigão do Oeste). These changes are seen and felt by the surrounding communities, NGOs or researchers and with the pressures they had suffered and are still suffering by the most distinct social actors (loggers, miners, squatters, among others) their way of life is going by new meanings and representations.

In spite of these obstacles the Paiter Suruí still hold a lot of their values, both as regards respect for culture and cosmogonic aspects, which are related with the culture of other Tupi Mondé ethnicities.

The action developed by Brazilian State also has other deployments with deep consequences for the indigenous ethnicities of Amazon, as the loss of part of their territory, as regards both state-own territorial reconfiguration and activity of illegal occupation by surrounding society, which it characterizes the indigenous desterritorialization and new apprehensions and world representations.

> [...] Appropriation and modification of the geographic space can be understand as processes of territorialization or depending of the circumstances they become conceived as deterritorialization or de(re)territorialization, which in the case of the indigenous populations it falls into the category of deterritorialization, this due to the loss of part of their space or when this space is mischaracterized from its original form, trough the action of State or by the social groups who possess the Capital (Almeida Silva & Leandro, 2010: 48).

By these means the role of Brazilian State, as attempt to soften the problematic existing and resulting from the "encounter of societies" and different cultures, has acted, although pressed, in the creation of indigenous lands, at the same time that Federal Constitution of 1998 recognizes the primary law to land and cultural permanency.

IV. THE MAPIMAI – CRIATION OF THE WORLD

The Mapimaí is a ritual that commemorates the creation of the world, and it happens as reconcilement and search for balance between human being, nature and culture, which it also alludes to the valorization of their culture. In this ritual the Paiter Suruí participate in the celebration divided in clans, which are represented by an indigenous leader. The responsibility of the preparations for commemoration is placed under responsibility of one of the clans, which it stays separated from the rest during the ritual.

The host clan offers the ritual – which it is also festive, and during the event is served a beverage know under the name of *chicha*[2] to the participants, whom must drink it until no longer tolerate more liquid and disgorge it. The strategy adopted is not permit the leader to be drunk, because this is viewed as sign of weakness and imbalance.

Thus all members of the clans try to drink as much as possible to preserve their leader, inducing him to drink the minimum quantity while the other ingest the beverage, which it is also considered as element of transcendence and purification of body, and they become drunk. The excess of *chicha*, when the natives disgorge it from their body, purifies body and spirit.

The Paiter Suruí are particularly known as the singer-natives and they produce handicrafts and musical instruments to be used during the festivity. We observed, during the entire celebration, how the symbolic is feeling, living, internalized and also manifested by the members of ethnicity in the beauty and uniformity of every song, which it is exclusive of its composer and cannot be played for any other person. They also confection necklaces, headdress and other artifacts in an isolated place from the host clan.

After these "marker"-objects are interchanged as a symbolic form of spiritual and cultural strengthening, or better, this integral act of the ethnicity lead us to the Mauss' enunciation (1968-1969 [1931a, b]; 1997 [1950], 2003) that refers the exchange and reciprocity concepts, which are directly related to the fundamental structure of kinship and affiliation, organization and experience of world shared for all natives.

In the cosmogonic order the Paiter Suruí participate of the same values and symbolic representations, their communities are divided into halves, one of them represents the spirits of the woods and the other represents the spirits of the *roçado* (a kind of small scale farming). Thus they organize agriculture as well obligations and duties, since kinship is one of the most important forms of social organization. That set of experiences between all the members can be stated, according to Dardel (2011: XII), as a

> [...] geographicity, which it expresses the geographic very essence of being-in-the-world. While it is the basis of the existence, the association between geographicity, place and landscape had been fertile, permitting a phenomenological comprehension of the geographic experience.

The Mapimaí, as a ritual, is a reference to the Paiter Suruí's organizational forms of the day-to-day activities, that is, it supplies the basis to produce a systemized agriculture, fishing and hunting so that all members help themselves collectively, and it is marked by reciprocity

[2] Fermented drink, it contents alcoholic strength. It contents as a raw material corn, or cará and/or other tubercles.

and the chance of re-discovering their origins and planning other odds against new internal/external challenges.

Before official contact the Mapimaí was celebrated for several weeks and it was organized in this way: the half who represents the woods stayed at an opening in the forest during summer, in an isolated place which it is situated about one km from village, while the other half who represents the *roçado* it would not entering that space.

This condition enabled the establishment of an indigenous agricultural calendar marked by turnover and the accomplishment of festive collective efforts for the performance of farming activities and harvest. The *roçado*-half was responsible for the production of food and *chicha* while the woods-half was responsible for beneficial actions (similar to *mutirões*, collective actions), which it was characterized as symbolic interchange.

After the contact the ritual stayed "asleep" for several years because the Paiter Suruí had to defend the territory, furthermore, Funai introduced the practice of individual *roças* (small farming) like the agriculture practiced by settlers. In 2000 the Mapimaí ritual was re-established in its ancestral practices – with the following supports: *Metareilá* Association (from the Paiter Suruí), Ethnoenvironmental Defense *Kanindé* and Environment Ministry – MMA.

Currently the Mapimaí has duration of three to seven days, a time well below if compared with the previous period to the contact; this is result of obligations and commitments undertaken by the ethnicity.

The ritual is performed by more than one ceremonies in a "frenetic" rhythm and all participants decorate themselves with necklaces, belts and paintings. During ritual the ceremonial chief's wife presents herself carrying a torch which it cannot be extinguished. The torch is fixed next to the ceremonial chief's reception throne (*yama*) and it stays there, which it is lighted by that chief and cannot be extinguished. The sacred fire will be extinguish by itself, otherwise the creator of humankind (*Palop*) will leave of visiting and protecting the village; if the torch was extinguished by forcefully it will still have another meanings, between them, the indication of someone who will die soon.

This reunion has the sense of strengthening of their cosmogonic cultural values and it is of utmost importance to keep the territory because it permits to the youngest to understand and narrow the ties with history and the struggled for land, as well as to comprehend the ties with the nature, cultural identity, spirituality and territoriality.

The Mapimaí is realized with the food-half which necessitates bigger small farms to share them, therefore they dedicate more time to collect and prepare the foods, and then they offer this meal to the guests. However the food-half establishes a relationship of interdependency with the half which represents the spirits of the woods, and when they are united they characterize the one ethnic identity, that is, they are "true people" or "ourselves".

The arrival to the camp is very active and the men make sounds in a festive atmosphere, and they transport their bows, arrows, feather ornaments and headdress which they are also utilized in the daily activities. The women carry pottery jars, necklaces and baskets produced by them and they even have "*tipóias*" (a kind of sling) in which they transport their children.

In the organization process the woods has senses, meanings and peculiar representations because it is the appropriate place to find raw material to produce handicrafts, tools of war and even food, and the search can happen individually or collectively.

In the forest there are straw to make baskets and houses, *taquara* (bamboo) to make arrows and flutes, genipap inks for the body paintings, rope and wood which are indispensable to make bows, and those spiritualized material elements compose the phenomenological set of the Mapimaí ritual. Thus, the forest with the sparrow-hawk and the river are inseparable parts from ritual, since they are constituted as unit where each representative element only has sense because it is intrinsically related to other.

During the Mapimaí happened and it still happens marriages following the cosmogonic orientation inherited by the Paiter Suruí. Polygamy is permitted. Contact with the culture of surrounding society and the influence of churches had brought other meaning to the polygamous practice but it was not enough to eliminate it.

Nowadays there are natives married with two or three wives, and in ancient times it was common man have a bigger number of wives. In married life wives use to live together in harmony and peace; they deny to be jealous of each other and they affirm that there is no submission or contempt feeling because they understand that they constitute the same family, which it includes similar cares with children from other women.

The celebration of the Mapimaí ritual starts with the entrance of clans in single file, the wives following the lead (the elders), one of which carries a torch which represents the fire of life. The rest of the natives, with bows and arrows and accompanied by their wives, follows the leader.

The Mapimaí is a ritual with songs, dancing, fraternizations, reciprocal activities that approximate the clans and permit the reflexion and interchange of backgrounds and experiences at the action space. The ritualistic and symbolic representation of Mapimaí in 2012 shows itself different from the previous due to the Paiter Suruí to use shorts with specific colours and the name of the clan to which the member belonged, in order to characterize with vehemence his or her identity and family territoriality.

In the place in which the host clan was waiting it was installed sculptures produced with banana stems which were represented a family of farmers: father, mother and children. At that moment, symbolically, the Paiter Suruí thrown into a climate of war, emitting shrill sounds, after they shot in some puppets and cut their heads. They continued their manifestation with loud sounds as a celebration for had won the war.

This symbolical content represented in the Mapimaí has the sense of spiritual and cultural strengthening of the collective, in a way to solidify the kinship ties and reaffirm the marks of territoriality and their connection to the land. That acting is not only a physical expression, but it consists in the interaction between human being and supernatural, according to Dardel (2011: 48):

> [...] the connection between human being and land received, in the temporal-space atmosphere of the magic-mythical world, a meaning essentially qualitative. Geography is more than a basis or element. It is a power. From land comes the powers that attack or protect human being, they determine his/her social existence and their own behavior, which are mixed with their organic and psychic life, to a such point that it is impossible to separate the outside world from the facts that are human properly.

This form of symbolic representation realized by the Paiter Suruí leads us to the reflection that, in fact, the ethnicity, in its process of apprehension of the cosmogonic phenomena, remembers aspects related to territorial conflicts against settlers, as a result of migration encouraged by Brazilian State from the 1960s, when thousands of migrants in search of opportunities – land, money, among others – were leading to the *Paiterey Garah* Indigenous Land.

In that direction, the representation of Mapimaí can be understood as if the invader was present or as a tentative of exorcize them from their territory. At the same time it signifies that the ethnicity is vigilant in relation to actions that may happen in their territory, such as the presence of loggers, miners, invaders of land, among others civil society actors[3].

Between one pause to another in the Mapimaí, the owners of ritual (the hosts) came and under the "*chapéu de palha*" (a house built of straw) they offered "*chicha*" in a large quantities until to start the evening. Then they joined together again and told their personal experience in the *Tupi Mondé* language, and they expressed laughs.

Thus we understand that the Mapimaí is the celebration of life, although, in a first moment, the organization of the ritual had been performed with the participations of clans in a separately way; the climax happens when all the attendants get together and results in the unit as identity and belongingness.

V - Not Conclusive Final Considerations

In this work we can perceive that fragmentation of space, of territoriality, it depends on political or economic joint and structure, in which external organizations act as propagators of ruptures of ethnic identity. The recognition of indigenous identity as a collective being became more than political right, in conformity with Cardoso de Oliveira (2006: 35):

> In those societies the dimension of ethnical identity related to the culture tends to create individual or collective crises. And with them particular social problems are raised which are susceptible of confrontation by public policies as the recognition policies, for example.

That fragmentation can be pointed when we see the existing houses in the village, which are not part anymore of the model of housing from their forefathers. Today their houses are built with "modern structures" and characteristics from a surrounding society, which it results in changes not only related to the houses, but in their spirituality through churches, in their education through schools. We even situated the media through television, newspaper and internet, which are indirectly related to the "structuring markers", since they also have an inappropriate influence.

The insertion of religious segments which are foreign to cosmogony, the insertion of languages, the reduction of territory through demarcation for inclusion in surrounding society, the pressure by obligatory displacement of a specific collective from its original space to other unknown space, they are important elements of those "markers".

---

[3] It is necessary to point that, in the present, the Paiter Suruí attempt to solve the conflicts with the outside actors through dialogue, even they are enabling themselves technically and politically for this purpose. Those dialogues had resulted in solid partnerships with government and non-governmental institutions, corporations as Google Earth, as well as they have elaborated a long term planning (Suruí Forest Carbon Project, which it is duly certified) with the aim of to maintain the forest and at the same time to safeguard the territory, culture and survival of the ethnicity.

The "structural markers" share the idea of building from a collective vision and involve the founding aspects of cosmogony. Then, the Mapimaí is one of those "markers", which it is built by the Paiter Suruí collective, which it is full of ancestrality, heritage, pertinency, identity and territoriality.

The existing clans, although with specificities in their contexts, form a single collective: the Paiter Suruí with identity, own cultural values, territoriality lived and experienced in the space of action, that is, in their particularities of building, seeing and understanding the world which, added to the conception/evolution from other people, it culminates in what we denominate human cultural diversity.

Thus, we understand that the Paiter Suruí territoriality exceeds the boundaries demarcated by state, as a result of the relationship that they establish with their cosmos, which it is much more than physical relationship. The territoriality is strongly supported in the collective memory, though with the reduction of their lands some of their burial grounds and sacred places are situated outside from institutionalized boundary – which, for them, it represents a violation of their rights and refusing of citizenship, as a tentative of invisibility.

Despite all the problematic found and cultural hibridity, the Paiter Suruí make of challenge their walking towards better days, according to *Labiway Esaga*, Almir Narayamoga Suruí:

> What is happening with our culture it is that every year every day culture advances because culture is not a thing that stationary, it is a thing that walks, it walks in a positive way or in a negative way, and therefore we are firmly working on the maintenance of our culture and on the utilization of the non-indigenous culture (Silva & Almeida Silva, 2012: 412).

We understand as one of the possible ways the permanency of their ethnoknowledges associated to scientific knowledge, through formal education, which nowadays it is one of the preoccupations of the Paiter Suruí in the quest for their rights as citizens.

References

Almeida Silva, Adnilson de. (2010). Territorialidades e Identidade do Coletivo Kawahib da Terra Indígena Uru-Eu-Wau-Wau em Rondônia: "Orevaki Are" (reencontro) dos "marcadores territoriais". (Tese de Doutorado em Geografia). Curitiba: UFPR/SCT/DG/PPGMDG. 301.

_____. (2012). A questão indígena em Rondônia e os projetos de desenvolvimento na Amazônia Ocidental. Ciência Geográfica, v. XVI. 8-14. Disponível em http://www.agbbauru.org.br/publicacoes/revista/anoXVI_1/agb_xvi1_versao_internet/AGB_abr2012_02.pdf. Acesso em 10 dez 2013.

_____. (2011). Representações Indígenas: Territorialidades e Identidade – Uma Aproximação Teórica. In: Revista RA'E GA - UFPR: n. 23 UFPR. 238-262. Disponível em http://ojs.c3sl.ufpr.br/ojs/index.php/raega/article/view/24839/16647. Acesso em 15 dez 2013.

_____. (2013). Espiritualidade, territorialidade: interfaces das representações culturais coletivas indígenas. In: Revista RA'E GA: o Espaço Geográfico em Análise - UFPR, v.

27. 111-139. Disponível em http://ojs.c3sl.ufpr.br/ojs2/index.php/raega/article/view File/30420/19697. Acesso em 10 out 2013.

_____ & Leandro, E.L. (2010). Questão Indígena na Amazônia, a especificidade de Rondônia: algumas considerações. In: Amaral, J.J.O. & Leandro, E.L. (orgs). Amazônia e Cenários Indígenas. São Carlos: Pedro e João Editores. 45-70.

Ávila, C.A.B. (2008). O componente social do plano Colômbia e a territorialidade da comunidade camponesa-indígena Awá do Departamento do Putumayo (Colômbia). Tese de Doutorado em Geografia. São Paulo: USP/FFLCH/Departamento de Geografia.

Brandão, C.R. (1982). Pesquisa Participante. São Paulo: Brasiliense.

Bonnemaison, J. (2002).Viagem em torno do Território. In: Rosendahl, Z. & Corrêa, R. L. (orgs.). Geografia Cultural: um século (3). Rio Janeiro: EDUERJ. 83-131.

Bosi, E. Memória e sociedade. (2005).13. ed. São Paulo: Companhia das Letras.

Cardoso de Oliveira, R. (2006). Caminhos da Identidade: Ensaios sobre etnicidade e multiculturalismo. São Paulo: UNESP.

Cassirer, E: Linguagem e Mito. (1992). São Paulo: Perspectiva.

_____. (1994 [1944]). Ensaio sobre o homem: introdução a uma filosofia da cultura humana. São Paulo: Martins Fontes

Claval, P. (2007). A geografia Cultural. Florianópolis: EdUFSC.

_____. (2011). Epistemologia da Geografia. Florianópolis: EdUFSC.

_____. (2008). Introdução: Uma, ou algumas, abordagem(ns) cultural(is) na geografia humana. In: Serpa, A.(org.). Espaços Culturais: vivências, imaginações e representações [online]. Anais do II NEER. Salvador: EDUFBA. 12-29. Disponível em http://static.scielo.org/scielobooks/bk/pdf/serpa-9788523209162.pdf. Acesso em 10 dez 2013.

Dardel, E. (2011). O Homem e a Terra: natureza da realidade geográfica. São Paulo: Perspectiva.

Galvão, E. (1979). Encontro de sociedades: índios e brancos no Brasil. Col. Estudos brasileiros, v. 29. Rio de Janeiro: Paz e Terra.

Gil, A.C. (2007)Métodos e Técnicas de Pesquisa Social. São Paulo: Atlas. http://pib.socioambiental.org/pt/povo/surui-paiter/1763. Acesso 10 ago 2013.

Kanindé Associação de Defesa Etnoambiental. (2011) Etnozoneamento Paiterey Garah: Terra Indígena Sete de Setembro. Porto Velho: Kanindé.

Mauss, M. Essais de Sociologie. (1968-1969 [1931a]). Paris: Éditions de Minuit (tomos 1 e 2 de Oeuvres).

_____. (1968-1969 [1931b]). Oeuvres. Paris: Editions de Minuit, vol. 3.

_____.(1997 [1950]). Essai sur le don: forme et raison de l'échange dans les sociétés archaïques. In: Mauss, M. Sociologie et anthropologie. Paris: PUF (ed. original: Année Sociologique, seconde série, tome 1, Paris, 1923-1924).

_____. (2003). Sociologia e Antropologia. São Paulo: Cosac & Naify.

Rocha, E. (1996). O que é mito. São Paulo: Brasiliense.

Sahlins, M. (1997). "O 'pessimismo sentimental' e a experiência etnográfica: porque a cultura não é um 'objeto' em via de extinção (parte I)". Mana [online]. vol. 3, n.1, 41-73. Disponível em http://www.scielo.br/pdf/mana/v3n1/2455.pdf. Acesso 15 nov 2011.

_____. (1997). "O "pessimismo sentimental" e a experiência etnográfica: por que a cultura não é um "objeto" em via de extinção (parte II)". Mana [online]. vol. 3, n.2, 103-150. Disponível em http://www.scielo.br/pdf/mana/v3n2/2442.pdf. Acesso 16 novembro 2011.

_____. 2003 [1985]. Ilhas de História. Rio de Janeiro: Jorge Zahar.

Silva, C.A. & Almeida Silva, Adnilson de. (2012). Paiter Suruí. Revista Pesquisa & Criação, 2012, vol. 11, Número Especial: Anais do XXI PIBIC/UNIR/CNPq. Porto Velho: UNIR. 406-414. Disponível em http://www.periodicos.unir.br/index.php/propesq/issue/view/222. Acesso 15 novembro 2013.

In: Spirituality
Editor: Edith C. Roberts

ISBN: 978-1-63482-370-8

Chapter 10

TOWARD A GLOBAL UNDERSTANDING OF SPIRITUALITY AND RELIGIOSITY: DEFINITIONS, ASSESSMENTS, AND BENEFITS

Sarah E. Koss and Mark D. Holder*
University of British Columbia; Psychology, IKBSAS, Canada

ABSTRACT

Throughout history, the terms spirituality and religiosity were often used interchangeably until the constructs were separated due in part to the rise of secularism and a shift in Western culture during the last few decades (Hill et al., 2000; Zinnbauer et al., 1997). Many researchers, theologians, and philosophers now consider these two terms as connected but separable constructs, and studies now endeavour to clarify this distinction (e.g., Emmons & Paloutzian, 2003; Hill et al., 2000; Holder, Coleman, & Wallace., 2010). However, researchers have yet to reach a consensus on the distinct meanings of the two terms (Emmons & Paloutzian, 2003; Hill et al., 2000; Zinnbauer et al., 1997). This lack of consensus contributes to inconsistencies in the literature and difficulty comparing findings across studies. To address these concerns, the present chapter compares a range of definitions for both spirituality and religiosity before proposing the following new definition of spirituality: "Spirituality is a feeling of Connectedness to something greater experienced by cultivating a relationship with oneself, one's community, one's environment, and one's perception of the transcendent." Using this definition as a reference, we examined current assessments of spirituality and religiosity, focusing on each one's ability to capture the construct on a global level. Additionally, the benefits of religiosity and spirituality, especially concerning subjective well-being and health, are discussed. Together, these considerations lead to ideas and possibilities for future directions of spirituality research.

* mark.holder@ubc.ca.

INTRODUCTION

Historically, religious ideas have provided frameworks and sets of principles for explaining the world and defining an ethical life (Kurtz, 2012). In the Western world, the Christian church's ubiquitous presence influenced everything from social relations to political schemes (Tappert, 1967), which paralleled Eastern religions, such as Buddhism where the term for *religion* was often synonymous with *law* (Toshio & Stone, 1996). More recently, the rise of secularism and modern critiques of theology have significantly diminished the societal influence of religion in Western society (Kurtz, 2012; Hill et al., 2000), though there has been a resurgence of religion in numerous other regions of the world (Pesut, Fowler, Taylor, Reimer-Kirkham, & Sawatzky, 2008). According to Kurtz (2012), the world is becoming more like a multicultural global village, and consequently the exclusivity of many religious ideas is being increasingly challenged. This challenging of religious ideas is undermining the traditional sources of ethical systems that enable individuals to coexist peacefully and justly within a society; yet, with this movement toward a global village, current society has a pronounced need for such an ethical system (Kurtz, 2012).

The situation may not be as dire as that identified by Kurtz. Historically, the terms spirituality and religiosity were often used interchangeably. However, the rise of secularism and modern science has caused a shift during the last few decades, especially in Western society, and the two terms are now considered related but separate constructs (Hill et al., 2000; Zinnbauer et al., 1997). Modern science initially avoided the topics of religion and spirituality, but there has been a more recent increase in studies of these constructs in many research disciplines (Emmons & Paloutzian, 2003). This research has led some to an understanding that to be human is to be spiritual, though individuals have the right to choose the degree to which they identify with the construct (Pesut, Fowler, Reimer-Kirkham, Taylor, & Sawatzky, 2009). Consequently, though the construct of religion is typically conceptualized in culture-specific ways (Worthington et al., 2014), the construct of spirituality may transcend cultural divides through focusing on common humanity. As a result, by understanding the construct of spirituality, it may be possible to bridge gaps in the global village caused by religion.

However, within academia, researchers, theologians, and philosophers have yet to reach a consensus on the separate meanings of religiosity and spirituality (Emmons & Paloutzian, 2003; Hill et al., 2000; Zinnbauer et al., 1997). This lack of consensus contributes to inconsistencies in the literature and difficulty comparing results across studies. To address these concerns, the present chapter compares a range of definitions for religiosity and spirituality before proposing a new definition of spirituality that is applicable across cultures and regions. Using this definition as a reference, we then examine assessments of spirituality and religiosity, focusing on each one's ability to capture the separate construct on a global level. Once definitions and assessments have been established, the benefits of religiosity and spirituality, especially concerning subjective well-being and health, are discussed. All together, these considerations lead to ideas and possibilities for future directions of spirituality research.

CONCEPTUAL DEFINITIONS

Research findings on religiosity and spirituality are often difficult to compare across studies due to inconsistencies in the conceptualization, definitions, and measures of these constructs. Although many researchers, theologians, and philosophers now consider religiosity and spirituality as connected but separable constructs (e.g., Holder, Coleman, & Wallace, 2010), there is still a lack of consensus on the separate meanings of the two terms (Emmons & Paloutzian, 2003; Hill et al., 2000; Zinnbauer et al., 1997). This lack of consensus is more pronounced in the definition of spirituality, as most studies now utilize similar definitions of religiosity, such as "The identification with institutional beliefs that adhere to specific traditions and doctrines of a religion" (Hill et al., 2000; Holder et al., 2010). Such definitions of religiosity free the endorsement of spirituality by recognizing that individuals can self-identify as being spiritual independently of following a specific religion.

Definitions of spirituality vary greatly across research disciplines. To be useful, the definition of spirituality must be valid and measurable for research purposes, as well as globally applicable. If the definition is vague, replicating studies is more challenging; if the definition is established within a particular theological understanding, it may unintentionally exclude diverse viewpoints (Pesut et al., 2008). Some researchers have argued that a globally applicable definition of spirituality is not possible (e.g., Fenwick & English, 2004). However, given that much research posits that part of being human is to be spiritual (Pesut et al., 2008), this chapter proposes that a global definition of spirituality is possible if the emphasis is on common humanity, viewed as the similarities of human experience. (This is not to be confused with humanism, which often emphasizes human rationality over faith [Herrick, 2005; Higgins, 2014].)

Several studies have utilized minimal definitions of spirituality such as "A search for the sacred" (Pargament, 1999), or "An inner belief system" (Holder et al., 2010). Although these definitions proved sufficient for the studies that employed them, both lack precise detail and are associated with traditional assumptions of the spiritual world (Pesut et al., 2008). Alternatively, some studies used definitions that emphasize a singular aspect of spirituality, such as "A meaningful purpose" or "A union with God" (Hill et al., 2000), but these do not encapsulate the entire construct of spirituality and the second is clearly rooted within Judeo-Christian theology. In contrast to a minimal or singular-aspect definition, many studies have employed a multidimensional approach to defining spirituality (Hill et al., 2000). However, there is no consensus regarding the dimensions of spirituality.

LaPierre (1994) described a model of spirituality recognizing six dimensions: i) *journey*—the search for purpose and meaning in life; ii) *encounter with transcendence*—the recognition that there is a level of reality beyond ordinary human experience, often referred to as God; iii) *community*—belonging to a group of individuals on a similar path; iv) *religion*—what an individual does in response to a belief in the divine; v) *the mystery of creation*—an experience of the natural world and its creator; and vi) *transformation*—a personal change that occurs through becoming more spiritual. These six dimensions have face validity, but the definition is strongly rooted in Christian theology and thus is not fully inclusive of global spirituality.

In contrast, Elkins, Hedstrom, Hughes, Leaf, and Saunders (1988) suggested a definition of spirituality consisting of nine dimensions: i) *transcendent dimension*—an experientially based belief in something greater; ii) *meaning and purpose of life*—an authentic sense that life is meaningful and one's own existence has a purpose; iii) *mission in life*—a sense of vocation; iv) *sacredness of life*—a sense of awe and belief that life is holy; v) *material values*—an understanding that ultimate satisfaction is not found in the material, but the spiritual; vi) *altruism*—a strong sense of social justice and a belief that we are all part of common humanity; vii) *idealism*—a commitment to the betterment of the world; viii) *awareness of the tragic*—valuing of the preciousness of life through being aware of suffering; and ix) *fruits of spirituality*—the effect that an individual's spirituality can have on many aspects of his or her life. This multidimensional definition appears globally applicable, being established with a focus on the human nature of spirituality, but it may not be valid beyond face value, as the logic behind the list is rather unsystematic. In addition, Elkins et al.'s dimensions cannot completely envelope the dimensions proposed by LaPierre and vice versa. For instance, Elkins et al.'s *mission in life* dimension is similar to LaPierre's *journey* dimension, but it is unclear whether Elkins et al.'s dimensions encompass LaPierre's *transformation* and LaPierre's dimensions encompass Elkins et al.'s *idealism.* This suggests that perhaps both multidimensional definitions are capturing some, but not all dimensions of spirituality, or alternatively that at least one definition is reaching dimensions beyond the core construct of spirituality.

Both Elkins et al. and LaPierre developed their definitions through extracting recurring ideas from the spiritual literature. However, given that the dimensions identified by different studies vary substantially, this may not be a fully successful approach. In contrast, Fisher, Francis, and Johnson (2000) created a four-domain definition of spiritual health by examining four principle relationships in life: the self, the community, the environment, and the transcendent. These relationships or "domains" integrate core aspects of human experience, as well as parallel most of the dimensions of spirituality proposed in other multidimensional definitions, such as those by Elkins et al. and LaPierre. The first, *personal domain*, is the relationship with oneself, and is often expressed through a sense of purpose in life; the second, *communal domain*, is the relationship with one's community and is often expressed through interpersonal relationships; the third, *environmental domain*, is the relationship with one's environment and is often expressed through awe and enjoyment of nature; the fourth, *transcendent domain*, is the relationship with one's perception of the transcendentand is often expressed through an understanding of some-thing or some-One beyond human level.

As Fisher et al. (2000) indicated, most people develop all four domains, but some individuals are particularly expressed in one domain. For instance, an individual might strongly relate to the environmental domain through a passion for gardening or the transcendent domain through a passion for music. However, according to Hill et al. (2000):

> "To say, 'I find my spirituality in gardening' or 'Music is my spirituality' might indeed suggest that a person finds great satisfaction and subjective well-being through gardening or playing music seriously… but unless such lifestyles are responses to a perception of the Sacred (e.g., the person gardens because caring for nature is a way of experiencing the creative forces of the universe, the person plays and listens to music because its beauty and the complex mathematical structures underlying the music cause the person to contemplate the beauty and order of God or the entire universe), then it is inappropriate to refer to gardening or music as 'spiritual'" (p. 65).

Recognizing the veracity of Hill et al.'s claim, this chapter proposes that spirituality consists of the four domains of spiritual health described by Fisher et al., but that these domains must also generate a specific sense of what Hill et al. refers to as the Sacred, which this chapter refers to as Connectedness. The term Sacred corresponds with religion (Sacred, n.d.), which limits its suitability in a global definition of spirituality. Alternatively, Connectedness corresponds with relationships and being human (Meezenbroek et al., 2012), making it a more conceptually accessible and cross-culturally inclusive term. Furthermore, Connectedness is often mentioned in the research literature in association with spiritual ideas and definitions (Bangert, 2014; Chiu, Emblen, Van Hofwegen, Sawatzky, & Meyerhoff, 2004). Therefore, situating Connectedness as the central component entails a reorganizing of the terms associated with spirituality, but not the addition of a new term. Fisher et al. (2000) alluded to the idea of Connectedness, but did not emphasize it. Without the concept of Connectedness within each domain, the four-domain definition of spiritual health does not fully capture the essence of spirituality. Bangert (2014) discussed Connectedness as a central component of spirituality, but did not include the four domains. Meezenbroek et al. (2012) created a definition based on Fisher et al.'s four domains and included the idea of Connectedness, but the wording of their definition is not concise and does not fully conceptualize Connectedness as an overarching, central component similar to the term Sacred. Therefore, the present chapter proposes Connectedness as the central component in spirituality and suggests the following succinct, multidimensional, globally-applicable definition of spirituality: "Spirituality is a feeling of Connectedness to something greater experienced by cultivating a relationship with oneself, one's community, one's environment, and one's perception of the transcendent."

Rather than emphasizing dimensions representing constructs related to spirituality, this definition emphasizes domains representing fundamental relationships in the human experience. Constructs related to spirituality can be incorporated in these domains, allowing for the relationship between spirituality and each construct to be acknowledged and examined without requiring different definitions. For example, meaning in life is often acknowledged as a component of spirituality (e.g., LaPierre, 1994); researchers have examined this claim and reported that spirituality is predictive of changes in meaning in life (Kashdan and Nezlek, 2012); and meaning in life can be incorporated in the personal domain of the proposed definition (Fisher et al., 2000). This is similar for other constructs and other domains, such as incorporating altruism in the communal domain, nature connectedness in the environmental domain, and prayer (a venture to create a connection with the divine [Ladd et al., 2007; Whittington & Scher, 2010]) in the transcendent domain.

Additionally, by conceptualizing Connectedness as a central focus, constructs related to spirituality that do not fit within a specific domain, such as forgiveness and meditation, can be included under the broader understanding of Connectedness. Forgiveness is often considered only a Judeo-Christian concept (Idler et al., 2003). However, forgiveness is a component in most religions (Kidwell, Wade, & Blaedel, 2012) and spiritual beliefs (Unterrainer, Nelson, Collicutt, & Fink, 2012), as well as a contemporary topic of study in psychology (Emmons, & Paloutzian, 2003). In response to the demand for a universal definition of forgiveness that is disassociated from religion, Toussaint and Friedman (2009) considered the work of research psychologists studying forgiveness (e.g., McCullough, 2001) as well as spiritual ideas from organizations (e.g., Foundation for Inner Peace, 2008) to create the following definition: "Forgiveness occurs when a person lets go of emotionally backed judgments, grievances, attack-thoughts and beliefs toward themselves and others so that they can perceive the goodness, worth, magnificence, innocence, love, and peace in both themselves and another person simultaneously" (p. 636).

This universally applicable definition of forgiveness can be related to each of the four domains of spirituality. It is related to the personal domain because the motivation behind forgiveness is often to free oneself from negative emotions (North, 1998), and because of self-forgiveness, which involves abandoning self-resentment while accepting that one is only human (Bauer et al., 1992). Forgiveness is related to the communal domain because it often involves forgiving other people, and because of collectivistic forgiveness, which occurs when individuals value collective goals over personal goals and desires in order to re-establish harmony within a community (Hook, Worthington, Utsey, Davis, & Burnette, 2012). Forgiveness is related to the environmental domain through circumstantial forgiveness, which entails forgiving situations, including environmental ones such as natural disasters (Toussaint & Friedman, 2009). And, forgiveness is related to the transcendent domain because the feeling of being abandoned by God can sometimes occur during times of struggle for those of monotheistic faiths (Idler et al., 2003), and because the motivation for forgiveness is often tied to perceptions of the transcendent within specific religions. For example, religions such as Christianity, Islam, and Judaism teach of a God who is forgiving of His followers and, in turn, they are required to extend forgiveness to fellow humans, while Buddhism and Hinduism take a slightly different approach by teaching forgiveness as a practice that encourages positive Karma (Kidwell, Wade, & Blaedel, 2012). These two approaches to forgiveness are similar in that they are in response to a transcendent concept, such as God or Karma, and can produce similar results (Tripathi & Mullet, 2010). Yet, forgiveness is not just related to each of the four domains; it also helps to restore Connectedness in general. For instance, a person who normally feels a greater connection to their community may lose their feeling of Connectedness if a transgression is perceived, but then through forgiveness Connectedness can once again be restored.

Similar to forgiveness, meditation is also related to all four domains and Connectedness. In general, meditation involves moment-to-moment attention to one's immediate experience, though the execution of the practice varies across types (Kristeller, 2011). According to Sedlmeier et al. (2012), people meditate for two reasons: for spiritual reasons such as gaining inner peace and enlightenment, and more recently for therapeutic reasons such as overcoming physiological problems. Many researchers avoid the spiritual context of meditation because religious associations cause it to be a sensitive subject (Kristeller, 2011). However, now that spirituality has been distinguished as separate from religion, it may be possible to distinguish meditation for spiritual purposes from religion as well. As a spiritual construct, meditation is similar to forgiveness because it is associated with all four domains of spirituality.

Meditation has the strongest relation to the personal domain, as the practice of meditation is, in general, a personal practice. Through meditation one can gain self-actualization (Alexander et al., 1991), insight into one's life (Walsh, 1983), and inner peace (Kristeller, 2011). There is also a community aspect to meditation. Practicing meditation can help cultivate interpersonal relationships (Carson, Carson, Gil, & Baucom, 2004; Shapiro, 2002), and according to Kristeller (2011), the shift in self-perception caused by mediation can be accompanied by a shift in relation to other people. Meditation is also related to the environmental domain, as meditating in a natural setting can increase one's connectedness to nature (Chambliss, 2013). Meditating can also cause one to feel a connection to a greater, transcendent dimension. For example, the meditation effect referred to as an anomalous experience or altered state causes feelings of floating and paravisual experiences (Cardeña, Lynn, & Krippner, 2014), which are often considered by meditators as signs of transcendent connection (Kristeller, 2011). Furthermore, similar to how forgiveness can restore spirituality, meditation has been shown to increase spirituality. For example, Bormann et al. (2006) found that individuals living with HIV who repeated a spiritual mantra for five minutes every day had increased spiritual faith and spiritual connectedness after ten weeks.

Overall, by allowing for various types of relationships between spirituality and other constructs, the proposed definition of spirituality sets itself apart from previous definitions. While many definitions provide definitive components, this definition provides a definitive framework with room for flexibility. As the empirical understandings of different constructs—from altruism to forgiveness—change, this chapter's definition of spirituality can recognize the new evidence and adapt the situating of components within the definition without requiring changes to the four domains and Connectedness framework.

Assessments

Having formulated separate definitions of religiosity and spirituality, the next concern involves the measurement of these constructs. Currently there are hundreds of measures of religiosity and spirituality (Emmons & Paloutzian, 2003). Hill & Hood (1999) compiled an extensive volume reviewing 125 measures and 14 years later Hill (2013) estimated that at least 100 additional measures have been developed. Included in this estimate are self-report measures assessing a variety of related topics, from religious fundamentalism to mysticism, as well as a few alternative methods to self-report, such as Nielsen and Webster's Simultaneous Objective/Subjective Assessment (Hill, 2013). Considering the large number of measures available, Hill (2013) echoed the earlier plea by Gorsuch (1984) that researchers not construct new measures, but rather utilize, and only if necessary modify, existing measures.

Nonetheless, Hill (2013) acknowledged that current assessments have limitations; a sentiment supported by other researchers (e.g., Kapuscinski & Masters, 2010). Brief scales are often desirable, but their reliability may be low if there are too few items (Hill, 2013). Even if a scale displays adequate reliability, the validity is often questionable because of problems in defining religion and spirituality, including inconsistency and overlap (Hill, 2013; Kapuscinski & Masters, 2010). In addition, there are cultural limitations; many of the religious and spiritual scales are framed within a Judeo-Christian perspective, making them culturally insensitive and of limited use for non-Judeo-Christian populations (Meezenbroek et al., 2012), and concepts related to religiosity and spirituality may be difficult to translate accurately (Casas, González, Figuer, & Malo, 2009). Furthermore, in developing measures of spirituality, more weight is often given to inner experiences including cognitive and affective components, while overt behavioural elements are not emphasized. Although spirituality is a personal experience, Kapuscinski and Masters (2010) argued that the exclusion of observable behaviour in spirituality scales seems unjustified from both a psychological and theological perspective.

Considering Hill and Gorsuch's appeals to researchers to not create new measures, while also recognizing the limitations of many scales, this chapter discusses current measures with the goal of finding two appropriate measures—one for religiosity and one for spirituality. Previous review articles and books have already reviewed existing measures (e.g., Hill & Hood, 1999; Hill, 2013; Kapuscinski & Masters, 2010; Meezenbroek et al., 2012). Subsequently, this chapter focuses on a smaller number of potentially suitable measures. Ideally, the appropriate measures will capture the essence of the religiosity and spirituality definitions with minimal overlap, be suitable on a global level, include both inner experience and outer behavioural components, and exhibit adequate reliability and validity.

Religiosity Measures

Scales that assess religiosity in a manner that is aligned with this chapter's definition (i.e., the identification with institutional beliefs that adhere to specific traditions and doctrines of a religion) are not prevalent. Many of the available scales assess dimensions related to religiosity, such as the Religious Maturity Scale (Dudley & Cruise, 1990) or the Religious Fundamentalism Scale (Altemeyer & Hunsberger, 1992, 2004), but are not designed to assess the general concept of religiosity. Of those that do focus more on the general construct, most utilize Christian terminology and ideas throughout, such as the Cross-Cultural Dimensions of Religiosity scale (Jong, Faulkner, & Warland, 1976), which includes the item "What do you believe about Jesus?" Consequently, this scale and others with items strictly pertaining to a specific religion are not as useful in assessing religiosity on a global level, and thus are not appropriate measures of religiosity as defined in this chapter.

A common practice to increase the inclusiveness of measures of religiosity is to replace the word "God" with "higher power" (e.g., Unterrainer, Nelson, Collicutt, & Fink, 2012). However, even if the language is made more inclusive, many of measures are still not globally applicable because they do not fully distinguish between the constructs of religiosity and spirituality. For example, the Multidimensional Inventory for Religious/Spiritual Well-Being (MI-RSWB; Unterrainer et al., 2012) consistently refers to the constructs together, as if they are interchangeable. Similarly, the Brief Multidimensional Measure of Religion and Spirituality (BMMRS; Fetzer Institute, 2003) includes the item, "I find strength and comfort in my religion" in the spirituality section; and the 20-item Beliefs and Values scale (King et al., 2006) scores the religious and spiritual items together, such that someone who is religious and spiritual will always score higher than someone who is equally devoted to his/her spirituality, but not religious.

The dearth of global, inclusive religiosity measures may suggest that a singular religiosity measure cannot be developed. One approach, given the marked differences in religious beliefs, is to develop religiosity measures tailored to specific religions. For instance, the Psychological Measure of Islamic Religiousness (Abu Raiya, Pargament, Stein, & Mahoney, 2007) assesses religiosity for those of the Islam tradition, while the Measures of Hindu Pathway Scales (Tarakeshwar, Pargament, & Mahoney, 2003) assesses religiosity for those of the Hindu tradition. However, the increasing movement toward a global village has created the demand for a religiosity measure that is culturally sensitive and can be used when sampling from a multicultural society. To meet this demand, the scale must focus on commonalities of the religious experience. A universal scale of religiosity cannot focus on specific beliefs, which can vary substantially across religions, but it can focus on commitment, which is applicable across religions. Therefore, rather than asking "Are you religious?" which implies examining one's beliefs, measures could ask "How religious are you?" which implies examining one's level of commitment. This change is supported by evidence that suggests being highly religious is strongly associated with being highly religiously committed (Worthington et al., 2003).

There are several available scales of religious commitment including the Salience in Religious Commitment Scale, first published in 1975 (Roof & Perkins). Since its conception, the scale has been used in several studies, including a few within the last 10 years (e.g., Bohus, Woods, & Chan, 2005; Rakos, Laurene, & Slane, 2008). The scale appears culturally inclusive as the questions simply ask about religious faith, but it may not fully encompass the construct of religiosity because there are only three items. In addition, the scale relies heavily on face validity and may be subject to a ceiling effect (Young, 1999). Therefore, though this scale has been used sufficiently as a brief measure of religious commitment, it may not be the most suitable scale for measuring general religiosity.

Another measure of religious commitment is the Santa Clara Strength of Religious Faith Questionnaire (SCSORF; Plante & Boccoccini, 1997a). With 10 items, the SCSORF appears to better cover the broad construct of religiosity. Although most of the items concern the internal experience, such as "I look to my faith as a source of comfort," some items do imply external behaviours, such as "I consider myself active in my faith or church" (Plante & Boccoccini, 1997a). Furthermore, the scale has strong psychometric properties, having shown excellent reliability and validity (Lewis, Shevlin, McGuckin, & Navratil, 2001; Plante & Boccoccini, 1997b). Nonetheless, one drawback of the SCSORF is that some items use Judeo-Christian terms, making the scale less culturally inclusive. One study adapted the scale for Muslims (Pakpour, Plante, Saffari, & Fridlund, 2014), but it has yet to be adapted to be globally suitable.

An additional religious commitment measure is the Religious Commitment Inventory—10 (RCI-10; Worthington et al., 2003). This scale also consists of 10 religiosity-related items, several of which are similar to those in the SCSORF (Plante & Boccoccini, 1997a). For example, the SCSORF item, "I enjoy being around others who share my faith" is similar to the RCI-10 item, "I enjoy spending time with others of my religious affiliation." However, the RCI-10 items are more balanced between internal experiences and external behaviours, containing items such as "Religion is especially important to me because it answers many questions about the meaning of life" and "I make financial contributions to my religious organization." The RCI-10 has shown strong internal consistency, 3-week and 5-month test-retest reliability, and construct and discriminant validity (Hill, 2013; Worthington et al., 2003). In addition, the measure has received modest support for its use with nonreligious individuals and individuals from a variety of religious traditions, including Buddhists, Muslims, and Hindus (Worthington et al., 2003). Consequently, of the potential religiosity measures discussed, the RCI-10 may be the most appropriate measure of religiosity as a global construct separate from spirituality.

Spirituality Measures

Compared with religiosity, a potentially suitable measure of spirituality in alignment with our proposed definition (i.e., spirituality is a feeling of Connectedness to something greater experienced by cultivating a relationship with oneself, one's community, one's environment, and one's perception of the transcendent) was more easily identified. As explained previously, this definition of spirituality is based on Fisher et al.'s (2000) four domains of spiritual health. These four domains also make up the foundation for Fisher's 20-item Spiritual Well-Being Questionnaire (SWBQ; Gomez & Fisher, 2003). This correspondence between the definition and measure make the SWBQ an obvious choice for the measure of spirituality, though it also shows potential for several other reasons.

The psychometric properties of the SWBQ have been extensively analysed with promising results. It has shown strong reliability, including internal consistency, variance extracted and composite reliability, as well as strong validity, including construct, concurrent, discriminant, and predictive (Gomez & Fisher, 2003). In addition, the SWBQ has undergone exploratory (Gomez & Fisher, 2003) and multi-group confirmatory (Gomez & Fisher, 2005b) factor analyses, which supported gender response equivalencies and factorial independence from personality, as well as verified the presence of the four domains and a single overarching spiritual well-being factor. The SWBQ has also been analysed using item response theory (IRT; Gomez & Fisher, 2005a). Although the IRT analyses suggested areas for improvement, Fisher (2010) noted that none of the improvement attempts (e.g., Moodley, 2008) have resulted in substantial improvement over the original 20-item SWBQ.

One difficulty with the SWBQ is that it has always been portrayed as a measure of spiritual health, not spirituality. Although similar, a spirituality measure should conceptually answer the question, "How spiritual are you?" while a spiritual health measure should conceptually answer the question, "How good do you feel about your spirituality?" However, literature suggests that while most spirituality measures rely solely on items regarding one's lived experience, spiritual health actually depends on one's world-view and beliefs as well (Fisher, 2010; Ross, 2006). Fisher subsequently modified the SWBQ and renamed it the Spiritual Health and Life Orientation Measure (SHALOM; 2010). The SHALOM utilizes the same 20 items as the SWBQ, but contains two sections. In the first section, respondents rate the 20 items according to their ideal; in the second section, respondents rate the same items according to their lived experience. The difference between respondents' "ideals" and "lived experience" gives an indication of their spiritual health. For example, if an individual does not feel the environment is necessary for spiritual health, s/he will likely score low on the item, "oneness with nature," but this will likely be congruent with his/her ideals for that item and thus will not be concerning (Fisher, 2010).

Consequently, with spiritual health conceptualized as the difference between the ideals and lived experience sections of the SHALOM, the lived experience section alone (i.e., the original SWBQ) can simply be viewed as a measure of spirituality. This is supported by research that successfully utilized items from the SWBQ as a measure of spirituality rather than spiritual health (e.g., Holder et al., 2010). Nonetheless, spirituality is by nature an individual experience (Kapuscinski and Masters, 2010), and thus assessing spiritual health is important. Consequently, this chapter supports the use of the SHALOM, as it provides a measure of spirituality through the lived experience section and a measure of spiritual health as a reference.

This chapter further supports the use of the lived experience section of the SHALOM as a measure of global spirituality because a religion-neutral version was recently published (Fisher, 2013). This version replaces the terms "God," "Divine," and "Creator" with "Transcendent," lessening its religious affiliation and allowing it to act as a measure of spirituality/spiritual health across a variety of worldviews. This new version of the SHALOM is statistically sound, although the model of fit for the original SHALOM is slightly better. As a result, Fisher (2013) suggested that the version of the SHALOM used for a study should be determined by the population under investigation. If the population is composed of individuals with a monotheistic understanding of religion and spirituality, then the original SHALOM is the recommended choice, whereas the use of the new SHALOM is preferable for a more diverse population.

Although this chapter recognizes the value of the SHALOM, the measure has room for improvement. Meezenbroek et al. (2012) doubted the interpretability of the term "developing" used at the beginning of each term. For example, they did not feel "developing" was the proper verb in the item, "Developing trust between individuals." In response to Meezenbroek et al.'s misgivings, perhaps the term "cultivating," which is used in the proposed definition of spirituality, may be more appropriate. "Developing" implies a lack then gain of a quality; "cultivating" implies the nurturing and growth of an already existing quality. Nonetheless, changing the verb could affect the meaning and psychometric properties of the SHALOM and thus this suggestion should be tested before being widely adopted.

In addition, Kapuscinski and Masters (2010) argued that more weight is often given to inner experiences than behavioural elements. Some items of the SHALOM suggest outward behaviour, such as, "Developing kindness toward other people" and "Developing awe at a breathtaking view." However, none of the items directly measure behavioural elements associated with spirituality. Considering that Kapuscinski and Masters deemed the exclusion of observable behaviour in spirituality scales unjustified on both a psychological and theological perspective, it may be prudent to add some items or a section specifically assessing spiritual behaviours to the SHALOM.

The SHALOM may be limited in assessing spirituality as defined in this chapter. Although some of the items do mention the idea of Connectedness (e.g., "Developing a connection with nature"), the concept is not emphasized for each of the domains. Therefore, this measure may not fully capture this chapter's definition in which Connectedness is emphasized. One possible solution would be to include additional items that ask about Connectedness. By adding instead of altering items, the original SHALOM and its psychometric properties may be preserved while the usefulness of the added items can be tested in comparison with the original measure.

Despite these three suggestions for improvement, the SHALOM has proven itself to be one of the better measures of spirituality and thus this chapter advocates its use in future studies of spirituality.

BENEFITS

Research on religiosity and spirituality, especially within the discipline of psychology, often focuses on their benefits by examining each construct's association with well-being, including health and subjective well-being (SWB). Health is "a state of complete physical, mental and social well-being and not merely the absence of disease or infirmity" (World Health Organization, 1948), while SWB is an overarching construct comprised of three distinct components: 1) a cognitive evaluation of one's life, including life satisfaction; 2) an affective appraisal of one's positive emotions, including happiness; and 3) the inclusion of negative emotions at a low, but situationally appropriate, level (Diener, 2006).

The relationship between religiosity and health is complex and not simply summarized. One review found that religiosity is correlated with lower rates of suicide and alcohol abuse (Myers, 2000). However, another study (Gorsuch, 1995) found that only nurturing and supportive religions are negatively associated with substance abuse, while restrictive and negativistic religions are positively associated with abuse. In addition, there is evidence that religiosity offsets the negative effects of stress (Krause & Van Tran, 1989); however, there is a positive correlation between religiosity and prejudice (Hunsburger, 1995), which is negatively correlated with the psychological well-being of those being discriminated (Schmitt, Branscombe, Postmes, & Garcia, 2014).

Research on the relationship between SWB and religiosity has also reported complex interactions. Tix, Dik, Johnson, and Steger (2012) found that the relationship between SWB and religious commitment varied across Christian traditions, with religious commitment predicting greater well-being for Evangelical Protestants, but greater anxiety for Mainline Protestants. Inconsistent results were reported in studies of components of SWB and religiosity. Several studies have reported a positive relationship between religiosity and happiness (e.g., Argyle, 2001; Francis, Robbins, & White, 2003; French & Joseph, 1999; Robbins & Francis, 2000), but other studies have found no significant associations between the constructs (e.g., Lewis, Maltby, & Burkinshaw, 2000; Lewis, Maltby, & Day, 2005). Complex results were also found for life satisfaction, as its relationship with religiosity varies with age, religion and denomination (Ellison, 1991). In addition, religious institutions can provide social support, which is associated with low levels of depression (Koenig, King, & Carson, 2012), but not fitting in with one's religious community is associated with isolation and high levels of depression (Kim-Prieto, 2014; Pearce, Little, & Perez, 2003). Furthermore, in their review, Lewis and Cruise (2006), cited evidence that religiosity is positively correlated with purpose in life, hope, and existential certainty, but also with anxiety, fear of death, and guilt.

To gain a clearer understanding, several studies have examined mediating and moderating variables. Some found that meaning in life can act as a mediating variable between religiosity and SWB (Myers, 2000), while others found that religious orientation can be a moderating variable, with intrinsic religious orientation associated more with positive well-being and extrinsic religious orientation associated more with negative well-being (Smith, McCullough, & Poll, 2003). Cultural and religious differences may also moderate the correlation between religiosity and well-being (Kim-Prieto, 2014). For example, there is evidence that religiosity predicts life satisfaction for Christians, Buddhists, and Hindus, but not for Muslims (Diener, Tay, & Myers, 2011). Furthermore, religious context and regulation moderate the relationship between religiosity and SWB, creating a paradox in which greater national religiosity is associated with higher negative affect, while individual religiosity is associated with higher positive affect (Diener et al., 2011). This apparent inconsistency may be attributable to greater national religiosity often being associated with restricted religious and personal freedom, whereas individual religiosity fulfills universal human needs and fosters virtues such as gratitude and kindness (Tay, Li, Myers, & Diener, 2014).

However, Tay et al.'s explanation of individual religiosity actually resembles spirituality more than religiosity according to the definitions utilized in the current chapter. In addition, meaning in life and intrinsic religiosity are correlated with spirituality (LaPierre, 1994;

Nelson, Rosenfeld, Breitbart, & Galietta, 2002), all of which suggests that spirituality mediates the relationship between religiosity and well-being. This is supported by studies indicating that, when examined separately, spirituality but not religiosity is a predictor of happiness (e.g., Holder et al., 2010). Nonetheless, this does not indicate that spirituality is superior to religiosity. Given that religion often acts as a repository for the spiritual (Hill et al., 2000), it is not possible for spirituality to be superior. Instead, the conflicting religiosity research suggests that strict religious rules and regulations, especially when integrated at a government level, can be detrimental to well-being, whereas focusing on the spiritual aspects of religion can be beneficial to well-being. This offers an explanation for many of the conflicting results previously mentioned, such as the study by Gorsuch (1995) in which nurturing and supportive religions were negatively associated with substance abuse, while restrictive and negativistic religions were positively associated with substance abuse.

That spirituality moderates the relationship between religiosity and well-being is further supported by literature focusing solely on spirituality, which reports a positive correlation with well-being. Much of the research on life satisfaction and spirituality is confounded by religiosity, but studies that separate the constructs show a significant positive relationship between spirituality and life satisfaction (e.g., Cohen, 2002; Kelley & Miller, 2007; Tate & Forchheimer, 2002). More research is available on the topic of spirituality and happiness. For example, using the Spiritual Well-Being Questionnaire (SWBQ; Fisher et al., 2000), Holder, Coleman, and Wallace (2010) found that spirituality accounted for up to 26% of the variability in children's happiness. Other studies have found comparable results in adults (e.g., Cohen, 2002). Considering that happiness is a multidimensional construct (Holder et al., 2010), the amount of variance explained by spirituality is substantial. A positive correlation between spirituality and happiness has also been found in other populations, including individuals with acquired brain injuries (Koss, Holder, & Jassi, 2013, June).

Additionally, spirituality is positively related to resilience and coping. Vahia et al. (2011) found a strong association between resilience and increased spirituality, which remained significant after controlling for demographic variables. Moreover, Kidwai, Mancha, Brown, and Eaton (2014) found that more spiritual individuals were less likely to be distressed following negative events. Spirituality's positive relationship with resilience and coping may explain why spiritual beliefs are important to individuals living with life-limiting and chronic illnesses (Dein & Stygall, 1997; Rafferty, Billig, & Mosack, 2014). Glover-Graf, Marini, Baker, and Buck (2007) found that many individuals experience an increase in their spirituality after the onset of chronic pain conditions and that their spirituality helped them accept their conditions. In addition, spirituality has been associated with better health outcomes in those with chronic illnesses, such as HIV (Mosack et al., 2005; Rafferty et al., 2014). Studies also suggest that spirituality is related to more general health (Coyle, 2001). Much of this research in the general population is confounded by religion (Matthews, McCullough, Larson, Koenig, Swyers, & Greenwold Milano, 1998), but one study of individuals with acquired brain injuries found that when examined separately, spiritual beliefs but not religious practices correlated with better physical health (Johnstone, Yoon, Rupright, & Reid-Arndt, 2009).

Spirituality Related Behaviors

There are numerous behaviors related to spirituality, many of which are also related to well-being (Coyle, 2001). Five examples of these behaviors are searching for and possessing meaning in life, practicing altruism, developing a connection with nature, praying, practicing forgiveness, and meditating.

Meaning in life is incorporated in the personal domain of spirituality. Adolescents with lower levels of meaning in life have shown elevated levels of drug use, unsafe sex, lack of exercise, and lack of diet control (Brassai, Piko, & Steger, 2011), and similar results have been found with adults (e.g., Nicholson, Higgins, Turner, James, Stickle, & Pruitt, 1994). In addition, searching for and possessing meaning in life predicted variance in perceived health above and beyond depression (Steger, Mann, Michels, & Cooper, 2009). Meaning in life is related to SWB, though the relationship is moderated by the level of search for meaning; those who rate low on meaning but high on searching experience the lowest levels of happiness (Cohen & Cairns, 2012) and life satisfaction (Steger, Oishi, & Kesebir, 2011). However, this moderated relationship varies across cultures. Searching for meaning when paired with low presence of meaning is associated with lower SWB in cultures that emphasize independence and view lack of meaning negatively, whereas searching for meaning is unrelated to SWB in cultures that emphasize interdependence and view lack of meaning more positively (Steger, Frazier, & Zacchanini, 2008; Steger & Kashdan, 2007; Steger, Kashdan, Sullivan, & Lorentz, 2008; Steger, Kawabata, Shimai, & Otake, 2008).

Altruism is incorporated in the communal domain of spirituality. Post (2005) noted in a literature review that altruism, as expressed through volunteering, is related to experiencing less major illness, greater longevity, lower mortality, and better general health. This relationship has also been seen cross-culturally (e.g., Krause, Ingersoll-Dayton, Liang, and Sugisawa, 1999). Additionally, altruism is associated with SWB. Not only is altruism positively correlated with happiness and life satisfaction (Post, 2005), but counting one's acts of kindness for a week was found to increase happiness (Otake, Shimai, Tanaka-Matsumi, Otsui, and Frederickson, 2006) and people who are perceived as kind are also perceived as happier than those who are not perceived as kind (Rimland, 1982).

Connecting with nature is incorporated in the environmental domain of spirituality. Nature connectedness is likely related to health (Howell, Dopko, Passmore, & Buro, 2011), as exposure to nature is correlated with improved cognitive recovery (Kaplan & Kaplan, 1995), increased longevity (Takano, Nakamura, & Watanabe, 2002), greater perceived general health (de Vries, Verheij, Groenewegen, & Spreeuwenberg, 2003) and many other restorative effects (see Howell & Passmore, 2013). Nature connectedness is also positively correlated with SWB, including positive affect, vitality, and life satisfaction (Capaldi, Dopko, & Zelenski, 2014). This positive relationship between nature connectedness and well-being is likely a global phenomenon, as the preference for natural environments over man-made ones exists across cultures (Shiota et al., 2007). However, the robustness of the relationship may vary, as certain cultures foster nature affiliation more than others (Howell & Passmore, 2013).

Praying is incorporated in the transcendent domain of spirituality. As with the behaviours in the other domains, prayer is also related to health and SWB. However, the empirical findings are not consistent. Some researchers have hypothesized that people who pray for their health are more prone to avoidance techniques when dealing with stress (Masters, 2007). However, one study found that people who prayed for their health actually engaged in more health promoting behaviours (Harrigan, 2011). In another study, coronary patients who were prayed for by strangers had a significantly better hospital course than those not prayed for, but critics have pointed out that there were no differences between the groups in terms of days in the hospital or mortality and that the study lacked adequate statistical control (Masters, 2007). Prayer has also been found to be associated with happiness, but once personality was controlled the association no longer remained (Robbins, Francis, & Edwards, 2008). This lack of association may have resulted from not differentiating between the six different types of prayer: 1) *adoration*, which involves worshipping God; 2) *confession*, which involves admitting to negative behaviour and asking for forgiveness; 3) *giving thanks*, which involves expressing gratitude toward God; 4) *supplication*, which involves asking for God to intervene in specific events; 5) *reception*, which involves awaiting God's guidance; and 6) *obligatory*, which is often a component of strict religions (Laird, Snyder, Rapoff, & Green, 2004; Whittington & Scher, 2010). Of these six types of prayer, adoration, giving thanks, and reception were strongly associated with life satisfaction (Whittington & Scher, 2010). These three types are egoless in nature and involve more positive affirmations, such as gratitude, whereas the other three types (i.e., confession, supplication, and obligatory) are more selfish and involve more negative affirmations, such as repentance. As with religion, prayer that is more tied with rules and regulations, such as obligatory prayer, is not related to well-being, while prayer that focuses more on spiritual aspects, such as thanksgiving prayer, is related to well-being. In addition, though prayer is seen across cultures, the prevalence of prayer types varies between cultures (Ladd et al., 2007). Given that prayer types vary in their relationship to well-being, it is likely that prayer is only related to well-being in some cultures.

Forgiveness is related to all four domains of spirituality and has the ability to restore Connectedness. Similar to the research on prayer, studies on forgiveness have found that forgiving because of religious motivations, rather than moral or interpersonal motivations, is correlated with higher stress and poorer health (Cox, Bennett, Tripp, & Aquino, 2012). Nonetheless, most forgiveness research reports a positive relationship with well-being. One experimental study found that people concentrating on unforgiving responses had greater cardiovascular reactivity than those concentrating on forgiving responses, suggesting that forgiveness decreases cardiovascular health risks (van Oyen Witvliet, Ludwig, & Vander Laan, 2001). Another study found that all types of forgiveness, including forgiveness of others and circumstances, are correlated with happiness, with the strongest correlation between self-forgiveness and happiness (Toussaint & Friedman, 2009). Negative cognitions regarding a transgression and delaying forgiving are related to decreased happiness within the last seven days, while positive feelings and behaviors related to forgiving are associated with longer term happiness (Maltby, Day, & Barber, 2005). Given that forgiveness is conceived similarly across cultures (Tripathi et al., 2010), it is likely that the relationship between forgiveness and well-being is similar cross-culturally.

Meditation is related to all four domains of spirituality and increases Connectedness. Research often focuses more on therapeutic meditation rather than spiritual meditation, but the boundary between the two is not clear-cut (Sedlmeier et al., 2012). This chapter focuses on the benefits of spiritual meditation, but recognizes that there is significant overlap. In general, meditation has a significant positive relationship with health. One study found that older adults with back pain who participated in an 8-week meditation program had greater pain acceptance and physical functioning than those in a wait-list control group (Morone, Greco, & Weiner, 2008). Meta-analyses have confirmed this positive relationship between meditation and health, indicating a medium effect size for meditation on mental and physical health (Grossman et al., 2004) and a strong effect size for meditation on stress reduction (Eberth & Sedlmeier, 2012). Meditation as an effective stress-reduction and coping technique has also been seen cross-culturally (Tyson & Pongruengphant, 2007). The few studies that examine the relationship between SWB and spiritual meditation report significant correlations (Sedlmeier et al., 2012; Shapiro, 2002). One study explored the impact of including a meditation practice in Fordyce's Personal Happiness Enhancement Program (PHEP) and found that the happiness of the meditation-plus-PHEP group increased more than the only-PHEP group (Smith, Compton, & West, 1995). Additional studies found that meditators tend to look happier than non-meditators to outside observers (Choi, Karremans, and Barendregt, 2012), and that there is an association between meditation and left prefrontal activation in the brain, an area that is positively associated with happiness (Davidson et al., 2003).

Overall, while the research on the benefits of religiosity varies, there is substantial evidence that spirituality and related constructs are positively correlated with, and in some cases directly impact, health and SWB.

FUTURE DIRECTIONS

Several ideas proposed in this chapter require empirical support, and some limitations found in the research literature require attention. First and foremost, the spirituality definition proposed in this chapter, "Spirituality is a feeling of Connectedness to something greater experienced by cultivating a relationship with oneself, one's community, one's environment, and one's perception of the transcendent," requires validation. In addition, the framework and inner flexibility of the spirituality definition needs to be assessed through exploring the relationships between Connectedness, the four domains, and related constructs. For example, research could explore whether gratitude correlates with one or more of the four domains and how it might be related to Connectedness.

Additionally, the assessment of religiosity and spirituality requires investigation. The effectiveness of the Religious Commitment Inventory–10 in assessing this chapter's definition of religiosity needs to be determined. This measure has shown reliability, validity, acceptability for use across cultures, and potential to assess cognitive, affective, and behavioural components of religiosity, but further evidence is required across all criteria. In addition, the use of the lived experience section of the SHALOM requires validation as a measure of spirituality as opposed to spiritual health. In response to the limitations of the SHALOM mentioned in the Assessments section, the validity of three proposed alterations to the SHALOM should be tested: 1) replacing the verb "developing" with "cultivating," 2) including items that measure spiritual behaviours, and 3) ensuring each domain contains items that measure Connectedness. Additionally, the global appropriateness of the SHALOM could be further examined.

Once the separate definitions and measures have been validated, assessing the benefits of religiosity and spirituality requires investigation. Perhaps the inconsistencies in the religiosity research are attributable to inconsistencies across definitions and assessments of religiosity. A consensus on definitions and assessment would be valuable in addressing these inconsistencies. In particular, future research should examine the differences between religions that emphasize rules and regulations versus those that act as repositories for and conveyers of the spiritual. Mediators and moderators of the relationship between religiosity and well-being also require further examination, especially culture as a moderator and spirituality as a mediator. Additional research on the benefits of spirituality that is not confounded by religiosity is necessary and could be aided by using this chapter's proposed definition. A further limitation of the research literature is that most studies sampled from primarily Christian populations from industrialized nations. Studies are now examining the benefits of spirituality across cultures to address this limitation.

Future research could focus on the subtleties of the relationship between spirituality and well-being. For instance, research could identify which dimensions of spirituality are most strongly related to well-being. In addition, the causal direction of the relationship between spirituality and well-being needs to be addressed. This research could help develop interventions aimed at increasing spirituality and well-being,

CONCLUSION

This chapter proposes a definition and measure of religiosity separate from spirituality. It also proposes a new, multidimensional definition and altered measure of spirituality separate from religion. Unlike previous definitions of spirituality, this chapter's definition conceptualizes Connectedness as an umbrella term encompassing four domains of spirituality: the personal domain, the communal domain, the environmental domain, and the transcendent domain. The relationships between spirituality and other constructs, including meaning in life and altruism, are not permanently located within the definition. As research further examines the relationships between spirituality and other constructs, especially regarding mediating and moderating variables, the proposed definition should be able to accommodate the findings without change.

Unlike many constructs related to well-being (e.g., gratitude and volunteering), spirituality is not a singular domain, but instead an overarching construct that is related to many aspects of people's lives. Consequently, spirituality seems to be unique in its contribution to well-being, and further understanding of this relationship could lead to effective well-being interventions.

Compared with spirituality, religiosity has shown contradictory relationships with well-being, perhaps because religion contains conflicting components. The rules and regulations of religion are often associated with more negative well-being, but the nurturing and spiritual aspects of religion are often associated with more positive well-being. In a related way, religions that are more nurturing and spiritual are associated with enhanced well-being. Yet, even the most nurturing and spiritual of religions will contradict beliefs in other religions, leading to exclusivity. Though religion within individual lives may be beneficial, religion on a national or global level may cause problems. In contrast, spirituality is incorporated within most religions, can be experienced by individuals who are not religious, and is consistently related to positive well-being. Therefore, in navigating the world movement toward a global village, focusing on spirituality may bridge disparities caused by religion, transcend cultural divides, and draw attention to common characteristics of humanity.

REFERENCES

Abu Raiya, H., Pargament, K. I., Mahoney, A., & Stein, C. (2008). A psychological measure of Islamic religiousness: Development and evidence for reliability and validity. *The International Journal for the Psychology of Religion, 18*, 291-315. doi:10.1080/10508610802229270

Alexander, C. N., Rainforth, M. V., & Gelderloos, P. (1991). Transcendental meditation, self-actualization, and psychological health: A conceptual overview and statistical meta-analysis. *Journal of Social Behavior & Personality, 6*, 189-247. Retrieved from http://search.proquest.com

Altemeyer, B., & Hunsberger, B. (1992). Authoritarianism, religious fundamentalism, quest, and prejudice. *The International Journal for the Psychology of Religion*, *2*, 113-133. doi:10. 1207/s15327582ijpr0202_5

Altemeyer, B., & Hunsberger, B. (2004). A revised religious fundamentalism scale: The short and sweet of it. *The International Journal for the Psychology of Religion*, *14*, 47-54. doi:10.1207/s15327582ijpr1401_4

Argyle, M. (2001). Religion. In *The Psychology of Happiness* (2nd ed., pp. 164–177). New York: Routledge.

Bangert, K. (2013). Religion, spirituality, and child well-being. In Ben-Aryeh, A., Frønes, I., Casas, F., & Korbin, J. E. (Eds.), *Handbook of Child Well-Being: Theories, Methods and Policies in Global Perspective* (pp. 1171-1207). Springer.

Bauer, L., Duffy, J., Fountain, E., Halling, S., Holzer, M., Jones, E., … Rowe, J. O. (1992). Exploring self–forgiveness. *Journal of Religion and Health, 31,* 149–160. doi:10.1007/BF00986793

Bohus, S., Woods, R. H., Jr., & Chan, K. C. (2005). Psychological sense of community among students on religious collegiate campuses in the Christian evangelical tradition. *Christian Higher Education*, *4*, 19-40. doi:10.1080/153637590507423

Bormann, J. E., Gifford, A. L., Shively, M., Smith, T. L., Redwine, L., Kelly, A., ... Belding, W. (2006). Effects of spiritual mantram repetition on HIV outcomes: a randomized controlled trial. *Journal of Behavioral Medicine*, *29*, 359-376. doi:10.1007/s10865-006-9063-6

Brassai, L., Piko, B. F., & Steger, M. F. (2011). Meaning in life: Is it a protective factor for adolescents' psychological health?. *International Journal of Behavioral Medicine*, *18*, 44-51. doi:10.1007/s12529-010-9089-6

Capaldi, C. A., Dopko, R. L., & Zelenski, J. M. (2014). The relationship between nature connectedness and happiness: A meta-analysis. *Frontiers in Psychology, 5*. eCollection. doi:10.3389/fpsyg.2014.00976

Cardeña, E., Lynn, S. J., Krippner, S. (Eds.) (2014). *Varieties of Anomalous Experience: Examining the Scientific Evidence (2nd ed.).*Washington, DC: American Psychological Association. doi:10.1037/14258-014

Carson, J. W., Carson, K. M., Gil, K. M., & Baucom, D. H. (2004). Mindfulness-based relationship enhancement. *Behavior Therapy, 35*, 471-494. doi:10.1016/S0005-7894(04)80028-5

Chambliss, K. M. (2013). *Beholding Nature: Contemplation and Connectedness* (Doctoral Dissertation). Retrieved from http://media.proquest.com/

Chiu, L., Emblen, J. D., Van Hofwegen, L., Sawatzky, R., & Meyerhoff, H. (2004). An integrative review of the concept of spirituality in the health sciences. *Western Journal of Nursing Research, 26*, 405-428. doi:10.1177/0193945904263411

Choi, Y., Karremans, J. C., & Barendregt, H. (2012). The happy face of mindfulness: Mindfulness meditation is associated with perceptions of happiness as rated by outside observers. *The Journal of Positive Psychology, 7*, 30-35. doi:10.1080/ 17439760.2011.626788

Cohen, A. B. (2002). The importance of spirituality in well-being for Jews and Christians. *Journal of Happiness Studies, 3*, 287-310. doi:10.1023/A: 1020656823365

Cohen, K., & Cairns, D. (2012). Is searching for meaning in life associated with reduced subjective well-being? Confirmation and possible moderators. *Journal of Happiness Studies, 13*, 313-331. doi:10.1007/s10902-011-9265-7

Cox, S. S., Bennett, R. J., Tripp, T. M., & Aquino, K. (2012). An empirical test of forgiveness motives' effects on employees' health and well-being. *Journal of Occupational Health Psychology, 17*, 330. doi:10.1037/a0028314

Coyle, J. (2002). Spirituality and health: towards a framework for exploring the relationship between spirituality and health. *Journal of Advanced Nursing, 37*, 589-597. doi:10.1046/ j.1365-2648.2002.02133.x

Davidson, R. J., Kabat-Zinn, J., Schumacher, J., Rosenkranz, M., Muller, D., Santorelli, S. F., ... Sheridan, J. F. (2003). Alterations in brain and immune function produced by mindfulness meditation. *Psychosomatic Medicine, 65*, 564-570. doi:10.1097/ 01.PSY.0000077505.67574.E3

de Jager Meezenbroek, E., Garssen, B., van den Berg, M., van Dierendonck, D., Visser, A., & Schaufeli, W. B. (2012). Measuring spirituality as a universal human experience: A review of spirituality questionnaires. *Journal of Religion and Health, 51*, 336-354. doi:10.1007/ s10943-010-9376-1

de Vries, S., Verheij, R. A., Groenewegen, P. P., & Spreeuwenberg, P. (2003). Natural environments…healthy environments? An exploratory analysis of the relationship between greenspace and health. *Environment & Planning A, 35*, 1717-1731. doi:10.1068/a35111

Dein, S., & Stygall, J. (1997). Does being religious help or hinder coping with chronic illness? A critical literature review. *Palliative Medicine, 11*, 291-298. doi:10.1177/02692163970 1100405

Diener, E. (2006). Guidelines for national indicators of subjective well-being and ill-being. *Applied Research in Quality of Life, 1*, 151-157. doi:10.1007/s11482-006-9007-x

Diener, E., Tay, L., & Myers, D. G. (2011). The religion paradox: If religion makes people happy, why are so many dropping out? *Journal of Personality and Social Psychology, 101*, 1278-1290. doi:10.1037/a0024402

Dudley, R. L., & Cruise, R. J. (1990). Measuring religious maturity: A proposed scale. *Review of Religious Research, 32*, 97-109. Retrieved from http://www.jstor.org

Eberth, J., & Sedlmeier, P. (2012). The effects of mindfulness meditation: A meta-analysis. *Mindfulness, 3*, 174-189. doi:10.1007/s12671-012-0101-x

Ellison, C. G. (1991). Religious involvement and subjective well-being. *Journal of Health and Social Behavior, 32*, 80-99. Retrieved from http://www.jstor.org/stable/ 2136801

Elkins, D. N., Hedstrom, L., Hughes, L. L., & Leaf, J. (1988). Toward a humanistic-phenomenological spirituality: Definition, description, and measurement. *Journal of Humanistic Psychology, 28*, 5-18. doi:10.1177/0022167888284002

Emmons, R. A., & Paloutzian, R. F. (2003). The psychology of religion. *Annual Review of Psychology, 54*, 377-402. doi:10.1146/annurev.psych.54.101601.145024

Fenwick, T. J., & English, L. M. (2004). Dimensions of spirituality: A framework for adult educators. *Journal of Adult Theological Education, 1*, 49-64. doi:10.1558/ jate.1.1. 49.36052

Fetzer Institute / National Institute on Aging Working Group (2003). *Multidimensional Measurement of Religiousness/Spirituality for Use in Health Research: A Report of the Fetzer Institute / National Institute on Aging Working Group* (2nd ed.). Retrieved from http://fetzer.org/resources/multidimensional-measurement-religiousnessspirituality-use-health-research

Fisher, J. (2010). Development and application of a spiritual well-being questionnaire called SHALOM. *Religions, 1*, 105-121. doi:10.3390/rel1010105

Fisher, J. (2013). You can't beat relating with God for spiritual well-being: Comparing a generic version with the original Spiritual Well-Being Questionnaire Called SHALOM. *Religions, 4*, 325-335. doi:10.3390/rel4030325

Fisher, J. W., Francis, L. J., Johnson, P. (2000). Assessing Spiritual Health via Four Domains of Spiritual Wellbeing: The SH4DI. *Pastoral Psychology, 49*, 133-145. doi: 10.1023/A: 1004609227002

Foundation for Inner Peace (2008). *A Course in Miracles* (3 ed.). New York, NY: Viking: The Foundation for Inner Peace.

Francis, L., Robbins, M., & White, A. (2003). Correlation between religion and happiness: A replication. *Psychological Reports,* 92, 51-52. doi:10.2466/pr0.2003.92.1.51

French, S., & Joseph, S. (1999). Religiosity and its association with happiness, purpose in life, and self-actualisation. *Mental Health, Religion & Culture, 2*, 117-120. doi:10.1080/ 13674679908406340

Glover-Graf, N. M., Marini, I., Baker, J., & Buck, T. (2007). Religious and spiritual beliefs and practices of persons with chronic pain. *Rehabilitation Counseling Bulletin, 51*, 21-33. doi:10.1177/00343552070510010501

Gomez, R., & Fisher, J. W. (2003). Domains of spiritual well-being and development and validation of the Spiritual Well-Being Questionnaire. *Personality and Individual Differences, 35*, 1975-1991. doi:10.1016/S0191-8869(03)00045-X

Gomez, R., & Fisher, J. W. (2005a). Item response theory analysis of the spiritual well-being questionnaire. *Personality and Individual Differences, 38*, 1107-1121. doi:10.1016/ j.paid.2004.07.009

Gomez, R., & Fisher, J. W. (2005b). The spiritual well-being questionnaire: Testing for model applicability, measurement and structural equivalencies, and latent mean differences across gender. *Personality and Individual Differences, 39*, 1383-1393. doi:10.1016/ j.paid.2005.03.023

Gorsuch, R. L. (1984) Measurement: The boon and bane of investigating religion. *American Psychologist, 39,* 228-236. doi:10.1037/0003-066X.39.3.228

Gorsuch, R. L. (1995). Religious aspects of substance abuse and recovery. *Journal of Social Issues, 51*, 65-83. doi:10.1111/j.1540-4560.1995.tb01324.x

Grossman, P., Niemann, L., Schmidt, S., & Walach, H. (2004). Mindfulness-based stress reduction and health benefits: A meta-analysis. *Journal of Psychosomatic Research, 57*, 35-43. doi:10.1016/S0022-3999(03)00573-7

Harrigan, J. T. (2011). Health promoting habits of people who pray for their health. *Journal of Religion and Health, 50*, 602-607. doi:10.1007/s10943-009-9293-3

Herrick, J. (2005). *Humanism: An introduction*. Amherst, NY: Prometheus Books

Higgins, C. (2014). The humanist moment. *Asia Pacific Education Review, 15,* 29-36. doi:10.1007/s12564-013-9294-5

Hill, P. C. (2013). Measurement in the psychology of religion and spirituality. In R. F. Paloutzian, & C. L. Park (Eds.), *Handbook of the psychology of religion and spirituality* (2nd ed., pp. 43-61) [Google Books version]. Retrieved from http://books.google.ca/

Hill, P. C., & Hood, R. W., Jr. (Eds.). (1999). *Measures of Religiosity*. Birmingham, AL: Religious Education Press.

Hill, P. C., Pargament, K. I., Hood, R. R., McCullough, M. E., Swyers, J. P., Larson, D. B., & Zinnbauer, B. J. (2000). Conceptualizing religion and spirituality: Points of commonality, points of departure. *Journal for the Theory of Social Behaviour, 30*, 51-77. doi:10.1111/ 1468-5914.00119

Holder, M. D., Coleman, B., & Wallace, J. M. (2010). Spirituality, religiousness, and happiness in children aged 8–12 years. *Journal of Happiness Studies, 11*, 131-150. doi:10.1007/s10 902-008-9126-1

Hood, R. W., Jr., Hill, P. C., & Spilka, B. (2009). *The psychology of religion: An empirical approach* [Google Books version]. Retrieved from http://books.google.ca/

Hook, J. N., Worthington, E. Jr., Utsey, S. O., Davis, D. E., & Burnette, J. L. (2012). Collectivistic self-construal and forgiveness. *Counseling and Values, 57*, 109-124. doi:10.1002/j.2161-007X.2012.00012.x

Howell, A. J., Dopko, R. L., Passmore, H., & Buro, K. (2011). Nature connectedness: Associations with well-being and mindfulness. *Personality and Individual Differences, 51*, 166-171. doi:10.1016/j.paid.2011.03.037

Howell, A. J., & Passmore, H. A. (2013). The nature of happiness: Nature affiliation and mental well-being. In *Mental Well-Being* (pp. 231-257). Amsterdam, Netherlands: Springer.

Hunsberger, B. (1995). Religion and prejudice: The role of religious fundamentalism, quest, and right-wing authoritarianism. *Journal of Social Issues, 51*, 113-129. doi:10.1111/j.1540-4560.1995.tb01326.x

Idler, E. L., Musick, M. A., Ellison, C. G., George, L. K., Krause, N., Ory, M. G., ... Williams, D. R. (2003). Measuring multiple dimensions of religion and spirituality for health research: Conceptual background and findings from the 1998 General Social Survey. *Research on Aging, 25*, 327-365. doi:10.1177/ 0164027503025004001

Johnstone, B., Yoon, D. P., Rupright, J., & Reid-Arndt, S. (2009). Relationships among spiritual beliefs, religious practices, congregational support and health for individuals with traumatic brain injury. *Brain Injury, 23*, 411-419. doi:10.1080/ 02699050902788501

Jong, G. F. D., Faulkner, J. E., & Warland, R. H. (1976). Dimensions of religiosity reconsidered: Evidence from a cross-cultural study. *Social Forces, 54*, 866-889. doi:10.1093/sf/54.4.866

Kaplan, R., & Kaplan, S. (1995). *The Experience of Nature: A Psychological Perspective.* Ann Arbour, MI: Cambridge University Press.

Kapuscinski, A. N., & Masters, K. S. (2010). The current status of measures of spirituality: A critical review of scale development. *Psychology of Religion and Spirituality, 2*, 191-205. doi: 10.1037/a0020498

Kashdan, T. B., & Nezlek, J. B. (2012). Whether, when, and how is spirituality related to well-being? Moving beyond single occasion questionnaires to understanding daily process. *Personality and Social Psychology Bulletin, 38*, 1523-1535. doi:10.1177/0146167 212454549

Kelley, B. S., & Miller, L. (2007). Life satisfaction and spirituality in adolescents. In R. L. Piedmont (Ed.), *Research in the Social Scientific Study of Religion, 18,* 233-262. doi:10.1163/ej.9789004158511.i-301.91

Kidwai, R., Mancha, B. E., Brown, Q. L., & Eaton, W. W. (2014). The effect of spirituality and religious attendance on the relationship between psychological distress and negative life events. *Social Psychiatry and Psychiatric Epidemiology, 49*, 487-497. doi:10.1007/s00127-013-0723-x

Kidwell, J. E., Wade, N., & Blaedel, E. (2012). Understanding forgiveness in the lives of religious people: The role of sacred and secular elements. *Mental Health, Religion & Culture, 15*, 121-140. doi:10.1080/13674676.2011.560598

Kim-Prieto, C. (2014). Introduction: Positive psychology of religion across traditions and beliefs. In C. Kim-Prieto (Ed.), *Religion and Spirituality Across Cultures* (pp. 1-18). doi:10.1007/978-94-017-8950-9

King, M., Jones, L., Barnes, K., Low, J., Walker, C., Wilkinson, S., ... Tookman, A. (2006). Measuring spiritual belief: Development and standardization of a Beliefs and Values Scale. *Psychological Medicine, 36*, 417-425. doi:10.1017/S003329170500629X

Koenig, H., King, D., & Carson, V. B. (2012). *Handbook of religion and health* [Google Book version]. Retrieved from http://books.google.ca/

Koss, S. E., Holder, M. D., & Jassi, A. (2013, June). *Power of belief: The relationship between spirituality and well-being in people with acquired brain injury.* Poster presented at the Third World Congress on Positive Psychology, Los Angeles, CA.

Krause, N., Ingersoll-Dayton, B., Liang, J., & Sugisawa, H. (1999). Religion, social support, and health among the Japanese elderly. *Journal of Health and Social Behavior, 40*, 405-421. Retrieved from http://www.jstor.org/

Krause, N., & Van Tran, T. (1989). Stress and religious involvement among older blacks. *Journal of Gerontology, 44*, S4-S13. doi:10.1093/geronj/44.1.S4

Kristeller, J. (2011). Spirituality and meditation. In J. D. Aten, M. R. McMinn, & E. L. Worthington Jr. (Eds.)., *Spiritually Oriented Interventions for Counseling and Psychotherapy* (pp. 197-227). Washington, DC: American Psychological Association. doi:10.1037/12313-008

Kristeller, J. L., & Johnson, T. (2005). Cultivating loving kindness: A two-stage model of the effects of meditation on empathy, compassion, and altruism. *Zygon®, 40*, 391-408. doi: 10.1111/j.1467-9744.2005.00671.x

Kurtz, L. R. (2011). *Gods in the global village: The world's religions in sociological perspective* (3rd ed.). [Google Books version]. Retrieved from http://books.google.ca/

Ladd, K. L., Ladd, M. L., Harner, J., Swanson, T., Metz, T., Pierre, K. t., & Trnka, D. (2007). Inward, outward, upward prayer and Big Five personality traits. *Archive for the Psychology of Religions, 29*, 151-175. doi:10.1163/008467207X188711

Laird, S. P., Snyder, C. R., Rapoff, M. A., & Green, S. (2004). Measuring private prayer: Development, validation, and clinical application of the multidimensional prayer inventory. *The International Journal for the Psychology of Religion, 14*, 251–272. doi: 10.1207/s15327582ijpr1404_2

LaPierre, L. (1994). A model for describing spirituality. *Journal of Religion and Health, 33,* 153-161. doi: 10.1007/BF02354535

Lewis, C., & Cruise, S. (2006). Religion and happiness: Consensus, contradictions, comments and concerns. *Mental Health, Religion & Culture, 9*, 213-225. doi:10.1080/13694670600615276

Lewis, C. A., Maltby, J., & Burkinshaw, S. (2000). Religion and happiness: Still no association. *Journal of Beliefs and Values, 21*, 233-236. doi:10.1080/713675504

Lewis, C. A., Maltby, J., & Day, L. (2005). Religious orientation, religious coping and happiness among UK adults. *Personality and Individual Differences, 38*, 1193-1202. doi:10.1016/ j.paid.2004.08.002

Lewis, C. A., Shevlin, M., McGuckin, C., & Navrátil, M. (2001). The Santa Clara strength of religious faith questionnaire: Confirmatory factor analysis. *Pastoral Psychology, 49*, 379-384. doi:10.1023/A:1010370728546

Maltby, J., Day, L., & Barber, L. (2005). Forgiveness and happiness, the differing contexts of forgiveness using the distinction between hedonic and eudaimonic happiness. *Journal of Happiness Studies, 6,* 1-13. doi:10.1007/s10902-004-0924-9

Masters, K. S., & Spielmans, G. I. (2007). Prayer and health: Review, meta-analysis, and research agenda. *Journal of Behavioral Medicine, 30*, 329-338. doi: 10.1007/s10865-007-9106-7

Matthews, D. A., McCullough, M. E., Larson, D. B., Koenig, H. G., Swyers, J. P., & Milano, M. G. (1998). Religious commitment and health status: a review of the research and implications for family medicine. *Archives of Family Medicine, 7*, 118-124. Retrieved from http://triggered.clockss.org/ServeContent

McCullough, M. E. (2001). Forgiveness: Who does it and how do they do it? *Current Directions in Psychological Science, 10*, 194-197. doi:10.1111/1467-8721.00147

Meezenbroek, E. deJ., Garssen, B., van den Berg, M., van Dierendonck, D., Visser, A., & Schaufeli, W. B. (2012). Measuring spirituality as a universal human experience: A review of spirituality questionnaires. *Journal of Religion and Health, 51*, 336-354. doi:10.1007/s10943-010-9376-1

Moodley, T. (2008). *The relationship between coping and spiritual well-being during adolescence* (Doctoral dissertation). Retrieved from http://etd.uovs.ac.za

Morone, N. E., Greco, C. M., & Weiner, D. K. (2008). Mindfulness meditation for the treatment of chronic low back pain in older adults: A randomized controlled pilot study. *Pain, 134*, 310-319. doi:10.1016/j.pain.2007.04.038

Mosack, K. E., Abbott, M., Singer, M., Weeks, M. R., & Rohena, L. (2005). If I didn't have HIV, I'd be dead now: Illness narratives of drug users living with HIV/AIDS. *Qualitative Health Research, 15*, 586-605. doi:10.1177/1049732304271749

Myers, D. G. (2000). The funds, friends, and faith of happy people. *American Psychologist, 55,* 56-67. doi:10.1037/0003-066X.55.1.56

Nelson, C. J., Rosenfeld, B., Breitbart, W., & Galietta, M. (2002). Spirituality, religion, and depression in the terminally ill. *Psychosomatics*, *43*, 213-220. doi:10.1176/appi.psy.43.3.213

Nicholson, T., Higgins, W., Turner, P., James, S., Stickle, F., & Pruitt, T. (1994). The relation between meaning in life and the occurrence of drug abuse: A retrospective study. *Psychology of Addictive Behaviors*, *8*, 24. doi:10.1037/0893-164X.8.1.24

North, J. (1998). The ideal of forgiveness: A philosopher's exploration. In R. D. Enright & J. North (Eds.), *Exploring Forgiveness* (pp. 15–34). Retrieved from http://muse.jhu.edu

Otake, K., Shimai, S., Tanaka-Matsumi, J., Otsui, K., & Fredrickson, B. L. (2006). Happy people become happier through kindness: A counting kindnesses intervention. *Journal of Happiness Studies*, *7*, 361-375. doi:10.1007/s10902-005-3650-z

Pakpour, A. H., Plante, T. G., Saffari, M., & Fridlund, B. (2014). The Santa Clara Strength of Religious Faith Questionnaire (SCSORF): A validation study on Iranian Muslim patients undergoing dialysis. *Journal of Religion and Health, 53*, 1185-1897. doi:10.1007/s10943-014-9856-9

Pargament, K. I. (1999). The psychology of religion and spirituality? Yes and no. *The International Journal for the Psychology of Religion, 9*, 3-16. doi:10.1207/ s15327582 ijpr0901_2

Pearce, M. J., Little, T. D., & Perez, J. E. (2003). Religiousness and depressive symptoms among adolescents. *Journal of Clinical Child and Adolescent Psychology, 32*, 267–276. doi:10.1207/S15374424JCCP3202_12

Pesut, B., Fowler, M., Reimer-Kirkham, S., Taylor, E. J., & Sawatzky, R. (2009). Particularizing spirituality in points of tension: Enriching the discourse. *Nursing Inquiry*, *16*, 337-346. doi:10.1111/j.1440-1800.2009.00462.x

Pesut, B., Fowler, M., Taylor, E. J., Reimer-Kirkham, S., & Sawatzky, R. (2008). Conceptualising spirituality and religion for healthcare. *Journal of Clinical Nursing*, *17*, 2803-2810. doi:10.1111/j.1365-2702.2008.02344.x

Plante, T. G., & Boccaccini, M. T. (1997a). The Santa Clara strength of religious faith questionnaire. *Pastoral Psychology*, *45*, 375-387. doi:10.1007/BF02230993

Plante, T. G., & Boccaccini, M. (1997b). Reliability and validity of the Santa Clara strength of religious faith questionnaire. *Pastoral Psychology*, *45*, 429-437. doi:10.1007/BF02310643

Post, S. G. (2005). Altruism, happiness, and health: It's good to be good. *International Journal of Behavioral Medicine, 12*, 66-77. doi:10.1207/s15327558ijbm1202_4

Rafferty, K. A., Billig, A. K., & Mosack, K. E. (2014). Spirituality, religion, and health: The role of communication, appraisals, and coping for individuals living with chronic illness. *Journal of Religion and Health.* Advance online publication. doi:10.1007/s10943-014-9965-5

Rakos, R. F., Steyer, K. R., Skala, S., & Slane, S. (2008). Belief in free will: Measurement and conceptualization innovations. *Behavior and Social Issues*, *17*, 20-39. doi:10.5210/bsi.v17i1.1929

Rimland, B. (1984). The altruism paradox. *Southern Psychologist, 2*, 8-9. Retrieved from http://www.amsciepub.com

Robbins, M., & Francis, L. J. (2000). Religion, personality, and well-being: the relationship between church attendance and purpose in life. *Journal of Research on Christian Education*, *9*, 223-238. doi:10.1080/10656210009484908

Robbins, M., Francis, L. J., & Edwards, B. (2008). Prayer, personality and happiness: A study among undergraduate students in Wales. *Mental Health, Religion & Culture, 11*, 93-99. doi:10.1080/13674670701702548

Roof, W. C., & Perkins, R. B. (1975). On conceptualizing salience in religious commitment. *Journal for the Scientific Study of Religion, 14*, 111-128. Retrieved from http://www.jstor.org/

Ross, L. (2006). Spiritual care in nursing: An overview of the research to date. *Journal of Clinical Nursing, 15*, 852-862. doi:10.1111/j.1365-2702.2006.01617.x

Sacred. (n.d.). In *Merriam-Webster's online dictionary.* Retrieved from http://www. merriam-webster.com/dictionary/sacred

Sedlmeier, P., Eberth, J., Schwarz, M., Zimmermann, D., Haarig, F., Jaeger, S., & Kunze, S. (2012). The psychological effects of meditation: A meta-analysis. *Psychological Bulletin, 138*, 1139-1171. doi:10.1037/a0028168

Schmitt, M. T., Branscombe, N. R., Postmes, T., & Garcia, A. (2014). The consequences of perceived discrimination for psychological well-being: A meta-analytic review. *Psychological Bulletin, 140*, 921-948. doi:10.1037/a0035754

Shapiro, S. L. (2002). Meditation and positive psychology. In S. J. Lopez, C. R. Snyder (Eds.), *Oxford Handbook of Positive Psychology* (2nd ed., pp. 601-610). New York, NY: Oxford University Press.

Smith, T. B., McCullough, M. E., & Poll, J. (2003). Religiousness and depression: Evidence for a main effect and the moderating influence of stressful life events. *Psychological Bulletin, 129*, 614-636. doi:10.1037/0033-2909.129.4.614

Smith, W. P., Compton, W. C., & West, W. B. (1995). Meditation as an adjunct to a happiness enhancement program. *Journal of Clinical Psychology, 51*, 269-273. doi:10.1002/1097-4679(199503)51:2<269::AID-JCLP2270510217> 3.0.CO;2-0

Steger, M. F., Frazier, P. A., & Zacchanini, J. L. (2008). Terrorism in two cultures: Stress and growth following September 11 and the Madrid train bombings. *Journal of Loss and Trauma, 13*, 511-527. doi:10.1080/15325020802173660

Steger, M. F., & Kashdan, T. B. (2007). Stability and specificity of meaning in life and life satisfaction over one year. *Journal of Happiness Studies, 8*, 161-179. doi:10.1007/s10902-006-9011-8

Steger, M. F., Kashdan, T. B., Sullivan, B. A., & Lorentz, D. (2008). Understanding the search for meaning in life: Personality, cognitive style, and the dynamic between seeking and experiencing meaning. *Journal of Personality, 76*, 199-228. doi:10.1111/j.1467-6494.2007.00484.x

Steger, M. F., Kawabata, Y., Shimai, S., & Otake, K. (2008). The meaningful life in Japan and the United States: Levels and correlates of meaning in life. *Journal of Research in Personality, 42*, 660-678. doi:10.1016/j.jrp.2007.09.003

Steger, M. F., Mann, J. R., Michels, P., & Cooper, T. C. (2009). Meaning in life, anxiety, depression, and general health among smoking cessation patients. *Journal of psychosomatic research, 67*, 353-358. doi:10.1016/j.jpsychores.2009.02.006

Steger, M. F., Oishi, S., & Kesebir, S. (2011). Is a life without meaning satisfying? The moderating role of the search for meaning in satisfaction with life judgments. *The Journal of Positive Psychology, 6*, 173-180. doi:10.1080/17439760.2011.569171

Takano, T., Nakamura, K., & Watanabe, M. (2002). Urban residential environments and senior citizens' longevity in megacity areas: The importance of walkable green spaces. *Journal of Epidemiological Community Health, 56*, 913-918. doi:10.1136/jech.56.12.913

Tappert, T. F. (Ed.). (1967). *Table Talk: Luther's Works, 54*. Philadelphia, PA: Fortress Press.

Tarakeshwar, N., Pargament, K. I., & Mahoney, A. (2003). Measures of Hindu pathways: development and preliminary evidence of reliability and validity. *Cultural Diversity and Ethnic Minority Psychology*, *9*, 316-332. doi:10.1037/1099-9809.9.4.316

Tate, D. G., & Forchheimer, M. (2002). Quality of life, life satisfaction, and spirituality: Comparing outcomes between rehabilitation and cancer patients. *American Journal of Physical Medicine & Rehabilitation*, *81*, 400-410. doi:10.1097/00002060-200206000-00002

Tay, L., Li, M., Myers, D. G., & Diener, E. (2014). Religiosity and subjective well-being: An international perspective. In C. Kim-Prieto (Ed.), *Religion and Spirituality Across Cultures* (pp. 163-175). doi:10.1007/978-94-017-8950-9

Tix, A. P., Dik, B. J., Johnson, M. E., & Steger, M. F. (2013). Religious commitment and subjective well-being across Christian traditions. *Journal of Psychology and Christianity*, *32*(1), 20-29.

Toussaint, L., & Friedman, P. (2009). Forgiveness, gratitude, and well-being: The mediating role of affect and beliefs. *Journal of Happiness Studies, 10*, 635-654. doi:10.1007/s10902-008-9111-8

Toshio, K., & Stone, J. I. (1996). The imperial law and the Buddhist law. *Japanese Journal of Religious Studies, 23*(3-4), 271-285. Retrieved from https://nirc.nanzan-u.ac.jp/en/publications/jjrs/

Tripathi, A., & Mullet, E. (2010). Conceptualizations of forgiveness and forgivingness among Hindus. *The International Journal for the Psychology of Religion*, *20*, 255-266. doi:10.1080/10508619.2010.507694

Tyson, P. D., & Pongruengphant, R. (2007). Buddhist and Western perspectives on suffering, stress, and coping. *Journal of Religion and Health*, *46*, 351-357. doi:10.1007/s10943-006-9104-z

Unterrainer, H., Nelson, O., Collicutt, J., & Fink, A. (2012). The English version of the Multidimensional Inventory for Religious/Spiritual Well-Being (MI-RSWB-E): First results from British college students. *Religions, 3*, 588-599. doi:10.3390/ rel3030588

Vahia, I. V., Depp, C. A., Palmer, B. W., Fellows, I., Golshan, S., Thompson, W., … Jeste, D. V. (2011). Correlates of spirituality in older women. *Aging & Mental Health*, *15*, 97-102. doi:10.1080/13607863.2010.501069

van Oyen Witvliet, C., Ludwig, T. E., & Vander Laan, K. L. (2001). Granting forgiveness or harboring grudges: Implications for emotion, physiology, and health. *Psychological Science*, *12*(2), 117-123. doi:10.1111/1467-9280.00320

Walsh, R. (1983). Meditation practice and research. *Journal of Humanistic Psychology, 23*, 18-50. doi:10.1177/0022167883231004

Whittington, B. L., & Scher, S. J. (2010). Prayer and subjective well-being: An examination of six different types of prayer. *International Journal for the Psychology of Religion, 20*, 59-68. doi:10.1080/10508610903146316

World Health Organization (1948). *WHO definition of health*. Preamble to the Constitution of the World Health Organization as adopted by the International Health Conference, New York, 19-22 June, 1946; signed on 22 July 1946 by the representatives of 61 States

(Official Records of the World Health Organization, no. 2, p. 100) and entered into force on 7 April 1948. The definition has not been amended since 1948. Retrieved from http://www.who.int/about/definition/en/ print.html

Worthington, E. L., Jr., Lavelock, C., Van Tongeren, D. R., Jennings, D. J., II, Gartner, A. L., Davis, D. E., ... Hook, J. N. (2014). Virtue and positive psychology. In K. Tempe & C. A. Boyd (Eds.), *Virtues and their vices* (pp. 433-458). doi: 10.1093/ acprof:oso/978019964554 1.003.0021

Worthington, E. L., Jr., Wade, N. G., Hight, T. L., Ripley, J. S., McCullough, M. E., Berry, J. W., ... O'Connor, L. (2003). The Religious Commitment Inventory—10: Development, refinement, and validation of a brief scale for research and counseling. *Journal of Counseling Psychology, 50*, 84. doi:10.1037/0022-0167.50.1.84

Young, P. D. (1999). Salience in religious commitment scale. In Hill, P. C., & Hood, R. W., Jr. (Eds.), *Measures of Religiosity*. Birmingham, AL: Religious Education Press.

Zinnbauer, B. J., Pargament, K. I., Cole, B., Rye, M. S., Butter, E. M., Belavich, T. G., ... Kadar, J. L. (1997). Religion and spirituality: Unfuzzying the fuzzy. *Journal for the Scientific Study of Religion, 36*, 549-564. doi:10.2307/1387689

Zinnbauer, B. J., Pargament, K. I., & Scott, A. B. (1999). The emerging meanings of religiousness and spirituality: Problems and prospects. *Journal of Personality, 67,* 889-919. doi:10.1111/1467-6494.00077

In: Spirituality
Editor: Edith C. Roberts

ISBN: 978-1-63482-370-8

Chapter 11

"SPIRITUAL BUT NOT RELIGIOUS": SOME CONTEMPORARY INFLUENCES AND THEIR IMPACT ON HEALTH

Christian R. Bellehumeur,[1*] Ph.D., psychologist and associate professor, and Lakshmi Sundaram[2†], M.A., C.C.C., Private Practice and lecturer

[1] School of Counseling, Psychotherapy and Spirituality
Faculties of Human Sciences and Philosophy,
Saint Paul University, Ottawa, Ontario, Canada
[2] Saint Paul University, Ottawa, Ontario, Canada

ABSTRACT

In Western societies, many people call themselves spiritual but not religious; this emerging religious stance inevitably gives rise to various societal attitudes and spiritual practices. Nowadays, many argue that spirituality is perceived as being highly personal and subjective. Some authors suggest that it can also be part of collective practices and shared beliefs which are not explicitly associated with conventional or institutionalized religions but rather, to a so called "implicit religion" (Gollnick, 2005). In light of this new paradigm, this chapter on being "spiritual but not religious" has three main objectives. First, it aims to provide reference points in order to contextualize the emergence of the term "spiritual but not religious" (SBNR) by presenting aspects of contemporary social contexts such as secularism and other new forms of spirituality. The second objective is to present factors which appear to be associated with this religious stance, SBNR, and its related emerging spiritual practices. Notably, three factors, trends or approaches will be discussed: a) the importance of holistic health; b) the socio-ecological approaches to spirituality and c) the influence of Eastern philosophy, such as the growing interest in

* Email: cbellehumeur@ustpaul.ca.
† Email: lakshsundaram@gmail.com.

mindfulness practices, in Western societies The third objective is to discuss the positive impact of these factors, trends and approaches on health, as well as some possible limitations to the understanding of a "healthy" spirituality in secular Western societies, particularly with respect to SBNR.

"We are not human beings having a spiritual experience; we are spiritual beings having a human experience."

Pierre Teilhard de Chardin in Le Phénomène Humain (1955)

INTRODUCTION

Today, many authors use the term *religion* to refer to an organized institution of collectively shared beliefs and practices that prescribe a way of being, acting and thinking for its supporters (Gollnick, 2005). As for spirituality, it is understood to be a singular, individual and private experience, whether or not related to religion. Spirituality could result in a way of being which offers meaning and purpose to a person's existence. However, in Western societies many people are moving away from beliefs and practices associated with religious institutions and calling themselves spiritual but not religious (Fuller, 2001). The term "spiritual but not religious" can be called a religious stance - just like being atheist, agnostic or a-religious can be considered a religious stance - and seems to echo this trend to withdraw from organized religion and to present religion and spirituality in a polarized manner.

It may be dangerous to put too much emphasis on polarizing the two terms when defining spirituality as separated from any main religious institution and/or tradition. Gollnick (2005) pointed out the tendency to put them in opposition: organized religion versus personal spirituality; substantive religion versus functional spirituality and mundane harmful religion versus lofty helpful spirituality. In essence, contrasting religion and spirituality in such a way reflects the idea that spirituality is good and religion is bad. These views are reductive and simplistic in that spirituality does not exist in a social vacuum and the quest for the sacred is never purely personal or isolated from the social context (Gollnick, 2005).

In a recent work, Casey (2013) explored the research and practice implications of being spiritual but not religious (SBNR). She suggests that definitions of spirituality are heterogeneous and that religiousness and spirituality are not the same construct. She also indicates the need to better operationalize these two concepts in order to fully investigate their roles, including that of SBNR, in both psychiatry and health research. This chapter focuses on being "spiritual but not religious" by attempting to deepen understanding of this new religious stance with regards to health. Three main objectives will be addressed: firstly to provide reference points to help contextualize the emergence of the term the "spiritual but not religious" (SBNR) by presenting aspects of contemporary social contexts such as secularism and other new forms of spirituality. Secondly, to present some factors which seem to be associated with this religious stance, SBNR, and its related emerging spiritual practices. Notably, three factors, trends or approaches will be discussed: a) the importance of holistic health; b) the socio-ecological approaches to spirituality and c) the influence of Eastern philosophy, such as the growing interest in the mindfulness practice, in Western societies.

The third objective is to discuss the positive impact of these factors, trends and approaches on health, as well as some possible limitations to the understanding of a "healthy" spirituality in secular Western societies, particularly in relation to SBNR.

Contemporary Social Contexts: Secularism and New Forms of Spirituality

Secularization of Western society is characterized, amongst other things, by the development of science, human rights charters, the democratic revolution and the autonomy of reason. In modern society, religion does not play the central role it did in traditional societies (Gollnick, 2005). Today, many individuals turn away from inherited forms of Christianity or other religions that no longer meet their aspirations, nor help them to make sense of their lives, nor remain current or suitable for their spiritual needs. For example, some see contemporary Catholicism as a legalistic and normative religion which is sad and cold (Daviau, 2014).

However, as many people distance themselves from mainstream or traditional religions, one needs to look at the various meanings of secularism (Taylor, 2007). The first meaning of a secular society is related to redefining the relationship to a transcendent God, who is no longer at the center of social life and public spaces. The second meaning is related to the decline in faith in God along with the decline in religious belief and practice. In addition, Taylor (2007) addresses a third meaning of secularism, in opposition to the first and second meanings, which corresponds to new conditions of belief. According to him, what is common to both believers and non-believers is that secularism conditions the experience of our quest towards wholeness. In short, the universal search for a higher good is the pinnacle of human development.

Furthermore, in Western secular societies, the majority of Americans and two-thirds of Europeans call themselves believers, but only a third of those regularly practice their religion (Lenoir, 2003). Although less rooted in religion than ever before, this populace do not appear tempted to adopt radical atheism or to join fundamentalist or sectarian groups (Lenoir, 2013). Rather, many people appear to accept uncertainty, cultivating instead a dialectic relationship placed on a broad spectrum between faith and scepticism which overwhelms or challenges all the traditional religious identities (Lenoir, 2003). According to Lenoir (2003), two major trends are observed in modern secular societies: ultra-religious individualism, and the globalization of religion. The current period would be characterized by freedom of choice, the desire for personal achievement, the quest for meaning, the reign of authenticity, spiritual nomadism, the primacy of subjectivity and interpersonal relationships. But paradoxically, as Lenoir (2003) points out, this ultra-modernity is also marked by a strong desire for "re-enchantment of the world" with hints of cosmic – or archaic – religiosity: astrology, angels, spiritualism, magical thinking, neo-shamanism, holistic medicine, and so on. All these new forms of spirituality have led Lenoir (2003) to conclude that God (along with religion) is not dead, but rather, has been transformed.

According to Taylor (2007), the characteristics of this new spiritual landscape are that the barriers between different religious groups have fallen, that the existing ghetto walls have been taken down, as they were for the English Catholic Church after Vatican II. At another level, the range of beliefs in something higher widens: fewer people say they believe in a personal God, and more describe believing in something like an impersonal force. More and more people are expressing religious beliefs that are outside of Christian orthodoxy. Along the same lines, we see the expansion of non-Christian religions, especially Eastern beliefs and the proliferation of New Age practices which are at the border of humanism and spirituality. Davie (1994) speaks of "believing without belonging." The focus has become about the individual and his experience. Spirituality must speak to that experience; and, the fundamental mode of spiritual life is the quest. As opposed to "religion" this type of search is often called "spirituality" by adherents. This opposition reflects the rejection of the "institutional religion," that is to say, the claimed authority of the churches which consider it their duty to guide the search and/or to maintain it within specific boundaries while dictating a certain type of conduct.

Furthermore, even if many would argue that spirituality is perceived as being highly personal and subjective, some authors, such as Gollnick (2005), suggest that it can also be part of collective practices and shared beliefs which are not explicitly associated with conventional, institutionalized or organized religions, but rather to a so called "implicit religion."

Consequently, Gollnick (2005) proposes that there is a relationship between spirituality and religion: implicit religion. There may be a common area between spirituality and religion concerning identity elements, values and worldview. For example, a commitment to preserving the environment because the person believes the earth is sacred. At the same time, such implicit religion might not offer a broader vision of a spiritual world, or even any conscious thought of it. "Examples of non-spiritual elements in implicit religion might include peak experiences, such as sexual ecstasy or the elation of cheering for one's football team when these experiences are not viewed as part of a larger spiritual universe" (Gollnick, 2005, p. 33).

In portraying these aspects of the contemporary social contexts, notably by referring to secularism (Taylor, 2007) and new forms of spirituality (Lenoir, 2003), we observe more and more people today calling themselves spiritual but not religious, known by the acronym SBNR. This term is used to self-identify to a religious stance, embracing spirituality while rejecting conventional or traditional organized religion as the sole means of fostering spiritual growth (Fuller, 2001). Although the term is encountered world-wide, it is most prominent in Northern America; in the United States, percentages may range from 10 to 33 % of people who identify as SBNR (Stark, 2005; survey on Gallup.com). This appears more likely amongst younger people than amongst older ones. However, there are considerable differences amongst people defining themselves as SBNR; they vary in their personal spiritual philosophies and practices and their referencing to some form of higher power or transcendence without religious belonging.

Based on the perspective of William James, Fuller (2001) cites two key elements which distinguish attitudes, ideas, lifestyles and practices as truly spiritual. The first element refers to seeing the visible world as a larger part of a spiritual universe which offers meaning. The second element refers to making it one's goal in life to live in harmony with the spiritual world. According to these criteria, Fuller (2001) mentioned that "many forms of questioning and commitment could be considered spiritual, such as wonder about where the universe comes from, why we are on earth, what happens when we die, or commitment to the values of love and beauty which seem to reveal a meaning beyond the visible world" (Gollnick, 2005,

p. 30). At the same time, according to these two criteria, adopting beliefs, interests, and activities that fail to address concerns within a wider reality, could not therefore be considered spiritual (Gollnick, 2005).

In order to expand on the understanding of the new SBNR religious stance and its related emerging spiritual practices, we will take a closer look at the relationship between spirituality and the contemporary importance of holistic health, through the development of alternative therapies and new medicines.

THE IMPORTANCE OF HOLISTIC HEALTH

According to Levin (2001), the craze surrounding studies linking spirituality and health can be explained partly by the combination of the positive impact of religion and spirituality on the lives of Western seniors, and a holistic approach to health and well-being which has developed considerably since the 1970s. In fact, there is increasing evidence that spiritual values and goals in life bring an undeniable contribution to physical and mental health as well as to overall life satisfaction.

Two factors could explain the growing interest in combining spiritual concerns with healthcare services (Astrow, Puchalski & Sulmasy, 2001). The first factor is related to the recognition that scientific medicine is limited and seems to have reduced the patient to an object of analysis and research which cannot resolve the end of all sufferings. The second factor relates to the results of many stringent scientific studies which have demonstrated the beneficial effects of religious practice and spirituality on health. Without denying the scientific medical advances in the diagnosis and treatment of diseases (Simard, 2006), many have noted that the development of a technological medicine has rationalized disease at the expense of the ailing (Philibert, 1998). This is explained by the fact that modern medicine has tended to put technology at the service of a reductionist conception of health, namely, the health of the body and often a manipulated body (Simard, 2006).

In its evolution and in the course of its action, scientific medicine has often confined itself to what is measurable and objectifying, and has excluded what is not within those categories (Simard, 2006). In doing so, it has forgotten to address questions about the meaning of life and of both personal and collective visions of the world and of life; questions which are taken more seriously by alternative medicinal therapeutic approaches (Simard, 2006). Finally, the scientific vision of medicine has faced serious restrictions, such as the exorbitant cost of new technologically advanced treatments, and the precipitating exclusion of the poor (Simard, 2006). With the development of alternative therapeutic approaches expanding to include concepts of health, illness and healing, traditional scientific medicine, without being rejected, is being challenged over its silence to address fundamental existential questions. Hence, there is a growing interest in the spirituality of the suffering, in palliative care, and in the importance of the caring relationship between health care professionals and patients. Elements which are now understood in a broader sense and which are becoming an integral part of the healing process, encompassing a heart-body-soul harmony (Simard, 2006). Furthermore, the introduction of the concept of "total" pain by Saunders (1981) has forced scientific medicine to treat not only physical, but also psychosocial and spiritual suffering. This has caused a fundamental reconsideration of medical practice, and has brought back an awareness of the need for both caregivers and those ailing to consider the importance of spirituality (Simard, 2006).

Because wellness and health are increasingly important to people, post-modern approaches are seeking to bring facets of the human being back into a holistic balance. Our society has never been sicker, and new ways of understanding the human body are increasingly and urgently needed. For example, Statistics Canada and the Public Health Agency calculate that, from 1970 to 2007, incidence rates for all primary cancer cases combined increased 0.9% per year in males and 0.8% per year in females (Public Health Agency of Canada, 2013). Although the biomedical model presently in place in western medical facilities is equipped to help with acute health problems, it is not as well equipped to handle chronic illness such as cancer. As psychotherapy is an important adjunct to caring for people who suffer from chronic disease, a spiritual orientation to therapy is a valid lens through which to see the problems human beings live with. "In sum, the empirical evidence suggests links between health and spiritual and religious factors, although the mechanisms by which such effects are produced are not fully understood [...]" (Sperry & Shafranske, 2005, p. 12).

Finally, although medical practice and research can offer invaluable aid to treat diseases and to improve quality of life, one cannot reduce human life to its mere physical dimension. We are also a spiritual beings in search of meaning and fulfillment. It is only by considering this spiritual quest and by accepting human finiteness – especially expressed in sickness and death – that medicine can really contribute to human emotional and spiritual maturation (Simard, 2006).

THE SOCIO-ECOLOGICAL APPROACHES TO SPIRITUALITY

The human need for nature is not a new concept: our wellbeing and association with the natural world is part of the never ending human quest of who we are and what we are supposed to be. For many authors, nature is seen as a portal to spirituality (Besthorn, Wulff & St. George, 2010; Coates, Gray & Hetherington, 2006; Sundaram, 2014). Many decades ago, famous writer and psychiatrist Carl Jung described in his own terms the tendency of the modern man to become disconnected from nature; he suggested that madness would result if human beings did not reconnect with the two important parts of themselves, the primitive man and the modern man (Sabini, 2002; Sundaram, 2014). He stated that primitive man was awake and aware but, that in modern western culture, that was no longer the case.

We have become increasingly disconnected from the natural world, our evolution towards city living happened quickly and it seems that human beings have not yet fully adapted (Buzzel & Chalquist, 2009; Miyazaki, 2006). The result of this separation is stress. Stress arising from the numbing of our senses. We have become rigid and unfocused, distracted by attachments to pleasure and avoidance of pain. Our culture appears to cultivate a fear of uncertainty and yet uncertainty (as primitive man well knew) is always around the corner, often disguised in the mundane events of our daily lives. This is why many seek psychotherapy and counselling to get better. However, modern psychology, just like scientific medicine, has not only been criticized for its tendency to study the human person as an object rather than an evolving, living participant (Croteau, 1981); it has also been neglecting the relationship between humans and nature (Roszak, 1992). A modern, integrated psychology must take into account this fundamental relationship with nature in considering the whole person (Buzzel & Chalquist, 2009; Jordan, 2009; Sundaram, 2014). Humans are, after all, spiritual beings and our spirituality, our sense of being connected to something bigger than ourselves, affects the way in which we mature as human beings (Besthorn, Wulff & St. George, 2010; Brazier, 2011, Buzzel & Chalquist, 2009; Coates, Gray & Hetherington, 2006; Rozak, 1992; Rozak, Gomes & Kanner, 1995; Wilson, 1984). Our human experience is rooted in nature and culture and if we consider E.O Wilson's Biophilia hypothesis, nature is programmed into our genes and is essential to our overall well - being (Wilson, 1984).

We all inherently know this. Think of a time at the beach or a camping trip, think of your animals, or depictions of nature in art and advertising. Studies show consistently that nature is good for our physical, psychological and spiritual health. It seems a natural evolution then, that we return to nature in order to reconnect with ourselves.

More than two decades ago, the term ecopsychology was coined by historian Theodore Roszak. Roszak (1992) maintained that recognizing our innate association with nature would allow us to then transform our relationship with the earth. In breaking down the term ecopsychology into its derivatives, *oikos*, meaning home and *psyche* meaning soul, This earth, this omnipotent Other we inhabit, becomes home for the soul (Sundaram, 2014) or as Roszak (1992) suggests, nature and humans share an ensouled world. In his award winning book, the Holy Longing, Catholic priest and theologian Ronald Rolheiser (Rolheiser, 1999) shares this view and offers his definition of spirituality, " Spirituality is more about whether or not we can sleep at night than whether or not we go to church. It is about being integrated or falling apart, about being within community or being lonely, about being in harmony with Mother Earth or being alienated from her" (Rolheiser, 1999, p. 6-7). This concept is a familiar one to aboriginal peoples around the world, the sacred landscape which we share with nature being essential to our fundamental well-being. From the perspective of this innate interconnected relationship with earth, it is not surprising that our modern disconnection with nature can result in mental health issues (Berry, 2009; Coates et al., 2006; Jordan, 2009; Sackettt, 2010; Sundaram, 2014).

On a spiritual level, becoming increasingly disconnected from the natural world has led us to become more disconnected from each other. On the other hand, spending quality time in nature, either gardening, outdoors, or in the wilderness, can help us step away from ourselves and cultivate empathy towards all that is other, expanding and developing one's maturity to support self-transcendence (Clinebell, 1996; Jordan, 2009). As a catholic ecotheologian, Thomas Berry (1988) suggests that our relationship with nature may increase the awareness of our experience. Bradley Holt (2005) describes spiritual formation as being "in the first instance, about experience, not theory" (Holt, 2005, p 22). Thus, by experiencing nature we may awaken the senses that are often anesthetized by modern life and perhaps awaken the spiritual aspects of ourselves and that elusive divine interconnectedness with all that is other.

Many ecotherapists report similar findings from their work with a deep sense of belonging, reflecting a sense of place, emerging when clients speak of their experiences in nature (Brazier, 2011; Buzzell & Chalquist, 2009; Chalquist, 2007; Jordan, 2009; Sackett, 2010; Stein, 2013). At the heart of ecotherapy, a term coined by Clinebell (1996) is the notion that our relationship with nature is one of reciprocity. We live in this earth, not simply on it (Sundaram, 2014). We benefit from the gloriousness of its flora and fauna and are sustained by the bounties of the earth; in return, we take care of the earth (Clinebell, 1996; Jordan,

2009). We cannot deny that we are part of nature, part of something vast and inexplicable and yet our modern Western culture has supported a split between spirit and matter, psyche and nature. Ecotherapy addresses this rift between humanity and earth by opening the door to our deep ecological instincts or ecological consciousness (Besthorn, Wulff & St. George, 2010; Brazier, 2011; Buzzel & Chalquist, 2009; Coates et al., 2006; Roszak, 1992; Wilson, 1984). We are after all dependent on nature for our well being, perhaps not as much as primitive man, but nevertheless the health of the planet seems to reflect the health of our psyches and despite all the power we purport to encompass, we seem unable to stop the extinction of species and the degradation of our planet. A beautiful description of this is provided by psychoanalyst Martin Jordan (2009) who, at the forefront of the nature based therapy movement, sees ecopsychology as "coming into relationship with nature in ways that celebrate the complexities of our emotional worlds, acknowledging not only the destructive tendencies of the human race, but also its capacity for love and reparation, and directing this capacity towards the natural world" (Jordan, 2009, p. 30).

In summary, by bearing witness to the changes and transformations in nature we may begin to recognize the impact we have on the earth and on others and thus take steps towards our own spiritual transformation (Berry, 2009). The importance of nature in one's spirituality can be translated in various practices such as any action and commitment to the preservation of ecology, encouraging local and organic farming, or a personal orientation towards a concern for health, well - being and harmony with nature; for both present and future generations. Another emerging practice is observed among many people choosing to create new ways to preserve the environment. These people value and encourage local and organic economy which resonates with values such as mutual aid, volunteering, resource sharing and justice. Acting against the current industrialization of food, these people, called culturally creative, by Ray and Anderson (2000), are willing to pay more money or taxes in order to promote health values, organic farming and local economy, reducing the distance and cost of the transport of goods.

The Influence of Eastern Philosophy Such As Mindfulness

Spanning a history of 2500 years, the practice of mindfulness is gradually becoming commonplace in Western societies. In fact, this millennial practice has interested Western scientists for about the last four decades (Shapiro & Carlson, 2009). It is found among others in the fields of medicine, psychotherapy and personal growth (Shapiro & Carlson, 2009). Cognitive-behavioural therapeutic approaches integrating mindfulness mediation practices have been developed and evaluated (Bondolfi, 2004). These approaches include the most cited, the "Mindfulness Based Stress Reduction" program (MBSR; Kabat-Zinn, 1982, 1990), dialectical behaviour therapy ('Dialectic Behaviour Therapy, DBT; Linehan, 1993), acceptance and commitment therapy (Acceptance and Commitment Therapy, ACT, Hayes, Strosahl, & Wilson, 1999) and more recently, Mindfulness Based Cognitive Therapy (MBCT; Segal, Williams & Teasdale, 2002, 2006).

These approaches suggest that by integrating the practice of mindfulness, those suffering can benefit from a therapeutic tool which may facilitate, for example, healing and improvement of many anxiety symptoms (Segal et al., 2006). Today, interest in the practice of mindfulness exceeds even the scientific sphere and the therapeutic arena; mindfulness is now popular with the media. . For the general public, there are many books that deal with the benefits of mindfulness meditation (Ricard, 2008). "The Power of Now", the bestseller by Tolle (2000) – sanctioned by famous American TV host Oprah – reflects this contemporary craze for mindfulness.

This originally Buddhist approach (Brazier, 2009) maintains that, as humans, we want to feel secure. When we are uncomfortable or insecure, our behaviours are often distracted away from the present moment by our senses (eye, ears, nose, tongue, body and mind's eye or thoughts), we use these distractions as psychological defenses and we become attached to them and form an identity around them (Brazier, 2009; Brazier, 2011). We then often fall into the trap of thinking that identity is permanent and part of our self. When life inevitably happens, that identity becomes threatened and it sends us into a state of seeking oblivion (essentially diagnosable psychological pathologies). Jon Kabat-Zinn (Kabat- Zinn, 2003) defines mindfulness as "the awareness that emerges through paying attention on purpose, in the present moment, and nonjudgmentally to the unfolding of experience moment by moment"(Kabat-Zinn, 2003, p. 145). Mindfulness allows you to put aside your thoughts while promoting the adoption of an observer position, which emerges with its own cognitive processes (Segal et al., 2006). More particularly, mindfulness is based on the fact that there are regions in the brain which are more active and developed than other regions. The narrative circuit is responsible for all human thoughts and interpretations; the chatter of white noise that sometimes prevents us from experiencing the present moment. When this narrative circuit is going, our senses may not be as able to read what is going on in the environment, leaving us less aware of our surroundings. On the other hand, the experiential circuit refers to when we are more in contact with our senses, in the present moment, with heightened awareness (Brazier, 2009, Monteiro & Musten, 2013). Studies have shown that individuals that practice mindfulness meditation have the ability to change circuits and may focus more easily in the present moment (Kabat-Zinn, 1994).

Salmon, Sephton, & Weissbecker (2004) summarized in five points the elements of the practice of mindfulness. These elements are actually intra-psychic processes (thoughts, behaviours, emotions, feelings, attitudes): "a) conscious allocation of attention in the service of (b) non-judgmental awareness; ideally cultivated (but not necessarily limited to) a state of (c) physiological hypo-arousal; with the intention of (d) enhancing present-moment awareness and (e) diminishing habitual patterns of cognitive, behavioral and psychological reactivity"(quoted in Toneatto & Nguyen, 2007, p. 261).

In summary, with full awareness, we try to be in contact with ourselves; in Sanskrit, Samma sati – right mindfulness – means the vigilant awareness of our own cognitive processes. Mindfulness or right mindfulness means to bring attention to the present moment, in the here and now, that is to say taking care to bring attention back to the subject of concentration when our mind wanders (Segal et al., 2006). This helps to decrease the influence of verbal and conceptual rules of the past (i.e. ruminations) and expectations of the future (Hayes & Smith, 2005). Mindfulness allows the practitioner to realize that the spirit ("mind's eye") is often going to comment or judge. The goal is to become an observer as opposed to a prisoner of one's own thoughts by letting them go without repudiating them (Hayes & Smith, 2005). This mindfulness is not limited to a meditation practice, but could be useful at any time of human activity, without the need to sit or to focus on breathing, but by paying attention to what is happening in the present moment.

THE POSITIVE IMPACT OF HOLISTIC APPROACHES, NATURE AND MINDFULNESS ON HEALTH

Western scientific medicine has made tremendous progress in improving and prolonging quality of life, decreasing the rate of infant mortality, inventing immunization practices and so forth. However, traditionally, medicine was mostly concerned with curing the body, with little emphasis on the soul. As a result, some people have turned to complementary and alternative medicine (CAM) to address their health issues. Such approaches are defined in various ways, but generally have three characteristics: "1) they tend to focus on aspects which are not usually emphasized in conventional medical care, 2) there is typically little clinical research to support claims of efficacy or safety, and 3) they tend to be provided within a holistic philosophy that emphasizes the spiritual, relational, emotional, and physical aspects of health and healing" (O'Mathúna, 2001).

The holistic conception of health resonates with what Taylor (2007) mentions regarding the contemporary quest for spiritual integrity, that which is often closely linked to the search for a better overall health. This holistic approach, used in many forms of alternative or non-traditional medicine, is seen in various forms, such as yoga, mindfulness meditation, hypnosis, reiki, acupuncture and so forth, in an attempt to heal the mind and body in ways that traditional medicine cannot. In sum, it may be helpful for health professionals and clinicians trained in scientific medicine to ascertain their patients' use of these types of CAM and to integrate all forms of care used to manage health problems, such as cancer (Hsiao, Wong, Miller et al., 2008).

Furthermore, it is common sense to admit that a good walk in nature, along a river or on trails in the wilderness can help someone feel rejuvenated and calmer. According to Miyazaki (2006) this makes perfect sense. A pioneer of empirical studies on the benefits of nature on health and well-being, Miyazaki (2006) points out that for about 99.9 % of evolutionary history, human beings have lived in nature. It is not until recently that we have begun to adapt to an urban lifestyle. This transition and bombardment of our senses by electronic and other non- natural stimuli generates stress. As mentioned previously, C. G. Jung wrote of this transition to urban areas and industrialized environments and the need for modern man to maintain connection with primitive man in order sustain an authentic, creative and balanced whole. This lack of balance results in stress (Sabini, 2002; Sundaram, 2014).

Stress is essential as it gets us primed up to protect ourselves and is ultimately responsible for our survival. Stress is also part of human nature, and it can be seen as an adaptation strategy which helps us scan for threat; its purpose is to keep us aware, attuned to our senses and thus to the surrounding environments, to fight or flight in the presence of danger (Berman, Jonides & Kaplan, 2008: Buzzell & Chalquist, 2009). Modern stress appears in a less dangerous form, an ever pervasive, chronic stress fuelled by numbing of the senses, distraction, worry, tension, business etc. Nature offers a space to rest physically, psychologically and spiritually, a space where our senses can open fully without having to filter or multitask. The link between nature and physical well - being and even healing has been demonstrated in many recent studies. The notion that our urban alienation from nature may be at the root of our increasing physical, psychological, spiritual challenges provides much fodder for research. The high rates of stress in urban environments are a growing concern: stress, anxiety, depression, burnout, sick leave... are words that fill headlines worldwide.

Using continuing clinical trials on more than 1000 participants, Miyazaki (2006) studied participants engaged in the practice of Forest Bathing or 'bathing the mind and the body in the forest' which essentially involves spending time in the forest. His results showed that after less than an hour in the forest there was a significant improvement in health markers, a 12.7 % decline in cortisol levels and an increase of parasympathetic nervous system activity. Results also revealed a boost to the immune system which along with the decrease in cortisol levels, lasted for up to a week following immersion in the forest (Miyazaki, 2006; Sundaram, 2014). Other studies have shown that time spent in nature can increase serotonin levels, decrease heart rate, depressive symptoms, and aggression as well as stimulate right hemisphere brain activity (Corazon, Stigsdotter, Jensen & Nelson, 2010; Selhub & Logan, 2012; Sundaram, 2014). In urban environments, our senses become overloaded, we are constantly distracted and we learn to filter out or numb our awareness in order to prevent a sort of sensory burnout. (Berman et al., 2008; Brazier, 2009; Buzzell & Chalquist, 2009; Kabat-Zinn, 1994; Kaplan, 1995; Miyazaki, 2006).

According to Berman et al. (2008), this overload can drain the brain of its executive functioning capacity. The prefrontal cortex is responsible for decision making, creativity and abstract thinking and filtering out constant distractions can lead to what they call directed attention fatigue (Berman et al., 2008; Sundaram, 2014). Nature fosters mental clarity by allowing an attunement of the senses which in turn fosters flexibility, experiential openness and more creativity (Berman et al., 2008; Sackett, 2010; Sundaram, 2014).

At the psychological level, studies conducted by Hegarty (2010) on the emotional benefits of nature-connectedness, revealed that most participants sought contact with nature during the challenging times of their lives. Participants reported feeling a sense of connection with something greater than themselves, often describing their experiences as mystical or transcendental (Hegarty, 2010; Sundaram, 2014). Andrew Howell and his team (Howell, Dopko, Passmore & Buro., 2011) delved deeply into the question of our connectedness with nature and how it can be measured as a reflection of our well- being. Drawing from Wilson's Biophilia hypothesis (Wilson, 1984) that human beings have an instinctive, emotional and genetic need to be in contact with nature, Howell and his team conducted empirical studies and produced convincing results demonstrating that connection to nature may be more beneficial to our emotional and social well being than previously realized. Interestingly, in a second study nature connectedness was found to be significantly correlated to mindfulness (Howell et al., 2011).

Mindfulness also appears to have an impact on our emotional and social well-being. At the behavioural level, mindfulness has been linked to improving concentration through emotional regulation, increasing empathy and compassion, fostering the ability to step back from automatic reactions and acting more consciously under pressure. Literature also attests to the merits of mindfulness on health. From a neurological perspective mindfulness affects the brain in a similar manner that nature affects the brain. A recent study out of Harvard University reports that mindfulness exercises practiced for less than half an hour each day results in an increased thickness of the cerebral cortex which increases the brains plasticity in areas associated with psychological flexibility, awareness, emotional regulation and compassion (Holzel, Carmody, Vangel, Congleton, Yerramsetti, Gard & Lazar, 2011). A by -

product of this is decreased stress and increased immune system functioning (Kabat- Zinn, 1994).

Mindfulness teaches us that we are not what we are thinking, that we can live our experiences without being submerged in our experience. Our experiences are considered neither good nor bad, they are simply experiences. Mindfulness helps bring us to the present moment where it is then possible to objectively evaluate and make conscious choices regarding the external information we receive and process. It is through our senses that we receive information and become conscious of our world. In a similar manner that nature helps us open to our experience, mindfulness helps us awaken those senses and reconnect with our bodies (Brazier, 2009; Kabat-Zinn, 1994; Monteiro & Musten, 2013). By practicing mindfulness techniques we begin to feel a sense of harmony with others, we become less focused on ourselves and a natural compassion emerges (Brazier, 2009; Kabat-Zinn, 1994; Monteiro & Musten, 2013).

Researchers have proposed different mechanisms of action which may explain why the practice of mindfulness can help reduce symptoms and/or stimulate behavioural changes within various clinical disorders, such as anxiety, mood disorders, stress reduction, depression, chronic pain, sleep disorders, borderline personality disorder, addiction disorders and many more (Brazier, 2009; Bowen, Chawla & Marlatt, 2011; Germer, Siegel & Fulton, 2013; Hayes, Folette & Lineman, 2004; Segal et al, 2002). For example, Segal and colleagues (2002) argue that the practice of mindfulness develops the ability to better manage or transform irrational thoughts, unpleasant feelings and negative emotions with an attitude of acceptance and non-judgment. Techniques of heightening awareness and experiencing bodily sensations, thoughts and emotions are practiced with particular attention paid to the labelling of experiences as good or bad. The practice of simple observation can then be carried through into walking meditation, body scanning and eventually transposed into all aspect of life (Brazier, 2009; Kabat-Zinn, 1994; Monteiro & Munsten, 2013).

Some Limitations to the Study of "Healthy" Spirituality

This section presents some limitations to the understanding of a "healthy" spirituality in secular Western societies. As suggested by Koenig (2008), the first limitation has to do with the problem of tautology in some empirical studies. According to Koenig (2008), a medical doctor, mental health researcher and epidemiologist, some empirical findings that claim that "spirituality" is beneficial for mental health have been criticised on the grounds that definitions of spirituality have been stretched to imply mental health by definition. Attempts have been made to redefine the term in a more inclusive manner, accommodating those from diverse religious backgrounds and to those with no religion. Such research has broadened the term to incorporate a wide range of psychological notions such as social connectedness or interdependence with others, purpose and meaning in life, hopefulness, inner peace and general well- being. This may become problematic for researchers when assessing the relationship between "spirituality" and mental health since, by most definitions, mental health implies that a person has some purpose in life, is hopeful, socially connected, peaceful and has a sense of general well-being. According to Koenig (2008), when defining spirituality with terms related to mental health, it becomes a meaningless tautology to say that the two concepts, spirituality and better mental health, are linked.

The second limitation is related to the nature of empirical studies per se. According to the scientific paradigm, research seeks to establish facts, or causal relationships between variables. Thus, in the case of religion and spirituality, studies are often conducted in order to measure and identify their influence on health (Zinnbauer, 2013).

For example, some research will operationalize spirituality as hope or optimism, social support, meaning of life, or will use spiritual activities such as prayer, meditation, feeling of being comforted or abandoned by God, and so forth (Pargament, 2013). As for health, it may be measured by the levels of lipids in the blood, hormone levels, brain activity, blood pressure, psychotic symptoms, anxiety, clinical signs and behaviours and so forth. In all these studies, using associations or causal relationships between variables and multiple possible combinations, researchers seek to clarify, support or invalidate associations between health factors and spiritual factors from various sources. This may create a body of theories and research which may be equally interesting as it is fragmented.

However, given the importance of studying spirituality understood in terms of experience (Fontaine, 2014), one cannot stick to a scientific reduction which considers the representations of a person as a material, anatomical and biophysiological body. Researchers today need to be concerned with a person's subjective experience, while taking into account the scientific context that lingers in the review of objective phenomena and universals which are identifiable and measurable across populations. Taking spirituality into account, researchers must carry their interest into the singular, complex phenomena which is impossible to simplify, reduce, or contextualize in a world order that is beyond the strict control of variables. Considering spirituality in its entirety and complexity becomes difficult to grasp in scholarly categories uprooted by the singular experience of individuals. The study of spirituality is thus open to dialogue, uncertainty, disorder and contradictions, and thus the conceptual frameworks, the underlying assumptions, and the truths and preconceptions remain partial.

In the area of health, it is also important to clarify that while making space for spirituality, it is assumed that one needs to cope with multiple theories and knowledge that may emerge from an episode of illness and suffering. This allows the inclusion of totality and holism. Moreover, we understand why this introduction to the topic of spirituality occurs mainly in the area of palliative care, where clinicians and researchers already accept the limits of scientific medicine (Vonarx, 2014).

Furthermore, in the field of social and health sciences research, there exists a way of knowing strongly supported by a reduction process that tends to simplify spirituality to the first idea of experience, which fades along the way. To understand this, let's take into consideration the distinction between religion and spirituality previously mentioned. By separating spirituality from religion, some social and health scientists claim that they do not have to take a stand in favour of any belief systems and representations which are proposed by religions. For example, these researchers will look at the purpose of life, relationships or connections to something other than oneself, self-transcendence, values, worldviews, hope in the form of presence or absence, needs and suffering. In principle, these multiple phenomena can be studied as detached from religious traditions, or not having to deal with these traditions or organizations, or in the least, not having to really understand them.

In support of this latter point, Bibby (1988) has coined the term "religion à la carte" where everyone selects beliefs or practices that meet his own needs. However, as Bibby (1988) points out, this phenomenon may result in various ruptures such as the emergence of plural beliefs which co-exist between traditional religious beliefs, cosmic beliefs, sublimated ego seen as a parcel of divinity; privatization of religious experience and the current tendency to detach the spirituality of religion. To illustrate the following, two examples speak of the tendency to psychologize spirituality without taking into consideration the symbolic and religious context of some of those concepts.

The first example refers to the growing popularity of Eastern philosophy in Western societies. For instance, it is well known that the idea of reincarnation is often seen for some in the West as a second chance, rather than a consequence of failing to successfully reach the state of *nirvana*, or the extinction of self. Furthermore, the recuperation of mindfulness in the West is also subject to a contextual interpretation (Bellehumeur & Malette, 2010). When someone realizes that mindfulness is part of the Eightfold Noble Path, its practice is not as easy and straightforward. Indeed, in what is considered by Buddhist tradition as the fourth truth of the Four Noble Truths, namely the path leading to the cessation of suffering (dukkha), mindfulness is the seventh part of the eight that is usually presented in three categories: wisdom (right understanding, right thought); ethics (right speech, right action, right lifestyle); and meditation (right effort, fair consciousness, right concentration) (Huxter, 2007; Chiesa, 2013 cited in Iezzoni, 2013).

Kang and Whittingham (2010) point out that in a Buddhist perspective, mindfulness is an integral part of *dukkha* so that as such it could not be taken in isolation. Especially as these categories are interrelated: "Ethics relies on mindfulness […] ethics is the foundation or basis for the two latter trainings: those of concentration and wisdom. This quality of mindfulness which is so important for ethics is important for these also" (Tsering cited in Kang & Whittingham, 2010, p. 173). Whether described as "just" reveals that mindfulness calls for ethical discernment, it requires a judgment of what is considered kusula (healthy) or akusala (unhealthy). This seems absent from the perspective of many western clinical psychological and medical approaches integrating mindfulness practices (Iezzoni, 2013). In these approaches, mindfulness has been reduced to a mere postural awareness, an acceptance and non-judgment of any experience whatsoever, dependent on a limited understanding of *vipassana.* They have inspired third wave psychotherapeutic approaches (Kang & Whittingham, 2010) which resemble a humanistic type of unconditional acceptance of the present moment. This western psychological reduction of mindfulness does not take into account the vision of the world which is rooted in the mindfulness practice: "Far from a simple technique or type of consciousness that we might call mindfulness, we are dealing with an entire mode of knowing and of being in the world composed of many interdependent synergistic facets which are simultaneously ways of entering the whole and themselves part of the enlightened awareness itself" (Rosch, 2007, p. 261).

A second example which we present briefly has to do with the experience of forgiveness. In many studies in psychology of religion and in clinical psychology, forgiveness is linked to personal wellbeing, inner peace and more positive emotions (Pargament, 2013). Although these positive outcomes are part of the experience of forgiveness, the latter may not be solely a personal and subjective matter. Forgiveness is essentially a phenomenon that may have a social and collective dimension which impacts the common good of all societies. In our view, a purely psychological definition of forgiveness putting the emphasis on subjective wellbeing and on the personal self tends to echo the individualistic society. Spirituality which encourage journeying on the path of forgiveness may appear, in some cases, as vertical or centered on itself and not as open to others (Carson, 1989). For instance, some people argue that it deprives the person of the wisdom and shared lessons of the community.

Furthermore, organized religions, such as monotheist religions and many Eastern spiritual traditions, have some forms of religious practice which may benefit churchgoers' wellbeing and health in several ways. These may be providing social support, attachment to a loving God or a positive Divine Energy, the organized practice of prayer, positive psychological states of mind, coping strategies, optimism and hope, gratitude, humility, purpose in life and so on (Pargament, 2013). In many main conventional religions, altruistic acts and compassion towards the poorest people are socially valued, fostered and encouraged. Given the fact that less poverty has been identified as the first determinant to improve health worldwide (Torpy, 2007; Leon & Walt, 2001; Chossudovsky, 2003), humanitarian helping associations often run by religious organizations, have been and may still be a considerable way to ensure better life conditions and health in many situations.

More recently, a British study conducted by King, Marston, McManus and his colleagues (2013) looked at the relationship between spirituality and mental health using a more traditional understanding of the term to avoid the above mentioned problem of tautology. In this study, King and his colleagues (2013) examined 7,403 interviews with British people, of whom 35% had a religious understanding of life, 19% had a spiritual but not religious one, and 46% had neither a religious nor spiritual outlook. These terms were explained in the following way: "By religion, we mean the actual practice of a faith, e.g. going to a temple, mosque, church or synagogue. Some people do not follow a religion but do have spiritual beliefs or experiences. Some people make sense of their lives without any religious or spiritual belief." (King et al, 2013, p. 69). Participants were also interviewed in depth about their mental health, alcohol and drug use, social support, use of psychotropic medication, gambling, and were asked about their overall happiness. Results showed that people who were "spiritual but not religious" were more vulnerable to mental disorders [dependence on drugs, abnormal eating attitudes, anxiety, phobias and neuroses]. These differences still held even when taking into account social support and physical health, as well as age, sex, and ethnicity.

Although the nature of the causal relationship between spirituality and mental disorders remains currently unknown, some explanations are suggested. One possible reason is related to the fact that not having a religious framework for one's beliefs could lead to mental disorders in people who have a need for a spiritual understanding of life (King, Weich, Nazroo, & Blizard, 2006). Alternatively, having a mental disorder might prompt a person to engage in a spiritual quest in the hope of mental healing. However, exploring one's spirituality without the support of others might lead to an inner obsession that, for some people, may end up spiralling out of control. On another note, personal crises may drive people to seek spiritual solace that by itself, if pursued in isolation, does not address the underlying psychological problems or distress; the resources of a healthy spiritual tradition or religion could then provide or point to the means of addressing psychological concerns or issues. With wisdom and careful spiritual advice, with psychological issues being addressed if needed, genuine spiritual growth becomes possible (Zinnbauer, 2013).

According to King et al. (2013)'s study, other reasons may explain why some spiritual but not religious people are so troubled. Perhaps, there are some people who are simply not successful in pursuing their spiritual quest. King et al. (2013) found that participants who said they were spiritual but not religious rated the importance of their beliefs and of the practice of their faith lower than the religious people, indicating perhaps a lack of self-discipline on the part of those who claim to be SBNR.

Many other variables would need to be measured to fully appreciate the results of King et al. (2013)'s study. For example, this study did not examine the specific content of the beliefs and practices of the SBNR people. It seems obvious that the content of one's spiritual beliefs (e.g. either a positive God image or negative one; see Schaap-Jonker, Eurelings-Bontekoe, Zock, & Jonker, 2008) could well affect one's mental health. Another variable could be related to personality traits. According to Saucier & Skrzypińska (2006), people who were more focused on subjective spirituality and less interested in religiosity tended to show different personality characteristics compared to those with a more conventional religious orientation. As opposed to people describing themselves in conventional religious terms, who tended to be fairly conservative in their attitudes and beliefs, people who were more spiritual and less religious tended to be more non-conforming and even peculiar in their outlook and personal traits. They were more likely to describe themselves as **weird** and **crazy and** tended to believe in a range of "alternative" ideas (such as astrology, witchcraft, psychic powers and magical thinking).

CONCLUSION

In this chapter, we have attempted to provide sociological, anthropological and psychological factors to better understand the religious stance of being 'spiritual but not religious,' SBNR. The term studied by Fuller (2001) is now so commonplace that it has spawned its own acronym ("I'm SBNR") and website: www.SBNR.org. We propose that some factors, trends or approaches are associated with this new spiritual stance. First, we have presented the importance of holistic health which is evident in complementary and alternative medicine. Secondly, the socio-ecological approaches to spirituality which may well be considered as an implicit religion (Gollnick, 2005) allowing for new forms of nature-based therapies. Lastly, we have discussed the influence of Eastern philosophy in Western societies reflected by the growing interest in mindfulness practice in modern daily lives and in clinical psychology and medicine.

In contemporary western societies where religious practice is often less common and moral rules are increasingly complex and plural, human beings have a need to develop their own spirituality and ethical reflection. Given the fact that today's western societies are more individualistic, and since modern individuals have less need of a group for their survival than was the case in traditional society (Bégin & Bellehumeur, 2002), individuals enjoy more freedom, spiritual and otherwise; On the other hand, individuality leads to less solidarity.

As expected, the practice of being spiritual but not religious has been mostly criticized by those who participate in organized religion. Some say it may lead to egotism, self-centeredness, complacency, or neglecting the poor because there is no common community and shared solidarity. However, as Taylor (2007) has elegantly pointed out, an ethic of authenticity prompts the individual to seek within himself the model of his own life, to be faithful to his own originality, to 'be himself' rather than trying to imitate an exterior model.

This ethic of authenticity may not necessarily result in narcissism, subjectivism and withdrawal ("repli sur soi"); it may all depend on how people view life. For some, being sincere and genuine with themselves will lead them to connect to some form of transcendence – some form of existence that goes beyond themselves – to engage in profound and meaningful loving relationships, to have a responsible social life and a committed religious attitude. Others, on the contrary, will fall in the narrowest narcissism and develop a selfish attitude. In essence, this points to an inevitable paradox: any increase of freedom will consequently lead people to reach a lower or higher life (Taylor, 2007).

Another paradox may lie in the expression, "spiritual but not religious". As the term is sometimes feared for the tendency to be too focused on the self, for its psychologizing propensity or even worse, to turn into spiritual narcissism. It is sometimes understood as being too de-centered from the person's religious individuality, too eclectic or scattered in multiple forms of religiosity or lacking in critical thinking with regard to various religious currents. Being SBNR may either refer to some centrifugal forces for some people, or centripetal forces for others. Important questions such as psycho-spiritual integration, Jung's individuation, or psycho-spiritual growth remain a challenge for all human persons.

In sum, the new forms of spiritualities such as being SBNR seem to reflect the sense of security of the will and consciousness of humans; a complete trust in human potential. It also seems to show a fear of moral authority, as if recalling dogma and religious heritage could be a threat to the individuality of the person. In their book, Daviau and Lavoie (2008) point out that the reduction of the spiritual life to the inner life is the aspect of the spirituality of those surveyed (midlife people, men and women) which has more similarities with the new spiritual quest. These authors speak of the primacy of conscience, particularly, the consciousness, the body and the imagination which have become places from which the inner life may develop and without which it is impossible - according to the followers of the new spiritualities - to reach the state of perfection and goodness which is inherent to the Cosmos. Never, perhaps, has individual consciousness been affirmed as powerfully as in the new forms of contemporary spirituality (Daviau & Lavoie, 2008). Furthermore, the emergence of a new paradigm based on the ability of consciousness to transform and transcend itself appears to Daviau and Lavoie (2008) as an attempt to reconcile the religious and spiritual quest with the values of autonomy and freedom. Indeed, there is neither magisterium or beliefs or requirements, or rituals imposed in this new paradigm. Everyone is free to invent a spirituality that suits him or her, as everyone is free to draw on the traditions of his or her choice.

Finally, considering the increasing prominence in modern society of people who consider themselves spiritual but not religious, more in-depth research is needed to understand fully why SBNR people might appear to be particularly vulnerable to mental illness (King et al., 2013). Overall, spirituality is also rich and calls to be fostered in everyone's life, we cannot overlook this precious dimension of humanity. Let us remember that the Latin, Greek and Hebrew roots of the spiritual term refer to *spiritus* meaning breath of life, *pneuma,* also with the breath in mind, and *ruach,* wind, a breath which we do not know where it comes from, nor where it goes.

REFERENCES

Astrow, A. B., Puchalski, C.M. & D.P. Sulmasy (2001). Religion, Spirituality, and Health Care: Social, Ethical, and Practical Considerations, *The American Journal of Medicine, 110*, 283-287.

Bellehumeur, C.R., & J. Malette (2010). Regards psychosociaux sur les défis de la pratique de la pleine conscience. *Counseling et spiritualité, 29* (1), 67-89.

Bégin, B., & Bellehumeur, C. R. (2002). Le counseling pastoral au risque des défis de la famille contemporaine. *Sciences pastorales, 21*(2), 313-337.

Berman, M.G., Jonides, J., & Kaplan, S. (2008). The cognitive benefits of interacting with nature. *Psychological Science,* 19(12), 1207-1211.

Berry, T. (1988). *The Dream of the Earth.* San Francisco: Sierra Club Books.

Berry, T. (2009). *The Scared Universe*: *Earth Spirituality, and Religion in the Twenty-First Century.* New York: Columbia University Press.

Besthorn, F.H., Wulff, D., & St. George, S. (2010). Eco-Spiritual Helping and Postmodern Therapy: A Deeper ecological Framework. *Ecopsychology*, 2(1), 23-32.

Bibby, R. W. (1988). *La religion a la carte. Pauvreté et potentiel de la religion au Canada* (traduit de l'anglais par Louis-Bertrand Raymond, S.J.), Montréal, Fides.

Bondolfi, G. (2004). Les approches utilisant des exercices de méditation de type «mindfulness» ont-elles un rôle à jouer? *Santé mentale au Québec*, 29 (1), 137-145.

Bowen, S., Chawla, N., & Marlatt, G.A. (2011). *Mindfulness-Based Relapse Prevention for addictive Behaviors: A Clinician's Guide.* New York: Guilford Press.

Brazier, C. (2009). *Other - Centred Therapy: Buddhist Psychology in Action.* Washington: O-Books.

Brazier, C. (2011). *Acorns Among the Grass: Adventures in Eco-therapy.* Washington: O-Books.

Buzzell, L., & Chalquist, C. (2009). *Ecotherapy: Healing with nature in mind.* San Francisco: Sierra Club Books.

Carson, V. B. (1989). *Spiritual Dimensions of Nursing Practice*, Philadelphia, W.B. Saunders.

Casey, P. R. (2013). I'm spiritual but not religious: Implications for research and practice. In Cook, Christopher (ed.). *Spirituality, Theology and Mental Health: Interdisciplinary Perspectives.* SCM Press.

Chalquist, C. (2007). *Terrapsychology: Reengaging the Soul of Place.* New Orleans: Spring Journal Books.

Chiesa, A. (2013). The Difficulty of Defining Mindfulness: Current Thought and Critical Issues, *Mindfulness*, 4 (3), 255-268.

Chossudovsky, M. (2003). *The Globalization of Poverty and the New World Order.* Second edition. Pincourt, Quebec: Global Research, CRG.

Clinebell, H. (1996). *Ecotherapy: Healing Ourselves, Healing the Earth: A Guide to Ecologically Grounded Personality Theory, Spirituality, Therapy and Education.* Minneapolis, MN: Fortress.

Coates, J., Grey, M., & Hetherington, T. (2006). An 'Ecospiritual' Perspective: Finally, a Place for Indigenous Approaches. *British Journal of Social Work*, 36, 381-399.

Corazon, S.S., Stigsdotter, U.K., Jensen, A.G.C.J., & Nilsson, K. (2010). Development of the Nature-Based Therapy Concept for Patients with Stress - Related Illness at the Danish Healing Forest Garden Nacadia. *Journal of Therapeutic Horticulture*, 20, 34-50.

Croteau, J. (1981). *L'homme : sujet ou objet? Prolégomènes philosophiques à une psychologie scientifico-humaniste.* Coll. « Recherches-Philosophie », no 25. Montréal, Bellarmin, et Tournai, Desclée et Cie.

Daviau, P. & L.-C. Lavoie (2008). *La spiritualité au mitan de la vie. Étude comparative du féminin et du masculin.* Québec, Qc : Les Presses de l'Université Laval.

Daviau, P. (2014). Transmettre une spiritualité en famille : est-ce possible ? In K. Demasure, E. Champagne, R. Martinez de Pison, M. Rovers (Eds.). *Family's Many Faces – La famille au pluriel. (pp. 183-197).* Leuven, Belgium : Peeters.

Davie, G. (1994). *Religion in Britain Since 1945: Believing Without Belonging (Making Contemporary Britain).* Oxford, UK: Wiley-Blackwell.

Fontaine, M. (2014). Expériences humaine et spirituelle ou comment s'interpellent secularization et spiritualité. *Spiritualitésanté, 7* (2), 36-39.

Fuller, R. C. (2001). *Spiritual But Not Religious: Understanding Unchurched America*, Oxford, Oxford University Press.

Germer, C.K., Siegel, R.D., & Fulton, R.F. (2013) *Mindfulness and Psychotherapy, second edition.* New York: Guilford Press.

Gollnick, J. (2005). *Religion and Spirituality in the Life Cycle.* New York, NY: Peter Lang.

Hayes, S. C., Strosahl, K., & Wilson, K. G. (1999). *Acceptance and Commitment Therapy: An experiential approach to behavior change.* New York: Guilford Press.

Hayes, S.C., Folette, V.M., & Lineman, M.M. (2004). *Mindfulness and Acceptance: Expanding the Cognitive - Behavioural Tradition.* New York: Guilford Press

Hayes, S.C., & Smith, S. (2005). *Get out of your mind and into your life: The new Acceptance and Commitment Therapy.* Oakland, CA: New Harbinger.

Hegarty, J.R. (2010). Out of the consulting room and into the woods. Experiences of nature connectedness and self-healing. *European Journal of Ecopsychology*, 1, 64-84

Holt, B.P., (2005). *Thirsty for God: A Brief History of Christian Spirituality.* Minneapolis: Fortress Press

Hölzel, B.K., Carmody, J., Vangel, Congeleton, C., Yerramsetti, S.M., Gard, T., Lazar, S.W. (2012). Mindfulness practice leads to increases in regional brain gray matter density. *Psychiatry Research – Neuroimaging*, 191 (1), 36-43.

Howell, J.A., Dopko, R.L., Passmore, H., & Buro, K. (2011). Nature connectedness: Associations with well- being and mindfulness. *Personality and Individual Differences*, 51(2), 166- 171.

Hsiao, A.F., Wong, M.D., Miller, M.F., Ambs, A.H., Goldstein, M.S., Smith, A., Ballard-Barbash, R., Becerra, L.S., Cheng, E.M. & Wenger, N.S. (2008). Role of religiosity and spirituality in complementary and alternative medicine use among cancer survivors in California. *Integrative Cancer Therapies, 7*(3), 139-146.

Huxter, M. J. (2007). Mindfulness as Therapy from a Buddhist Perspective, in D. A. Einstein (éd.), *Innovations and Advances in Cognitive–Behaviour Therapy* (pp. 43-55). Brisbane: Australian Academic Press.

Iezzoni, N. (2013). Measuring mindfulness? *Counselling and Spirituality*, 32(2), 13-31.

Jordan, M. (2009) Nature and Self - an Ambivalent Attachment. *Ecopsychology*, 1(1), 26-31.

Jordan, M., & Marshall, H. (2010). Taking counselling and psychotherapy outside: Destruction or enrichment of the therapeutic frame? *European Journal of Psychotherapy and Counselling*, 12 (4), 345-359.

Kabat-Zinn, J. (1982). An outpatient program in behavioral medicine for chronic pain patients based on the practise of mindfulness meditation, *General Hospital Psychiatry*, 4, 33-47.

Kabat-Zinn, J. (1990). *Full Catastrophe Living: Using the Wisdom of your Body and Mind to Face Stress, Pain and Illness*, Delacorte, New York.

Kabat- Zinn, J. (1994). *Wherever You Go There You Are - Mindfulness Meditation in Every Day Life*. New York: Hyperion.

Kabat-Zinn, J. (2003). Mindfulness-Based Interventions in Context: Past, Present, and Future, *Clinical Psychology: Science and Practice*, 10 (2), 144-156.

Kang, C. & K. Whittingham (2010). Mindfulness: A Dialogue between Buddhism and Clinical Psychology, *Mindfulness,* 1 (3), 161-173.

Kaplan, S. (1995). The Restorative Benefits of Nature: Toward an Integrative Framework. *Journal of Environmental Psychology*, 15, 169-182.

King, M., Marston, L., McManus, S., Brugha, T., Meltzer, H., & Bebbington, P. (2013). Religion, spirituality and mental health: results from a national study of English households. *The British Journal of Psychiatry, 202*(1), 68-73.

King, M., Weich, S., Nazroo, J., & Blizard, B. (2006). Religion, mental health and ethnicity. EMPIRIC – A national survey of England. *Journal of Mental Health, 15*(2), 153-162.

Koenig, H. G. (2008). Concerns about Measuring "Spirituality" in Research. *The Journal of Nervous and Mental Disease, 196*(5), 349-355.

Leon. D.A. & G. Walt (eds.) (2001). *Poverty, inequality, and health: an international perspective.* New York, NY: Oxford University Press.

Lenoir, F. (2003). *Les métamorphoses de Dieu. La nouvelle spiritualité occidentale*. Paris, France : Éditions Plon.

Levin, J.S. (2001). Preface in : Koenig, H. G., McCullough, M. E., & D. B, Larson. *Handbook of Religion and Health.* New York: Oxford University Press.

Linehan, M., (1993), *Cognitive-behavioral Treatment for Treating Borderline Personality Disorders*, Guilford Press, New York.

Miyazaki, Y. (2006). *Science of Natural Therapy.* Chiba: Chiba University.

Monteiro, L., & Musten, F. (2013). Mindfulness Starts Here: An eight week Guide to Skillful Living. Victoria: Friesan Press.

O'Mathúna, D. P. (2001). Spirituality and Alternative Medicine in the New Millennium. The Center of Bioethics & Human dignity. Trinity International University. https://cbhd.org.

Pargament, K. (2013). *APA Handbook of Psychology, Religion and Spiritualiy, vol. 2, An Applied Psychology of Religion and Spirituality.* Washington, DC, American Psychological Association.

Philibert, P. (1998). Changements de signification de la santé et des soins de santé, *Concilium, 278.* 13-20.

Public Health Agency of Canada (2013). *Cancer incidence, mortality and survival trends in Canada, 1970-2007.* http://www.phac-aspc.gc.ca /publicat/cdic-mcbc/33-2/ar-03-eng.php

Ray, P. H., S. R. Anderson (2000). *The Cultural Creatives: How 50 Million People Are Changing the World* (illustrated ed.). New York: Harmony Books.

Ricard, M. (2008). *L'art de la méditation*. Paris: Nil.

Rolheiser, R. (1999). *The Holy Longing: Guidelines for a Christian Spirituality*, New York: Doubleday.

Rosch, E. (2007). More Than Mindfulness: When You Have a Tiger by the Tail, Let It Eat You, *Psychological Inquiry: An International Journal for the Advancement of Psychological Theory*, 18 (4), 258-264.

Roszak, T. (1992). *The Voice of the Earth*. New York: Simon & Schuster.

Roszak, T, Gomes, & M.E., Kanner, A.D. (1995). *Ecopsychology: Restoring the Earth, Healing the Mind*. San Francisco: Sierra Club Books.

Sackett, C. (2010). Ecotherapy:A Counter to Society's Unhealthy Trend? *Journal of Creativity in Mental Health,* 5,131-141

Sabini, M (Editor) (2002). *The Earth has a Soul: C.G. JUNG on Nature, Technology & Modern Life*. Berkeley: North Atlantic Books.

Salmon, P., Sephton, S. & Weissbecker, I. et al. (2004). Mindfulness meditation in clinical practice. *Cognitive Behavioral Practice. 11*(4), 434-446.

Saunders, C. M. (1981). The Philosophy of Terminal Care, In. C.M. Saunders, *The management of Terminal Disease, (pp. 193-202)*. London, E. Arnold.

Saucier, G., & Skrzypińska, K. (2006). Spiritual But Not Religious? Evidence for Two Independent Dispositions. *Journal of Personality, 74*(5), 1257-1292.

Schaap-Jonker, H., Eurelings-Bontekoe, H. M., Zock, H. & E. Jonker (2008). Development and validation of the Dutch *Questionnaire God Image*: Effects of mental health and religious culture. *Mental Health, Religion & Culture, 11* (5), 501-515.

Segal, Z.V., Williams, J.M.G., & Teasdale, J.D. (2002). *Mindfulness-based Cognitive Therapy for Depression: A New Approach to Preventing Relapses*, Guilford Press, New York.

Segal, Z.V., Williams, J.M.G., & Teasdale, J.D. (2006). *La thérapie basée sur la pleine conscience pour la dépression : Une nouvelle approche pour prévenir la rechute. Bruxelles, Éditions de Boeck.*

Selhub, E.M., & Logan, A.C. (2012). *Your Brain on Nature: The Science of Nature's Influence on Your Health, Happiness, and Vitality*. Mississauga: Wiley.

Simard, N. (2006). Spiritualité et Santé. Reflets : revue d'intervention sociale et communautaire, Volume 12, numéro 1, 2006, p. 107-126.

Shapiro, S.L., & Carlson, L.E. (2009). *The art and science of mindfulness: Integrating mindfulness into psychology and the helping professions*. Washington, APA.

Sperry, L. & E. P. Shafranske (2005). *Spiritually Oriented Psychotherapy*. Washington, DC : American Psychological Association.

Stark, R. (2005). *What Americans Really Believe*, Baylor University Press.

Stein, J.E. (2013). Nature and Soul; Reflections from an Ecopsychology Perspective. *The Journal of Holistic Psychology,* 2, 283-293.

Sundaram, L. (2014). Let's take it Outside: Nature as a dynamic Partner in the Therapeutic Relationship. *Counselling and Spirituality*, 33(1), 51-69.

Taylor, C. (2007). *A Secular Age*, Harvard University Press.

Tolle, E. (2000). *Le pouvoir du moment présent*. Éditions Ariane.

Toneatto, T. & Nguyen, L. (2007). Does mindfullness meditation improve anxiety and mood symptoms? A review of the controlled research. *La revue canadienne de psychiatrie, 52*(4), 260-266.

Torpy, J. M. (2007). Poverty and Health. *JAMA*. 298(16):1968.

Vonarx, N. (2014). Sens et thérapies au pluriel: quand les personnes atteintes du cancer se font thérapeutes. *Les Cahiers francophones de soins palliatifs, 10* (1), 17-24.

Wilson, E.O. (1984). *Biophilia: The human bond with other species.* Cambridge, MA: Harvard University Press.

Zinnbauer, B. J. (2013). Models of healthy and unhealthy religion and spirituality. In K. Pargament (Editor-in-Chief). *APA Handbook of Psychology, Religion and Spiritualiy, vol. 2, An Applied Psychology of Religion and Spirituality. (pp. 71-89).* Washington, DC, American Psychological Association.

In: Spirituality
Editor: Edith C. Roberts

ISBN: 978-1-63482-370-8

Chapter 12

THE SPIRITUAL DIMENSION OF ANOREXIA NERVOSA: CLINICAL AND THERAPEUTIC IMPLICATIONS

Rosa Behar and Marcelo Arancibia
Department of Psychiatry, Universidad de Valparaíso, Chile

ABSTRACT

Background: Spirituality and asceticism are relevant characteristics of patients suffering from anorexia nervosa.

Objective: To describe the evidence on spirituality and asceticism in anorexia nervosa related to clinical features and therapeutic approaches.

Method: Medline/Pubmed, Scielo databases and specialized textbooks were used to look for evidence on asceticism and spirituality in anorexia nervosa and its clinical and therapeutic implications.

Results: From a historical perspective, spirituality and ascetic behaviours showed by medieval saints, and those observed in modern anorectics, share common features; however, the former wanted to reach sainthood and the latest seek thinness so valuable in Western sociocultural context. Contemporary Protestantism and anorexia nervosa display distinctive characteristics of protestant ethics, mainly self-discipline, self-control, self-sacrifice, rationality, efficiency and goals achievement. Although asceticism in these patients has been significantly correlated to worse outcome, more treatment dropouts, perfectionism, immaturity and purging, it is also associated to creative and adjustment skills and its connection to spiritual and religious proneness might improve the outcome of psychopathological and/or behavioural symptoms in anorexia nervosa.

Conclusions: The timeless occurrence within the historical Western framework of the anorectic syndrome pathogenic essence suggests that factors like age, personality and/or psychosocial environment pathoplastically model it. Spirituality would stimulate the motivation, contention and increase therapeutic adherence in patients suffering from anorexia nervosa. It should be considered as a helpful and eventually routine therapeutic tool in the treatment of anorectic patients.

PRELIMINARY CONSIDERATIONS

Fasting has been a core expression of the asceticism practiced by some rigorous adherents of a faith. The religious connotations of asceticism have remained relatively unexplored in terms of the understanding and they might contribute on the pathogenesis or psychodynamics of eating disorders, particularly the anorectic syndrome (Rampling, 1985). In her classical description of anorectic psychodynamics, Bruch (1974) illustrates how voluntary abstinence from food is a prescribed ritual in many religious traditions as an effort to liberate oneself from selfish, materialistic concerns, and to purify body and soul.

Mogul (1980) wrote: “What distinguishes adaptative asceticism from pathological states is not so much its extent, or even the subjective experience of gratification from it, but the degree to which the asceticism becomes an end in itself”, and adds that food refusal has been used as a means to different aims in diverse historical periods (moral purity, fame, attention, thinness), but always it also becomes an end in itself, and the consequent starvation is both deliberate and nonvolitional. Reber (1985) defines asceticism as: “A way of living based upon voluntary abstention from sensual, physical pleasures and emphasising simplicity and self-discipline. The ascetic usually professes to be focussing on a higher moral/religious value system”.

There are several definitions for the notions of *religion* and *spirituality*; nevertheless,the scientific and theological researches are divided on how they typify them (Larson, Swyers & McCullough, 1997). According to Huguelet & Koenig (2009), the word *religion* points to specific behavioral, social, doctrinal, and denominational characteristics, it involves belief in a supernatural power or transcendent being, truth or ultimate reality, and the expression of such a belief in behaviour and rituals. Moreover, ritualistic religious fasting is time-limited and tends to focus on avoiding specific foods completely or not eating during specific time intervals and thereby does not typically result in emaciation. It lacks the persistent and pervasive nature of food refusal that characterizes the form of fasting observed in medieval religious ascetics or modern-day anorectics. In addition, weight loss generated from other physical and psychological conditions is often distressing to the affected individual, even Rieger, Touyz, Swain & Beumont (2001) also report that there are other contemporary cases in which ego-syntonic and deliberate emaciation would not represent an eating disorder or any other form of psychopathology, but it may be used as an effective means of protest (i.e., hunger strike).

On the other hand, *spirituality* is linked to vital questions about life’s meaning as it relates to the transcendent, which may or may not emerge from formal religious traditions. Hence, spirituality’s meaning is more subjective, broad and difuse, less measurable; but from a clinical perspective, it helps to establish a dialogue with patients who may or may not consider themselves religious (Huguelet & Koenig, 2009).

Spiritual and religious issues are sometimes neglected or misrepresented in the field of psychiatry (Huguelet & Koenig, 2009) and the general attitude toward religion belief, practice and experience has been ambivalent by mental health professionals, although it offers a different way of viewing psychiatric illnesses; what is more, evidence also exists showing that religion may help patients with psychiatric conditions. Whereas further research on this debate is deeply needed, growing support demonstrates that religion/spirituality is an important issue for patients with psychiatric conditions and may be beneficial or damaging to their illness. According to Mardsen, Karagianni & Morgan (2007), generally, awareness of patients' spirituality is just a component of holistic care, but links between religious asceticism and eating disorders imply that interactions between faith and illness can be everlasting and indissoluble.

THE CONCEPT OF ASCETICISM

Asceticism and Spirituality

Most religions embrace special ascetic cults or ideals. Asceticism (from the Greek *askesis,* exercise) involves spiritual exercises (self-denial, renunciation of immediate or sensual gratifications) in the pursuit of virtue and the achievement of perfection (Fassino, Pierò, Gramaglia, AbbateDaga, Gandione, Rovera, et al., 2006). Its origins antedate and extend beyond the confines of Judeo-Christian tradition, although it is within the context of the Catholic faith that ascetic practices have influenced the moral values of Western civilisation, through their demonstration in the lives of the saints and other venerated persons (Rampling, 1985). Huline-Dickens (2000) highlights the relationship between self-indulgence and virtue, stating that as greed had caused sin, abstinence from food can thus be seen as both penitential and the means to redeem the sinner. Greed, in the form of gluttony, is one of the seven capital vices or sins in Catholic theology.

Psychopathological Dimensions

The preeminence of morality and spirituality is maintained by subordinating the body in all the appetences. Starvation (by abstinence) not only subdues libidinous desires, but induces a state of psychological alertness said to be favorable to mystical experience, as an advance towards its perfection (Rampling, 1985).

Apart from perfectionism, Menninger (1938) identified four dimensions of asceticism: Aggression, a desire to be punished, an erotic motivation, and a self-destructive impulse. Therefore, anger seems to play a relevant and often underestimated role in ascetic behaviours. In fact, extreme asceticism (*epaskesis*) has been considered as a culmination of rage, inhibited in its outward expressions and turned toward oneself. Furthermore, Fassino et al. (2006) believe that asceticism has often been referred to as a deviant behaviour motivated by subconscious guilt or masochism. As said by Fenichel (1945), in the pursuit of asceticism, masochistic satisfaction can be procured from renunciation and self-mortification, and has described how mortifying the flesh can be a distorted expression of blocked sexuality, and repressed drives may increase inner destructiveness or be acted out in self-destructive ways.

Other authors have highlighted the similarities among the saints' asceticism and some psychological traits of anorectics (currently diagnosed according to DSM-5), particularly self-discipline, self-denial, rituals, social protest, frustration of physical needs, closeness to death, control over instincts, and aspiration to immortality (Lacey, 1982). Huline-Dickens (2000) has identified that ascetic saints and anorectics are connected conceptually in the process of idealization and are comparable in their pursuit of perfection through the above mentioned methods; but, from a teleological viewpoint, the saints attained perfection to be akin to the God of Christianity; while anorectics seem to reach perfection to model themselves in the shape of an internal ideal God.

As has been held by Klein (1940), idealisation is related with the splitting of the object into good and bad and is a mechanism of defence against anxiety, a salient process in the developing anorectic. Idealisation as a psychological mechanism may be associated with the development of anorexia nervosa, and in society it is a necessary process for the existence of religious ideals.

However, from a clinical perspective, fasting in anorexia nervosa, is commonly based on a disorder of body image, or at least on placing excessive importance on body shape and weight for self-esteem (American Psychiatric Association, 2000), and seems to represent the common final pathway for an intrapsychical, family, and social disorder (Gabbard, 2000).

Medlicott (1969) describes how under the stimulus of the ascetic ideal, the fullness of life is denied, the flesh becomes corrupt, and the world is seen as negative and evil, promoting a state of regression. He exposes two major consequences of the ascetic condition of mind: interference with ego functioning, and, distortions of drive. Regression would be the primary response of the ascetic ego to the detachment from the material world, with the renunciation of sensual satisfaction and genital sexuality. Regression undermines relationships with the real world and generates a retreat from reason, splitting and paranoid projection. Ultimately, reality testing is abandoned, ego boundaries fade and concepts of identity are lost.According to Medlicott, a withdrawal into asceticism reactivates primitive levels of functioning, which may lead to aggressiveness, sado-masochistic fantasies, omnipotence and omniscience.

Asceticism and Anorexia Nervosa

Crisp (1980) has recognized that asceticism may be an important attribute in anorexia nervosa, but the relationship between religion and anorexia has remained as an obscure research topic.

In line with Huline-Dickens (2000), this is not to say that empirical evidence is likely to show that religious themes are prominent in all individual cases of anorexia nervosa. Neither can be expected to find an ascetic lifestyle in all anorectic patients. As well as religious influences are important, socio-cultural and psychological are factors to consider in this disorder, and there are many psychopathological features common to both the anorectic and the religious ascetic. Notions of sacrifice, suffering, ritual, idealism and heroic feats, guilt, introspection, inhibitions, vigilance and relentless discipline and perfectionism, are all found in the Judeo-Christian religious tradition, which is a system of idealisation, and also in anorectics.

Furthermore, anorexia nervosa is described by anorectics themselves through testimonies as a form of *askesis*, a discipline of the body for the sake of a higher purpose (Behar, 2012). Along with Corrington (1986), like asceticism, anorexia nervosa is a form of control, it enables women to resist the prevailing values of societies which they do not control, while at the same time making them acceptable to those societies.

Consistent with Rampling's reflections, possibly the special relevance of the Christian ascetic tradition for the modern problem of anorexia nervosa lies in the allegorisation of feeding. The sacrificial rejection of food is steady and ego-syntonic with those acceptable personality traits centred in an altruistic and reverential ideology. But, this author thinks that the asceticism of anorexia nervosa may appear perverse rather than good, dishonored rather than noble, foolish rather than heroic, but even in its most misguided forms it may contain within itself a permanent mystical element (Rampling, 1985). Despite these considerations,

Riegeret al.(2001) emphazises the fact that there are other contemporary cases in which ego-syntonic emaciation would not represent an eating disorder or any other form of psychopathology. For instance, deliberate self-starvation may be used as an effective means of protest, like anorectic patients and (Brumberg, 1989), this can be differentiated from nonpathological forms of intentional self-malnourishment. Individuals who engage in these kind of behaviours do so as a means to an end and when it is reached, the self-imposed starvation ceases.

From a feminist view, food and sex, are considered as symbols of male power and rejected, in favor of a higher or inner form of "nourishment". The association of fasting with asexuality, and the bodily image of the anorectic, pale skeletal, nearly "bodiless", are reminders of those earlier female ascetics for whom severe fasting and other austerities were a means of erasing their female, bodily nature and a way of achieving an asexual spiritual union with God (or Christ), the only form of dominance they would accept. Striving towards the ascetic image is a source of satisfaction and liberation from imprisonment of the body and its subjugation to an unacceptable world, in a society in which women are subordinate. In both cases, *askesis* is not experienced as self-destructive, but as self-liberating. Hence, since food is seen by others as a source of power and strength, refusal of food is perceived by anorectics and ascetics both as a rejection of dominance by others and, paradoxically, as a source of power for themselves, a triumph of the will over bodily limitations, and the forging of a new identity. Consequently, the path of the modern anorectic may be even harder than that of her earlier counterpart, in that her society regards her behaviour as aberrant(Corrington, 1986).

Asceticism Assessment

The importance of ascetic tendencies in anorexia nervosa is confirmed by the fact that one of the most widely used questionnaires for the study of eating disorders – the Eating Disorders Inventory-2 (EDI-2) (Garner, 1984) – includes a specific subscale for the assessment of asceticism that measures the tendency to pursue spiritual ideals such as self-discipline, self-denial, self-limitations, hypercontrol over body needs, and self-sacrifice to increase one's worth. From a conceptual side, asceticism is strongly correlated to perfectionism and to drive for thinness EDI subscales. In a study, asceticism, as assessed with the EDI-2, was correlated with the outcome in anorexia nervosa: patients with higher degrees of asceticism were more likely to belong to the not improved group of patients after six months of multimodal treatment (Fassino, AbbateDaga, Amianto, Leombruni, Garzaro, &Rovera, 2001).

Psychopathological and Behavioural Variables

Despite several investigations on this issue (Banks, 1992; Banks 1997), it is still not clear which personality and psychological features underlie asceticism in anorexia nervosa, as it is expressed in current Western culture. Specifically, it is not well-defined what kind of relationship exists between asceticism and perfectionism, whether asceticism depends on less specific disorders in personality development, on psychosomatic alterations due to low body weight and illness duration, or on the individual's cultural background (Behar, Gramegna & Arancibia, 2014). Multiple linear regression models have showed that asceticism is related to angry temperament, high control over anger, perfectionism, maturity fears, and number of vomiting episodes per week. These results suggest that self-discipline and hypercontrol of anorectic patients are related to a temperament proness to angry feelings in subjects with a fear of becoming adult and with a trait of pathologic perfectionism (Fassino et al., 2006).

The relationship between symptoms like perfectionism, anger, and maturity fears, on the one hand, and asceticism, on the other, have been explained as follows by Fallon&Howath (1993): asceticism has been considered positively for its creative and adaptative implications and as a means to achieve personality growth and perfection. But when the subject shows high perfectionism and maturity fears, there may be difficulty accepting and integrating some impulses. Fasting and self-control exercises may then be turned against oneself aggressively with the aim to disintegrate lower personality structures and inhibit lower-level impulses (Dabrowski, 1967).

Perfectionism

Because of its association with ritualism, self-discipline, and absolute self-control, asceticism could be considered a reflection of the perfectionism characteristic of Western cultures which have experienced an apparent increase in the prevalence of anorexia nervosa in the past last decades (Fairburn & Harrison, 2003; Gordon, 1991).

Maturity Fears

Maturity and adulthood imply that the subject has to face new social roles (including the sexual one), strong impulses, and instincts. These last need to be managed, and asceticism may be used for the attainment of self-control and for the inhibition of lower-level impulses (Dabrowski, 1967). Moreover, in a sample of nonresponder anorectic patients after six months of multimodal treatment, a strong correlation emerged between asceticism and maturity fears, the last being a typical psychological trait of eating disorders, which is also related to outcome in anorexia nervosa (Fassino et al., 2001; Behar &Arancibia, 2013).

Anger

Anger also seems to strengthen ascetic behaviours. An angry temperament and excessive control over anger characterize those anorectic patients displaying high levels on asceticism. From this standpoint it can be understood why the fasting of anorectic patients resembles that of many medieval saints; in both cases fasting represents an angry protest against expectations, pressures, and the social role imposed on women (Katzman& Lee, 1997),where both, religious asceticism and illness seem to allow a socially and culturally acceptable way to complaint (Morgan, Marsden &Lacey, 2000).

Bulimic Behaviours

In a sample of bulimic patients, more severe vomiting was associated with higher degrees of asceticism (AbbateDaga, Pieró, Gramaglia, &Fassino, 2005). This result may seem contradictory, because asceticism is a struggle for control and vomiting is instead an impulsive behaviour. However, vomiting usually follows binges (objective or subjective ones) and should be considered a means to compensate for the release of lower impulses seen in the binge, as well as physical exercise and dieting. In religious language, vomiting becomes a type of expiation.

ASCETICISM WITHIN THE WESTERN HISTORY

Historical Cases of Anorexia Nervosa

Cases of deliberate yet nonvolitional self-starvation, sometimes resulting in recovery, at times resulting in death, and primarily affecting young adolescent girls, exist in numerous historical periods (Russell, 1997). Specific cases of anorexia nervosa that cannot be attributed to the influence of Western ideals have been reported in the Middle East, the Indian subcontinent, and East Asia, where a plurality of motivations for food refusal has been described both across and within sociohistorical contexts (Littlewood, 1995; Russell, 1997).

The historians Bell (1985) and Bynum (1987) have both argued that religion informed the food refusal of women in history: Bell sought to find evidence in his extensive study of the writings of medieval women which suggested that "holy anorexia" was a rebellion against patriarchy; Bynum described how women rejected both body and family through food practices as a means to control both themselves and their circumstances.

Prior to the formal recognition of anorexia nervosa as a distinct syndrome, several reports in the medical literature suggest its existence (Keel &Klump, 2003) since XVI to XIX centuries.

The Renaissance

For possible cases of anorexia nervosa in the sixteenth century, McSherry (1985) suggested that Mary, Queen of Scots (1542–1587), suffered from this eating disorder. However, too little information is included in the short report to examine the supposition and cases of self-starvation were recorded by hagiographers from the eighteenth century back to the twelfth century.

Enlightenment

Throughout the seventeenth and eighteenth centuries, "miraculous maids" were girls between the ages of 14 and 20 who engaged in self-starvation, modeling themselves explicitly after ascetic medieval saints (Bemporad, 1996).

Victorian Era

In 1860, Chipley (1860) described cases of extreme emaciation among females who actively refused to eat (*sitomania*) despite spasms of hunger and attributed the deliberate self-starvation to a desire for attention and notoriety and concluded that motivations behind *sitomania* overlaps with those attributed to so-called fasting girls of the eighteenth and nineteenth centuries. All over this period, cases of fasting girls gained great attention in the popular media throughout America and Europe (Brumberg, 1989; Vandereycken & Van Deth, 1994; Bemporad, 1996). Typically, these cases involved adolescent girls who abruptly refused to eat and generated a mixture of medical concern and religious admiration. According to Brumberg (1989) Anglo American girls during the Victorian era were well-acquainted with the religious fasting of medieval saints, and St. Catherine of Siena's biography was included in inspirational books for girls. Meanwhile, psychiatrists ratified the continuity between the extreme fasts leading to death among adolescent girls in the United States, England, France, and Germany and the recently identified syndrome of anorexia nervosa (Keel &Klump, 2003).

Contemporary Period

The presence of religious motivation does not exclude the presence of weight concerns as evidenced by modern cases of "spiritual starvation" (Bynum, 1988; Banks, 1992; Banks, 1997; Katzman & Lee, 1997; Morgan et al., 2000). Some cases (Banks, 1992; Banks, 1997) involve women who fasted to engender spiritual purity and thus display a striking resemblance to historical cases of fasting performed by medieval religious ascetics.

It is not necessary to revisit the fourteenth century to collect evidence for a spiritual dimension in anorexia nervosa. Simone Weil, acknowledged by some authors as the greatest mystic, philosopher and writer of the twentieth century, died at the age of 34 of anorexia nervosa (Weil, 1951). She also saw eating as a form of sexual dominance and the acceptance of power. The refusal to eat as a deliberate rejection of power so that one may be totally consumed (eaten) by God (Corrington, 1986).

Rampling (1985) has assumed that it is within the context of Catholic faith that ascetic practices have influenced the moral values of the West, and yet the Protestant puritan tradition could also be seen to be influential. Weber (1930) lays emphasis on what he saw as the peculiar spirit of economic enterprise among early Protestants, a spirit characterized as disciplined, rational and highly ascetic, and demonstrated that religious ethics were part of a complex of forces that inluenced economic action. Similarities are therefore evident between puritan character and the anorectic: both exercise constant vigilance and self-control with prohibitions on sensuality and spontaneity, both experience a burden of guilt and are driven to effciency and achievement (Huline-Dickens, 2000). Vandereycken & van Deth (1996) also describe how legislation and Protestant and Catholic doctrines reinforced the Victorian traditions of patriarchy and sexual repression to produce a bourgeois family characterized by intense emotional involvement and religiously inspired care for the moral well-being of its members. The sacred ritual of the family meal, these authors argue, became a metaphor for this peculiar mixture of intimacy and hierarchy.

Other authors have called attention on the medicalization of fasting practices and thus the historical configuration of anorexia nervosa (Tait, 1993).

Medieval Ascetic Women

In *Holy anorexia*, Rudolph Bell (1985) argued that a historically significant group of thirteenth century female Italian saints exhibited an anorectic behaviour in response to the patriarchal social structures in which they were submitted. He describes how, by the suppression of physical urges and basic feelings such as fatigue, sexual drive, hunger and pain, they appeared to liberate the body and achieve daring aspirations.

"Holy Anorexia" and "Anorexia Nervosa": Bell (1985) distinguishes between "holy" and "nervous" anorexia, depending on the culture in which the young woman is striving to gain control over her life. In twentieth century Western Europe, highly valued societal goals are bodily health, thinness and self-control; in medieval Christendom these were spiritual health, fasting and other forms of self-denial. Nevertheless, Bynum (1987) argued for a plurality of meaning for self-starvation among the fasting saints throughout this period such that extreme asceticism was alternately viewed as a mark of God's grace, demonic possession, fraud, and illness within the lifetimes of all fasting saints; for instance, St. Clare of Assisi (death 1253) and St. Catherine of Siena (death 1380) were revered for their self-starvation whereas Sister Domenica (death 1553) and Catherine Vannini (death 1606) were viewed with significantly greater suspicion. Thus, self-starvation in pursuit of a religious ideal was not unambiguously approved in medieval times any more than self-starvation in pursuit of a thin ideal is sanctioned in modern times (Keel &Klump, 2003).

As has been seen, several authors such as Bell (1985), Rampling (1985) and Bruch (1974) have suggested parallels between the anorectic and the ascetic attitudes. There are certainly many features common to both contemporary anorexiaand the religious ascetic and they highlight the pursuit of an impossible or unrealizable ideal, passivity and sacrifice for others, and heroic behaviours such as relentless self-discipline and self-denial.

Historical and Socio-cultural Context: Corrington(1986) calls attention to the historical socio-cultural contexts in the emergence of both types of anorexia nervosa. The author describes that in the patristic and medieval periods, women adopted a rigorous self-denial originally promoted by and for men, to become a new ascetic ideal. Similarly, modern anorectics, faced with a cultural mandate to deny the traditional roles and even body shapes of women in order to focus upon male competitiveness and power, resist what they see as attempts to impose authority on them from the outside. Hence, eating and non eating become symbols of power and control: refusal to eat is a repudation to any authority over the body other than one's own. Additionally, fasting also provided women with a means of transcendence. The practice of starvation for sainthood is also accompanied by desire for union with God (or Christ) as an escape from the unacceptable desires of the flesh (Corrington, 1986). Whether motivated by hatred of the body or performed in order to suffer on account of sins perpetrated, ascetics in the early Christian world believed that the prelapsarian state of Adam and Eve had been corrupted in such a way that the twisted will of men had crammed the body with unnecessary food which generated excessive energy manifest as appetite, anger and lust for the flesh (Brown, 1988). Feelings of guilt have, as their origin, the concept of transgression and can thus be seen to represent self-administered punishment.

Sainthood and Gender Differences: Weinstein & Bell (1980) identify why did the sexes not share these ideal values. Bell thinks that this is due to differing perceptions of the locus of sin, and Weinstein describes how, for male saints, the occasion of sin most often was a response to an external stimulus, but that for females, sin seemed to arise from the depths of woman herself. For a woman, who had few options, choosing the monastic profession may have been a rebellion against social conditions. For a man, there were many other ways of achieving autonomy in a culture that approved of male self-determination and it is unclear whether the current criteria for anorexia nervosa can be appropriately applied. Nonetheless, parallels are evident; both “holy anorectics” and “nervous anorectics” dislike the consequences of eating; both represent ideal states of being (holiness in medieval Italy, thinness in contemporary Europe) and avoidance of sex and selfishness as well as food. In both types are described excessive activity, perfectionistic tendencies and constant vigilance; a disinterest in ordinary human relationships, a self-suficiency, and a preference for caring for others rather than receiving care for themselves. They are never satisfied with their efforts to pursue their ideal, whether to be holy or thin (Davis, 1985).

A Psychosocial Approach

Anorectic patients may use cultural symbols to give meaning to their personal concerns with growth, separation, and sexuality and to communicate their suffering in a socially acceptable and understandable way.

Culture and Symbolization

Clinicians working with contemporary women with anorexia nervosa have commented on the ascetic component in the disorder, meaning their self-denial, heightened morality, opposition between body and spirit, asexuality, and denial of bodily death (Mogul, 1980; Palazzoli, 1978; Rampling, 1985; Sabom, 1985; Turner, 1984). Banks (1997), from the psychological anthropology, points out that while these clinicians have commented on the asceticism in contemporary anorexia nervosa, they have little to say about the role of culture in subjective experiences of this asceticism which challenge a strict and opposing dichotomy between the conscious and unconscious, between culture (seen as "public") and the individual mind (seen as "private" and idiosyncratic). Obeyesekere's idea of "the work of culture”, (Obeyesekere, 1990) highlights that symbolic regressive forms existing at the cultural level are created and recreated through the unconscious thoughts of individuals, transforming the archaic motivations of early experience and foresighting to their realization in experience of the sacred, and Stephen & Suryani's (2000) concept of the "autonomous imagination" suggests that the dramatic nature of the initiatory sufferings in shamanism could combined to give a misleading prominence to the role of an initiatory madness. Both postulates are especially useful in understanding how contemporary anorectics use in imaginative ways cultural symbols, such as notions of asceticism about food and the body that are a part of religion, to give meaning to their personal concerns with growth, separation, and sexuality, transforming cultural symbols and language to express their starvation and deep anxieties. These cases allow support to views that culture and religion, as symbolic systems, have reinforcements in deep motivation (Obeyesekere, 1981, 1990; Spiro, 1965, 1987).

In addition, Garrett (1996) explains that Durkheim's explanation of asceticism offers a brand new interpretative support in which anorexia nervosa and its recovery are understood as the negative and positive phases respectively of a ritual of self-transformation. Participants in this study referred to anorexia nervosa as a spiritual quest and for them recovery involved a re-discovery (or creation) of a threefold connection: inner, with others and with "nature". These links are, for them, the defining features of spirituality. The negative phase of the ritualistic quest (anorexia nervosa) involves a confrontation with the inevitability of death as a condition of the positive phase (recovery) in which people actively choose life. This theoretical approach provides a non-medicalized understanding of the condition and simultaneously enables a re-interpretation of the fasting of medieval women saints.

Spiritual and Religious Attitudes

Although Warren, Jackson, Thornton, Russell, Touys &Beumont (1994), found that religiosity did not appear to be important in their sample of anorectic and bulimic patients when compared with control groups; in contrast, Wilbur & Colligan (1981), observed that their anorectic patients had higher scores on religious fundamentalism than control groups when measured using the Minnesota Multiphasic Personality Inventory (MMPI). On the other hand, Joughin, Crisp, Halek & Humphrey (1992) administering a Religious Beliefs Questionnaire to anorectics noted that the degree of weight loss was associated with the level of importance of religion as assessed by the questionnaire. This effect was particularly pronounced for Anglicans, in whom, they concluded, asceticism was more prevalent, and the authors speculated that asceticism is used by individuals to justify weight loss, but their findings did not support the suggestion that religious upbringing predisposes to the development of anorexia nervosa. Further, Jacobs-Pilipski,Winzelberg, Wilfley, Bryson & Taylor (2005) verified that women with strong spiritual/religious beliefs and practices cope with body dissatisfaction differently than women without them. Participants with strong spiritual/religious beliefs were significantly more likely to pray, meditate, or read religious/spiritual texts to cope with body image distress. Participants without strong beliefs and practices were more likely to cope utilizing distraction.

Religious Background

Jacoby (1993) detected a higher incidence of anorectic abstainers who were Protestant and a higher incidence of bulimics who vomited among Roman Catholics. He hypothesized that these findings were linked to the more internalized drive control in Protestants and that this was associated with the Protestant ethic described by Weber (1930); while Sykes, Leuser, Melia & Gross (1988) noticed that there was a higher prevalence of both bulimia and anorexia nervosa in patients of Jewish and Catholic backgrounds than in the general population, and a lower prevalence in Protestants.

Family Dynamics

Whilst empirical evidence for religious themes in anorexia nervosa is not strong, in the family therapy literature there are signals of ethical codes of sacrifice, loyalty and sexual denial in the families of anorectics (Huline-Dickens, 2000). White (1983), for example, stresses the strong demand for loyalty within families and considers that women in such families are expected to be sensitive, devoted and self-sacrifycing. Several authors have remarked that families appear to need their anorectic child for purpose and stability.

Becker, Körner & Stöffler (1981), stand out that “the family atmosphere is described by the patients as largely performance-orientated and sexually repressive to a frequently anachronistic degree (…)The family is quite obviously dominated by one of the parents, who also dictates the usually ascetic family ideal…". The patients themselves conform to the family ideal of hard work and performance orientation to an unusually high degree, striving to better themselves socially and, at the beginning of their illness, usually keeping to the ideal of sexual abstinence. Minuchin, Rasman & Baker (1978) have written of the rigidity and over-protectiveness of families of anorectics, and the "usually strong religious or ethical code...used as a rationale for avoiding conflict".

Sykeset al. (1988) believed that the higher prevalence of eating disorders in Jewish and Catholic patients might be related to the importance of food in some way in these religious groups and hypothesized that the family dynamics of eating-disordered patients resembled those in families which had "survival guilt" (i.e. a general inability to enjoy life), self-punitive behaviours, unresolved losses, and a wish to be taken care of. They considered that centuries of being an ostracized minority led to isolation and an emphasis on ritual, with corresponding denial and avoidance of feelings, similar to the underlying dynamics of families with a member with an eating disorder. Nonetheless, it is dificult to see how this hypothesis could apply equally to Jews and Catholics.

Within the context of family dynamics,Mogul (1980), in viewing anorexia nervosa in the light of adolescent issues, especially the development of self-discipline, he argues that asceticism has an important role in establishing a sense of strength and freedom from dependence on the parents, and therefore can be seen to have an adaptive function.

Femenine Sexual Role and Religious Experience

Bridges & Spilka (1992) describe how the Judeo-Christian heritage is operative implicitly in the lives of those in the West, and how religious symbols and images shape individual's gender role concepts and reinforce traditional sex roles. Religious commitment is associated with acceptance of conventional female roles, and socialization of women in this culture has traditionally inculcated high levels of powerlessness and guilt. Negative views of the self are inevitable when women are considered to be the cause of sin and evil, and Tiller et al.(1995) mention Bridges and Spilka's hypothesis that supports this argument by citing a number of studies demonstrating that self-destructive passivity, intropunitiveness, frustration and anger can be associated with such religious values, and possibly as a consequence, depression, agoraphobia and eating disorders are observed to be more common in women. In fact, it has been shown that patients with anorexia nervosa are more likely to direct hostility inwardly and that intropunitiveness is associated with depression.

THERAPEUTIC IMPLICATIONS

Research on psychological processes involving religion is neutral with respect to the existence or nonexistence of God or any other supernatural being. In the context of care, clinicians facing a patient addressing a religious topic, should consider it in terms of meaning, coping its relationship to current therapeutic goals and recognize that religion includes multiple dimensions, i.e., beliefs, experience, afiliation, commitment, organized religious activity, private religiosity, and coping behaviors or cognitions designed to help people adapt to difficult life situations (Koenig, McCullough & Larson, 2001).

Multilevel Interdisciplinary Paradigm

Palouzian& Park (2005) define a multilevel interdisciplinary paradigm as a framework that allows an accurate description of religious phenomena by recognizing "the value of data at multiple levels of analysis while making non-reductive assumptions concerning the values of spiritual and religious phenomena". As an example of the usefulness of this paradigm, these authors describe the case of religious conversion, which can be examined both at a neuropsychological level and at a socialpsychological level.The multilevel interdisciplinary model can embrace subdisciplines of psychology, but also other domains such as evolutionary biology, neurosciences, anthropology, philosophy, other allied areas of science, and pastoral care.

Spirituality and Clinical Care

Spiritual interventions are rarely used in contemporary treatment programs and little empirical evidence is available concerning their effectiveness (Richards, Berrett, Hardman & Eggett, 2006).

Culliford (2002) has clearly argued that biopsychosocial care covers the "spiritual values and skill (…) recognized as necessary aspects of clinical care". In accordance with this statement, Morgan et al. (2000) suggest that motivational interviewing may be improved by consideration of patients' spiritual constructs of their illness, varying between respect for God given appetitive functions to extreme asceticism, and Lacey(1982) strengths that spiritual constructs may be underestimated where clinicians feel uncomfortable in a spiritual domain due to deficits in education, resources, and conflicting personal beliefs.

Marsden et al. (2007) maintain that once engaged in treatment, spirituality may enhance patients' motivation, provide containment and improve treatment adherence. For patients with strong religious faith, spiritual practice is helpful in recovery, and spiritual maturation goes together with positive psychological changes. Conversely, psychological maturation may challenge spiritual beliefs and either result in failure of treatment or loss of faith. Awareness of the spiritual dimensions of patients' beliefs was essential to avoid forcing patients into a choice between psychological therapies and religious faith. Spiritual practice appears to be helpful for some patients in recovery from eating disorders, and spiritual development is synchronous with positive psychological changes.

Religious and Spiritual Therapies

Several religious/spiritual therapies were found to be helpful for patiens, supporting the further use and research on these therapies (Hook, Worthington, Davis, Jennings, Gartner & Hook, 2010). Berrett, Hardman, O'Grady & Richards (2007) propose that both trauma and eating disorders can distance women from their own spirituality, which undermines a potentially important treatment resource, and offer suggestions based on their clinical experience for helping eating disorder patients who have suffered trauma to rediscover their faith and spirituality.

Richards et al. (2006), infered that patients in a spirituality group tended to score significantly lower on psychological disturbance and eating disorder symptoms at the conclusion of treatment compared to patients in cognitive and emotional support groups, and higher on spiritual well-being. On weekly outcome measures, participants in the spirituality group improved significantly more quickly during the first four weeks of treatment. This study provides preliminary evidence that attending to eating disorder patients' spiritual growth and well-being during inpatient treatment may help reduce depression and anxiety, relationship distress, social role conflict, and eating disorder symptoms.

Joughin et al. (1992), found that anorectics reporting a religious conversion experienced less severe weight loss than those who had not converted. They suggested that conversion provided a channel within which subjects initiated a supportive structure and set of moral guidelines, hence lessening the illness severity.

Theistic Approach

Richards, Smith, Berrett, O'Grady & Bartz (2009) mentioned a psychological treatment for women with eating disorders who have theistic spiritual beliefs and they illustrate how a theistic approach can complement traditional treatment.

On the other hand, Marsden et al.(2007) in studying associations between eating disorders and religious asceticism in adult Christian women receiving inpatient treatment for anorexia or bulimia nervosa, described five dominant categories emerged: locus of control, sacrifice, self-image, salvation, maturation. They also determined that appetitive control held moral connotations. Negative self-image was common, based more on sin than body-image. Medical treatment could be seen as salvation, with religious conversion manifesting a quest for healing, but treatment failure threatened faith. Beliefs matured during treatment, with prayer, providing a healing relationship. Religious beliefs impact on attitudes and motivation in eating disorders. Clinicians' sensitivity determines how beliefs influence clinical outcome. According to the authors, treatment modifies beliefs such that theological constructs of illness cannot be ignored.

Yoga

In the XXI century the mindfulness techniques of yoga have been adapted as an adjunct to the treatment of individuals with eating disorders (Douglass, 2011). Qualitative data have reported improvements in body satisfaction and disordered eating due in part to yoga and its associated spirituality (Dittmann&Freedman, 2009).

Adolescence

Manley & Leichner (2000), reported the profound anguish and despair frequently experienced by adolescents struggling with eating disorders. They proposed a practice perspective which emphasizes empathic listening, the development of a strong therapeutic alliance and also suggested cognitive therapy, topical developments in the areas of spirituality and motivational enhancement and involving the distressed adolescent's family as well.

For older children and adolescents, Huline-Dickens (2000) recommends that religious beliefs should be examined rationally.The themes of guilt, masochism and denial are evidently strong in the anorectic patient and commonly lead to treatment difficulties and it is often perceived clinically that the illness represents in some ways a solution to the problem of excessive guilt as it allows for gain through suffering and thus an placation of a masochistic drive.

Outcome

The narratives suggest that long-term recovery involves spiritual or political commitment and purposeful engagement with communities larger than the self (Matusek & Knudson, 2009). Recovery from anorexia nervosa, as a very complex process, goes well beyond conventional treatment; self-acceptance, determination, and spirituality are in the same way essencial elements (Espíndola & Blay, 2009). In other studies, asceticism has been found to correlate with outcome (Fassinoet al., 2001) and high levels of asceticism are associated with a greater likelihood of treatment drop out in anorexia nervosa, though stronger predictors are temperament and character dimensions, and management of angry feelings (Fassino, AbbateDaga, Pierò&Rovera, 2002).

Recommendations and Proposals

Religion, spirituality and globalization have a vital impact on wellness and quality of life for a growing number of people worldwide. The World Health Organization has rightly regarded religious, spiritual and personal beliefs as a component of quality of life. This growing awareness may enhance the study of religion and spirituality in psychiatric training, research and practice (Verhagen, 2010).

In accordance with Hook et al. (2010), there are limited evidence that religious/spiritual therapies have outperformed established secular therapies; hence, they recommend that the decision to use an religious/spiritual therapy may be an issue of client preference and therapist comfort. Even so, Jacobs-Pilipski et al. (2005), call attention to the fact that spiritual and religious beliefs and practices may be underutilized resources for coping with body image concerns.

Clinicians involved in psychiatry have many reasons for their reluctance to address spiritual/religious issues with patients. As affirmed by Neelman & King (1993), clinicians' own religious involvement (or lack of it) may infuence the value they place on religious/spiritual issues. They are generally less involved in religious activities than their patients and are less likely to be interested in discussing these issues; further, there is widespread lack of knowledge about how to address religion or spirituality in clinical practice, since there has been historical conflict between psychiatry and religion. At the same time, some clinicians may fear that addressing issues pertaining to religion may represent walking into unknown territories, thus risking harm to patients. Additionally, psychiatrists may feel uncomfortable being involved in a social/care network in which roles are not well defined between clinicians and clergy.

Clinicians need to be aware of the spiritual dimension of eating disorders in their patients and it should be part of routine biopsychosocial formulation, and repeated throughout treatment. This may present an obstacle to treatment, or may improve motivation and therapeutic adherence. Treatment of any disorder with biological, psychological, and social components may modify patients' religious beliefs. As the therapeutical management progresses, it is important to revisit these areas of concern to assess the continuing interplay between psychopathology and religious attitudes. This is particularly relevant in eating disorders, where schematic deficits in self-concept may overlap with religious constructs. Health care professionals need to be sensitive to the effect of changing beliefs, including spiritual crises, and not dismiss them as minor aspects to medical treatment (Mardsen et al., 2007).

Psychiatric care often involves a multidisciplinary/multilevel model of care: the comprehensive paradigm is the bio-psycho-social model which aims at addressing the whole person and underlines the need to consider disorders from a holistic perspective, thus avoiding a reductionistic view that considers only biological (i.e., pharmacological treatments) or psychological characteristics of the person. This model involves integrating religion/spirituality into the social perspective, approaching patients from a bio-psycho-social-religious/spiritual points of view. This is recommended because religion/spirituality affects social, psychological, and even biological aspects of human life, and all domains affect each other, including the spiritual (Engel, 1977).

REFERENCES

AbbateDaga, G., Pierò, A., Gramaglia, C. &Fassino, S. (2005). Factors related to severity of vomiting behaviors in bulimia nervosa. *Psychiatry Research, 134,* 75–84.

American Psychiatric Association. (2000). Working group on eating disorders: practice guideline for the treatment of patients with eating disorders.*American Journal of Psychiatry, 157,* 1–39.

Banks, C. (1992). "Culture" in culture-bound syndromes: the case of anorexia nervosa. *Social Science & Medicine, 34,* 867–884.

Banks, C. (1997). The imaginative use of religious symbols in subjective experiences of anorexia nervosa. *Psychoanalytic Review, 84,* 227–236.

Becker, H., Körner, P. &Stöffler, A. (1981). Psychodynamics and therapeutic aspects of anorexia nervosa. *Psychotherapy and Psychosomatics, 36,* 8–16.

Behar, R. (2012). Spirituality and asceticism in anorexia nervosa. *Revista Chilena de Neuro-Psiquiatría, 50,* 106–118.

Behar, R., Gramegna, G. & Arancibia, M. (2014). Perfectionism and body dissatisfaction in eating disorders. *Revista Chilena de Neuro-Psiquiatría, 52,* 103–114.

Behar, R. & Arancibia, M. (2013). Maturity fears in anorexia nervosa. *Mexican Journal of Eating Disorders, 4,* 143–152.

Bell, R. (1985). *Holy anorexia.* Chicago: University of Chicago Press.

Bemporad, J. (1996). Self-starvation through the ages: reflections on the pre-history of anorexia nervosa. *International Journal of Eating Disorders, 19,* 217–237.

Berrett, M., Hardman, R., O'Grady, K. & Richards, P. (2007). The role of spirituality in the treatment of trauma and eating disorders: recommendations for clinical practice. *Eating Disorders, 15*, 373–89.

Bridges, R. & Spilka, B. (1992). Religion and the mental health of women. In Schumaker, J. (Eds.), *Religion and mental health,* (43-53). New York: Oxford University Press.

Brown, P. (1988). *The body and society: men, women and sexual renunciation in early christianity.* New York: Columbia University Press.

Bruch, H. (1974). *Eating disorders: obesity, anorexia nervosa and the person within.* London: Routledge&Kegan Paul.

Brumberg, J. (1989). *Fasting girls: a history of anorexia nervosa.* New York: Plume.

Bynum, C. (1987). *Holy feast and holy fast. The religious significance of food to medieval women.* Berkeley: University of California Press.

Bynum, C. (1988). Holy anorexia in modern Portugal. *Culture, Medicine, and Psychiatry, 12,* 239–248.

Chipley, W. (1860). On sitomania. *Journal of Psychological Medicine and Mental Pathology, 13,* 266–270.

Corrington, G. (1986). Anorexia, asceticism and autonomy: self-control as liberation and trascendence.*Journal of Feminist Studies in Religion, 2,* 51–61.

Crisp, A. (1980). *Anorexia nervosa: Let me be.* London: Academic Press.

Culliford, L. (2002). Spirituality and clinical care. *British Medical Journal,* 325:1434–1435.

Dabrowski, K. (1967). *Personality-shaping through positive disintegration.* London:J. & A. Churchill.

Davis, W. (1985). Epilogue. In *Holy anorexia,* (181-183). Chicago, IL: University of Chicago Press.

Dittmann, K.&Freedman, M. (2009). Body awareness, eating attitudes, and spiritual beliefs of women practicing yoga. *Eating Disorders, 17*, 273–92.

Douglass, L. (2011). Thinking through the body: the conceptualization of yoga as therapy for individuals with eating disorders.*Eating Disorders, 19*, 83–96.

Engel, G. (1977). The need of a new medical model: a challenge for biomedicine. *Science,196,* 129–136.

Espíndola, C.&Blay, S. (2009). Anorexia nervosa treatment from the patient perspective: a metasynthesis of qualitative studies. *Annals of Clinical Psychiatry, 21*, 38–48.

Fairburn, C. & Harrison, P. J. (2003). Eating disorders. *Lancet, 361,* 407–416.

Fallon B. &Howath E. (1993). Asceticism: creative spiritual practice or pathological pursuit? *Psychiatry, 56,* 310–316.

Fassino, S., AbbateDaga, G., Amianto, F., Leombruni, P., Garzaro, L., & Rovera,G. (2001). Nonresponder anorectic patients after 6 months of multimodaltreatment: predictors of outcome. *European Psychiatry, 16(8),* 466–473.

Fassino, S., AbbateDaga, G., Pierò, A., &Rovera, G. (2002). Dropout from brief psychotherapy in anorexia nervosa. *Psychotherapy and Psychosomatics, 72,*126–134.

Fassino, S., Pierò, A., Gramaglia, C., AbbateDaga, G., Gandione, M., Rovera, G., et al. (2006). Clinical, psychological, and personality correlates of asceticism in anorexia nervosa: from saint anorexia to pathologic perfectionism. *Transcultural Psychiatry, 43,* 600–614.

Fenichel, O. (1945). *The psychoanalytic theory of neurosis.* London: Routledge&Kegan Paul.

Gabbard, G. (2000). *Psichiatria psicodinamica.* Milan: Cortina Editore.

Garner, D. (1984). *Eating Disorder Inventory 2.* Florence: OrganizzazioniSpeciali.

Garrett, C. (1996). Recovery from anorexia nervosa: a durkheimian interpretation,*43,*1489–506.

Gordon, R. (1991). *Anoressia e bulimia: anatomia di un'epidemiasociale.* Turin:Cortina.

Hook, J.,Worthington, E.,Davis, D., Jennings, D.,Gartner, L.& Hook, J. (2010). Empirically supported religious and spiritual therapies. *Journal of Clinical Psychology, 66*, 46–72.

Huguelet, P. & Koenig, H. (2009). Introduction: key concepts. In Huguelet, P., & Koenig, H. (Eds.). *Religion and spirituality in psychiatry,* (1-5). Cambridge: Cambridge University Press.

Huline-Dickens, S. (2000).Anorexia nervosa: some connections with the religious attitude. *British Journal of Medical Psychology,*73, 67–76.

Jacobs-Pilipski, M., Winzelberg, A.,Wilfley, D., Bryson, S.&Taylor, C. (2005). Spirituality among young women at risk for eating disorders. *Eating Behavior,* 6, 293–300.

Jacoby, G. (1993). Eating disorder and religion. *Psychotherapy, Psychosomatic Medicine and Psychology, 43,* 70–73.

Joughin, N., Crisp, A., Halek, C. & Humphrey, H. (1992). Religious belief and anorexia nervosa. *International Journal of Eating Disorders, 12*, 397–406.

Katzman, M. & Lee S. (1997) Beyond body image: the integration of feminist and transcultural theories in the understanding of self starvation. *International Journal of Eating Disorders, 22(4),* 385–394.

Keel, K. &Klump, K. (2003). Are eating disorders culture-bound syndromes? Implications for conceptualizing their etiology. *Psychological Bulletin, 129,* 747–769.

Klein,M.(1940).Mourning and its relation to manic depressive states. *International Journal of Psychoanalysis, 21,* 125–153.

Koenig, H., McCullough, M. & Larson, D. (2001). *Handbook of religion and health.* Oxford: Oxford University Press.

Lacey, J. (1982). Anorexia nervosa and a bearded female saint. *British MedicalJournal, 285,* 1816–1817.

Larson, D., Swyers, J. & McCullough, M. (1997). *Scientific research on spirituality and health: a consensus report.* Rockville, MD: National Institute for Health Research.

Littlewood, R. (1995). Psychopathology and personal agency: modernity, culture change and eating disorders in south asian societies. *British Journal of Medical Psychology, 68,* 45–63.

Manley, R.&Leichner, P. (2003). Anguish and despair in adolescents with eating disorders—helping to manage suicidal ideation and impulses. Crisis, *24,*32–6.

Marsden, P.,Karagianni, E.&Morgan, J. (2007). Spirituality and clinical care in eating disorders: a qualitative study. *International Journal of Eating Disorders, 40*, 7–12.

Matusek, J.&Knudson, R. (2009). Rethinking recovery from eating disorders: spiritual and political dimensions.*Qualitative Health Research, 19*, 697–707.

McSherry, J. (1985). Was Mary, queen of scots, anorexic? *Scottish Medical Journal, 30,* 243–245.

Medlicott, R. (1969). St. Anthony Abbott and the hazards of asceticism: an analysis of artists' representations of the temptations. *British Journal of Medical Psychology, 42,* 133–140.

Menninger, K. (1938). *Man against himself.* New York: Harcourt, Brace & World.

Minuchin, S., Rasman, B. & Baker, L. (1978). *Psychosomatic families: anorexia nervosa in context.* Cambridge, MA: Harvard University Press.

Mogul, S. (1980). Asceticism in adolescence and anorexia nervosa. *Psychoanalytic Study of the Child, 35,* 155–175.

Morgan, J. F., Marsden, P. &Lacey, J. (2000). 'Spiritual starvation?': a case series concerning christianity and eating disorders. *International Journal of EatingDisorders, 28(4),* 476–480.

Neeleman, J. & King, M. (1993). Psychiatrists' religious attitudes in relation to their clinical practice: a survey of 231 psychiatrists. *ActaPsychiatricaScandinavica, 88*, 420–424.

Obeyesekere, G. (1981). *Medusa's hair. An essay on personal symbols and religious experience*. Chicago and London: University of Chicago Press.

Obeyesekere, G. (1990). *The work of culture. Symbolic transformation in psychoanalysis and anthropology.* Chicago: University of Chicago Press.

Palazzoli, M. (1974). *Self-starvation. From individual to family therapy in the treatment ofanorexia nervosa.* New York: Jason Aronson.

Palouzian, R. & Park, C. (2005). *Handbook of the psychology of religion and spirituality.* New York: Guilford Press.

Rampling, D. (1985). Ascetic ideals and anorexia nervosa. *Journal ofPsychiatric Research, 19,* 89–94.

Reber, A. (1985). *Dictionary of psychology.*Harmondsworth: Penguin Books.

Richards, P., Berrett, M., Hardman, R. &Eggett, D. (2006). Comparative efficacy of spirituality, cognitive, and emotional support groups for treating eating disorder inpatients. *Eating Disorders, 14*, 401–15.

Richards, P., Smith, M., Berrett, M., O'Grady, K.&Bartz, J. (2009). A theistic spiritual treatment for women with eating disorders.*Journal of Clinical Psychology, 65*, 172–84.

Rieger, E., Touyz, S. W., Swain, T., & Beumont, P. (2001). Cross-cultural research on anorexia nervosa: assumptions regarding the role ofbody weight. *International Journal of Eating Disorders, 29,* 205–215.

Russell, G. (1997). The history of bulimia nervosa. In Garner, D., &Garfinkel, P. (Eds.), *Handbook of treatment for eating disorders,* (11-24). New York: Guilford Press.

Sabom, S. (1985). The gnostic world of anorexia nervosa. *Journal of Psychology andTheology, 13*,243–254.

Spiro, M. (1965). Religious systems as culturally constituted defense mechanisms. In Spiro, M. (Ed.). *Context and meaning in cultural anthropology,* (100-113). New York: The Free Press.

Spiro, M. (1987). Religion. Problems of definition and explanation. In Kilborne, B., &Langness, L.(Eds.). *Culture and human nature,* (187-222). Chicago and London: University of Chicago Press.

Stephen, M. &Suryani, L. (2000). Shamanism, psychosis and autonomous imagination *Culture, Medicine and Psychiatry,* 24,5–40.

Sykes, D., Leuser, B., Melia, M. & Gross, M. (1988). A demographic analysis of 252 patients with anorexia nervosa and bulimia.*International Journal of Psychosomatics, 35,* 5–9.

Tait, G. (1993). 'Anorexia nervosa': asceticism, differentiation, government. *Australian and New ZealandJournal of Sociology, 29,* 194–208.

Tiller, J., Schmidt, U., Ali, S. & Treasure, J. (1995). Patterns of punitiveness in women with eating disorders. *International Journal of Eating Disorders, 17,* 365–371.

Turner, B. (1984). *The body and society. Explorations in social theory.* Oxford and New York: Basil Blackwell.

Vandereycken, W. & Van Deth, R. (1994). *From fasting saints to anorexic girls: the history of self-starvation.* New York: New York University Press.

Vandereyecken, W. & van Deth, R. (1996). *From fasting saints to anorexic girls. The history of self-starvation.* London: Athlone Press.

Verhagen, P. (2010). General Introduction: Religion and science. In Veerhagen P., van Praag H, López-Ibor JJ, Cox J, Moussaoui D.(Eds.). *Religion and psychiatry: beyond boundaries* (1-10).Oxford: Wiley-Blackwell.

Warren, W. G., Jackson, C., Thornton, C., Russell, J., Touys, S. W. &Beumont, P. (1994). A study of the relation between eating disorder and death concern. *Australian and New Zealand Journal of Psychiatry,28,* 463–468.

Weber, M. (1930). *The protestant ethic and spirit of capitalism.* London: Allen and Unwin.

Weil, S. (1951). *Waiting on God.*Routledge&Kegan Paul, London.

Weinstein, D. & Bell, R. (1980). *Saints and society: the two worlds of Western Christendom 1000–1700.* Chicago, IL: University of Chicago Press.

White, M. (1983). Anorexia nervosa: a transgenerational perspective. *Family Process, 22,* 255–273.

Wilbur, C. &Colligan, R. (1981). Psychological and behavioural correlates of anorexia nervosa. *Journal of Developmental and Behavioural Paediatrics, 2,* 89–92.

In: Spirituality
Editor: Edith C. Roberts

ISBN: 978-1-63482-370-8

Chapter 13

RELIGIOSITY OF PSYCHOTHERAPISTS IN SANTIAGO DE CHILE: RESULTS OF A SURVEY

Ramón Florenzano, MD, MPH*

Facultad de Psicología, Universidad del Desarrollo, Santiago de Chile, Chile

ABSTRACT

This study compares the religiosity of representative samples of the Chilean psychiatrists, psychologists and psychoanalysts with the general population. A questionnaire inquiring into religious and spiritual beliefs was anonymously applied through a web based survey: there were more non-believers among psychoanalysts (62, 8%) than among psychiatrists (42,8%) and psychologists (33,6). The three professional groups were less religious than the Chilean population (87%). Results are compared with the study by Shafranske et al in the U.S: 73% of psychiatrists and psychologists believed in God, compared with 96% of the population, and by Hofman & Walach in Germany, where 57% of the psychotherapists belonged to a religious denomination.

This research was done receiving a grant in aid of the Research Advisory Board of the International Psychoanbalytic Association.

INTRODUCTION

In the last decade, the interface between spiritual and religious practices and mental health has become a subject of systematic exploration, with a growing awareness than they are key in the emotional life of individuals and societies [1]. Psychology, psychiatry and psychoanalysis are professions that emerged at the end of the XIX century, and have expanded quickly in the last 100 years. They represent a societal confidence that emotional problems can be subdued through scientific knowledge. They can be seen as competing with the traditional role of religions in offering answers to life cycle themes: birth, marriage, death,

* E-mail address: rflorenzano@gmail.com.

areas that were the domain of religious practitioners for a long time. Now, they are in the realm of medical or social sciences.

Sigmund Freud offered explanations to some of the main religious phenomena: God was seen by him as a projected father-figure, and religious rituals as the obsessional neurosis of humanity [2]. He saw religions as infantile, irrational or neurotic activities. However, spiritual life and the pursuit of religious truth have something in common with psychoanalysis: both in religion and in psychotherapy people seek salvation or sanation, try to solve their problems and search for happiness.

The role of religious beliefs has become an important subject for mental health research and practice in the last decadesm and the American Psychological Association and the World Psychiatric Associations have created special Task Forces centered on the subject. Kelly has distinguished between the term *spirituality,* that refers to transcendent experiences with understandings about God or other forces in the universe, and the term *religiosity* refers to institutionalized systems of beliefs, values and activities based on spiritual creeds [3].

Most Chileans, and most South-Americans, are very religious. The "Encuesta Nacional Bicentenario" was carried out in a national sample of the Chilean population over 18 years (n=2037 people living in the 86 most populated towns) [4]. 86,6% of Chileans said they belonged to a religious denomination (Catholics 65,5%, other Christian churches 18,3%, other churches 2,5%); 12,1% said they did not belong to any; and 1,6% declared themselves atheists. Among the religious, 21,1% of the surveyed declared that attended churches or temples at least once a week (14,2% of men and 26,4% of women). In the ages 15 to 24 years, the percentage of weekly or more attendance decreased to 13,3%, in comparison to 28,1% in the group over 60 (Chi2=164,94;30 df;p=0,0001).

The religiosity of mental health practitioners has been studied in several countries. Shafranske (2000) studied the religiosity of mental health practitioners in USA, surveying a random sample of 355 psychiatrists belonging to the American Psychiatric Association: he sent a mailed questionnaire about their beliefs, the answers of 117 of them were compared with data from 253 members of the American Psychological Association and a national sample of the US population, taken from the General Social Survey of 1990 (n=1253) [5]. He found belief in life after death in 48% of the psychiatrists, 54% of the psychologists, and 71% of the public at large; belief in God or an Universal Spirit in 73% of the psychiatrists, 73% of the psychologists, and 96% of the public; attended church or temple weekly 26% of the psychiatrists, 28% of the psychologists, and 43% of the public at large. With regards to salience of religion, 38,2% of the psychiatrists, 26% of the psychologists, and 58% of the public at large consider religion as very important in their lives. With regards to the need to explore and be aware of patient´s religious issues, 50% of the psychiatrists and 87% of the psychologists considered it important. Both psychiatrists and psychologists felt that religious and spiritual issues were very rarely or not at all covered in their training.

The purpose of this piece of research, funded by the Research Advisory Board of the International Psychoanalytic Association, was to study the religious and spiritual beliefs and practices of mental health practitioners in Chile, and compare them with the beliefs and practices of the Chilean General population.

Methods

A questionnaire inquiring into the spiritual and religious beliefs and practices of mental health practitioners, was adapted from the "Encuesta Nacional Bicentenario 2007", with 30 items related to religious beliefs and practices. This survey was applied to a representative sample (n=2033) of the general population of Chile in 2007. A five item scale, that explored religious practices, developed by Barber, Stolz, & Olsen at the University of Tennessee, was adapted to Spanish in Colombia and Chile and formed part of the CNAP Plus) was added to the questionnaire [6]. Sample items are: Also, a seven item socio-demographic questionnaire was applied requesting data about age, gender, marital status, education and place of residence.

The questionnaire (available on request), was applied to representative samples randomly chosen of psychologists from the *Colegio de Psicólogos de Chile* (n=77), psychiatrists from the *Sociedad Chilena de Neurología, Psiquiatría y Neurocirugía* (n=35) and psychoanalysts from the *Asociación Psicoanalítica Chilena* (n=24)

Sampling was done from the memberships rosters of those three professional bodies, using a random number generation program from SPSS 17.0. The surveys were answered in the web, and analysed with the same statistical package The *Colegio de Psicólogos de Chile* (Chilean College of Psychologists) is the organization that certifies training of practitioners in Chile. The *Sociedad Chilena de Neurología, Psiquiatría y Neurocirugía* (Chilean Society of Neurology, Psychiatry and Neurosurgery, Psychiatry Branch), is the scientific organization that gathers 600 practicing psychiatrists, and is a full member of the World Psychiatric Association. The *Asociación Psicoanalítica Chilena* is the Chilean branch of the International Psychoanalytic Association, and gathers about 93 full members.

The instrument was sent by e-mail to the randomly chosen members of the three associations, allowing four weeks to receive a response. Data were analyzed with descriptive statistics. Data obtained from the three professional groups were compared with the general population obtained with the the national application of above described Encuesta Nacional Bicentenario.

Table 1. Sociodemographic Characteristics of Mental Health Professionals Surveyed in Chile, 2009-2010 (n=136)

	Psychologists (n=77)	Psychiatrists (n=35)	Psychoanalysts (n=24)	Statistical Significance
Mean Age	43	49	52	
SD	12	11	8	
Gender	%	%	%	Chi 2=16,712; 2 df; p=0,000
Females	70,1	31,4	41,7	
Males	29,9	68,6	58,3	
Single	16	20	0,0	Chi 2=14,217; 6 df; p=0,27
Living together	8	5,7	0,0	
Married	61,3	74,3	91,7	
Divorced	14,7	0,0	8,3	

Table 2. Religious adscription, mental health professionals compared with general population, chile 2009, (n=134)

	Chileans (%)	Psychologists (%)	Psychiatrists (%)	Psychoanalysts (%)
Catholics	65	56	51,4	37,5
Other Christians	20	4	2,9	0
Other Religions	3	8	2,9	0
Agnostics/without religious preference	12	32	42,9	62,5

Chi^2 = 9,195; df = 6; p = 0,163.

Results

The mean age of psychoanalysts was higher (52 years with a standard deviation of 8) than the one of psychologists (43 years and SD 12); and psychiatrists (49 years and SD 11). Females predominated among psychologists (70,1%) in comparison to psychiatrists (31,4%) and psychoanalysts (41,7%) The differences were significant (Chi2=16,712; 2 df; p=0,0001). With regards to marital status, 61,3% of the psychologists were married, compared with 74,3% of the psychiatrists, and 91,7% of the psychoanalysts (Table 1).

The predominant religion in Chile is Catholicism. This applies to the general population and to the different mental health professionals in our sample. In the latter, the percentage of non-believers was not similar between groups: the percentage of agnostics increased from 12% in the general population, to 62,5% between psychoanalysts (Table 2). The amount of believers was higher among psychologists (68%), followed by psychiatrists (57,1%) and psychoanalysts (37,5%). The three professional groups were less religious than the general population (87%) as can be seen in Table 3.

If we observe religious preferences, the percentage of catholics in the general population was the highest (65%), compared with the sample of psychologists (56%), psychiatrists (51,4%) and psychoanalysts (37,5%). Other Christians denominations were represented in lower amount: among psychologists (4%), psychiatrists (2,9%). There was no one of them among psychoanalysts. This compares with 20% among Chileans in general.

Table 3. Comparison in percentages of believers and non believers, mental health professionals, CHILE 2009 (n=134)

	General Population	Psychologists	Psychiatrists	Psychoanalysts
Believers	87	68	57,1	37,5
Non Believers	13	32	42,9	62,5
Total	100	100	100	100

Chi^2 = 7,159; df = 2; p = 0,028.

The self appraisal of inner (intrinsic) spirituality is different from the (extrinsic) participation in specific religious practices, Table 4 shows the answer to the question "How religious do you consider yourself?": 14,3% of the psychologists felt they were very religious, compared with 3,1% of the psychiatrists, and 4,2% of the psychoanalysts. Somewhat religious were 63,6% of the psychologists, compared with 68,8% of the psychoanalysts, and 58,3% of the psychoanalysts. Not religious at all were 22,1% of the psychologists, 28,1% of the psychiatrists, and 37,5% of the psychoanalysts.

Table 4. Self evaluation of degree of religiosity, Chilean mental health professionals, Chile 2009. Answer to the question: How religious do you consider yourself?

	Psychologists	Psychiatrists	Psychoanalysts
Very	14,30%	3,10%	4,20%
Somewhat	63,60%	68,80%	58,30%
Not at all	22,10%	28,10%	37,50%

Chi2=5,764; df;p=0,217.

Table 5. Religious beliefs and practices, Chilean Mental Health Professionals, Chile 2009

	Psychologists	Psychiatrists	Psychoanalysts	Statistical Significance
Knows Holy Mary by heart	75,3%	74,3%	83,3%	Chi2=0,777; 2 df;p=0,678
Believes that Faith can move mountains *	67,5%	48.5%	30,0%	Chi2=10,405; 4 df;p=0,006*
Believes in God	72,7%	45,7%	41,7	Chi2=11,558; 2 df;p=0,003*
Prays when afflicted *	72,4%	45,7%	20,8%	Chi2=21,840; 2 df;p=0,0001*
Believes in Mary *	48,1%	25,7%	12,5%	Chi2=12,210; 2 df;p=0,002
Believes in miracles	39%	25,7%	4,2%	Chi2=10,980; 2 df;p=0,004
Believes in saints	39%	28,6%	8,3%	Chi2=8,157; 2 df;p=0,017
Believes in eternal life	41,6%	37,1%	4,2%	Chi2=11,661; 2 df;p=0,003
Believes in Marian Miracles *	36,4%	20,0%	0,0%	Chi2=13,470; 2 df;p=0,001
Believes in going to Heaven after death	32,5%	25,7%	4,2%	Chi2=7,668; 2 df;p=0,022
Religious readings in the last month	28,4%	22,9%	4,2%	Chi2=6,084; 2 df;p=0,048
Has participated in Marian pilgrimages	19,5%	17,1%	16,7	Chi2=0,145; 2 df;p=0,930
Visits relatives in the Cemetery by All Saints day	20,8%	5,7%	8,3%	Chi2=5,297; 2 df;p=0,071
Meditation in the last month	84,4%	74,3%	75%	Chi2=2,037; 2 df;p=0,361

P=0,05

The former self-evaluation compares with the religious participation or practices: attended more than monthly religious services 17,6% of the psychologists, 18,2% of the psychiatrists, 5,9% of the psychoanalysts, and 37,4% of the Chilean population. Specific religious beliefs and practices appear in table 5. Of interest, the belief in Holy Mary and Marian practices are important: most professionals (even psychoanalysts) report that they know Marian prayers by heart. The difference between the professions is also marked by practices linked to Mary and the depth of faith: psychoanalysts in a statistically significant way believe less than faith can move mountains, pray less when afflicted, believe less in Mary and her miracles. These differences appear in table 5.

CONCLUSION

There are few studies in developing countries that explore in depth the characteristics of spirituality and religiosity of mental health professionals. This paper surveyed on line [7] representative samples of Chilean psychiatrists, psychologists and psychoanalysts, finding that the last groups was the less religious. This does not mean necessarily that they do not spiritual: even if they did not adhere to established creeds, many of the psychoanalysts meditated weekly. The initial anti-theistic stance of Sigmund Freud seems to be kept by his Chilean followers even today: this can be related, as we proposed in a previous paper ([2]) to the slower growth of psychoanalysis in deeply religious South American countries in the Pacific coast, such as Chile, Peru and Ecuador; in comparison to Atlantic ones (such as Argentina and Brazil).

Marital status is a variable that can that influences religiosity: the survey of Chilean general population found that, as in other countries, women and married persons, are more religious. The socio-demographic characteristics of the professionals sample differ, with more women among psychologists and psychoanalysts, and more men among psychiatrists. The percentage of married is higher among psychologists and psychoanalysts, but they also have more respondents that were separated and divorced.

The fact that the Chilean general population is predominantly religious and specifically Catholic is related to a strong cultural tradition that expresses religiosity extrinsically through group rituals. Only in the last 40 years other Christian denominations have been growing in South America, a culturally catholic continent from the days of Spanish rule. Professionals groups bred in a positivistic and rationalist world view might have an intrinsic spirituality, or suspend their opinions as many of them do in this study.

Cultural sensitivity and attunement to the client beliefs is crucial in psychosocial therapies. In a setting where many people express problems in a religious context, using metaphors or recurring to religious healing rituals, it is important the knowledge of the therapists of those practices and belief systems. Most professionals surveyed memorized traditional Marian prayers. This could mean that they had a religious upbringing, and therefore were able to understand the religious background of their patients.

These findings show that mental health professionals are less religious that the general population in Chile. This can be understood as that professionals with more years of education are more secularized, especially in an activity that has replaced some of the traditional roles of the clergy, such as giving advice and promoting personal change. The fact that this trend is stronger among psychoanalysts is of interest. The relationship between psychoanalysis, philosophy and religion has been described as *"a triangle of hostility"* by

Cottingham [8]. This view comes from Sigmund Freud himself that liked the idea that he, together with Copernicus and Darwin, had dethroned the centrality of God in modern thought. At the same time, Cottingham asserts that "*contemporary philosophical thought is on the whole inimical to psychoanalytic ideas*". Our data confirms that in a country where the majority of the population is Christian, mental health professionals and specially psychoanalysts do not share the majority view. Therefore it is important their training them in this area, to become more close to the cultural sensitivity of the majority of their clients.

REFERENCES

[1] Lambert MJ (2004) *Bergin´s and Garfield's Handbook of Psychotherapy and Behavior Change.* New York, John Wiley and Sons.

[2] Florenzano R. (1990) Psicoanálisis y Religión. In: *Cuarenta Años de Psicoanálisis en Chile.* Eds: Eleanora Casaula, Jaime Coloma y Juan Francisco Jordan. Editorial: Ananke, Santiago, Chile.

[3] Kelly EW. (2004) *Spirituality and spirituality in counseling and psychotherapy. Alexandria Virginia American Counseling Association.*

[4] Instituto de Sociología Pontificia Universidad Católica de Chile y CEP Adimark (2007). *Encuesta Nacional Bicentenario* .

[5] Shafranske EP (2000) Religious Involvement and Professional Practices of Psychiatrists and Other Mental Health Professionals. *Psychiatric Annals* 2000; 30(8):525-532

[6] Barber,B.K., Stolz, H.E, Olsen J.A. (2005). Parental support, Psychological control and Behavioral control: Assessing relevance across time, methods and culture, *Monogr Soc Res Child Dev* 70, N.4,

[7] S.D. Gosling, & J.A. Johnson, (ed.) Advanced methods for conducting online behavioral research (pp. 3-8). Washington, DC: American Psychological Association.

[8] Cottingham J. (2007) *A triangle of hostility?* In: Braddock L and Lacewing M (Eds). *The Academic Face of Psychoanallysis: Papers in Philosophy, the Humanities and the British Clinical Tradition.* Routledge, London, 2007 Pp: 92-110.

INDEX

B

C

D

E

F

G

H

I

J

K

L

M

S

T

U

V

W

Y